TWO
CENTURIES
OF FAITH

The Boston College Church in the 21st Century Series

Patricia De Leeuw and James F. Keenan, S.J.,
General Editors

The Church in the 21st Century Center at Boston College seeks to be a catalyst and resource for the renewal of the Catholic Church in the United States by engaging critical issues facing the Catholic community. Drawing from both the Boston College community and others, its activities currently are focused on four challenges: handing on and sharing the Catholic faith, especially with younger Catholics; fostering relationships built on mutual trust and support among lay men and women, vowed religious, deacons, priests, and bishops; developing an approach to sexuality mindful of human experience and reflective of Catholic tradition; and advancing contemporary reflection on the Catholic intellectual tradition.

TWO CENTURIES OF FAITH

The Influence of Catholicism
on Boston, 1808–2008

THOMAS H. O'CONNOR, EDITOR

A Herder & Herder Book
The Crossroad Publishing Company
New York

Cover illustration: The construction of Holy Cross Church, Franklin Street, Boston, was completed in 1803. The design for this first Catholic church in Boston was provided free of charge by Charles Bulfinch, the town's leading architect, as a tribute to Bishop Jean Cheverus and the Catholics of Boston. Courtesy of the John J. Burns Library, Boston College.

The Crossroad Publishing Company
www.cpcbooks.com
www.crossroadpublishing.com

© 2009 by The Trustees of Boston College

In continuation of our 200-year tradition of independent publishing, The Crossroad Publishing Company proudly offers a variety of books with strong, original voices and diverse perspectives. The viewpoints expressed in our books are not necessarily those of The Crossroad Publishing Company, any of its imprints or of its employees. No claims are made or responsibility assumed for any health or other benefit.

Printed in the United States of America.

The text of this book is set in 10/12 Sabon.

Library of Congress Cataloging-in-Publication Data

Two centuries of faith : the influence of Catholicism on Boston, 1808–2008 /
    Thomas H. O'Connor, editor.
        p.   cm.
    "A Herder & Herder book."
    Includes bibliographical references and index.
    ISBN-13: 978-0-8245-2531-6 (alk. paper)
    ISBN-10: 0-8245-2531-0 (alk. paper)
    1. Catholic Church – Massachusetts – Boston – History. 2. Boston (Mass.) –
Church history. 3. Catholic Church – Influence. 4. Boston (Mass.) – Religious
life and customs. I. O'Connor, Thomas H., 1922–   II. Title.
BX1418.B7T86 2009
282'.74461 – dc22

                                                            2009000645

Contents

Presentation

I am delighted to present *Two Centuries of Faith: The Influence of Catholicism on Boston, 1808–2008* to Cardinal Seán O'Malley, O.F.M.Cap., as a contribution to the bicentennial celebration of the Archdiocese of Boston. Boston College and the Archdiocese have long had a mutually beneficial relationship, and this volume acknowledges the history and bonds linking our institutions and the Catholic community in the greater Boston area. On behalf of the 150,000 alumni of Boston College, I offer congratulations and best wishes to the Archdiocese of Boston and its faithful.

Sincerely,
William P. Leahy, S.J.
President

Office of the President
Boston College

Introduction

Thomas H. O'Connor

The two hundredth anniversary of the Archdiocese of Boston is a truly historic occasion that is deserving of serious reflection as well as joyous celebration. As a scholarly gesture of congratulation to Cardinal Seán P. O'Malley, archbishop of Boston, on the occasion of this bicentennial event, Rev. William P. Leahy, S.J., president of Boston College, authorized the Office of the University Historian to undertake the compilation of a series of essays focusing upon the various influences the Catholic Church has had upon Boston over the course of the past two hundred years. An advisory committee of twelve prominent faculty members from a variety of academic fields of study at Boston College selected a number of recognized scholars in the Greater Boston area who would be capable of elaborating on the variety of influences that Catholicism has produced on the life and society of Massachusetts.

"Sometimes we rhapsodize about the past, glamorize history, and remember only what is pleasant," said Cardinal O'Malley in the course of his homily on December 2, 2007, during the Mass at the Cathedral of the Holy Cross inaugurating the archdiocesan bicentennial year. "As a Catholic community in New England," he continued, "we should know that our beginnings as a local Church were fraught with hardship and hostility, and with enormous sacrifices." It is precisely those hardships and hostilities that made the early years of Catholicism in New England so precarious, but also made its subsequent achievements so remarkable.

Although a great many Roman Catholics made their way from Ireland to different parts of North America during the 1700s, few of them came to Massachusetts, where they knew they would find themselves in an openly hostile environment. The English Puritans who founded the Massachusetts Bay Colony were especially opposed to Catholicism. They had rooted out all traces of "Papism" in their own religious practices, forbade the presence of Catholic priests under pain of death, and refused to accept anyone who did not follow the Congregational form of worship.

It was not until after the American Revolution, and the subsequent alliances with France, that a number of French and Irish Catholics came out of hiding and formed a small congregation that depended on French naval chaplains and transient priests for their religious services until Bishop John Carroll sent Father François Matignon to Boston, followed several years later by a younger priest named Jean-Louis Lefebvre de Cheverus.

1

Drawing upon his affection for Boston as well as his own academic background, François Gauthier describes in his chapter the fascinating odyssey of the twenty-four-year-old Cheverus, who would be named the first bishop of Boston in 1808. Despite what might well have been a disastrous collision of opposing religious cultures in the Puritan town, the Cheverus years provided a surprisingly tolerant interlude during which the early Catholic Church was able to establish its roots in the rocky soil of New England. His ability to engage in civil dialogue about religious differences without being offensive earned him the respect of his Protestant neighbors, who admired his charitable errands of mercy not only on behalf of his parishioners in Boston, but also among the Native American peoples of northern Maine who were still loyal to the faith brought to them earlier by the French Jesuits from Canada. Long after Cheverus had returned to France, as Gauthier points out, the arrival of the "Quebecois" and the subsequent establishment of numerous French-speaking parishes throughout the Archdiocese of Boston carried his spiritual legacy well into the future.

The tolerance of the Cheverus episcopacy proved all too brief, however. By the time Benedict Fenwick replaced Cheverus as second bishop of Boston in 1825, the number of Irish Catholic immigrants had grown from a few hundred to more than five thousand, rekindling old fears about the threat of Papism to American democratic institutions.

Lacking any semblance of political influence, Boston's Catholics were powerless to protect themselves against either verbal assaults or physical harassment. In chapter 2 Thomas H. O'Connor describes how, during the 1840s and 1850s, Bishop John Fitzpatrick avoided violence by convincing the Irish to refrain from retaliation, while persuading his Brahmin friends to observe the constitutional rights of immigrant Americans. During the last half of the nineteenth century, Archbishop John Williams continued the same kind of cautious standoff between Catholics and Protestants in order to maintain the peace and assure a steady measure of progress.

The opening of the twentieth century brought changes in the political status quo. By 1910 Catholics not only constituted more than half the population of the Greater Boston area, but were also moving into positions of social and political influence. Convinced that "the day of the Puritan has passed," the new archbishop, William Henry O'Connell, was not at all hesitant about using the power of his position to ensure that public policies were consistent with Catholic beliefs. As time went on, the size of the Catholic electorate and the popularity of Cardinal Richard Cushing virtually guaranteed a close relationship between church and state. After the 1960s, however, financial difficulties, demographic changes, liturgical controversies, and clerical sexual scandals badly damaged the social and political structure upon which the church had depended for nearly a century and created serious challenges for the future.

Even as early Boston Catholics struggled to secure some measure of political expression, church leaders also sought ways of meeting the pressing needs of their impoverished people. Justice and charity, writes Father Bryan

Hehir, were seen as "pillars of Christian discipleship" and a "fundamental dimension of Christian life." Because they feared that local Protestant charity groups would endanger the religious faith of young children, Catholics at first developed their own separate agencies until, by the early twentieth century, their professionalized services began working more closely with non-Catholic groups. With the coming of the New Deal and the expansion of state and federal charitable agencies, rules and regulations began creating issues that often conflicted with long-held positions in Catholic moral teaching, while the vast changes from early industrialism to modern globalization forced Catholic leaders to greatly enlarge the scope of their social vision.

As Father Hehir traces the development of Catholic Charities in the Archdiocese of Boston during the late twentieth century, he summarizes events that have affected the church at large and suggests some innovative responses. In order to maintain their integrity, however, he indicates that Catholic charitable agencies must find more creative ways of responding to the new and complex religious issues they are confronting as the result of a greater religious and moral pluralism throughout the American legal system.

Catholics in Boston were concerned not only with developing special charitable agencies to meet the needs of their members, but also with creating educational institutions that would help preserve their faith. As long as the Irish were most numerous during the first part of the nineteenth century, most Catholic families preferred to send their children to the public schools where they would become Americanized and where speaking English would not be a problem. When other European immigrants arrived in America during the later nineteenth century, however, they pressed for separate national churches and also looked for a Catholic educational system that would appreciate their native languages and respect their religious traditions.

Father Joseph O'Keefe describes the successful ways in which the parochial school system provided the most widespread and sustained example of bilingualism and biculturalism for Catholic students outside the dominant Anglo-Saxon-Protestant culture of the times. With the additional emphasis on parochial education provided by Cardinal O'Connell and Cardinal Cushing, Catholic schools experienced an unprecedented growth during the mid-1940s.

Starting in 1966, however, as a result of escalating costs, declining vocations, and changing demographics, enrollments in Boston parochial schools suffered a steady decline. By the 1990s, according to Father O'Keefe, traditional native-language schools had suddenly become virtually nonexistent and were replaced by programs that are monolingual and monocultural in order to accommodate the increasing enrollment of African American, Hispanic, and Asian students. What these social, cultural, and economic changes will mean to the traditional mission and purpose of parochial education is something that requires serious reflection in the very near future.

As outsiders, arriving impoverished and illiterate in a city hailed as the "Athens of America," Boston Catholics were generally regarded as lower-class immigrants who might benefit from a basic education, but who could never reach a respectable level of literacy. It came as a distinct surprise to many, therefore, when a series of Catholic writers produced something of a "golden age of Catholic literature" in the late nineteenth century. Focusing largely on the influence of John Boyle O'Reilly, creative editor of the *Boston Pilot* during the 1880s, Libby MacDonald-Bischof also analyzes the literary works of other contemporary writers in tracing a "Catholic literary movement" that acquired considerable recognition, but that never fully materialized.

These were professional writers who were practicing Catholics and who achieved success in the world of Boston letters while remaining true to their faith. According to Bischof, they did not attempt to conform to a particular vision of what constituted "Catholic" literature, but preferred to let their religion naturally pervade their work in order to maintain a "free intellectuality and creative gentility" among Catholic Bostonians. She is of the opinion that John Boyle O'Reilly and the other Catholic writers of the period were largely successful in achieving this measure of intellectual freedom because of the unassuming nature of Archbishop John Williams, who did not seek to shape or control the Catholic literary movement. She contrasts this attitude with that of Archbishop William O'Connell, whose concern with centralization, including literary productions, led him to consider Catholic writers more acceptable if their work were stamped with some mark of "ecclesiastical approval" and conformed to some designated parochial purpose.

In the course of these essays, the Catholic Church in Boston has been almost universally identified as an "Irish church." In his essay on diversity, William Leonard agrees that the church in Boston always had a distinctive Irish flavor, but he also points out that ethnic and racial minorities have always played an important role in the history of the archdiocese. Various white European ethnic groups — the Germans, the French, the Italians — established their national churches, while small clusters of Catholics from Africa and the Caribbean were also a part of the early church.

After World War II, when the number of African Americans in Boston increased substantially, efforts by church leaders to assimilate black Catholics into the archdiocesan structure were frustrated by the struggle over school desegregation during the 1960s and the bitter busing crisis of the 1970s. By the 1980s, however, changing demographics had begun to further transform the racial and ethnic makeup of the Boston archdiocese, as immigrants began to arrive in great numbers from the Caribbean, Central America, and South America. Parishes in former Irish and Italian neighborhoods were transformed almost overnight as Catholics from Puerto Rico, Haiti, Brazil, Venezuela, and Vietnam established their own religious communities. With an estimated five hundred thousand Hispanics living within its boundaries in 2004, "the face of Boston Catholics is changing," writes Leonard, and certainly represents one of the most serious challenges the leaders of the Archdiocese of Boston will face in the coming century.

In addition to a growing measure of ethnic and cultural diversity within the Catholic Church in the Greater Boston area, there has also been a gradual but significant growth in the influence of gender. Starting with small groups of sisters who were brought into Boston during the early nineteenth century to do heroic work for impoverished families and abandoned children, Carol Hurd Green traces the careers of the leaders of various women's religious orders who became principals of secondary schools, directors of orphanages, and administrators of hospitals throughout the archdiocese. By the twentieth century, Catholic women, both sisters and members of the laity, had become successful literary figures, recognized scholars and theologians, and founders of colleges for women. Increasingly women became energetic community leaders, parish organizers, and successful fundraisers for charitable programs, foreign missions, and numerous building projects. And in the years following Vatican II, laywomen have also been given greater responsibilities within the church itself, serving as lectors, teachers of religious education, Eucharistic ministers, and even parish administrators.

In detailing the emergence of Catholic women as increasingly visible and highly influential members of the archdiocese, Carol Hurd Green points out that in recent years Catholic women have also been elected to important political offices at both the state and national levels, and that for the first time in American history an American woman has been appointed as U.S. ambassador to the Holy See. In retrospect Green has assembled the disjointed fragments of the images with which she begins her scholarly essay into a much more substantial portrait of the Catholic woman in the Archdiocese of Boston, who now forms an encouraging symbol of hope for the twenty-first century.

Over the course of two centuries, the nature of the Catholic parish and the responsibilities of the pastor have also changed with time and circumstances. When it was first created in 1808, the Diocese of Boston was immense, extending from northern Maine to southern Rhode Island, with indistinct boundaries and a handful of priests. In Boston itself, it was the laity who organized the first local parish and operated it in a congregational fashion until a resident priest was appointed.

As time went on, the role of the laity as parish administrators diminished as the powers of the bishops and pastors steadily increased. By the late nineteenth century, the parish had become what Father William Schmidt describes as "a natural extension of home and family" — the place with which every parishioner would personally identify from birth to death. The unity and solidarity of parish life within the hierarchical structure of the Archdiocese of Boston flourished in the years between the two world wars, according to Schmidt, and reached something of a "Golden Age" under Cardinal Cushing. After the 1960s, however, a combination of financial problems, demographic changes, and liturgical controversies, aggravated by sexual abuse scandals, created a serious loss of trust in the leadership of the church and a breakdown in the whole diocesan structure.

By the end of the century, churches were closing, old boundary lines were being eliminated, and parishes were organized into clusters. Many parishes had to rely on a single priest, with the prospect that some might have no resident priest at all. As Father Schmidt's narrative of parish life comes full circle, it appears in many ways that the archdiocese may be assuming some of the same characteristics of the first diocese in 1808, two hundred years ago, with lay people taking on legal, financial, and administrative responsibilities formerly exercised by bishops and pastors.

The concluding essay, by James O'Toole, provides an overview of episcopal leadership in the Archdiocese of Boston by analyzing the persons and personalities of the surprisingly small number of prelates (only nine in two hundred years) who have charted the course of the Catholic Church in Boston.

During the first century of its existence, Catholic bishops not only had to profess the faith and build the churches, but they also had to respond to the hostility of a dominant Protestant society. Without power or privilege, the early bishops like Fitzpatrick and Williams had to depend upon quiet tact and personal diplomacy to avoid violence and to shepherd a new generation of Catholics into social and political maturity.

By the time that William Henry O'Connell became archbishop of Boston in 1907, the growing Catholic majority meant that caution and deference were no longer necessary. Using the dignity of his position and the force of his personality, O'Connell shaped a "triumphalist" Catholic subculture, supported by a responsive political system. While his successor, Richard J. Cushing, employed a more democratic style, he continued to use the unquestioned power of the church to ensure a public policy that would be consistent with Catholic moral values.

Not long after the death of Cushing, however, his successor, Humberto Medeiros, was faced with a crippling debt, a serious decline in the number of priests, disturbing controversies over the implications of Vatican II, and a period of bitter racial conflict in the city. Many of the same problems continued to plague Bernard F. Law after 1984, leading to the closing of churches, the disruption of parishes, and disputes with public officials over questions of public policy. The explosive crisis of clergy sexual abuse in 2003 seriously undercut the close relationship between church and state, led to the resignation of the archbishop, and weakened the trust of Catholics at all levels in the competence and integrity of their leaders.

As the archdiocese moves into the twenty-first century, Professor O'Toole suggests that it will be incumbent upon the future leaders of the archdiocese to study the social, demographic, and political changes that have taken place in Greater Boston since the 1960s and assess their effects upon the traditional attitudes of the church and its people in planning for the new century.

Considering the fact that throughout the colonial era, for some two hundred years, members of the Catholic religion in the Massachusetts Bay

Colony were denied both political representation and social recognition, their accomplishments during the following two hundred years must be seen as nothing short of remarkable. This collection of scholarly essays describes a number of the ways in which Boston Catholics were able to overcome years of repression and intolerance to become a positive and respected influence in the life, the culture, and the institutions of the Commonwealth.

In preparing these essays, I would like to acknowledge my sincere appreciation to those scholars who took time out of busy professional and academic schedules to contribute their considerable talents to this volume, which celebrates the bicentennial of the Archdiocese of Boston. I am grateful to Father William P. Leahy, S.J., president of Boston College, for his personal support and encouragement; to Robert R. Newton, special assistant to the president, for his advice and counsel; and to Patricia De Leeuw, vice-president for faculties, for her guidance and assistance in the publication process. Sandra M. MacDonald, staff assistant in the office of the university historian, was indispensable for her assistance in editing the manuscripts and preparing them for final publication.

From Jean de Cheverus to Jacques Maritain

Two Centuries of French Presence
in the Archdiocese of Boston

FRANÇOIS GAUTHIER

TRANSLATED BY HANNAH LUBIN

At the center of the coat of arms of the Archdiocese of Boston stands a cross whose branches end in the fleurs-de-lys. A symbol of the French monarchy, this ornament in fact testifies to the gratitude felt by the diocese toward the French religious figures who brought it so much and in particular gratitude to the first bishop of Boston, Jean Lefebvre de Cheverus.

It is fitting that the celebration of the two hundredth anniversary of the diocese also be the occasion for us to recall this heritage and through the celebration of the memory of Bishop Cheverus to highlight the value as well as the uniqueness of what this French missionary brought to New England's cultural and social landscape.

But beyond Cheverus and that founding moment, the French presence in the religious life of the Diocese of Boston has continued, and, even today, the exchanges between Catholics of New England and French Catholics are many and strong.

This essay will attempt first of all to touch on this "Cheverus moment," the major stages of the life and work of a man who was both French missionary and American bishop, a veritable "pastor of two worlds." Under difficult conditions and in a sensitive environment, Cheverus succeeded very quickly in standing out and in earning the esteem and affection not only of the Catholics of Boston, then greatly in the minority, but in all parts of society in the city and surrounding region. In many respects, his actions and his vision would make him one of the great figures of New England history and, as a result, one of the most "original" witnesses to its French heritage. A true cultural mediator, the bishop of Boston began, and then fostered, a fertile Franco-American relationship. He turned out to be a precursor, too, for this relationship has lasted long and become more varied. It has deepened through waves of immigration, most notably those who arrived from French Canada. It has never ceased being intellectual in nature, involving institutions of learning and individual thinkers, as well as believers capable of nourishing religious dialogue. This we shall see in the second part of this essay.

Jean-Louis-Anne-Madeleine Lefebvre de Cheverus: French Missionary, American Bishop, Pastor of Two Worlds

The life of Cheverus has been the subject of many studies to which this essay will not attempt to add new information. It is nonetheless necessary to note that one has to go back almost fifty years to find the most recent biography of Bishop Cheverus, published upon the occasion of the 150th anniversary of the archdiocese.[1] I shall leave it to the historians to judge whether or not the findings of their research at that time show a need for a new study of this important figure in the building of the American Catholic Church. For those who are interested in the life of Cheverus, there are indeed too few publications readily available.[2]

A brief overview sheds light on three major stages in the life of the prelate: the first is that of his formative years, from his childhood in the provinces up until his departure for England prompted by the need to escape the violence of the French Revolution. The second, the longest and the most eventful stage, is that of his missionary activities, first with a short stay in London and then, from 1796 to 1823, in Boston and New England, with the development of the American church and the building of the diocese.

There, Cheverus would turn out to be a remarkable apostle and builder. Finally, there came the period that I refer to as the completion of his journey, beginning with his return to France, his being named to the bishopric of Montauban, and the conclusion of his mission in Bordeaux, where, recognized as one of the most eminent figures of the church in France, he was named cardinal in 1836, shortly before his death.

The Formative Years

The future bishop of Boston was born in Mayenne, a small town in western France, on February 28, 1768, and spent his happy childhood there. His family, of ancient nobility of the robe, belonged to the local elite and raised young Jean, his two brothers, and three sisters according to traditional values. He was intelligent, with a talent for his studies, and his religious vocation was aroused early on. At the age of twelve he received the tonsure in the Church of the Calvary. His precocity drew the interest of the hierarchy, and the young abbot received his first benefice in the following year, with the priory of Torbechet, and, perhaps more importantly, the promise of a grant to continue his studies in Paris, at the prestigious College Louis-le-Grand, where he would begin in 1781.

Settled into the heart of Paris's Latin Quarter, the young Cheverus dedicated himself with passion to his studies and earned many awards in the disciplines he cherished the most: philosophy and the humanities, Latin, and Greek. He was the best student of the college, the principal would later say of him. He loved his studies, and this formative period was fecund and would determine his lasting interest in intellectual thinking, as much as it would arm him with the tools necessary for debate and the exchange and confrontation of ideas. Cheverus is often depicted as a man of action and projects; he was also an intellectual and a scholar, which he would indeed have the opportunity to prove on many occasions in Boston. It is no surprise that upon leaving the college, he was accepted with distinction to the Oratory seminary of Saint-Magloire.

Having completed his theological studies at the Sorbonne, which was close by, Cheverus confirmed his vocation for the priesthood and enriched his knowledge of scripture, learned Hebrew, and even applied himself to the study of English. He had indeed come far from the small town of Mayenne and was opening up to a much wider world!

As much as from his teachers, Cheverus learned a great deal from his friends, and there were many who appreciated the unusual young clergyman. These included René Legris-Duval, who would become the king's chaplain and the last confessor of Louis XVI, the Irish Abbot McCarthy, who introduced Cheverus to his large library of English books, and the Abbé Matignon, one of his professors at the Sorbonne, who would later call him to his side in America. And his qualities were noticed well beyond this immediate circle, given that the superior of the Seminary of Saint-Sulpice offered him a position — which he would turn down, however, out of loyalty to the Oratory.

Cheverus would indeed remain faithful to that institution. The year 1790 marked the break between the Revolution and the church, and on July 12 the Civil Constitution of the Clergy was passed, eliminating the Concordat and forcing priests to take an oath of loyalty to the constitution. The hierarchy, as well as more than half of the priests in France, refused, entering little by little into disaccord, which would result in one of the most severe crises ever endured by the church in France.

Ordained as a priest, thanks to a special dispensation concerning his age, on December 18, 1790, during the last public ordination carried out in Paris during the Revolution, Cheverus returned immediately to Mayenne, where, welcomed by his uncle, the local priest of the principal parish, he celebrated his first Mass on Christmas night. In this troubled environment, he took on his first pastoral responsibilities. Now a vicar, he was intensely active in his parish, and demonstrated a rarely found energy. But conditions became more and more difficult for resistant priests who were being denied the right to public worship and finally forced into exile or deportation. Forbidden from aspiring to the succession of his uncle, the parish priest of Mayenne, and assigned to reside in Laval with the other un-sworn priests of the region, Cheverus at that point contemplated exile, and on September 11, 1792, he left France and headed to England. This was the beginning of his adventures abroad.

The second, English stage of the young priest (he was then twenty-four years old) saw Cheverus forge his early missionary vocation. In crossing the Channel, Cheverus found himself not only in a different country, but he discovered also a different religious culture, where Catholicism was marginalized, and a new language that required mastering. With energy and determination, he was able to overcome these two obstacles very quickly and draw lessons from this experience, lessons that he would brilliantly apply in Boston.

Just as many other French emigrants from the aristocracy and the clergy, whose numbers increased after the massacres of September (which he had miraculously escaped), Cheverus earned his living by teaching; and he proved so successful that he was soon able to gather the means to open a small chapel in Tottenham and to dedicate himself to the apostolate.

He also learned English, the language that he would soon say had become more familiar to him than French. If his successes made him aware of the extent of his own capabilities, Cheverus hesitated nonetheless about what to do next: Should he return to France and become involved in the fight against the revolutionary undertaking (we know that he considered taking part in the Quiberon landing, organized by royalist exiles), or apply himself to the service of missionary work, relying on his talent for new undertakings and his newly acquired English? A letter from the Abbé Matignon, his professor at the Sorbonne who had subsequently settled in Boston, would convince him to cross the Atlantic and to give the American adventure a try. On October 3, 1796, Cheverus arrived in Boston, the capital of New England.

The Mission: The "Cheverus Method"

In many respects, it was not a foreign land that Cheverus encountered upon arriving in the New World. In the extremely large parish that welcomed him, a parish that spanned the area of the states that today make up New England, but that despite this then counted fewer than a thousand Catholics, the French influence, present since the beginning of colonization, had left significant traces, above all for Catholics.

New England was in a sense, "Catholic" even before becoming "New England," for the first Christian presence was owing to the French. Starting in 1604, the French colonists, including Samuel de Champlain, had established a settlement in what is now northern Maine, on the island of Ste. Croix, a point of departure for Catholic evangelization among the region's Native American tribes. The Catholic presence was indeed felt in Boston, and the first public Mass was celebrated there by the chaplain of the French fleet, the Abbé de la Poterie, a unique character and a knight of the Holy Sepulcher, to whom we owe the precious relic of the Holy Cross being in Boston, as well as the name of the first cathedral. In fact, the history of Catholicism in the last years of the eighteenth century is almost exclusively that of French clergy and Catholics.

This presence strengthened with the independence of the United States, because the head of the young American church, Bishop Carroll of Philadelphia, sought to bring foreign priests to the new republic. For Carroll had only twenty-four priests to attend to a thousand times that number of Catholics. Carroll had studied in France, at the Collège de Saint-Omer, before entering the Jesuit order and coming back to America in 1774 after the suppression of the order in France. He had seen very clearly how the French Revolution had forced the emigration of a large part of a clergy whose members he knew well. Upon his appeal, a hundred or so French priests settled in the United States, and among them was Father Matignon in Boston.

Warmly welcomed by Matignon, his former teacher, Cheverus did not indulge in unrealistic hopes; he knew his mission would be difficult. He would have to overcome many things: prejudice against Catholics, the need to increase the number of Catholics, and finally, the challenge of simply keeping the church going, in the face of an almost total lack of means. Cheverus would prove equal to all of these challenges.

It was not easy to be Catholic in Boston in the final years of the eighteenth century. Both members of the elite and of the common people remained suspicious, or even hostile, toward the "Papists," and there were legal handicaps that prevented the complete equality of citizens of different religions. Even if they were in the minority and formed a small community, Roman Catholics lived within a majority culture that looked upon them with hostility. Followers of a faith considered fanatical and obscurantist, these Christians had the additional fault of being either foreign (and French, for the most part, to boot) or non-Europeans (the Indian tribes of northern New England having been in large part converted by the French Jesuits) or else were to be found among very recent immigrants, such as the Irish. In a fictionalized account, Michael C. White described the extent of the prejudices of which New England Catholics — veritable second-class citizens — were then the victims. Cheverus would, in spite of everything, become their courageous and able spokesman.

The Garden of Martyrs tells the story of the iniquitous trial in which Dominic Daley and James Halligan, two Irish immigrants, were the victims of a miscarriage of justice when, in Northampton, Massachusetts, in June of 1806, they were falsely accused of murder, tried, and sentenced to death.[3] Not permitted to testify and to present their own defense, they paid for ethnic intolerance and prejudice with their lives. Cheverus would be the first to take up their cause, intervening on their behalf, securing better conditions for them while they were being held, and arguing for reconciliation between immigrants and "Yankees." He was not, however, able to save their lives.

In the face of what one might call "Puritan prejudice," Cheverus developed a skilled strategy of dialogue, teaching, openness, and listening that would yield its fruits, with the people as with the elite. The two, then three priests who covered the area that would later become the diocese, led simple and austere lives, close to the poor and to their parishioners, fully integrated into their new country. During the yellow fever epidemic that struck Boston in 1798, Father Cheverus was constantly at the bedside of the sick, bringing relief to some, comforting the families of others, and never tiring of being at the service of all. Later, in 1812, while the rumors of a British attack were causing alarm in the city and while its defenders mobilized, Father Cheverus was active in organizing his parishioners to help fortify the city, himself wielding shovel and trowel (*la pelle et la truelle* as we say in French). During his visits to the Indian tribes of Maine, he shared the life of his flock, sleeping on the ground, drinking "the broth that was prepared and eating the meat which was presented to him on the bark of a tree, the only crockery of the savage."[4]

His reputation as a protector of the poor would always remain with him, and the many anecdotes that his biographers would later recount in this regard do not belong to hagiography, but indeed to history.

Beyond his charity, naturally put to evangelical use, one of Cheverus's even more remarkable traits was his commitment to the debate of ideas, the importance of which he well understood, especially in Boston, rightly called then, and still now, the "Athens of America."

Without a doubt his training at the Oratory and at the Sorbonne prepared him well for the battle for the hearts and minds of men, as did his stay in England, which made him familiar with Protestantism. As Professor Michel Gauthier of Bordeaux notes, "It was in the desire to favor also the integration of his parishioners that he undertook to participate actively in the intellectual life of the city of which he became one of the most visible ornaments." Certainly, Boston hadn't yet reached its cultural height (which it would in the middle of the nineteenth century), but it had never forgotten that its first inhabitant, the scholar Blaxton, of Cambridge, had brought a library with him, and thus, in the elegant words of Van Wyck Brooks: "There were books on the slopes of Beacon Hill while wolves howled still at the summit."[5]

The French priest mixed with ease among the intellectual circles of the city and frequented, as their equal, the greatest minds of Boston. A recent exhibition at the Boston Atheneum testified to the role of Cheverus in the birth of that famous institution, to which, at its creation, he was the second most important contributor. A friend of such notables as John Adams and Josiah Quincy, Cheverus fostered contacts with the academic milieu, including, most obviously, Harvard. That celebrated university in fact recruited, during the period in which Cheverus was in Boston, a French priest, Father Brosius, to teach mathematics. It was also to the famous Boston architect Bulfinch that he would entrust the design of the Church of the Holy Cross, the first Catholic edifice of the city of Boston.

The impact of this intellectual apostolate was considerable because it contributed not only to diminishing religious antagonism by giving the Catholic Church an image defined by dialogue and humility (an excellent orator, Cheverus was even invited on more than one occasion to preach at Protestant meeting houses), but also in bringing about conversions. For instance, the role he played in the spiritual evolution of Elizabeth Seton, "Mother

Seton," with whom he corresponded regularly throughout his life, is well known. In Boston and in the region, Cheverus managed to convert several well-known Protestants to Catholicism.

It is important to underline this aspect of Cheverus's work, because in a way it established, as we shall see, a tradition of French intellectual influence within the diocese.

The priest never avoided public debate, claiming a sort of right of response to the anti-Catholic press published in Boston. He did so without being aggressive or unduly polemical, but rather with simple humility and pedagogical flair.

To those who scoffed at the veneration of holy relics, he reminded them of the respect that one felt when looking upon the ancient monuments: "one is in awe before an ancient marble work, and yet one cannot similarly be in awe before the remains of the founders of the faith!"[6] To those who attacked the practice of indulgences, he referred to the actions of the Church Fathers and protested, "If in so doing we are giving permission to sin, let our church be overthrown!"[7] And, finally, to those who accused the Catholic Church of intolerance, he responded that it was Protestant intolerance that had forced the original settlers, the Puritans, to seek refuge in America: "Read, I pray you, the eloquent speech of the immortal Burke to the electors of Bristol in 1780."[8] This method of argument proved convincing.

Bit by bit, Catholics would obtain access to full political freedom and the constitutional guarantee that they would be treated as full citizens. A first victory was reached in the new state of Maine, which had become independent of Massachusetts in 1819 and whose lawmakers, following a petition strongly inspired by Cheverus, recognized political equality for Catholics. Massachusetts would follow shortly thereafter, allowing Catholics to hold public office. (It would not be until 1841, however, that a Catholic would be elected to the state legislature.) In both cases, Cheverus played an influential role. This progress also reflected the growing number of Catholics in New England.

Upon his arrival in Boston, Cheverus could almost certainly put a name to the face of each of his parishioners: there were only 57 baptisms and only 17 Catholic marriages in 1798 in Boston, where 210 parishioners took communion at Easter. Among them were very few compatriots: the French families living in Boston, immigrants from Saint-Domingue or even France, were few and no longer made up the majority of parishioners. The majority instead consisted of Irish immigrants, whose numbers continued to grow. The Irish would soon be the main presence in the diocese, and would also transform the face of the American Catholic Church.

Outside of Boston, there were places where the Catholic presence was kept alive and active: most notably in Salem and New Bedford in Massachusetts, in Claremont in New Hampshire, and in Damariscotta and Lincoln County in Maine. Cheverus visited these places often and encouraged the local parishioners to build their own churches.

As for the Catholics among the Indian tribes in northern Maine, the Penobscots and the Passamaquoddys, they remained, but without great numbers or power. Beginning in the seventeenth century, French Jesuits, the "Black Robes," had converted many, and they remained loyal to their Catholic faith after the retreat of their French allies. When they requested that Father Cheverus be assigned to them to attend to their religious needs, their request was granted by Bishop Carroll of Baltimore. Cheverus, as we have elsewhere seen, took this new responsibility to heart, earning and maintaining as a result the loyalty of these populations. He eventually was able to secure the naming of a new missionary, Father Romagne, also French, for a full-time ministry for them.

Thanks to these efforts, the number of Catholics rose considerably, and by the time Cheverus left his diocese in 1823, the area he covered counted more than forty-five hundred faithful. Their visible presence was reinforced by new means of action and influence.

The intellectual and missionary work of Cheverus was complemented by his work as a practical man and builder, guaranteeing the diocese the institutional and physical foundations upon which its future development would depend.

A principal pride of a pastor is to give his faithful a church worthy of their commitment. Before the arrival of Cheverus, the Catholics did not yet possess their own edifice. Throughout the eighteenth century, services were held in the homes of the faithful, or a room was temporarily transformed into a chapel, where hospitality was offered to the priest passing through. Then, during the war for independence, and upon the request of the French troops stationed in Boston, a former Huguenot parish (then located at 18 School Street) was offered to the French priest Bouchard de la Poterie. It was he who would celebrate there the first official Catholic Mass in Boston. The building proved over time to be inadequate for the growing parish, and Cheverus dedicated himself to finding the means to build a true church. In 1803 he succeeded in doing this through a campaign to collect funds, which illustrated his method particularly well: widening the appeal of what might have been presented as a narrow sectarian cause, he attracted the support of many non-Catholics. President John Adams was his first contributor, and along with Adams several notable Protestant families made generous donations. He commissioned the great architect Charles Bulfinch, who worked mainly in and around Boston and was a Protestant, to design the Franklin Street building, unfortunately no longer standing today. *Suaviter in modo, fortiter in re* might have been his motto (Gentle in manner, resolute in execution). "A charm of manner that recalled Catholics to their duties and disarmed Protestants of their prejudices" wrote Bishop Carroll when he recommended Cheverus to Rome for the nomination of bishop.

To this first church of Boston, the other pillars with which Cheverus wanted to endow his community progressively were built; five churches would be added to the Cathedral of the Holy Cross in the years following, to house the parishes of the diocese. Cheverus was also concerned with the young and especially with the transmission of beliefs and knowledge from one generation to the next. He summoned from Canada nuns of the Ursuline order, and it was these nuns who opened both the first Catholic convent of Boston and the first parochial school, which in 1820 welcomed close to one hundred students. His training efforts were fulfilled when, in 1817, he had the joy of ordaining his first seminarian, the Irishman Denis Ryan. Bishop of Boston since 1808, Cheverus could then exclaim that he had indeed accomplished his mission. Looking upon all that he had achieved, Cheverus could take pride in these accomplishments and look toward returning to France, where the church clergy were clamoring for him.

After long hesitation, Bishop Cheverus finally accepted an appointment by Louis XVIII, the restored king of France, to lead the Diocese of Montauban. Cheverus left the United States on October 1, 1823, to the great distress of Boston's Catholics, and beyond that to a great number of others, people simply living within the bounds of the diocese. Cheverus then began the last stage in his life's journey, a stage that would bring him to the archbishopric of Bordeaux and, shortly before his death, earn him the title of cardinal, bestowed upon him by King Louis-Philippe in 1836.

Boston would remain his major accomplishment: he had established its cathedral, its first churches, a first crop of priests and nuns in training, soon to be at the service of a community undergoing great expansion. Along with his fellow French missionaries, he had in effect succeeded, over several years, to provide the Catholic Church of New England with a solid foundation. More than that, he had managed, at least for a time, to modify the local perception of the Catholic Church. The "Cheverus Method" had changed mentalities and established Catholicism as an active participant in the local religious landscape. "In this city and in other places where a few years ago the name Catholic Church was, so to speak, infamous, we are now looked on with veneration and friendship, kindly regarded and kindly treated," Cheverus wrote in a report he sent to Rome on February 7, 1817. And many were the testimonials of his contemporaries that confirmed this change: "What a difference from the past! Twenty years ago, they would have hanged me without ever the fear of a trial...," wrote the bishop of Quebec after a visit to Boston upon the invitation of Cheverus and, as we can see, pleasantly surprised at the welcome he received in the city.

The return of the bishop to France would even provoke a petition addressed to France's Grand Aumonier signed by 226 eminent Protestant Americans to ask that Cheverus be allowed to remain: "We hold him to be a blessing and a treasure in our social community which we cannot part with and which, without injustice to any man we may affirm, if withdrawn from us can never be replaced."[9]

Much like the fragment of the Holy Cross given to Boston by the Abbé de La Poterie, this small fragment of the church bequeathed by Cheverus and his French associates to the whole diocese would remain a source of great strength.

A Renewed Heritage?
Continuity and Change in the French Presence

The return of Bishop Cheverus to France was as much in response to the intense pressure from the French authorities to reclaim an exceptional administrator at a time when the church of France was also renewing itself, as it was at the same time adapting to the new situation within the American church.

The growth of the Irish immigration, as well as the ability of the young American Catholics to take their development and future into their own hands, made recourse to French clergy less necessary by this point. Although no fewer than thirty-five French bishops, among them Bishop Cheverus, would be part of America's hierarchy in the nineteenth century, the church's demographic makeup was changing.

As we have seen, the first bishop of Boston was indeed well aware of this need for renewal and change and understood early on how to encourage vocations among the youth of his diocese. His successor, Bishop Benedict Fenwick, was born in Maryland.

In fact, after the death of Abbé Matignon in September 1818, painfully felt by Cheverus, and after the departure of the Penobscots' chaplain, Father Romagne, and, finally, after the return of Cheverus to France, the French sources for senior clergy would dry up and other currents would irrigate the growth of the diocese.

Nevertheless, in various forms, the French influence would remain; it would continue to nourish the Catholic community of Boston. The most visible and impressive of these influences was that of the Quebec immigration, beginning in the middle of the nineteenth century. As an indirect bearer of French culture it would enrich the life of New England, and that of course included the Diocese of Boston. It was also accompanied by the establishment of religious orders of French origin, in addition to the Ursuline sisters called by Cheverus. The Ursulines, highly esteemed by Cheverus's successors, would play an important role in the development of educational and social initiatives of the diocese and its charitable works. On yet another level, that of intellectual debate and exchange, including theological debate, the contribution of the French Catholic intellectuals would be significant, continuing to nourish the exchanges on both sides of the Atlantic.

"He who loses his languages loses faith"

The veritable exodus of the Quebecois who would emigrate toward the south beginning in the second half of the nineteenth century reached great proportions. "From 1840 to 1930, approximately 900,000 left Quebec for the United States, of which close to two-thirds went to New England."[10] These fervent Catholics brought with them their religion and their priests and very quickly expressed the need for parishes of their own in their new towns, where they could, in their own language, foster their faith. Here is not the place to recount all the obstacles and the difficulties they encountered in this endeavor, especially in the face of interrogations from the hierarchy on the creation of "national parishes" and in the face also of the incomprehension and fears of the Catholics of Irish origin. What is important to note, however, is that the Diocese of Boston benefited from the contribution of these ardent, practicing Catholics and gave these new arrivals the opportunity to express their faith in French. The first French parish was established in 1868 in Lowell, where the Oblates of Mary Immaculate served at the Church of St. John the Baptist.

Boston even saw the creation, under the impetus of the French priest Léon Bouland, of a "French national parish," placed under the patronage of Our Lady of Victories. After some vicissitudes, this parish was taken over in 1883 by the Marists, who had come from France and took up residence on Isabella Street. It is still today an active community, where one can admire, within this beautiful Gothic church, panes of stained glass from Chartres, one of which is dedicated to Bishop Cheverus. The parish still holds the title of "French national parish."

The initiative spread: another French parish opened in Cambridge in 1892, and yet another in Chelsea in 1908. In 1907 there were seventeen French parishes in the diocese, and by 1938 there would be twenty-five.

These churches were often adorned with objects imported from France and often dedicated to saints highly venerated in France: Our Lady of Lourdes, St. Joan of Arc, and the Curé of Ars have all found their place. French was spoken, prayer was conducted in French, and traditional French hymns were sung. It was the golden age for the French influence in the diocese.

This imprint was further strengthened by the arrival, once again, of French religious representatives in significant numbers. Just as the Revolution of 1789 had brought about the emigration of many priests, one hundred years later another moment of crisis in France — that of the end of the Concordat and the adoption of secular law — would have great effects on the American church.

The Third Republic had indeed undertaken a complete reform of the public education system, along with a ban prohibiting clergy from teaching. In 1904 a law was passed that excluded members of religious orders from schools. Hundreds of clergy and religious people, kept from such pedagogical service, turned to emigration in order to be allowed to continue their teaching.

At the prompting of the Quebecois and American hierarchies, opportunities were offered to the members of these congregations, particularly in New England, where the "Francos," or French Canadians, awaited them.

The Marists, as we have seen, acquired not only Our Lady of Victories in Boston but other parishes throughout the region. It was a French priest, Father André Garin, an Oblate of Mary Immaculate, who founded St. John the Baptist in Lowell. The expansion of the social and charitable work of the diocese called upon the skills and competencies that other French congregations had the reputation of mastering. It was thus that the Little Sisters

of the Poor took residence in 1870 at the request of Bishop Williams, who
assigned a group of six nuns from Paris to the management of a home for
the aged. The Sisters of Charity of St. Vincent de Paul, including St. Elizabeth Seton, under the influence of Cheverus had founded their American
branch and established themselves in the diocese as well. The Brothers of
Charity of Montreal followed in 1872 and opened the House of the Angel
Guardian. New congregations sprang up locally at the initiative of French
clergymen. The Alsatian Father Marie-Clément Staub founded in December
1914 at Assumption College in Worcester, the congregation of the sisters of
St. Joan of Arc. Their vocation was to help priests in the rectory; they would
always count among their ranks a majority of Franco-American sisters.[11]

Through these several examples we can see the immense contribution
made to the diocese by the French clergy and by the Franco-American
Catholic community that came from Canada. It followed in the spirit of
the missionary accomplishments of Cheverus.

The process of assimilation that the "Francos" would undergo would
eventually render this contribution less perceptible, especially in Boston,
where, unlike in other towns in the diocese, the community formed a small
group, less united, less geographically concentrated, without the "Little
Canadas" that one found in Lowell and Manchester. Over a few years, the
French parishes of Boston and its surroundings lost their homogeneity and
progressively disbanded. From 1908 to 1914 the decline within the parish of
Our Lady of Victories was significant: 135 baptisms were recorded in 1908,
and only 48 in 1912. In 1890, 60 children received their First Communion,
but by 1909 that number was down to 10. After 1912, these numbers were
no longer recorded. The sacrament of confirmation, which had been con-
ferred every two years before 1900, was given to 190 children in 1891, but
to only 29 in 1911. After 1914, the numbers had so dwindled that those
who remained were sent to the Cathedral of the Holy Cross.[12]

After Cheverus, after the decline of the identity of the Franco-American
community, did the French influence find new channels of expression? The
response that French thinkers and theologians have gotten from Catholic
intellectuals and academics of the diocese allow us to answer this question
in the affirmative.

A Contemporary Dialogue

As we saw earlier, the young American church depended in great part on the
French clergy to train its seminarians. French Sulpicians and Jesuits made
up the bulk of the teaching faculty of the seminary in Baltimore, the first
American Catholic seminary. Throughout the nineteenth century, in fact,
the French factor would continue to be present in the training of American priests. It is quite remarkable that in the case of the Diocese of Boston,
from Bishop Cheverus to Bishop O'Connell, all the bishops up until the
twentieth century received training that was in large part French. The successor of Cheverus, Bishop Fenwick, had attended the Sulpician seminary
of Baltimore; Bishop Fitzpatrick, who replaced him in 1846, completed his

theological studies at the Saint-Sulpice seminary in Paris, having first attended the Sulpician college of Montreal. And, finally, Bishop Williams, consecrated in 1866, was also an alumnus of both the seminary in Montreal and Saint-Sulpice in Paris, where he was ordained to the priesthood in 1845. It is thus understandable that the first archbishop of Boston appealed to the French congregations to help him in his endeavors. Finally, Bishop O'Connell studied at St. Charles College in Maryland, a seminary run by French Sulpicians.

It was no surprise that in the summer of 1884 a group of Sulpicians arrived from both Paris and from Maryland to make up the faculty of the new seminary of the diocese, the Seminary of St. John.

This remarkable situation would not last, however, and the influence of French professors would wane, as had the influence of Cheverus himself. The French were replaced by new American professors. After the period of supervision and substitution, one of cooperation and dialogue was finally being ushered in.

It was in this spirit that the relationship between French Catholics and the Catholics of the Diocese of Boston would be built upon a constant exchange and debate of ideas.

As the young French historian Florian Michel has shown, brilliant contemporary French Catholic intellectuals showed real interest in the United States and developed a network of work and friendship here. Boston was one of their favored destinations. We see this, for example, in the case of historian and philosopher Etienne Gilson, who came to the United States for the first time in 1926 on the occasion of an international philosophy conference that took place in Boston. He immediately took a liking to Boston, and, thanks to an agreement linking the Sorbonne and Harvard, he secured a position teaching in Cambridge for three semesters. This brilliant exegete of the Middle Ages and advocate of neo-Thomism enjoyed the esteem of his colleagues at Harvard and was invited to speak on the occasion of the university's tercentenary in 1936.

French Catholic thought would have yet another illustrious representative in the diocese: Jacques Maritain. "The greatest Catholic intellectual of the century," according to the *Dictionnaire des intellectuels français,* was, indeed, a friend and admirer of the United States.[13] His *Reflections on the United States,* published in 1958, is a testament to this. As Florian Michel remarks, Maritain was at the center of a Franco-American milieu made up of scholars, musicians, and diplomats who strove to reinforce the links between the two countries. Maritain spent over fifteen years in the United States. After being in New York from 1940 to 1944, he settled for a time in Princeton. He had discovered America in 1933 while on a trip to Boston, where he had been invited by Harvard professor Daniel Sargent. His links to Boston would only gain strength thereafter, culminating in 1958 when Boston College granted him the title of *doctor honoris causa,* bestowed upon him by Archbishop Cushing.

Gilson and Maritain, through the university circles of Boston, contributed greatly much both to secular society and to the local Catholic community: a renewed interest in Thomism, metaphysics, and theology. Florian Michel notes that the connections with Maritain are not purely academic. Maritain knew quite well Bishop John Wright, auxiliary bishop of Boston. Wright would go on to become bishop of Worcester and cardinal of the Curia. At a time when Maritain was contemplating his plans for the future, Bishop Wright played a little-known role in convincing him not to return to France: "Your work must be done here," he was told by the bishop. And Maritain followed this advice.[14]

Maritain's hesitation was reminiscent of that of Cheverus almost a century and a half before. From Cheverus to Maritain, to those who today salute their memory, a close relationship between France and the Archdiocese of Boston has truly flourished over many long years. This friendly relationship continues to this day, as we can see, for example, in the recent display of the relics of the Curé of Ars in the archdiocese.

Conclusion

Over the course of these two centuries, on various levels the French influence has always been present within the life of the Archdiocese of Boston. It has enriched and broadened its cultural heritage. Indeed, it is part of its collective memory. This influence reminds us that New England was also New France and that the French presence in North America has helped to shape, perhaps more than is often recognized, the human and cultural makeup of the region.

The French heritage is far more than just a few names on a map (out of the six states of the region, two have French names: Maine and Vermont). It is far more than a few buildings in Back Bay. It goes well beyond such visible traces.

The French historian Jean-Baptiste Duroselle liked to speak of the "mysterious charm of the Franco-American relationship." This charm can be found in the pages of a remarkable religious history written, together, by the Catholic communities of our two countries.

2

Papism and Politics in Massachusetts

Thomas H. O'Connor

The history of the Catholic Church in North America has many fascinating examples of ways in which the character, the beliefs, and the traditions of the venerable mother church in Rome, with its ancient religious precepts and conservative European customs, came into conflict with the newer ideas and more populist impulses of the Catholic communities that came into being in the United States. The question of rendering unto Caesar what is Caesar's and to God what is God's, for example, was a conundrum that took on special significance in a nation whose concepts of personal freedom were based upon individual rights and constitutional principles. To what extent those principles could be reconciled with a religious institution that derives its faith from divine revelation and ecclesiastical authority makes for an interesting and often complicated question well into the twenty-first century.

At first, of course, Roman Catholics had no political rights — indeed, no rights at all — in the openly hostile Puritan environment of the Massachusetts Bay Colony.[1] It was the coming of the American Revolution that actually brought about some remarkable and totally unexpected changes in the traditional status of Papists. While most of these changes were clearly designed to persuade the French monarchy to support the colonies in their rebellion against the British, the unintended consequences gave the small community of French and Irish immigrants their first measure of political acceptance. When General George Washington arrived in Cambridge in November 1775 to take command of the Continental Army, for example, he issued an order prohibiting his officers and men from taking part in that "ridiculous and childish" custom known as Pope's Night. He pointed out the "impropriety" of insulting the religious beliefs of their French Canadian allies in such a "monstrous" and inexcusable fashion.[2]

Once under way, the Revolution also provided many Bostonians with their first opportunity to become personally acquainted with French officers and state officials who came into the port of Boston aboard naval vessels. But a number of Bostonians, too, traveled to other cities and towns where they encountered many of their own countrymen with whom they had never been associated. John Adams met Charles Carroll of Carrollton, for example, a prominent citizen of Maryland, who had become a member of the Continental Congress and subsequently signed the Declaration of Independence. Adams was greatly impressed not only by the gentleman's liberal education, but also by the fact that although he was a dedicated Roman Catholic, he also appeared to be a patriotic American. Adams went so far as to approve sending Carroll's cousin, John, "a Roman Catholic Priest and a Jesuit," to work among the people of Canada for the rebel cause.[3]

These various changes in the local religious climate, especially after 1778 when France recognized the United States of America and concluded a military and commercial alliance, help explain why, when Massachusetts delegates met in September 1779 to draft a new state constitution, they composed a Bill of Rights that guaranteed "equal protection of the law" to all religious denominations. Few were under the delusion, however, that Catholics would actually receive any such equal treatment, since the new constitution required all state officials to take an oath that they were not subject to the jurisdiction or authority of any "foreign prince, person, prelate, state, or potentate." Since Protestants naturally assumed that Catholics were subject to both pope and prelate, this clause automatically excluded them from holding public office in Massachusetts.[4]

In 1801, although he had been in Boston only five years, young Father Jean Cheverus saw clearly the limitations still imposed upon Roman Catholics. In a letter to Bishop John Carroll, he summed up the prevailing situation sadly, but with a touch of Gallic realism: "Papists are only tolerated," he told the bishop. "As long as our ministers behave, we will not disturb them, but let us expect no more than that."[5] In 1820, however, when Maine was separated from Massachusetts as a result of the Missouri Compromise, Cheverus was pleased to learn that the Massachusetts clause preventing Catholics from holding public office was absent from Maine's new constitution. "Now," said the French cleric who by this time was bishop of Boston, "Catholics, Jews, and Moslems can hold public office here."[6]

Although the Constitution of the United States was formally ratified in 1788, no provisions had been made for political parties. Nevertheless, by 1794 controversies over national policy between Alexander Hamilton of New York (President Washington's secretary of the treasury), and Secretary of State Thomas Jefferson of Virginia, had produced two separate and distinct political factions.[7] Generally speaking, the rank and file of the Irish in Boston did not need too much persuasion to become staunch supporters of the Jeffersonian Republican Party. The homespun image of Jefferson himself, the strong agrarian nature of his political views, and his support of the French revolutionary ideals were all factors that appealed to immigrant Irish Catholics. Interestingly enough, local church leaders like Father François Matignon and Bishop Jean Cheverus, both of whom had escaped from a revolutionary regime that had secularized their church and sent clergymen to the guillotine, took a much different view. They were generally more sympathetic to the conservative principles of Hamilton, and opposed to the liberal secularism of Jefferson.[8] As a result, in a pattern that would last well into the future, the political objectives of the common people were often at variance with those of the members of their church's hierarchy. Fortunately, the American principle of separation of church and state, whether stated or implied, made it possible for the Irish to hold completely different and sometimes conflicting political views than those of their bishops, while continuing to submit loyally and obediently to their ecclesiastical authority in religious matters.[9]

From only a few hundred, when the first congregation was formed, the number of Irish Catholics in Boston had risen to some two thousand by 1820, to more than five thousand by 1825, and to just past the seven thousand mark by 1830, not long after Andrew Jackson of Tennessee had become the presidential candidate of the newly formed Democratic Party.[10] Along with their countrymen in other parts of the nation, the Boston Irish hailed Jackson's entrance into national politics. Not only did he seem to represent many of Jefferson's appealing rustic virtues, but his close identification with the "real people" made him even more appealing to immigrant voters. Emphasizing the distinction between the workingman and the businessman, Old Hickory created a political and social alliance that would keep the Irish in the Democratic Party for generations to come.[11]

Then, too, there was the fact that Andrew Jackson was a self-proclaimed Irishman — a theme the old general played upon with great political savvy. Those who supported President John Quincy Adams for reelection expressed disgust with the way in which Jackson agents were welcoming immigrants "with open arms," while searching out new recruits in "the kennels and the gutters" of the Irish districts. Although Whig newspapers assured their subscribers that Adams would surely sweep the Northeast and go on to victory, it came as a tremendous shock when the news arrived in November 1828 that Andrew Jackson had defeated John Quincy Adams for the presidency of the United States. Whigs bemoaned the fact that "all Broad Street" (the Irish section of Boston) would be invited to come to Washington to attend the inauguration as "the peculiar favorites of the *Irish* [sic] President."[12]

Perhaps it was the strong commitment of Irish Catholics to the democratic principles of Thomas Jefferson and the egalitarian politics of Andrew Jackson that created a tentative feeling in some quarters that quite possibly Catholicism, as it began to develop in the uniquely free American environment, might gradually assume more democratic characteristics. Charles Carroll, for example, had already established his patriotic credentials, and his cousin John had served the American cause in Canada before being named the first Catholic bishop in the United States. Once in office, Bishop Carroll had accommodated himself to the prevailing practice of placing church property in the hands of lay boards of trustees who were responsible for administering the legal and financial affairs of parishes at a time when Catholic priests would not be accorded official recognition.[13]

In the town of Boston, since no Catholic priest had been allowed to reside in the Bay Colony, lay people organized their first religious community along the lines of the prevailing congregational model, with lay trustees assuming legal responsibility for church finances and property rights. As early as 1831, as John McGreevy has pointed out in his study *Catholicism and American Freedom*, Alexis de Tocqueville, the observant French visitor, felt that he could sense a new "Catholic style" in America, suggesting the possibility that in time Catholicism might well become a powerful contributor to the "maintenance of a Democratic Republic in the United States." And about the same time, another visitor, Harriet Martineau, encouraged her British readers to believe that the Catholic religion in America was being modified by the "spirit of the time," and that its members were no longer a set of men "who can be priest-ridden to any fatal extent."[14]

Occasional speculation that the Catholic Church in America might be moving into a more "congregational" direction was put to rest before too long, however, when the Vatican stepped in after the death of Bishop John Carroll in 1815 and began appointing more conservative bishops. Neither members of the Roman hierarchy, nor an increasing number of the newly appointed bishops, found the "congregational" style of lay trusteeship acceptable as a permanent arrangement. Bishop Henry Conwell of Philadelphia, for example, complained that if this *democratic* [sic] method of ruling the church were ever to be approved by the Holy See, then "it would mean the quick collapse of the American church."[15] During the 1830s and 1840s, there was hardly an American parish that did not experience angry clashes between those who wanted to retain the earlier democratic procedures they had started out with, and those "ultramontanes" who looked ("beyond the mountains") to Rome for guidance in establishing a more centralized form of governance. Like Bishop John Hughes in New York, who announced that "episcopal authority comes from above and not from below," most bishops gradually eliminated the original boards of lay trustees and formed their own advisory boards.[16]

The reassertion of Vatican influence, the emergence of episcopal authority, and the unparalleled growth of the Catholic population during the late 1830s convinced many Protestants that they were no longer contending with a small and diffuse group of immigrants, but a growing organism of truly sinister proportions, whose members would "lay their inexperienced hands upon the helm of our power" and eventually destroy American liberties.[17] For proof of their conspiratorial theories, local Protestants could point to evidence that the Boston Irish were already creating a hostile political bloc. In 1843, the *Pilot,* the city's Catholic weekly, organized its estimated seven thousand subscribers and launched a campaign to defeat certain members of the state legislature who had not supported legislation to pay damages caused when an angry mob of workingmen burned down the Ursuline convent in Charlestown some nine years earlier.[18] Although the newspaper failed in its bid to change the membership of the legislature, its efforts revived old-time fears among many Boston natives who saw the fine hand of the Catholic hierarchy behind the scenes — a fear that was further inflamed the following year by reports that the Catholic issue in New York had caused the defeat of the Whig candidate, Henry Clay, in the presidential elections of 1844. The *Boston Courier* blamed the election of Democrat James K. Polk directly on the influence of Catholic priests who were out to bring the United States "under the subjection to the Holy See."[19]

The fear of growing Catholic political influence in Massachusetts became even more intense several years later when word circulated that the bishop of Boston was using his political influence to help defeat several changes being proposed at the state constitutional convention in 1853.[20] The issue rose when Democratic representatives from the western counties of Massachusetts made a number of constitutional proposals that would take away a good deal of power and patronage from the Whig establishment in the eastern part of the state. Ordinarily, immigrant voters in the East Coast cities voted almost automatically in favor of the Democrats, but in this particular case they feared that anti-Catholic rural voters in the west would gerrymander them out of existence and agreed with the *Pilot* that the proposals were "unfair, unjust, and undemocratic."[21] As a result, in an uncharacteristic move, the Irish switched their support to the upper-class Whigs, who were anxious to retain their dominant position in the urban areas. This uncustomary change in the Irish vote was attributed by most Yankees to the influence of the Catholic bishop and his desire to keep the immigrant voting power intact in the major cities of the east.

A native of Boston, and a graduate of the Boston Latin School, Bishop John Fitzpatrick had not only won the affection of his own immigrant flock when he took office in 1846, but also the respect of the Brahmin community. "Although two-thirds of the City are still Protestant," observed a visiting French cleric, "Boston cheerfully hailed the arrival of its new Bishop, whom the Bostonians are proud to designate a countryman of their own."[22] As bishop of Boston, Fitzpatrick regularly called upon his immigrant parishioners to forget about political dissension back in the Old Country and focus on their responsibilities to their adopted land. "This is our country now," he advised them. "Ireland is only a recollection." He urged them to become citizens as soon as possible, to vote regularly, and to assume the liberties of American citizens. At a time when Irish Catholics held no public offices in the Commonwealth and exercised very little influence in political affairs, Bishop Fitzpatrick took it upon himself to defend his parishioners from what he regarded as infringements of their basic constitutional rights.[23] In lodging his protests, the bishop was careful to frame his arguments in the kind of political and constitutional terms that could be readily understood by the predominantly Anglo-Saxon society of Boston, rather than resorting to the religious precepts of canon law that would have had little or no influence upon his listeners at that time. Instead of representing the religious beliefs of Roman Catholics, as such, he made it clear that he was upholding their constitutional rights as American citizens.

When he learned, for example, that indigent Catholic patients in the hospitals and almshouses were being denied the consolation of priests, he paid a personal visit to Mayor Josiah Quincy Jr. to protest such discriminatory practices.[24] When city authorities complained about the size and dimensions of Catholic burial sites, Fitzpatrick put the members of the Common Council on notice that he would use all his powers as bishop of Boston to protect his people from illegal harassment.[25] And when a boy named Thomas Wall had his hands badly beaten with a rattan by a public school teacher for refusing to read aloud the Protestant version of the Ten Commandments, Fitzpatrick advised his parents to bring legal charges against the headmaster of the school, while he himself sent a strongly worded letter to the members of the Boston School Committee protesting the violation of the personal liberties of Catholic Americans.[26]

It was one thing for the well-known bishop to speak out on behalf of his parishioners; it was quite another thing, however, for him to apparently encourage Irish-Catholics to organize their political power in an attempt to defeat an amendment to the state constitution. When the proposed revisions were eventually voted down in November 1853, it was assumed by most Bostonians that the personal influence of Bishop John Fitzpatrick had played an influential role in the defeat. "To this result," wrote former governor George S. Boutwell, "the influence of Bishop Fitzpatrick has contributed essentially," and the *Daily Commonwealth* agreed that for the first time in the history of Massachusetts, "the Catholic Church has taken the field as a power."[27]

More conscious than ever of the growing number of Irish-Catholic voters, especially after the frightening upsurge of immigration that followed the Great Famine of the mid-1840s, native Bostonians were now absolutely certain that a major Catholic voting bloc was in the making. Extraordinary measures were necessary to save the Commonwealth — and, indeed, the nation — from the power of immigrant voters.

Those extraordinary measures came almost immediately with the formation of the "American Party," a national political organization designed to protect the United States from the "insidious wiles of foreigners." Highly secret, with passwords, handshakes, and special oaths, by the fall of 1854 the so-called Know-Nothing Party had swept to power throughout the states of the North. In Massachusetts, it succeeded in electing the governor, all state officers, the entire membership of the Senate, and all but four members of the House. Once in office, the legislators pushed forward a program of "Temperance, Liberty, and Protestantism" and declared themselves ready to eliminate "Rome, Rum, and Robbery." Energized by their swift successes, during the summer of 1856 Know-Nothing leaders made plans to nominate their own candidate for the presidency of the United States.[28]

Fortunately for immigrant Americans, the Know-Nothing movement collapsed almost as suddenly as it had begun. The explosion of violence between the free-soil and pro-slave factions that rocked the Kansas Territory during the spring of 1856 drove the American Party from the national headlines, and caused the abysmal defeat of its presidential candidate, Millard Fillmore, in the November elections. It had become clear to all that human slavery, not foreign immigration, was the issue that would tear the nation apart in a contest of wills that eventually led to the disruption of the Union and the outbreak of civil war.[29]

Ironically, just as the Revolutionary War had first made it possible for Catholics to exist at all as part of the civic community, it was the Civil

War that provided them with their first real opportunity to exercise those political powers they had previously been denied. As a result of their willingness to fight for the preservation of the Union, Irish Catholics emerged from the conflict with a degree of civic tolerance that would have been unthinkable a decade earlier. And there were concrete results from this new attitude. The Massachusetts legislature, for example, instructed all school committees that no students could be required to read from any version of the Bible that went against "the conscientious scruples" of their parents or guardians. City authorities also announced that patients in the Boston City Hospital could now be attended by a clergyman of their own choosing.[30] This type of legislation, the *Pilot* observed, was "a long stride" from the intolerance of the Know-Nothing years and a clear acknowledgment of the loyalty displayed by the "adopted citizens in this hour of national trial."[31]

Not only did the national conflict reflect a welcome change in the social status of Irish Catholics, but it also marked a decided improvement in their depressed economic circumstances. Whether it was a bounty for service in the armed forces, income from war work in factories, armories, and shipyards, or salaries from construction projects laying out the South End or filling in the Back Bay, for the first time many Irish men and women were able to bring home a day's pay on a regular basis. This improvement in their financial income allowed many Irish families to abandon the congested areas along the Boston waterfront and move into the nearby neighborhoods of Charlestown, Brighton, Dorchester, and West Roxbury in such large numbers that by 1873 all of these districts had been annexed to the city of Boston.[32]

Despite a greater degree of tolerance and a higher level of financial security, however, it was not at all clear that Roman Catholics would enjoy any more substantial political power than they did before the war. After Appomattox, the Republican Party was clearly dominant. It was the party of Lincoln, the Constitution, emancipation, and victory. The Democratic Party, on the other hand, was the party of the Confederacy, secession, slavery, and defeat, supported only by a handful of old-line Yankee Democrats and a growing number of loyal but still powerless Irish Americans. The political future certainly did not look bright at all.[33]

By the 1870s and 1880s, however, the Boston Irish were no longer the impoverished, infirm, and illiterate exiles who had dragged themselves ashore during the 1840s and 1850s. Numbering well over seventy thousand, they now constituted a growing and maturing community that was becoming increasingly conscious of its size and assertive of its powers.[34] One of the first significant signs of a new political consciousness occurred on August 18, 1868, when a group of young Irishmen met at Boston's Parker House and formed the Young Men's Democratic Club, with the intention of reinvigorating and reshaping the Democratic Party so that Irish Americans, for the first time, could play a substantive role. The sons of Irish immigrants, most of these young men had managed to acquire an education and had become accepted into the middle-class professional community of Boston.[35]

The undisputed leader of this emerging group was Patrick A. Collins, whose mother had brought him to Massachusetts in 1848 after his father had died during the famine. He attended the public schools in Chelsea, was a regular communicant at St. Rose Church, and later worked as an upholsterer. Studying nights at the Boston Public Library, young Collins eventually received a law degree from Harvard Law School, and in 1868 was elected to the Massachusetts House. Two years later he became the youngest member of the state Senate, where he worked to abolish remaining forms of anti-Catholic discrimination.[36]

No longer content to be silent partners in a civic process still dominated by what was fast becoming a Yankee minority, Collins and his young friends were ready to assume an aggressive role in state government without counsel or direction from church leaders. There was no distinguishable anticlericalism about this, however. They simply regarded things like political elections, party programs, and legislative policies as separate and apart from the spiritual concerns of the Catholic Church.[37] Most men remained on good terms with members of the clergy, and Collins himself became a charter member of Archbishop Williams's new lay organization called the Catholic Union. Conscious of the rise of laymen in political and financial circles, the archbishop himself attended the weekly meetings of the Catholic Union, making it quite clear in his deliberate fashion that although he did not want "aggressive" Catholics, neither did he want "cowardly" ones. He wanted Catholics, he told the members, who would "stand on their rights as American citizens; no more."[38]

This was certainly consistent with the view of Patrick Collins, who had moved from the state legislature in 1882 to begin the first of three terms in the United States Congress. As proud as he was to be a Catholic, Collins was equally proud to be a Democrat, according to his friend Michael Curran, and expressed the belief that Thomas Jefferson was to Democracy what St. Paul was to Christianity. As a younger man, traveling through New England during the mid-1860s as an agent for the Fenian Brotherhood, he had come under fire from several Catholic clergymen, and responded sharply to what he regarded as an unfair attack upon his work for Irish independence: "A clergyman has no more right to mark out for an Irishman his course in Irish politics than he has to dictate to an American whether he shall vote the Republican or the Democratic ticket."[39] Some forty years later, it was still evident that Collins had not modified his political views regarding the separation of church and state. Shortly after his inauguration as mayor of Boston, on January 4, 1902, he was approached by several of his supporters. "General," said one of them, "you can do a great deal for your Catholic friends." Turning on the man, Collins made it clear where his political responsibilities lay: "I want you to understand, I am first an American, second a Democrat, and third a Catholic."[40]

Despite the fact that Democratic politics and the Catholic religion in Boston were beginning to move along separate but parallel tracks after the Civil War, there were few occasions when their respective concerns came into actual conflict during the nation's "Age of Big Business." This was a time of vast technological and industrial change that opened up numerous job opportunities for unskilled immigrant laborers. Large numbers of these workers, however, were badly exploited in the factories, the mills, the mines, and the sweatshops of the period and, after working long hours at little pay, went home to unheated apartments and overcrowded tenements.[41]

Providing solutions to the numerous social problems associated with the exploitation of workers and their families soon became the objective of various social agencies and charitable institutions. Catholic Church leaders tended to avoid the institutionalized agencies, however, generally preferring to deal with the problems of "their own people" in their own ways. Still suspicious of old-time Protestant proselytizing, they were now concerned that government involvement would diminish the primacy of parental authority in American families. Then, too, there was the belief that if government institutions took over the care of the poor, the homeless, the widow, and the orphan, then individual Catholics would be deprived of the opportunity to practice the virtue of charity, from which they could expect to gain eternal grace.[42]

Irish-Catholic politicians, especially in the Northeast, also agreed that the pressing social issues of the day were best handled locally, by those who knew the poor and the needy personally and directly. This certainly was the case with those local political figures known as ward bosses who had moved into positions of power and influence in the various districts of Boston, and who saw a direct relationship between the delivery of benefits and the delivery of votes.[43] While the boss regarded his position as a source of personal political advancement, he also saw it as an opportunity to help families, friends, and neighbors obtain the bare necessities of life without having to go through the humiliating experience of what Martin Lomasney, the boss of Ward Eight, once referred to as "the inquisitorial terrors of organized charity."[44] And with the election in 1884 of Hugh O'Brien as the first Irish-born mayor of Boston, local political leaders could take satisfaction in knowing that their political views would prevail.

On the state and national levels, as well, Democratic leaders also continued to believe that solutions to social problems should be constrained within the limits of local and familiar structures. As staunch Jackson Democrats, they continued to emphasize limited government, states' rights, and local controls. Even after the Civil War, they continued to oppose a national banking system, a gold standard, and a protective tariff. Believing in a natural balance of powers, embodied in the two major political parties, New England Democrats refused to be stampeded into supporting the more radical movements being promoted by Greenbacks, Populists, and Progressives throughout the Midwest that would give the federal government more power in controlling monopolies, managing railroads, and regulating trusts.[45] Most Irish Catholics sensed a sort of socialism or anarchism in these movements, which they were not ready to accept and of which few Catholic Church leaders would approve.[46] Patrick Collins, for example, expressed the view that as long as the American people still had the political rights guaranteed to them by the Constitution, then there was no need of "radical" solutions. Despite the evangelistic fervor of William Jennings Bryan and his progressive followers during the presidential campaign of 1896, Collins remained a conservative "Cleveland-Democrat" in the face of populist demands and progressive theories.[47]

When he returned to Boston after serving four years as American consul-general to London, Patrick Collins was persuaded to run for election as mayor of Boston. His successful campaign in 1902 made it abundantly clear that Irish Catholics had effectively taken over the Yankee city, and his sweeping reelection two years later helped to confirm his genuine popularity among both Protestants and Catholics. It was with great shock and grief, therefore, that Bostonians reacted to the news that on September 14, 1905, Mayor Patrick Collins had died suddenly in Hot Springs, Virginia, where he had gone for a rest.[48]

While the city went into mourning, John F. Fitzgerald, the forty-two-year-old boss of the North End, went into action and in November 1905 succeeded Collins as mayor of Boston. Fitzgerald's election ushered in a new phase of Boston's political history. The city's two former Catholic mayors, Hugh O'Brien and Patrick Collins, had been born in Ireland and regarded America as their "adopted land." Always deferential to the Brahmin traditions of Boston, they were willing to establish an accommodationist relationship with Yankee Democrats and Liberal Republicans whenever the situation warranted it. Starting with Fitzgerald, however, a new generation of Boston-born Irish political leaders would display little of the early deferential attitude or the accommodationist spirit in their drive to monopolize the agencies of municipal government.[49]

In the Catholic Church there was an almost simultaneous change in traditional attitudes and relationships. Throughout most of the nineteenth century, the general tendency of Boston's hierarchy toward the city's political establishment had been one of what historian Paula Kane has described as "withdrawn retrenchment."[50] The town's first bishop, Jean Cheverus, established remarkably cordial relations with the Yankee community, and later such prelates as John Fitzpatrick and John Williams worked successfully with tact and diplomacy to maintain a peaceful coexistence between their insecure immigrant flock and a hostile native-born population.[51] With the arrival in 1907 of William Henry O'Connell as archbishop of Boston, however, the days of passivity and accommodation were over. Vigorous and determined, O'Connell let it be known at the outset that a new age had arrived: "The Puritan has passed; the Catholic remains," he announced. "The child of the immigrant is called to fill the place which the Puritan has left."[52]

O'Connell set to work to make sure that this prediction came true. While Irish political leaders continued to concern themselves with winning elections, distributing favors, and focusing on local political issues, the archbishop established a pattern of separatism throughout the Archdiocese of

Boston that was carefully designed to disentangle Catholics as much as possible from all forms of Protestant influence. Separate Catholic Boy Scout and Girl Scout troops were set up for young people, and the establishment of the Catholic Youth Organization (CYO) was designed to reduce the influence of such suspect agencies as the YMCA and the YWCA. The new archbishop strongly urged pastors and parents to make sure their children attended parochial schools and Catholic colleges, and warned the faithful to avoid Protestant churches and all forms of non-Catholic ceremonies. In this way, according to Paula Kane, O'Connell created a "separatist Catholic subculture," designed to make Catholics more confident and secure in their own unique history and heritage.[53]

In shaping the religious values of Boston Catholics, the archbishop was trying to shape their political attitudes as well. He spoke out often about his own deep love for America and refused to accept the charge that Catholics could not be good Americans because they owed allegiance to Rome. O'Connell's own brand of Americanism took the form usually associated with the Republican Party in the early twentieth century, although he carefully refrained from involving himself in political campaigns or supporting any candidate for public office. When issues arose that he felt involved matters of Catholic Church doctrine or infringed upon the morality of Catholic family life, however, O'Connell did not hesitate to speak out strongly. This was particularly true in the years after World War I, when he saw the rise of totalitarian movements — Fascism in Italy, Nazism in Germany, and Communism in Russia — which he felt could endanger the freedoms of America and the sacredness of the American family.

O'Connell's apprehensions concerning the dangers of centralized power of government help explain his strong opposition during the 1920s and 1930s as the federal government became increasingly involved in social legislation.[54] Following the assassination of President William McKinley in 1902, the elevation of Theodore Roosevelt to the presidency had marked the beginning of a new era. Convinced that the national government should observe the rights of the worker as well as the employer, Roosevelt initiated antitrust suits, increased government regulation of railroads, broadened federal inspection of food, drugs, and meat, and launched an ambitious program of national conservation. After 1912, under Woodrow Wilson, government directives affecting public utilities and private enterprises became even more expansive, and in 1916 the Democrats were the first to pass a federal law regulating the working conditions of children.

These were precisely the kinds of extraordinary powers that caused the archbishop of Boston (elevated to cardinal in 1911) grave concern. He had personal misgivings about giving women the right to vote, but when the Nineteenth Amendment was finally passed in 1920, he accepted the decision with good grace and urged Catholic women to use their vote wisely.[55] In 1924, however, when a Massachusetts ballot question inquired whether Massachusetts should ratify a constitutional amendment approving federal laws to restrict child labor, O'Connell organized a vigorous campaign to defeat it. Along with most of the state's Irish political leaders, O'Connell opposed any child labor bill on the grounds that it would give unprecedented powers to the federal government — powers, he said, that would menace family life, endanger parental control, and diminish the sovereignty of the states. Contacting pastors and parishes throughout the archdiocese, he ordered sermons to be delivered reminding parishioners of their "solemn duty" to protect the interests of their children from the hidden dangers of a child labor law. When the ballot came up, the Massachusetts vote was overwhelmingly in opposition to the measure, and the proposed child labor amendment eventually went down to defeat.[56]

The studious avoidance by Irish political leaders of federal solutions to what they still regarded as uniquely local problems, however, was changed suddenly and dramatically by the economic collapse of 1929. The twelve terrible years of depression, according to William Shannon, brought to an end the world of the American Irish and "broke the rationale they had lived by." The Great Depression shattered their dreams, thwarted their ambitions, and challenged their confidence in the American free enterprise system.[57]

Although church leaders had done little to prepare Catholics for social action in any coherent fashion, the appearance of Pope Pius IX's encyclical *Quadragesimo Anno* in 1931 helped provide a set of broad moral guidelines. Expanding upon the social principles outlined by Leo XIII's *Rerum Novarum* forty years earlier, Pius declared that the vast differences between "the few who hold excessive wealth" and "the many who live in destitution" constituted "a grave evil in modern society." This was a theme that convinced many Catholics to reject the prevailing "gospel of wealth" in favor of a "social gospel" that would bring Christian ideals into modern industrial society. Some supported the Catholic Worker movement, which generated active social reforms and provided assistance for the poor and the unemployed. Others joined the Catholic trade union movement, which promoted unionism and informed Catholics about the social ideals of the church. And with the creation of the Catholic Welfare Conference in 1919, Monsignor John A. Ryan of Catholic University pioneered in developing a progressive social program for the church.[58]

Increasingly, Irish American political leaders turned to the New Deal policies of President Franklin D. Roosevelt to remedy the sufferings of the poor, the aged, and the unemployed through such measures as social security legislation, child labor laws, and public housing. In supporting government action to bring justice into the industrial system, Catholics also found encouragement in the views of the "radio priest," Father Charles E. Coughlin, whose radio broadcasts reached millions of listeners. A staunch supporter of FDR during his first term in office from 1929 to 1932, Coughlin deplored "want in the midst of plenty" and argued convincingly that the New Deal was, indeed, "Christ's Deal." And young John W. McCormack, beginning his long career in the U.S. Congress, never failed to assure his Irish-Catholic audiences that the New Deal programs were consistent with the principles of the papal encyclicals.[59]

There may have been an instinctive movement among some younger Irish American politicians during the 1930s to adopt federal solutions, but in local ecclesiastical circles there was little indication that the cardinal archbishop of Boston had any interest in becoming involved in national politics. O'Connell expressed his view that it was inappropriate for Catholic priests to involve themselves in social questions or economic controversies when they should be talking about things that were "purely religious."[60] Indeed, O'Connell made no secret of the fact that he had little use for political figures in general, and even less for most Boston politicians, whom he regarded as uncultured and uncouth.[61] As he became increasingly aware of the significance of his ecclesiastical position and the power of his own commanding presence, he realized that he did not really need political supporters or organized campaigns to make his positions known on moral issues affecting public life. He had only to speak out, make his moral principles known, and the results would follow.

When the Eighteenth Amendment went into effect in 1920, for example, O'Connell saw the measure as one more instance of excessive government power. Following the position taken by earlier prelates, in 1926 the cardinal enunciated what he called the "true Catholic viewpoint" by favoring voluntary abstinence and denouncing government-imposed Prohibition as contrary to scripture and tradition. Ignoring those who disagreed with him, he declared his happiness in seeing Prohibition "wiped from the constitution" when the amendment was finally repealed in 1933.[62] Two years later, when a bill for a fairly popular state-supported lottery came up in the state legislature, O'Connell spoke out in opposition to gambling, which he declared to be "a very serious moral problem." Once the cardinal had spoken, the bill's numerous supporters in the legislature hastily withdrew their support, and the measure went down to defeat.[63]

The cardinal's insistence on morality in public life became even more pronounced by the late 1930s and early 1940s, when attempts were made to change the Massachusetts statutes regarding birth control. Even here, however, O'Connell himself took no overt political action, but employed the legal services of Frederick W. Mansfield to fight the bill during the 1941 session of the state legislature, while he himself let it be known that it would be absolutely immoral for any Catholic to support such a bill. Although Mansfield's arguments in the legislature failed to prevent the measure from being placed on the 1942 election ballot in the form of a referendum allowing doctors to prescribe contraceptives to married women, the statute was roundly defeated statewide by some two hundred thousand votes.[64] Historian James O'Toole suggests several good reasons for O'Connell's decision not to launch an all-out campaign to defeat such an issue — his advanced age, his failing eyesight, the country's preoccupation with the Second World War.[65] But one has to also consider the accumulated power of a venerable church statesman whose solemn pronouncements on public issues could hardly be questioned, much less challenged, in a predominantly Irish-Catholic state like Massachusetts. When "Number One" spoke, no further discussion was necessary.

On Saturday, April 22, 1944, Cardinal William O'Connell died quietly in his bed at the age of eighty-four. Five months later, on September 28, 1944, word arrived from Rome that Richard J. Cushing, age forty-nine, would be the new archbishop of Boston. An affable and sometimes unpredictable cleric from South Boston, Cushing was a striking contrast to his more conservative predecessor, welcoming publicity, mingling with all sorts of people in all sorts of places, and clearly at home in the complex political atmosphere of Boston. He was also attuned to the interests of second- and third-generation Americans, many of whom emerged from World War II better educated, more self-assured, and more widely traveled than their parents. Working in the postwar spirit of ecumenism, Cushing sought to reduce the separation that existed between Catholics and Protestants and pledged to refrain from "all arguments with our non-Catholic neighbors."[66]

Coincidentally, but significantly, the new archbishop's ecumenical approach during the 1950s and 1960s was in tune with a new spirit of political accommodation that followed in the wake of the defeat of James Michael Curley in November 1949. On January 2, 1950, John B. Hynes was sworn into office as mayor of Boston and embarked upon a new period of government, urging the citizens of Boston to put aside their political and ethnic differences and work together for the renewal and reconstruction of the city.[67]

Rather than maintaining his predecessor's disdain for the political process, Archbishop Cushing thoroughly enjoyed the friendship of politicians at all levels of government and tended to see politics as one more instrument by which the church could strengthen the moral character of the community and promote worthy candidates to public office. In addition, Cushing felt that a revitalized Christian community could serve as an effective bulwark against the dangerous inroads of "godless" and "atheistic" Communism during the Cold War years.[68]

Dramatic evidence of the effectiveness with which Archbishop Cushing could marshal the city's political forces to achieve a moral purpose came in 1948 with the reappearance of the birth control issue. Although attempts to liberalize birth control legislation had been defeated in 1942, proponents of change made another attempt during the 1948 session of the state legislature. While Frederick Mansfield once again failed in his legal efforts to prevent a new referendum from being placed on the November ballot, Cushing launched a highly organized effort to defeat the measure at the polls. Under his direction, the *Pilot* published editorials and special features emphasizing the importance of a large voter turnout, while priests delivered sermons pointing out the moral duty of Catholics to exercise their right to vote. A special committee was organized to defeat the referendum, using the slogan "Birth Control is *still* God's Law" to emphasize that birth control was not a "Catholic" issue or a "religious" issue, as such, but a "moral" issue in which non-Catholics could participate. As election time drew closer, the *Pilot* published sample ballots and voting instructions, while directives went out to pastors to deliver sermons specifically on Question Four and on the moral obligation of parishioners to vote against birth control.[69]

On election day, November 2, 1948, Harry Truman won an upset victory over Republican candidate Thomas E. Dewey, while in Massachusetts, Democrat Paul A. Dever won the governor's race. A slate of Democrat-Catholic candidates (except for Leverett Saltonstall) captured all the statewide offices, and Question Four, the birth control referendum, went down to defeat by some 278,000 votes statewide. The decisive defeat of the birth control referendum was a clear demonstration that the political process could, indeed, be used to establish moral principles, as well as to influence voters to cast their ballots on the basis of moral judgments. The impressive outcome also demonstrated the political power that was at the disposal of the archbishop of Boston whenever he chose to use it, making it clear to officeholders throughout the Commonwealth that, despite current social and generational changes, they could not afford to ignore the position of the Catholic Church on issues of public policy.[70]

At the time that Richard J. Cushing was elevated to the status of cardinal by Pope John XXIII in November 1958, the Archdiocese of Boston would seem to have been at the apex of its religious power and its political influence. With its 2 million Catholics, its 406 parishes, and its 2,500 priests, the encouraging number of young people still going into religious life offered a promising future. Parishes were vigorous and active; churches were filled to overflowing on Sundays and Holy Days; retreats, novenas, and devotional services were well attended. Societies for men and women were active outlets for public displays of Catholicism, as well as sources of financial aid for the cardinal's numerous charities and ambitious building programs.[71]

In November 1960, the pride and self-assurance of Catholics throughout the nation, but especially in the city of Boston, was further enhanced with the election of John F. Kennedy as president of the United States. While on the one hand, his election appeared to represent the final building block in the close relationship between the Archdiocese of Boston and the heavily Irish political structure, on the other hand Kennedy's victory on the national scene was made possible in large measure by his solemn assurances that as president he would be completely free of Vatican control. "I believe in an America where the separation of church and state is absolute," he told the ministers gathered in Houston, "where no Catholic prelate would tell the president — should he be a Catholic — how to act and no Protestant minister would tell his parishioners for whom to vote." This passionate endorsement of the separation of church and state may not have had a great deal of relevance at a time when Cardinal Cushing could invite JFK (his "best friend") to recite the rosary with him over the radio, but at a later time, under different circumstances, these words would take on a much more significant meaning.[72]

Despite what appeared to be an eminently stable situation, however, there were already on hand a series of disturbing developments that suggested serious problems for the future. The changes Vatican II brought about in the Catholic Church during the 1960s, for example, were truly extraordinary. Few aspects of Catholic life and customs, devotion, or piety, remained untouched. The celebrant of the Mass now faced the congregation, Catholics were allowed to use the vernacular instead of Latin, a number of obligatory rituals and customs became voluntary, and laymen and laywomen were encouraged to take a more active role in the life of the church.[73]

Some Catholics greeted the changes with enthusiasm; others were clearly unhappy with many of the unfamiliar innovations they were asked to accept. Bitter and sometimes violent reactions took place in many parishes among those who insisted that the changes went too far and those who complained that they did not go far enough. Pastors disagreed with their curates, parishioners fought with each other, pastors took issue with their bishops over the speed and extent with which the new changes would be implemented. And the theoretical controversies led to some disturbing practical results. During the 1960s, a number of diocesan priests left the priesthood to get married or to seek another vocation. At the same time, there was a precipitous drop in seminary enrollments that raised serious questions about the ability of the archdiocese to staff its churches in the very near future. To make matters worse, as the health of Cardinal Cushing began to deteriorate steadily and as major donations declined, the archdiocese found itself facing the prospect of bankruptcy with a debt of some $45 million.[74]

It was precisely during the 1960s, too, that the issue of race became a serious factor in both the political as well as the religious life of Irish-Catholic Boston. Except for a few notable exceptions, during the nineteenth century most members of Boston's small, self-contained African American community had been predominantly Protestant. Although immigration from various parts of the Caribbean and the West Indies increased the number of Catholics during the early twentieth century, the overall size of the black community was still remarkably small for a city of Boston's size and importance. It was not until after World War II that Boston's African American population doubled in only a decade, rising from some twenty-three thousand in 1940 to over forty thousand in 1950, with the number of black Catholics going up proportionately.[75]

Recognizing the significance of this development, Cardinal Cushing established St. Richard's parish in Roxbury to meet the spiritual needs of the black population of the archdiocese. Although many members of the city's African American community welcomed the idea of having their own church, others complained that it was one more example of racial segregation. This came at a time when black people were achieving civil rights successes in the South and demanding equal rights in housing, employment, and education in the North. While Cushing displayed sympathy for the cause of civil rights and in 1964 spoke out forcefully against racism in Boston, he was clearly uncomfortable with such confrontational methods as strikes, boycotts, public demonstrations, and protest marches used by civil rights advocates to promote their cause.[76]

At this point, however, events in Boston were moving faster than the ailing archbishop could respond. Overwhelmed by age, ravaged by cancer, depressed by financial problems, and devastated by the tragic death of President John F. Kennedy, he was no longer able to function. It was agreed that he would retire in August 1970, on the occasion of his seventy-fifth birthday. Contrary to all expectations, the Vatican announced that Humberto Sousa Medeiros, bishop of Brownsville, Texas, would succeed Cardinal Cushing as archbishop of Boston.[77]

After a succession of prelates who came from the Boston area and were of Irish parentage, the appointment of an archbishop who was born in the Portuguese Azores and who had no previous connection with Boston came as a complete surprise to most Bostonians. It is still not clear whether he had been chosen to reconcile racial differences in the city after his successful experiences with the migratory workers in Brownsville; whether it was because of his loyalty to the Holy See in opposing more liberal views after Vatican II; or whether it was because it was felt that his unusual intelligence could be employed in reorganizing the affairs of the archdiocese. In any case, after his installation as archbishop of Boston, Humberto Medeiros assumed the burden of resolving many of the problems that faced the archdiocese.[78]

Setting to work with prayer and determination, Medeiros turned his attention to the huge financial debt of the archdiocese. By establishing the Cardinal's Stewardship Appeal, through which he assessed each parish a certain amount of money, and by cutting back judiciously on various programs and expenditures, he was able to reduce the debt to a manageable $15 million. The new archbishop also established a series of episcopal regions, each under a regional bishop who would report regularly to the archbishop, thus creating a more effective network of information and control.[79]

While he was dealing with serious problems of finance and management, Archbishop Medeiros was also implementing the liturgical changes called for by Vatican II. He established a pastoral office of spiritual development, promoted vocations among young people, and restored the permanent diaconate to encourage increased lay involvement in the life of the church. At the same time, however, he refused to discuss such questions as clerical celibacy or the ordination of women, reinforced church teaching against birth control, and came out strongly against the "new barbarism" of abortion. In contrast to his immediate predecessors, however, Medeiros declined to use political activities to impose his views on public morality. He had neither the time nor the temperament for the give-and-take of politics and little confidence in the seriousness of politicians. The complex nature of the problems confronting the Catholic Church he felt warranted prayerful reflection and spiritual solutions. It was in obvious recognition of the dedication and loyalty of the archbishop of Boston that on February 2, 1973, Pope Paul VI named Humberto Medeiros to the college of cardinals.[80]

Considering Medeiros's obvious distaste for the political process, it was highly ironic that the pitfalls of racial politics would prove the undoing of this deeply spiritual prelate. Even before Medeiros had assumed office as archbishop in 1970, the city's growing African American community had already become a factor in Boston's political life, starting with the 1967 mayoral race, when Kevin White contended with Louise Day Hicks, school committee member and vocal opponent of school desegregation. Although White managed to defeat Hicks by a narrow margin, it was clear that Boston faced a showdown on the race question as African American leaders continued to press their demands for the desegregation of Boston's public schools.[81]

In 1971, only a year after he arrived in Boston, Archbishop Medeiros issued a strongly worded pastoral letter denouncing racism and calling for equality in housing and education. In April 1974, he went to the State House and testified in support of the state's Racial Imbalance Law. Two months later, when federal judge Arthur W. Garrity Jr. declared the Boston public school "unconstitutionally segregated" and ordered a program of busing to achieve a proper balance, Medeiros urged the people of Boston to accept the process with "calm and quiet."[82]

The cardinal's outspoken denunciation of the "sin of racism," followed by his apparent acceptance of forced busing, caused many longtime Catholics to react with dismay, protest, and even vilification. Parents and grandparents who had grown up in the 1930s and 1940s remembered when Cardinal O'Connell inveighed against the perils of federal power and warned against the loss of parental authority. Now they felt betrayed, as their church leaders seemed to support policies that threatened to divide their families and endanger their children. Despite his sincere efforts at the kind of mediation that had worked so successfully in Brownsville, Texas, Medeiros found that, as the writer J. Anthony Lukas so aptly put it, there was absolutely no "Common Ground" in Boston over the busing issue. Criticized by antibusing leaders because he declined their requests to join them in their meetings or lead them in their prayers, the cardinal was also criticized by African American leaders for not taking a more forceful stand in behalf of the constitutional rights of their children.[83]

It was all too much for the beleaguered prelate. In addition to his years of hard work reducing the crippling debt, reorganizing the management of the archdiocese, and loyally sustaining traditional church doctrine in a highly challenging atmosphere, the strains and tensions of the bitter racial conflict in Boston took a particularly heavy toll on his weakened constitution. After a period of declining health and undergoing open-heart surgery, Cardinal Medeiros died on September 17, 1983, at the age of sixty-eight, after holding office for thirteen years.[84]

As a replacement for Medeiros, once again Rome did the unexpected. Bypassing several local candidates, on January 24, 1984, the Holy See announced that fifty-two-year-old Bernard F. Law, bishop of Springfield–Cape Giradeau, Missouri, would become the eighth bishop and fourth archbishop of Boston. Born in Torreón, Mexico, the son of an Air Force officer, Law attended schools in North America, South America, and the Virgin Islands, before graduating from Harvard University in 1953. After attending the seminary in Ohio, he was ordained in 1961. For three years he served as executive secretary of the Bishops' Committee for Ecumenical and Inter-religious Affairs before being named bishop in Missouri. Although few Bostonians knew anything about their new archbishop, they greeted him with genuine enthusiasm. With his Harvard degree, his congenial presence, and his outgoing personality, he seemed a return to the earlier style of prelate with which Bostonians were more comfortable.[85]

By the time Bernard Law reached Boston, the turmoil over forced busing had begun to subside, but there were still many serious problems awaiting his attention. Concerned with putting the management of the church on a more cost-effective basis, he retained the system of regional bishops, created a more efficient cabinet system, and established the Stewardship Appeal of ten collections a year to reduce costs and balance the budget. Despite his successes, however, there were ongoing demographic changes that challenged his efforts at stability. Old churches in depopulated areas of the city had to be torn down, while new churches in suburban areas had to be constructed.[86] Old "national churches" built by French, German, and Italian Catholics gave way to new congregations of Latino and Asian Catholics. And all the time, older diocesan priests were retiring or dying off, while the number of seminarians was declining at an unprecedented rate. In March 1998, Cardinal Law (named a cardinal in 1985) assembled some three thousand clergy and lay leaders at Boston's World Trade Center to inform them to expect the closing of from forty to sixty parishes by 2008 because of the lack of priests, and to anticipate using a greater number of lay people in running their churches.[87]

In bringing the interests of the Catholic Church to bear on social issues, financial problems, or interreligious matters, Cardinal Law became an influential powerbroker in the city, meeting around what he liked to call a "table of trust" with businesspeople, social activists, or representatives of various ethnic and racial groups. When it came to firmly establishing the doctrinal position of the Catholic Church on such controversial religious questions as the marriage of priests or the ordination of women, however, the archbishop adopted a much more aggressive stand. Unlike Cardinal O'Connell, he did not wait for newspaper reporters to find out what "Lake Street" thought; Cardinal Law went public and announced it himself. This was particularly true on the subject of abortion, which he called "the primordial evil of our day." In 1984, for example, Law made a dramatic and unprecedented appearance on Beacon Hill at a State House pro-life rally, just as the Massachusetts legislature was about to consider an amendment that would restrict or prohibit abortion. When an observer suggested that he was meddling with the constitutional separation of church and state, he responded quickly: "If a preacher isn't meddling, then he isn't really preaching."[88]

Angry confrontations between pro-choice and pro-life groups reached a
critical level in December 1994, when a deranged young man broke into female health clinics in Brookline and killed two young women. Cardinal Law
met personally with the governor of the Commonwealth, William F. Weld,
to discuss ways in which peaceful confrontations could be assured without the danger of violence. For his part, Law subsequently urged Catholics
to modify their inflammatory rhetoric, but encouraged them to maintain
their constitutional right of freedom of speech in a peaceful and responsible manner.[89] The cardinal continued to use his own personal power and
commanding presence to achieve what he regarded as a moral purpose in
successfully opposing the revival of the death penalty in Massachusetts. In
1999, however, he failed to dissuade Governor Paul Cellucci from nominat-
ing Margaret Marshall and Judith Corwin to the state's Supreme Judicial
Court because he felt that both women had anti-Catholic attitudes.[90]

In 1998, as Bernard F. Law prepared to observe the twenty-fifth anniversary of his consecration as a bishop, his silver jubilee seemed like a glorious
moment in the history of the Archdiocese of Boston and in the brilliant
career of its cardinal archbishop. A series of celebratory programs and activities marked the course of the festive year, floods of congratulatory letters
and telegrams poured in from all parts of the archdiocese, and Cardinal Law
presided over a pontifical Mass at the Cathedral of the Holy Cross. Later,
at a gala reception in the new Seaport Hotel on the Boston waterfront,
Law received personal greetings from prominent members of the Catholic
hierarchy from around the world.[91]

And then, before anyone realized what had happened, it all came crashing
down in the wake of a series of catastrophic revelations about the sexual
abuse of children by Catholic priests. In 1992 a scandal had erupted in
the Diocese of Fall River involving a priest named James R. Porter, who
was found to have molested more than one hundred children. Most Boston Catholics accepted Cardinal Law's assurance that Porter's transgressions
constituted an "aberration" of a single depraved individual in another diocese, and that he had put into place new regulations so that allegations of a
similar nature would be aggressively dealt with. Blaming the anti-Catholic
bias of the local media for sensationalizing the issue, he announced, "We call
down God's wrath on the media, particularly the *Globe*."[92] Sketchy reports
about sexual abuses in the Boston archdiocese by a priest named John J.
Geoghan, however, led investigative reporters from the *Boston Globe* in
September 2001 to request that sealed records of lawsuits against the priest
be made public. In November, Superior Court judge Constance M. Sweeney
ordered the records released, deciding that the public's right to know took
precedence over the church's right to privacy.[93] These documents showed
that Cardinal Law and his aides had routinely disregarded warnings about
Father Geoghan and had reassigned him to other parishes where he repeated his crimes. In representing several abuse victims, Attorney Mitchell
Garabedian subsequently filed suit against Cardinal Law, five of his bishops,

and several other church officials, charging that they all had knowledge of Geoghan's misconduct and were therefore responsible for the results.[94]

Shaken by the extent of the abuses of one pedophile priest, prosecutors throughout the Commonwealth demanded the release of lawsuits against other priests that had been impounded by judges. While Cardinal Law agreed to turn over to authorities the names of priests accused of sexual abuse, prosecutors said that was not enough. They insisted on full disclosure — not just names. Thomas F. Reilly, attorney general of Massachusetts, Martha Coakley, district attorney of Middlesex County, Kevin Burke, district attorney of Essex County, and other prosecutors whose jurisdictions covered the archdiocese sent a letter to the cardinal's lawyers containing a thinly veiled threat to bring church leaders before a grand jury if they did not turn over more information.[95]

While similar disclosures of clerical sexual abuse were surfacing in all parts of the United States, it was Boston that instantly became the storm center of the scandal, not only because the story broke there first and because of the sheer number of priests involved, but also because Boston was viewed as one of the most distinctly Irish-Catholic cities in America. "Nowhere has the impact of the scandal been more deeply felt," wrote the *Boston Globe,* "and nowhere else has the erosion of deference traditionally shown the church been more dramatic."[96] Newspaper polls indicated that many longtime Catholics had lost confidence in the institution, that attendance at Mass was falling off sharply, and that parishioners were withholding money from archdiocesan fundraising campaigns. Instead of the usual deference with which they had treated church leaders, Catholic public officials now responded with outrage, not only at the abuse itself, but also with the cardinal's coverup of the scandals. Demands for Law's resignation began to rise steadily. In April 2002, Marian Walsh, a state senator from West Roxbury and an ardent Catholic, became the first state lawmaker to openly call for the cardinal's resignation.[97] The following month, Acting Governor Jane Swift signed into law a bill requiring clergy to report any suspected case of child abuse, despite protests from the Massachusetts Catholic Conference that any such bill would destroy the confidential relationship between priest and penitent.[98]

The sex-abuse scandals had created a sudden and totally unimaginable change in the political culture of Massachusetts, not merely in the long tradition of deference usually accorded members of the Catholic hierarchy, but also in the whole political relationship between religion and public policy. In the past, it had been a foregone conclusion that the First Amendment's guarantee of separation of church and state prevented secular authorities from probing into the affairs of the church. The *Boston Globe* reported that on one occasion Bishop Thomas V. Daily said he had always taken it for granted that priests had immunity from civil and criminal prosecution for sexual abuse.[99] But now prosecutors insisted that elected officials, accountable to the public, should be the ones to decide the culpability of sexually abusive priests, not the cardinal and not the church. On May 8, Judge Sweeney, reportedly to prevent the Vatican from transferring the cardinal to Rome, ordered Law's immediate deposition, and Bernard F. Law became the first Catholic cardinal questioned under oath concerning actions taken while in office. Television viewers witnessed the embarrassing sight of a prince of the church being whisked into a back elevator in the underground garage of the Suffolk County Courthouse in an attempt to avoid the waiting cameras.[100]

Cardinal Law had clearly become the lightning rod for criticism and rebuke. His image appeared on the cover of *Newsweek* magazine; he was the constant focal point of newspaper reporters and TV cameras, a regular staple of the eleven o'clock news. By April 2002 he was under siege, virtually a recluse in his Lake Street residence, heckled constantly by demonstrators, increasingly marginalized by former friends and associates. Certainly a devastating personal blow came when some fifty-eight members of his own diocesan clergy signed a letter urging him to resign.[101] On April 12, Law traveled to Rome, presumably to see the pope and other Vatican officials to discuss the possibility of his resignation. Upon his return to Boston, it was still unclear what his decision would be as he consulted further with his bishops, as well as with close friends and advisers. A short time later, he returned to the Vatican, this time to attend a meeting of American cardinals called by the pope to discuss the issue of sexual abuse in the Catholic Church. Back in Boston, after a painful period of prayer and reflection, on December 13, 2002, the unthinkable finally happened. Cardinal Bernard F. Law resigned his post as archbishop of Boston.[102]

On July 3, 2003, news arrived that Seán Patrick O'Malley had been appointed archbishop of Boston, and on July 30, he was formally installed in his new office. Born on June 29, 1944, in Lakewood, Ohio, O'Malley was ordained a priest of the Order of Friars Minor Capuchin in 1970. After receiving a Ph.D. in Spanish and Portuguese literature at Catholic University, he developed ministries for the various Latino communities in the Washington, D.C., area until 1984, when he was appointed bishop of the Diocese of St. Thomas in the Virgin Islands. In June 1992, following the Father Porter sex scandals, O'Malley was installed as bishop of the Fall River diocese, where he subsequently settled more than one hundred abuse claims and developed a zero-tolerance policy against sexual abuse. After ten years in Fall River, in 2002 he was appointed bishop of the Diocese of Palm Beach, after two of its former bishops had resigned after admitting to acts of molestation. Just nine months later, at the age of fifty-nine, Seán O'Malley was appointed archbishop of Boston to replace Bernard F. Law.

Archbishop O'Malley arrived in Boston largely unknown, without an experienced staff, and without the kind of close relations with city and state political leaders enjoyed by his predecessors.[103] There were certain considerations that worked to his advantage, however. The fact that he was not from Boston, had not attended St. John's Seminary, and was not a diocesan priest, was dramatic evidence that he was not one of the old inner-circle of local clerics who had caused the problem. Furthermore, his successes in settling similar scandals in other dioceses had given him a reputation for honesty and accountability. O'Malley moved quickly and efficiently to address the crisis and soon managed to settle litigation against the archdiocese with a large number of claimants. On September 9, 2003, the Archdiocese of Boston signed an agreement to pay $85 million to victims of sexual abuse by Boston-area priests. The enormous cost of the settlement forced the archbishop to sell sixty-four acres of archdiocesan property in Brighton to nearby Boston College, while he himself moved from the cardinal's residence on Lake Street to more humble quarters near the Cathedral of the Holy Cross in Boston's South End.[104]

The complexities of the sexual abuse cases and the enormous size of the financial settlements made up only a small part of the problems confronting the new archbishop. Facing declining numbers of priests and seminarians, O'Malley was forced to undertake a further reconfiguration of parishes, which resulted in the closing of over seventy existing churches as well as a number of popular parochial schools — agonizing experiences for longtime Catholic parishioners, who blamed the crisis on the incompetence of church leaders.[105] Anticipating further church closings, confronting angry demonstrators, raising much-needed funds, supervising diocesan administration, and carrying out his required liturgical functions, O'Malley suffered from the absence of professional advisors and the lack of experienced political supporters. He seemed to go everywhere and do everything by himself, a singular figure in the brown monastic habit of his order, with only the small scarlet skullcap (*zucchetto*) to denote his exalted rank.[106]

It was at this time of turmoil and confusion that the explosive issue of same-sex marriage suddenly appeared on the Boston scene — perhaps the worst possible time for a highly disorganized and discredited archdiocese to confront a major political challenge to its moral authority and its traditional views on the sanctity of marriage. In November 2003, in the case of *Goodridge v. Public Health Department,* the Massachusetts Supreme Judicial Court, by a vote of 4 to 3, ruled that state laws excluding same-sex couples from marriage were unconstitutional. On February 4, 2004, by a similar margin, the court handed down an advisory opinion declaring that the only way to meet the state constitution's guarantee of equal rights was to grant same-sex couples full marriage rights.[107] The Catholic Action League of Massachusetts filed an *amicus* brief with the court protesting that the decision condoned unnatural sex acts, redefined the traditional understanding of marriage as a union between a man and a woman, and endangered the process of procreation and the responsibility of "transmitting new life."[108]

Considering the Catholic Church's devastating loss of political power and moral authority because of the sexual abuse scandals, it was obvious that it would have to adopt new political methods if it intended to defeat this latest attack upon its most basic views regarding the sanctity of marriage and the nature of the family. Since the 1960s, the Catholic Church in Massachusetts had been represented in public affairs by the Massachusetts Catholic Conference (MCC), under the direction of the archbishop of Boston and the bishops of the dioceses of Fall River, Springfield, and Worcester.[109] During the early years, according to Professor Maurice T. Cunningham, this tended to be a small, one-man lobbying operation that sought to influence the votes of individual state legislators.[110] By 1997, however, confronting controversies over such complex issues as abortion, the death penalty, assisted suicide, and stem-cell research, the bishops saw the need to substantially increase the size of MCC's operations in order to reach out much more effectively to pastors and parishioners. Even then, however, its efforts were fairly routine, until the gay marriage issue exploded on the scene and demanded an instant and bold response.[111]

There was no time to be lost. A joint meeting of both Houses of the state legislature had already been scheduled for February 11, 2004. Among the proposed constitutional amendments was one defining marriage, in the traditional sense, as the union between man and women. If this amendment were approved by a majority of two consecutive legislatures, it would go before the voters on a statewide ballot.[112] In anticipation of the convention, the four diocesan bishops issued a joint statement, to be read at all Masses throughout the archdiocese, denouncing same-sex marriage as intrinsically immoral, contrary to natural law, destructive of the norms of marriage, and harmful to the interests of the children. On December 16, 2003, Archbishop Seán O'Malley followed up with an address of his own, calling upon all priests to defend the church's position on the sanctity of marriage and the family and urging parishioners to contact their elected officials. On February 11, 2004, the constitutional convention assembled as scheduled, but when the delegates failed to reach a decision, it was recessed until later the next month. During the interim, church leaders stepped up their activities, with parish meetings, voter drives, letters, and sermons. After the constitutional convention reconvened on March 29, the delegates finally agreed to advance a constitutional amendment that linked the traditional definition of marriage with a provision for civil unions. This compromise proposal would have to survive a second convention of the next legislature before it could be placed on the ballot in November 2006.[113]

Although church leaders were satisfied with the definition of marriage that emerged from the convention, they were clearly disappointed with the prospect of civil unions. Nevertheless, it was at least a partial victory, especially considering the burden of the sexual-abuse scandals, and it encouraged them in their efforts to transform their spiritual message into a more effective political response by supporting a new organization called "Catholic Citizenship." A nonprofit, tax-exempt agency, initiated in June 2004 by former Boston mayor and Vatican ambassador Raymond Flynn, it was designed to mobilize the voting power of Bay State Catholics. By organizing parishes into voting precincts, publishing its own voter guides, and exerting pressure on state legislators, it encouraged Catholics to vote "Catholic first and Party second."[114]

Perhaps one of the new organization's most effective moves was to denounce the "judicial tyranny" of an unelected Supreme Judicial Court that had deprived Massachusetts citizens of their democratic right to vote on a major public issue affecting their lives. Opponents of gay marriage exerted increased pressure on legislative members of the constitutional convention to vote favorably on the amendment defining marriage as a union between a man and a woman, so that the measure could go to the next legislative session for a vote that would place it on the ballot.[115] Supporters of gay marriage, on the other hand, called for the legislators to support the ideals of the state constitution that guaranteed equal rights to all citizens of the Commonwealth. In January 2007, on the last day of their last session, lawmakers voted 134 to 62 to forward the question to the new legislative session scheduled for May 9, 2007.[116]

Tensions rose as both sides marshaled their forces and prepared for the final showdown on Beacon Hill. On May 9, 2007, the constitutional convention reconvened but then recessed until the following month. Then, on June 15, members of the legislature voted 151 to 45 against the amendment, which needed only 50 votes for the measure to go on the ballot. The adverse decision came as a stunning blow to the aspirations and expectations of the Archdiocese of Boston, whose spokesmen accused legislators of rejecting the will of the voters and endangering the welfare of their constituents.[117] Kris Mineau, president of the Massachusetts Family Institute, saw the defeat as the result of political arm-twisting by political leaders on Beacon Hill, while Edward Saunders, executive director of the Massachusetts Catholic Conference, complained about those public officials "who don't vote according to their faith or their values, but more for political correctness." Observing that only two elected officials from the entire city of Boston had voted for the traditional definition of marriage, former Boston mayor and Vatican ambassador Raymond Flynn sadly reflected on "how radically the city and state have changed."[118]

Certainly there had been strong political influences brought to bear to prevent the amendment from going to the voters. In less than six months, three highly placed opponents of gay marriage — Governor Mitt Romney, Senate President Robert Travaglini, and House Speaker Thomas Finneran — had been replaced by Governor Deval Patrick, Senate President Therese Murray, and House Speaker Salvatore Di Masi, who combined forces to defeat the measure. But even before that, there had also been a series of gradual and more subtle changes taking place in the political subculture of the state. "What happened between 2001 and 2007," according to *Boston Globe* reporter Yvonne Abraham, "was nothing less than a transformation on Beacon Hill and beyond."[119] For one thing, the repercussions of the child molestation scandals continued to reverberate throughout the archdiocese. It was, after all, less than six years since the revelations exploded on the Boston scene, and Catholics of all ages were still appalled at the extent to which the damaging effects permeated the ranks of the clergy. And the subsequent closings of churches and schools that followed in the wake of the scandals themselves raised further questions about the competency of church leaders to administer the diocese. The result was a loss of both social and theological credibility that weakened the efforts of the archdiocese in its struggle against gay marriage.

Second, as a consequence of the decline in personal deference toward priests and members of the hierarchy, as well as an increasing emphasis on the separation of church and state, many younger legislators and other public officials were much less intimidated by religious denunciations and threats of losing political office as a result of voting against public policies advocated by the church. And third, these were years when the human face of homosexuality became a more familiar part of local communities. The number of same-sex couples had grown more visible throughout the state, especially after nearly 10,000 gay and lesbian marriages had taken place in Massachusetts since May 2004, when the Supreme Judicial Court's ruling went into effect. In traveling through their districts, talking to people and listening to families, a number of state legislators, many of whom had previously opposed gay marriage, found themselves deeply affected by the fact that sons and daughters, brothers and sisters, aunts and uncles were among those who would be deprived of their rights and benefits as citizens. It was, indeed, true, as the *Boston Globe* observed, that what had happened in less than six years was nothing less than a transformation of Beacon Hill and beyond.

Conclusions

The gay marriage controversy brought into sharp and dramatic focus the changing circumstances regarding the separation of church and state in Massachusetts. For the greater part of the twentieth century, the Archdiocese of Boston had enjoyed a dominant position in both its religious stature as well as its political influence in a Commonwealth that had rapidly become overwhelmingly Catholic. During the 1930s and 1940s, Cardinal William Henry O'Connell enforced his political wishes regarding matters of public policy largely through the impact of his own commanding presence, while during the 1950s and 1960s, Cardinal Richard Cushing used his friendly relationships with prominent political figures to maintain a public policy that was comfortably consistent with Catholic teachings. After the transitional years of Cardinal Humberto Medeiros, the appointment of Bernard F. Law in 1984 seemed to offer a welcome corrective to what many Boston Catholics felt had become a lack of direction in church leadership.

The credibility of the hierarchy in Boston was badly shaken, however, when news of the sexual-abuse scandals became public. By the time Seán Patrick O'Malley arrived in Boston to take over as archbishop, the reassignment of local personnel had created a power vacuum that made it extremely difficult to respond effectively to the unexpected challenge of the gay marriage issue in 2003. When it became clear that traditional moral appeals from bishops and pastors might not be sufficient to arouse voters to defeat a measure that conflicted so dramatically with Catholic doctrine, the campaign focused on the undemocratic nature of the judicial decision that denied citizens the right to vote on a political issue. And it worked. Although still weakened from the effects of the sexual-abuse scandals, the remarkable ability of the archdiocese to motivate its parishioners to react against the gay marriage issue, according to Professor Maurice Cunningham, was "surprising evidence of its continuing vitality in the Massachusetts public square." Despite the fact that it failed to persuade the legislators to place the issue before the voting public, its supporters pledged to continue the fight until citizens could decide for themselves the proper definition of marriage.

In its struggle against gay marriage, the Catholic Church involved itself in a much wider range of political activities than ever before, appealing to parishioners to vote on the basis of their religious principles rather than upon their political convictions ("Catholic first and Party second") and calling for a popular vote to override an unfavorable constitutional decision. When state legislators decided to sustain the decision of the Supreme Judicial Court in direct opposition to the church's demand for a popular vote, it marked a decisive transformation in the traditional relationship between the Catholic Church and the political institutions of the Commonwealth. Whether this is a temporary aberration that will soon pass or the beginning of a new and more permanent relationship, only time will tell.

In seeking to once again establish a public policy that is consistent with Catholic doctrine, it remains to be seen whether or not the Archdiocese of Boston will be able to depend upon a loyal and compliant Catholic electorate. By the opening of the twenty-first century, it was clear that several of the factors that had virtually guaranteed a strong relationship between religion and public policy in Massachusetts in the past had undergone some critical changes. Rapid demographic changes, for example, have already transformed the racial and ethnic composition of the state's Catholic population; the mobility of residents and the closing of churches are eradicating long-established parish boundaries and disrupting the solidarity of older communities; many Catholics have been publicly raising questions about certain social teachings of the church without apparent concern for personal consequences. And, with their outrage at the extent of the sexual-abuse revelations, Catholic public officials are displaying a defiant independence that makes them an uncertain barometer of future political support.

Since there are few indications that any of these changes will cease to influence the political landscape, the archdiocese may well be forced to confront a future when it will be no longer possible to ensure a public policy that is consistent with its own religious beliefs or moral values. In an increasingly pluralistic society where constitutional guarantees of racial equality, ethnic rights, and religious freedom have become subjects of intense scrutiny, the conflict between religious beliefs and constitutional principles has become a highly controversial subject. To return to the policy of "withdrawn retrenchment" that characterized the church's political policy during the first century of its existence in Boston is, of course, unthinkable in this modern day and age. But to maintain the more "triumphal" policy of the twentieth century, when the growing predominance of Catholics in public office made it both possible and natural for the church to ensure that civil law would conform to moral law, becomes questionable in light of the kinds of changes that suggest a more pluralist and secular society.

As the Catholic Church recovers its strength and reestablishes its credibility, it will remain for its leaders, as they move into the third century of the history of the Archdiocese of Boston, not only to reinforce the religious beliefs and moral values of their own members, but also to contemplate more creative ways to influence public policy within the constitutional framework of a political community whose members no longer reflect the social, ethnic, and religious constituency of the previous century. Instead of calling upon the political voting power of its own parishioners to put into force a moral policy no longer acceptable to a changing community, both clergy and laity might work to transform the culture of that community through the kinds of intelligent appeals and instructional programs that could provide a working relationship between Catholic moral values and American political convictions.[120] The relationship between church and state has never been an easy or comfortable relationship in a pluralistic society, but such issues as individualism, diversity, and globalization have made it even more difficult. The Archdiocese of Boston, however, has shown great strength and resiliency in responding to complex social, religious, and political challenges during the course of the past two hundred years of its existence. There is every reason to expect that it will respond effectively to the new challenges that confront it as it enters the third century of its unique and historical role as Boston's center of Catholic faith and devotion.

3

Charity, Justice, and
the Church in Boston

The Work of Catholic Charities

J. BRYAN HEHIR

Catholic Charities, as its title indicates, had its foundation, its inspiration, and its role rooted in the wider ministry of the church of Boston. It was formally inaugurated by Archbishop John Williams in 1903, its creation was foreshadowed in the initiatives of charity already established in the U.S. Catholic community, and in the Boston archdiocese.[1] Once established, it became and remains an essential expression of the ministry of the church and a visible part of the social service world of the state of Massachusetts.

This essay about Catholic Charities of the Archdiocese of Boston is not primarily a historical survey. While history is inevitably part of the narrative, its principal focus is analytical, locating the work of Charities within the contemporary understanding of the church's social ministry and seeking to define the challenges and opportunities that confront this ancient work of the church (as old as the Sermon on the Mount and the Acts of the Apostles) in the setting of American society.

The design of the essay begins with an analysis of the relationship of the Catholic social vision to social ministry, then follows a section on how the American system of social policy and social welfare defines the work of Catholic Charities; the closing section focuses upon future challenges already visible for the ecclesial, social, and legal future of Charities in Boston and in the United States.

The Relationship of Social Vision and Social Ministry

The most direct, simple, and convincing description of the work of Catholic Charities is to be found in the New Testament. Whether one goes to the Sermon on the Mount in Matthew's Gospel or the Last Judgment scene in Mathew, or whether one uses Luke's Gospel — known as "the Gospel of the Poor" — with its well-known account of the Good Samaritan, the Gospels provide direct guidance for the Christian community. That guidance commands us to feed the hungry, to clothe the naked, to shelter the homeless, and to imitate the Good Samaritan's attention to those in need. Beyond

51

these direct, explicit imperatives (which are then reinforced in the Acts of
the Apostles), there is the pervasive theme in the Synoptic Gospels of Jesus
continuing the vocation and the teaching of the Hebrew prophets. The genius of the Good Samaritan was his ability to respond spontaneously and
generously to the immediate needs of the traveler by the side of the road.
The prophets, by contrast, directed the attention of Israel to deeper, systemic
conditions in society: patterns of land ownership, wages paid to workers,
methods of lessening conditions of inequality. Jesus in his opening discourse
of his public ministry (Luke 4:1–11) assumes the mantle of the prophetic
teaching and specifies its relevance for New Testament faith.

This teaching, focused on justice and charity as pillars of Christian discipleship, is addressed to the whole community of faith, to the church
institutionally and in the lives of its members. Catholic Charities exists so
that this fundamental dimension of Christian life will be visibly, effectively
carried forward in the life of the church at every level of its existence.

To be specific, the vision of faith is essentially incomplete if the work of
justice and charity is absent. The church lives by its vision, its understanding
of its vocation. In the Hebrew scriptures one finds the phrase, "Where there
is no vision people perish." Without vision the church can lose its way in
the midst of the complexities of history and the competing claims of voices
within the church and in the wider society. In the Christian tradition vision
is the reference point to which we return to clarify the purpose of the church,
to specify the standards of discipleship and to maintain our sense of identity,
personally and collectively, as we seek to live out the teaching and ministry of
Jesus the Christ. The vision of faith is received from the past, but it always
stands as a horizon ahead of us, toward which we move as the pilgrim
People of God. We use the vision of faith as an invitation to growth and
development, we use it also as a source of correction and guidance, and we
use it as a catalyst for action and service.

In the Catholic tradition, the vision of faith is evangelical and ecclesial;
that is to say, it is rooted in the scriptures (Hebrew and Christian) and it is
articulated in the teaching of the church. We read, hear, and reverence the
biblical tradition as it is interpreted and developed in the theology of the
church. This means that Catholic Charities is rooted not only in the com-
pelling mix of the prophets and the Gospels, but also in the social teaching
of the church from Augustine, Ambrose, and Chrysostom through Aquinas
and the Scholastics to the papacy of the twentieth century. The social vision
is an integral element of the Catholic vision; the social vision grounds and
guarantees the bond between the revelation of the scriptures and the contemporary ministry of Catholic Charities. A synthesis of how the social vision
is understood in our time is essential for an understanding of the mandate
of Catholic Charities in this opening decade of a new century.

Modern Catholic social teaching is a product of internal resources and
external challenges.[2] The challenges of modernity have called and compelled
the church to return to the religious, philosophical, and moral resources
of the faith to develop both pastoral and policy responses to the political,

economic, social, and international dimensions of the modern world. The Second Vatican Council in its document *Gaudium et Spes* summarized the significance of this task:

> At all times the Church carries the responsibility of reading the signs of the time and of interpreting them in the light of the Gospel, if it is to carry out its task. In language intelligible to every generation, she should be able to answer the ever recurring questions which men ask about the meaning of the present life and of the life to come, and how one is related to the other. We must be aware of and understand the aspirations, the yearnings, and the often dramatic features of the world in which we live.[3]

The social vision of Catholicism has been principally the product of the modern papacy, from Leo XIII (1879–1903) through John Paul II (1978–2005). The twin challenges that signify the world in which the vision has been developed are industrialization and globalization. The first, the product of nineteenth century change in the socioeconomic order, called forth the inaugural social teaching *Rerum Novarum* (1891); the second, a process we now experience and are seeking to understand its full dimensions, is both an extension of industrialization and a radically deeper and broader expression of it, which John Paul II sought to address in multiple texts, particularly *Centesimus Annus* (1991).

These two phenomena, industrialization and globalization, are analogous realities, possessing some common characteristics, yet differing significantly in their complexity, speed of development, and impact. The first impacted Europe and North America; the second has direct, powerful impact across the globe. The first was primarily socioeconomic in content; the second is political and cultural as well as socioeconomic. The first had been under way for almost half a century before the church addressed its moral significance; the second has been an object of analysis and attention from its beginning stages, principally through the leadership of John Paul II.

To synthesize the development of Catholic social vision in light of these two challenges it is useful to distinguish the *scope* of the evolving social teaching, its *substantive* elements, and its *style* of address.

The scope of the social teaching highlights the shift from industrialization to globalization. The first fifty years of the teaching (1891–1941) focused primarily on the challenges of the Industrial Revolution in the nations of Europe and the United States. There was scant attention paid to the rest of the world and even less attention to how industrialization functioned as a transnational force in human affairs. The social teaching of this period sought to provide moral direction to the deep changes industrialization catalyzed within the nations of the West.

The Second World War, its causes and its consequences, provoked the transition in Catholic teaching to a different level of analysis. Beginning with Pius XII (1939–58) and with much greater detail in the teaching of John XXIII (1958–63), Paul VI (1963–78), and John Paul II, the basic unit of analysis became the world as a whole. Paul VI captured the shift in his encyclical *Populorum Progressio* (1967) when he said, "Today the principal fact that we must all recognize is that the social question has become worldwide."[4]

This statement established the architecture of the modern social teaching; while John Paul II always stressed that the global context of all issues does not nullify the role and significance of the national and local agenda of social issues,[5] placing the social teaching in global terms stressed both the international and transnational dimensions of politics, economics, culture, and diplomacy. The impact of this shift in perspective became evident in the concepts of the church's own vocabulary. John XXIII introduced the idea of the "international common good" and the Synod of Bishops in 1971 stressed the idea of "international social justice." Where the early social teaching focused on appropriate national institutions for achieving social justice, Pius XII initiated the now longstanding Catholic interest in and engagement with the United Nations and the other postwar family of international institutions such as the World Bank, the IMF, and the agencies based in Brussels and Vienna.

The change in the level of analysis (from national to international) became evident in the substance of the social vision of the popes. The early social encyclicals were almost exclusively about socioeconomic issues; the postwar teaching, because it was international, devoted much attention to political-diplomatic issues, to questions of human rights, to international political economy, and to issues of war and peace. While it is possible to find some of these topics (e.g., war) treated in earlier Catholic theology and papal teaching, one enters a new period with the documents of Vatican II and the postconciliar period. John XXIII in *Pacem in Terris* (1963) provided a developed systematic statement of Catholic teaching on human rights within states and across the international community. John Paul II built upon this foundation and developed it extensively throughout his pontificate, beginning with his *Address to the United Nations* (1979). Vatican II refocused the attention of the church on the problems of modern warfare in *Gaudium et Spes* (part 2, chapter 5), thereby fostering a new generation of scholarship and engagement of Catholics in these questions.

Changes in scope and substance were accompanied in the social teaching by a change in style. The dominant style of papal teaching from Leo XIII through John XXIII was philosophical; the categories of the social tradition were drawn from Aristotle's theory of justice and Aquinas's doctrine of natural law. John XXIII brought this mode of teaching to its most systematic statement in *Pacem in Terris*. Vatican II marked a modification in the articulation of social vision; as with other areas of Catholic theology, the social teaching made greater room for explicit use of biblical categories and content. Beginning with *Gaudium et Spes* and continuing through the pontificate of John Paul II, the social vision was expressed in a mix of biblical and philosophical categories. This return to the scriptures gave the teaching a more prophetic tone while still preserving the precision of the philosophical categories. The balance was not a simple one to maintain and the complementarity of the two kinds of discourse worked more effectively on some topics (e.g., poverty) than others (e.g., war).

A century after industrialization catalyzed the church's moral response to it, the fact of globalization presented a more daunting reality. On the one hand it illustrated the wisdom of Paul VI's quote about the new social question; only at the level of global architecture could this process of globalization be understood. It was a mix of several factors: at its core lay material factors of instantaneous communication; the ability to move people, ideas, and money across boundaries, cultures, and geography; increased interdependence of economies and the political and cultural consequences of such integration. In the mantra of its supporters globalization meant integration "faster and farther." But, as with industrialization, the new massive political-economic-cultural change had significant moral consequences. The ability of globalization to produce wealth was amply demonstrated; the distributive effects of the process were not at all guaranteed. Globalization has its own logic, but not its own ethic. The social vision of the church is again challenged to help find the moral resources to impact and direct a momentous development in human society.

While the major issues in globalization often are its international consequences, there is a significant dimension of the process that directly affects the world in which Catholic Charities operates in the United States. One theme of the social vision not yet addressed in this essay is the attention given by Paul VI and John Paul II to "postindustrial" societies. The concept is not theirs, nor do they use the phrase; it originates from the world of social science, perhaps best known through the work of Professor Daniel Bell in his 1976 book *The Coming of Post-Industrial Society*. These societies are characterized in part by highly sophisticated economies, bureaucratized social systems, advanced technology and communication systems, and an increasingly educated work force corresponding to the idea of a postindustrial social system. Without ever invoking the phrase, Paul VI in his letter *Octogesima Adveniens* (1971) and John Paul II in *Centesimus Annus* (1991) both examine the moral questions arising from these societies. They are the drivers of globalization but they are also impacted by the process. These societies are democratic political systems and market economies; they are also religiously and culturally pluralistic. They generate what the late Senator Daniel Patrick Moynihan called postindustrial social problems.[6] John Paul II described their moral challenges as not simply quantitative but qualitative problems. They have issues of poverty, but not of the dimensions that afflict nations of the Southern Hemisphere.

Catholic Charities in the United States ministers in the midst of a postindustrial society — perhaps the world's most complex illustration of this kind of society. In Boston and throughout the United States, it works directly with those struggling to cope with and escape from poverty. Unlike much of the world, the poor are not a majority in the United States, but that often means their condition is less visible. Charities work at the intersection of ethnic, racial pluralism with communities that bear the burden of poverty in a wealthy society. Charities work also with the now volatile issue of immigration, itself a dimension of a globalized economy. The vision that sustains Charities remains a mix of the biblical narratives of God's care for the vulnerable of the earth and the legacy of the social teaching that seeks to bridge the chasm of time, place, and space between the scriptures and postindustrial society.

As Charities in Boston prepared to play its role in the two hundredth anniversary of the archdiocese, it was given a new resource from the church social vision: Benedict XVI's first encyclical, *Deus Caritas Est* (2007). In surveying the development of the social vision, I have thus far concluded it with the ministry of John Paul II. The rationale for that decision was, in part, the major contribution he made to the church's social teaching and social ministry. By word and deed, his pontificate embodied on a global stage the message of *Gaudium et Spes:* the church of Christ is called to live in the world and to make a difference in the lives of all, especially the poor.

The election of Pope Benedict XVI, while not totally unexpected, generated a stream of commentary comparing the two popes. One common expectation was that Benedict's background, theological orientation, and conception of the church's role would likely produce a less engaged style of leadership on social issues. Many of these same commentators were surprised by the pope's choice for his first encyclical, *Deus Caritas Est.* The letter was conceptually ambitious; its central theme is God's love for us and our expression of that love in human relationships. The theme of course is fundamental in Christian faith; the ambitious development of it by Benedict XVI involved an encyclical that first addressed love and sexuality and then turned to the expression of charity in social relationships with a specific focus on the role of Catholic social service agencies. This latter theme, to some degree an extension of the social teaching of the twentieth century, has its own distinctive style, and it seeks to provide direction for the ministry we know in the United States as Catholic Charities.

Benedict XVI combines theological reflection with practical direction in *Deus Caritas Est.* The fundamental theological principle that undergirds the entire letter is that any expression of Christian love is not simply obedience to a command, but is a response to the love God has first shown to us. When he turns to the work of charity in the church, Benedict argues that love must take shape in service to others and this service must become an organized activity at every level of the church's life. Perhaps the most decisive contribution of the letter is the pope's repeated assertion that this work of organized service to meet the needs of others, particularly the poor, is an "essential" expression of the church's ministry. Describing the development of the church's life in the apostolic and patristic eras, Benedict XVI says:

> As the years went by and the Church spread farther afield, the exercise of charity became established as one of her essential activities, along with administration of the sacraments and the proclamation of the word: love for widows and orphans, prisoners and the sick and needy of every kind is as

essential to her as the ministry of the sacraments and the preaching of the Gospel.[7]

The significance of this statement should be explicitly recognized. Along with a similar statement from the 1971 Synod of Bishops ("Action on behalf of justice and participation in the transformation of the world fully appear to us as a constitutive dimension of the preaching of the Gospel"),[8] Benedict's assertion establishes a broad and firm theological foundation for the social ministry of the church, that is, her engagement with the world in support of human dignity, human rights, and peace. Together these texts provide a synthetic statement of what it means to be Catholic: We are to be scriptural, sacramental, and social. To some degree, as the pope observes, this commitment to serve the needs of others is as old as the New Testament. But it is also true that the emphasis on engagement with the world has not always been as clearly understood as the first two elements of preaching the Word and celebrating the sacraments. The pope nicely brings together his theological principle (love is our response to God's prior love) and his ecclesiological principle (serving the needs of others is at the heart of what it means to be the church).

Having established this foundation, he moves on to what might be called his strategic-moral directions. The first involves the qualities needed for those who do the work of charity in the name of the church. Benedict XVI focuses on two requirements. The first is professional competence; this will be a welcome and universally accepted idea in the ranks of Catholic Charities, and a reassuring idea in the wider social work community in the United States. The pope's concern, that goodwill alone is not sufficient in the organized work of charity, was long ago recognized in the world of Catholic Charities in the United States. The professionalization of the staff of Catholic Charities in Boston and throughout the country was one of the principal characteristics of this ministry throughout the last century. The pope's second requirement is the need for "formation of the heart" for charity workers; this may take some interpretation in the United States because of the pluralistic character of the staff of Catholic Charities. While the degree of religious pluralism differs by diocese and region of the country, it is a basic characteristic of this ministry. Hence, when the pope speaks of the work of charity being a consequence of one's faith, it may be necessary to distinguish the faith-inspired work of the agency as a whole, the different meanings of faith held by staff members, and the need, in spite of religious pluralism, for an agreement within an agency about the *moral* principles that direct the work of each and all staff members and volunteers.

Beyond his directives for the professional staff, Pope Benedict moves to a broader plane of analysis describing the nature and role of the work of charity in the church. This is the section of the encyclical that has and will generate discussion and analysis in terms of how it relates to the tradition of social teaching summarized earlier in the essay. At the outset, it should be recognized that the organizing category of social teaching in the last century has been the concept of social justice. It has never been the exclusive category; John XXIII's *Pacem in Terris,* for example, described the four social values as truth, justice, freedom, and love.[9] Pius XI (1922–39) had stressed the idea of social justice in *Quadragesimo Anno* (1931), but had also included the notion of social charity,[10] which is an aspect of Benedict XVI's letter.

Benedict's focus is on the work of charity as a "proper work" of the church, something it must do throughout history and cannot hand off to other agencies to fulfill. In specifying the objective of this work, he distinguishes between the works of justice and charity. The theme is not new either in Catholic thought or in the broader horizons of Christian ethics.[11] Benedict's concern is less with the moral content of each category (the usual style of analysis) than it is to specify the appropriate agent in the achievement of each moral objective. He argues that justice is the work of the state, achieved through the instrumentality of politics. Charity is then understood as the proper contribution of the church to society. This basic distinction of agency is then qualified in three senses. First, by church here he seems to mean an organized institutional activity. Second, he then argues that while the state directly is responsible for a just ordering of society, the church has an "indirect" role to play: helping to define the meaning of justice in the complexity of social life and inspiring people to pursue it. Third, beyond these indirect roles for the institutional church, the laity should be directly involved in the political arena of working for justice.

Much of this is reflected in previous documents of the church and in theological debates about the appropriate social role for the church in society. Benedict's treatment may be controversial in theological and social policy circles if it is seen as drawing the voice of the church back from the work of social advocacy and direct participation in public policy debates in a society like the United States. Certainly the post–Vatican II era has seen the Catholic Church globally and in the United States take a quite specific role in public advocacy regarding issues of human rights, social justice, and peace. In the Catholic Charities movement in the United States, there was a conscious explicit effort in the 1970s and 1980s to join the classical work of charity (direct service to those in need) with a role for public policy advocacy. This effort fashioned a consensus that has been foundational for Catholic Charities throughout the country. The potential tension in *Deus Caritas Est* is that the ministry of Catholic Charities has never received a stronger endorsement than the ecclesiological principle of this letter, yet the description of charity — justice may be read as confining the work of charity more restrictively than other social teaching of the last century. I use the adjective "potential" tension because much depends on how the encyclical as a whole is received and understood. Certainly all would agree with the statement in *Gaudium et Spes* that the church has no specific political charism; Benedict is clear about "the autonomy of the temporal sphere."[12] Church and state inhabit distinct realms of human society. But another theme of *Gaudium et Spes,* highlighted in a commentary by John Courtney Murray, S.J., is that the church should pursue its properly religious ministry in such a way that it contributes to the protection of human dignity, the promotion of human rights, the fostering of unity in society, and the provision of meaning to all areas of life.[13] Contributing to these broad goals (often conflicted topics in society, at least in terms of how to pursue them) may imply a more activist agenda in terms of public advocacy than the pope's distinction envisions. As with most social encyclicals, the analysis and debate that follows them becomes part of the legacy.

There is no ambiguity, however, in the message of *Deus Caritas Est,* about the imperative for Catholic social agencies to respond to the needs of the poor and vulnerable. To cite the encyclical: "Love is therefore the service that the Church carries out in order to attend constantly to man's sufferings and his needs, including material needs."[14] How this service is fulfilled involves both constant characteristics (specified by the social vision of faith) and contingent characteristics shaped by the political, legal, economic, and cultural setting in which the church ministers. That setting requires analysis.

Social Context and Social Ministry

It will be evident to any reader of this chapter that the encyclical tradition in which the Catholic social vision is found is a singular literary form. Its abstract character, intensified by any attempt to summarize the tradition, leaves one with many ideas, but little sense of how the social vision looks in practice. The abstract nature of the social teaching (e.g., its recourse to concepts like common good, subsidiarity, and solidarity) is due in part to the unique challenge of writing an encyclical, an authoritative moral teaching that has as its primary audience over 1 billion Catholics living in every geographical-cultural community across the face of the earth. Beyond the primary audience, the social teaching seeks to be usable to those outside the church in political communities across the globe.

The Catholic social vision, therefore, cries out for translation, "inculturation," application, engagement with other ideas. The process of moving from the teaching of the universal church, uniquely embodied in papal and conciliar teaching, to the life of a "local" church (parish, diocese, national setting) involves at least two steps. The first lies at the level of ideas, an intellectual task of relating the Catholic vision to a specific political, legal, cultural setting. In American Catholicism, with its history of a minority immigrant community seeking acceptance and integration into the wider society, the intellectual task has been a continuing effort. The most cited effort in recent history was the work of John Courtney Murray, S.J., who labored with extraordinary skill and grace to address the charge that Catholicism was incompatible with American democracy. Murray rejected the proposition as wrongly formulated and then proceeded to illustrate not only compatibility but the possibility of enhancement of the American tradition from the resources of the Catholic social vision. Amazingly, in a story too complex to rehearse here, he simultaneously confronted the harder task of convincing Vatican skeptics that the Catholic tradition could learn from the ideas of Anglo-American democracy.[15]

Given the nature of Catholic faith, with its thick conceptual content, relating the ideas of Catholic vision to specific cultural contexts is an essential task. A second level of the same enterprise is more directly pertinent to this essay, namely, adapting the institutional structure of Catholic agencies to differing sociopolitical settings. This cannot be done without prior intellectual guidance, but it remains a task beyond the realm of ideas.

From the beginning, the American socio-political-cultural setting posed a new question for the Catholicism that Europeans brought to the United States. The very idea of religious freedom embodied in the First Amendment exemplified the challenge and the possibilities the new setting posed. The historical evolution and adaptation that ensued is a story not to be told in a chapter, so the alternative is an analytical cut at the contemporary issues facing Catholic social institutions, like Catholic Charities, today.

The analysis itself only can be a snapshot of a complex reality. It is useful to distinguish two levels of the complexity that shape the context for the work of Catholic Charities in Boston and throughout the country. First, a broadly structural assessment of the American sociopolitical setting; second, a commentary on the social policy context.

Structurally, the United States exhibits the following characteristics. Politically, it is a representative democracy in the liberal tradition. Economically, it is the most complex advanced capitalist economy in the world, one that drives the process of globalization and must then address the benefits and burdens of that process. Culturally, the United States is a liberal culture, marked by extensive religious and moral pluralism. Each of these structural characteristics creates both opportunities and challenges for Catholic social institutions. In the first decade of the twenty-first century, we are immersed in a narrative of adaptation with roots reaching back to the middle of the nineteenth century. The appropriate way to understand the significance of the narrative for the church and for American society is to locate "the Catholic social system" in the American social system. Catholic Charities, in Boston and nationally, is one dimension of the wider reality of the Catholic social system. The full dimensions of that "system" built by Catholics over the last 150 years includes Catholic education, Catholic health care, and Catholic Charities.[16] The system as a whole testifies to a historic Catholic characteristic reaching back to the emergence of the church from the Roman Empire. The characteristic has shaped the church's whole approach to its ministry of building the kingdom in history, its engagement with the world, continuing the salvific ministry of Christ. It is the conviction that long-term impact in the world requires an institutional presence in society. The church itself, of course, testifies to this conviction, combining within itself a community of people and the institutional structure that gathers the community.

This basic constitution of the church then was extended in time to incorporate other institutional structures, monasteries, schools, universities, social institutions; these do not belong to the structure of the church precisely defined, but they testify to the institutional character of Catholicism in history. The church in the United States built upon this institutional tradition and in two hundred years brought it to its most extensive expression in the modern history of Catholicism. It would be a huge mistake to portray this history as being rooted in a single coherent strategic vision. Nor is it my intent to use the term "system" to convey a highly integrated reality driven by a single planned design; I use the term analogously — there is a "system" of sorts here, but not in the sense that any American business school would affirm as a system. Each sector of the Catholic "system" has its own history; each has distinct motivating factors that brought it into existence.[17] The basic common driving motivation was a desire to serve a rapidly growing immigrant church along with a concern that Catholics not be lost in the larger culture or be without resources to live within it. Catholic Charities was a response to the fundamental material needs of an immigrant church, along with a concern for providing for Catholic children who were orphans and in need of adoption. The latter objective was Archbishop Williams's purpose in founding Catholic Charities of Boston.[18]

Over a century later Catholic Charities lives within a social system significantly different from the beginning of the last century. In Daniel Bell's canonical description, the United States is the world's prototypical postindustrial society. The church itself is both less apprehensive of being overwhelmed by the society and more interested in finding ways in which Catholic institutions can be seen as enhancing the welfare of all in society.

Catholic Charities, in Boston and elsewhere, works within a framework shaped by both the structural and social policy dimensions of the American social system. Politically, American democracy protects the fundamental truth of religious freedom. The right of religious freedom encompasses not only a personal right, but the right of religious communities to initiate institutions free to function in the wider society. The Catholic Church, as noted above, has used this protection extensively. It is the ground on which the Catholic social system has been built. Economically, the capitalism of the American system has produced a mixed economy; while the country argues incessantly about how mixed it is or should be, it has made room for, invited in, and even funded (within limits) religiously based social services. Culturally, the religious and moral pluralism of American society poses a challenge for both the Catholic social vision and its social institutions. Particularly in the Catholic health care system, but also in Catholic Charities, an increasing range of contested issues, principally involving bioethics and sexual ethics, collide with long-held positions in Catholic moral teaching. These issues are not only debated in society; they often are embodied in legislation or in decisions of the courts where they pose a threatening context for Catholic institutions.

Beyond structure lies policy. In the arena of social policy the American system, when compared with other postindustrial societies, may be described as expecting *less* of the state, *more* from the market, and a *great deal* from nonprofit social service institutions. While it is clear that the United States is a "welfare state," the engagement of the government in response to social problems like poverty and health care is far more restricted than in the other postindustrial market economies. The more restricted role of the state is, in part, due to the confidence that market-based solutions to these policy challenges are the most effective responses. Both the welfare reform debate of the 1990s and the continuing debates on national health care reflect the strong convictions about the role of the market in social policy. Even as such market-based ideas are advanced, however, virtually everyone acknowledges they will leave substantial gaps in social policy; since the state plays a modest role, the gaps are expected to be filled by what has come to be called the "nonprofit sector" of society. The terminology and categorization are a recent description, but roots of the nonprofit world can be found as early as Alexis de Tocqueville's analysis of American society. He focused on the tendency of Americans to form "voluntary associations" to fulfill multiple roles in society. These associations varied in purpose, size, and scope; they included religious, cultural, social, economic, and humanitarian purposes. In the twentieth century, in the academic and policy worlds these groups drew increasing attention. In terms of size, Michael O'Neill records a growth of nonprofit organizations from 27,500 to 744,000 in the years 1950–2000.[19] Lester Salamon, a foundational figure in the recent study of nonprofits, describes the sector as "a vast and diverse assortment of organizations."[20] He locates them in a central place in American social history:

> These organizations carry a life force that has long been a centerpiece of American culture — a faith in the capacity of individual action to improve the quality of human life. They thus embody two seemingly contradictory impulses that form the heart of American character: a deep-seated commitment to freedom and individual initiative and an equally fundamental realization that people live in communities and consequently have responsibilities that extend beyond themselves.[21]

Salamon goes on to specify the character of nonprofits as organizations that are "dedicated to mobilizing private initiative for the common good."[22] From the perspective of this chapter it is useful to note that both de Tocqueville's theme of voluntary associations and Salamon's description of nonprofits find complementary ideas (with quite different roots) in the Catholic social vision's principle of "subsidiarity" and its support for what are called in the social teaching "intermediate organizations." Both of these ideas (along with the concept of the "common good") are part of a normative social architecture in Catholic thought that resists the notion of complete state control of society and the economy. While the Catholic vision expects *more* from the state than prevailing American ideas, it also supports the development of organizations with public purposes that can fulfill the subsidiarity principle of meeting public needs through a pluralistic social structure.

Two qualifications are needed to fill out the development of analytical interest in the nonprofit sector. First, the paradox about the role of religion: religious organizations are the largest part of the nonprofit world in the United States, but often have been given marginal attention in academic analysis. Second, Salamon's definition of the sector is appropriately broad and diverse (from education to the arts and culture to social service) while the interest in this chapter is the social service dimension of the nonprofit world.

Both of these qualifications are needed to properly locate Catholic Charities among nonprofit agencies. It is a large, diverse entity (nationally and in Massachusetts) among nonprofits, and it is always explicitly defined as rooted in the Catholic social vision and the church's ministry. Catholic Charities of Boston in 2005 served over 200,000 people in eastern Massachusetts; its budget was $38,272,063; its funding from the government (federal, state, local) totaled $18,894,359, about half of its support and revenue; the world of Charities involved over 130 programs focused on children, families, refugees, and immigrants, but it also extended beyond them to those in need of counseling and various forms of emergency services. Charities of Boston is registered with the IRS as a 501(c)(3) organization and must abide by all the requirements that this tax-exempt status demands. It has a board of trustees with a chair appointed by the archbishop of Boston in consultation with the board. The corporate membership of Catholic Charities has the archbishop as its principal member, who possesses reserved powers that the board and organization recognize as constitutive of the agency and its mission.

None of this brief description has much similarity to the agency Archbishop Williams initiated at the opening of the last century. The evolution of the organization over the last century resulted from changes within the church and changes in American society. Internal change has principally involved professionalization of staff and a more complex bureaucratic structure, along with an unplanned distancing of Charities from direct involvement with parishes. External change has principally been the emergence of the United States as a welfare state. Samuel H. Beer succinctly describes a major consequence of this historic move: "In short, before Roosevelt the issue of national action to sustain and direct the economy did not arise. In Congress the question of 'government management of the economy' which in later years would stand out as one of the main issues evoking stable voting alignments, was simply not on the agenda."[23] A principal consequence of this national transformation for Catholic Charities would be the eventual collaboration between a government committed to an activist social policy with nonprofit agencies like Catholic Charities.

Internal and external changes have combined to produce, in Boston and throughout the nation, a strong vibrant network of social service agencies rooted in Catholicism, serving the wider society, funded by church and state, and recognized as a significant, crucial actor in the American social system.

To provide a deeper sense of how Charities conceives of its role today, it is useful to survey two debates, again external and internal, which shape the role of the agency, locally and nationally.

The Faith Based Initiative (FBI): This widely proclaimed and fiercely debated policy initiative of the Bush administration is best understood with a bit of history. In their uniquely valuable book, *The Poor Belong to Us,* Dorothy Brown and Elizabeth McKeown document the fact that as early as 1875 Catholic Charities of New York was receiving city funding for its work. The pattern was neither universal nor solely restricted to New York. The coming of the New Deal and its philosophy of federal responsibility for socioeconomic questions opened a chapter with new possibilities. While Brown and McKeown recount that Harry Hopkins prevented federal funding to nongovernmental agencies in the 1930s, by 1959 new legislation made it possible for the federal government to purchase services from nonprofits.[24] The Bush initiative, therefore, was not entirely new. Indeed it built upon the "Charitable Choice" provision of the Welfare Reform Act of 1996; this measure was designed to facilitate access by religiously based agencies to federal funding while also protecting their religious character. The Bush administration sought to expand this initiative through legislation (never passed) and through a series of executive orders to federal departments.

From the perspective of Catholic Charities, the FBI did not appear innovative. Charities, with its 501(c)(3) status and its desire to serve those in need far beyond the bounds of the faith community, had been a major recipient of government funding at all levels for decades.

Both Charitable Choice and the FBI raised substantive issues, however, which help locate the role of Charities in the social service arena. The issues involve constitutional, theological, and policy questions. None of these have reached final conclusions at this time, but it is possible to sketch their status. The constitutional question in simple form is whether the FBI breaches the nonestablishment clause of the First Amendment. There has not been a direct, clear test of this in courts, but that may be because the broad lines of an answer are available from previously established jurisprudence. If religious agencies receive federal funding, it should be used for secular purposes — in this case service of those in need — on a nondiscriminatory basis. Catholic agencies accept that premise without question; Benedict XVI in *Deus Caritas Est* explicitly ruled out any form of religious proselytizing in the ministry of Catholic agencies.[25] There have been and continue to be periodic challenges to religious agencies about the use of religious symbols, art, and crucifixes on the premises of social agencies. The FBI is designed in part to provide greater latitude for these expressions of religious identity. Catholic agencies, in my view, welcome this dimension of the FBI, but have not made it a major issue previously.

The theological question is not whether the state is permitted to fund religious agencies, but whether such funding poses a threat to the independence or integrity of the agencies. This question is answered differently by religious communities. In the Protestant social service world, there are churches that in principle oppose taking government funding. The conviction sustaining this view is that the best of governments still will not share much common ground with an explicitly Gospel-driven conception of ministry. The Catholic response to the issue, one that undergirds the Catholic social system as a whole, involves a broader principle than simply funding. The Catholic social vision has drawn a clear line between the secular and sacral spheres of society. The line has been clearer in principle than in practice over the centuries, but the relevant point here is that the secular power (the state) has not been seen in principle as a threat, but a potential collaborator with the church. Indeed the collaborative idea has been seen as a potential benefit to society as a whole. The state, through civil law, can set a positive tone for cooperation; the church through its institutions can enhance the capability of the state in the areas of education, health care, and social service. Collaboration always requires a firm structure of principles to protect the values and interests of both sides, but with that in place Catholicism judges state funding to be, in principle, a positive possibility.

The question of social policy is the least explored of the three. At stake here is an empirical question: Where can collaboration enhance present patterns of social service and where might it open new creative avenues of service. In the FBI debate multiple claims have been made about the comparative advantages of faith-based social service; the proposition clearly has its supporters, but it does not yet seem to command consensus in the policy community.

The question of Catholic identity, once taken for granted, today has a different tenor because of changes throughout the Catholic social system. From the middle of the nineteenth century through the middle of the twentieth, Catholic social agencies overwhelmingly served Catholics, were staffed by Catholics, and in great part were funded from Catholic sources. Today the constituency served (elementary education is somewhat different) is pluralistic, as is the professional community that staffs these institutions of Catholic social commitment. The move to pluralism of constituency and staffing has been the result of both religious commitment to serve the society as a whole and the product of secular funding that requires nondiscriminatory service in society.

At different levels of the Catholic social system, concerns were raised in the 1970s and 1980s about the possible erosion of an explicit sense of Catholic identity, precisely because of the changes that had occurred over twenty years. The American landscape in the three areas of education, health care, and social service contains multiple organizations that began under religious inspiration but are now totally secular in character. Given the fact that by the 1990s significant differences with Catholic teaching have developed in American law, culture, and professional practice — particularly in health care and social service — the possible erosion of Catholic identity could create severe problems in the realm of policy and practice.

In the 1990s the Catholic identity issue surfaced explicitly across the country.[26] It was an internal discussion, but it held the possibility of significant external consequences. John Paul II in many ways drove the debate, but the various sectors of the Catholic social system welcomed it — at first with some concerns but then with quite spirited engagement, particularly in Catholic higher education. Two key texts focused the discussion: for higher education, *Ex Corde Ecclesiae,* an apostolic letter from the pope setting out criteria for Catholic colleges and universities. *The Ethical and Religious Directives for Catholic Hospitals and Health Care Facilities,* a document of the National Conference of Catholic Bishops, was updated and used as the mandate for Catholic health care. There was no explicit document for Catholic Charities, but the wider themes of the identity debate encompassed them also. The identity discussion differed by sector; the most urgent area was health care, focused on issues of bioethics and pastoral care. In higher education, issues of authority and freedom, curricular content, and the role of theologians were principal concerns. In the social sector it was primarily services offered and the conditions of government funding for the work of Catholic agencies.

The identity discussion across the sectors was shaped by some common themes and then differentiated by specific moral issues. Thematically, the principal concern has been how to maintain a living connection with the original evangelical inspiration that began the ministry of education, care for the sick, and response to poverty and injustice. Keeping alive and at the center of complex modern institutions the Gospel inspiration of the Sermon on the Mount and the Good Samaritan takes constant cultivation and education. It also has to be done with an awareness of the pluralistic character of participants in the institutions. Thematic convictions about the role of faith and reason, the imperative to serve the poor, advocacy for social justice and peace, and a ministry focused on the needs of immigrants and children are simpler to sustain than some of the specific issues that institutions face.

The specific choices are most urgently faced in health care: issues about care at the inception of life and the end of life can generate debate because of the detailed, systematic ethic found in Catholic teaching and its differences with existing law, policies, or professional standards of care. In social service the potential clashes are less frequent, but two recent cases will be addressed below.

This review of the location of Catholic Charities in contemporary America reveals a stronger, larger, and more complex organization here and nationally than early periods of existence, but it also highlights a more complex atmosphere in which to function.

Vision, Ministry, and the Future

Defining the future for Catholic Charities in Boston is obviously a speculative enterprise. Certain elements are stable: the future of Charities will be solidly connected with and rooted in the broader ministry of the local church of Boston; its future will involve partnership with entities outside the church, i.e., the political community, the nonprofit community, and the corporate community; its primary constituency will be men, women, and children in need of collaboration and assistance as they struggle against poverty, illness, violence, and discrimination. These people will continue to be the defining reference point for Catholic Charities. The wider community of the church in Boston also has obligations and responsibilities for the fate and future of those in need, but that will be one of several responsibilities for the local church; for Charities the poor and the marginalized in society are the primary, essential focus.

One way to think about the future of Catholic Charities in Boston is to reflect on its relationship to three relevant publics: the church itself, the state, and the law.

The Church

Precisely because Charities is by nature, history, and structure a part of the Archdiocese of Boston, its future must be assessed in light of the basic challenges facing this local church in a new century. Two different kinds of challenges face Catholic Charities, some related to the wider life of the archdiocese, some specifically related to Charities itself.

Any analysis of the Archdiocese of Boston must begin with an understanding of the traumatic events of the sexual abuse crisis, which have dominated the closing five years of its second century (2002–7). This is not the place to analyze the events in detail, but a singular, pervasive consequence that is the legacy of the crisis is the loss of trust in the church itself. The loss is two-dimensional: loss of ecclesial trust and loss of public trust. Ecclesial trust is what binds the members of the church to its pastoral leadership, principally bishops and priests. Public trust is confidence the wider civil society has in the church as a partner in the life of society. The sexual abuse crisis severely eroded both species of trust. Social institutions (education, government, the military) require trust as a foundation of their work, but religious institutions, which depend upon voluntary participation, are uniquely dependent upon trust as the precondition of their ministry. The recovery of trust within the ecclesial and civil communities is, therefore, the single most urgent imperative facing the church of Boston. There is clearly no quick fix available for a challenge of this kind. It will take a multidimensional strategy encompassing organizational initiatives like the new financial reporting methods adopted by the cardinal and pastoral creativity at the parish and diocesan levels of activity. The road back to restored trust will be a long journey, likely to be met with some suspicion until promises made are fulfilled effectively and convincingly.

Catholic Charities has a distinct role to play in this broader strategy of restoring trust. Because its ministry builds a bridge between the church and civil society, and because its ministry involves direct, immediate address to

human need and suffering, Charities has the potential to contribute to ecclesial trust (people want to support it) and to public trust (it can act as
a consistently good citizen). To some degree Charities simply has to do its
work well to fulfill this role, but possessing a sense of its distinctive role and
potential will enhance its ability to meet the broader needs of the church at
this crucial moment in its history.

The second kind of challenge facing Charities exists independently of the
recent crisis. It is really an opportunity to recapture and renew a previous
characteristic of the life of Charities, its relationship with the parishes of the
archdiocese. This is a challenge that faces Catholic Charities at a national
level also. It results from one of those unintended consequences that occur
in large social institutions. As noted earlier, one of the principal characteristics of the development of Charities in the last century was the systematic
professionalization of its staff and its bureaucratic emergence as a distinct
agency within dioceses. The unintended but real result of both of these moves
was a slow separation between the work of Charities and the daily life of
parishes. Unlike parochial schools, which have remained embedded in parish structures, both health care ministries and social service agencies exist
virtually independent of parish life. The latter, in Boston and throughout
the country, do depend significantly on volunteers (and in some dioceses on
collections taken up in parishes), but there is both psychological and institutional distance between parishes and Catholic Charities to the detriment of
both. Charities could benefit from deeper ties with parishes (e.g., volunteers,
financial and moral support), and parishes would benefit morally and spiri-
tually from a more pervasive connection with this dimension of the church's
social ministry.

The State

In this essay the "state" refers to all levels of government, federal, state,
and local. As already discussed, Catholic Charities, on the basis of its social
vision and teaching, seeks a positive, structural, collaborative relationship
with the state. It does so not simply on the basis of state funding, but for
broader moral and social reasons. Both church and state have distinct but
complementary responsibilities for human welfare in civil society. Postindustrial societies do not have a majority of their population living in poverty
as that standard is defined globally or nationally. But they clearly do have
significant parts of the population struggling with issues of basic human
needs. At this writing, over 30 million Americans are classified by national
standards as living in poverty; over 40 million Americans do not have health
insurance; and both hunger and housing are substantial daily challenges in
every state of the union. Finally, immigration policy and the social conditions facing immigrants remain among the most contested political issues in
American society.

The ability of Catholic Charities to collaborate with the state is dependent upon the internal resources of Charities (including its vision) and broad
areas of American social policy. The latter has both national characteristics

and differentiation at the state level. Charities in Massachusetts generally encounter one of the more expansive social welfare policies in the nation. Even here, however, the direction of social policy is impacted by a series of factors that constrain the church-state collaboration in response to basic social needs. Those factors include a spectrum running from the impact of globalization to decisions about taxation and fiscal policy to lack of consensus about how to address both classic and postindustrial social problems. As noted above, American social policy depends upon nonprofit social service agencies to fill the gaps in the social safety net. This ability to do that, however, depends in part on the social policy context in which they work. That means that the relationship of Catholic Charities to the state must include both advocacy for a generous social policy vision *and* provision of social services.

The Law

The relationship of Charities and the state is always two-dimensional: the discussion just completed focuses upon positive possibilities through church-state collaboration. But the state, through federal and state law and the decisions of the courts at all levels of American society, also sets the legal framework within which Charities must function. On the whole, the history of this legal narrative has been one in which Charities could function without major conflicts. Inevitably much of this legal narrative is about administrative requirements, reporting requirements, and standards of care. Using its 501(c)(3) status along with appropriate legal and financial staffing, Charities has not found American law constricting or conflictive.

Over the last twenty-five years, however, a new problem has emerged. In one sense it is rooted in the religious and moral pluralism of American society. Pluralism requires a legal regime in which each community is protected in holding and expressing its convictions; it also requires that on issues that affect the public order of society some moral common ground must be found and expressed in law and policy. On the socioeconomic questions that are at the center of the work of Charities, the Catholic social vision, articulated in the language of natural law, has been a welcome voice in the policy debate and the nonprofit world.

In the last third of the twentieth century, however, a series of issues, less social than bioethical and sexual in content, came to influence the world of social policy. On many of these issues Catholic teaching does not command a consensus in the wider society; on some issues it is distinctly a minority position. Accommodating a minority view on religious-moral grounds is a continuing challenge for American pluralism. One of the instrumentalities invoked is a "conscience clause" or some form of exemption from prevailing law and policy. Perhaps the clearest example of such an exemption is provision of conscientious objection originally granted to "peace churches," then expanded to others. Two recent cases of the last decade pose troubling precedents for Catholic Charities. In each there were reasonable expectations that an exemption from prevailing policy would be granted. In neither case did this happen. The broader question is whether Catholic Charities needs to prepare for a future without protection provided by conscience clauses or legal exemptions when policy mandates of the state conflict with Catholic teaching.

The two cases can only be summarized here as examples of what the future could hold on similar issues. The issues were different in character: a California case about contraception and the Boston case about gay adoptions. The first affected the state of California and potentially the country; the second had immediate impact on Charities of Boston. The California Case was decided in the Supreme Court of California in 2004; it was appealed to the U.S. Supreme Court, which allowed the decision of the California court to stand. At issue was the "Women's Contraception Equality Act," which requires that employers providing prescription drug coverage in their health plans must include coverage for female contraceptives. Catholic Charities, in light of Catholic teaching about contraception, was being required to act against the religious-moral principles of the agency. The California court recognized a legitimate exemption for "religious employers" but judged that Charities was not covered by the exemption. The court held that the religious employer exemption in the law applied only to institutions that:

- ◆ have as their purpose the inculcation of religious values;
- ◆ primarily employ persons who share the religious tenets of the entity;
- ◆ primarily serve persons who share the religious tenets of the entity;
- ◆ qualify as a nonprofit agency according to the IRS Code of 1986.

Essentially the court's decision held that the religious exemption would cover a diocesan administrative office or a parish staff or a school but not Catholic Charities. The irony of the decision is that to qualify as a religious entity Charities would have to serve primarily Catholics and employ few if any persons beyond the Catholic community. Since the California law is similar to those in many other states, this decision can have broad implications. Thus far, agencies when faced with such laws have been observing them under implicit or explicit protest.

The Boston case surfaced in 2005–6; since it centered on the right of gay couples to adopt children, it attracted nationwide attention in part because Massachusetts is the only state in the union where gay marriage is a constitutionally protected right. Distinct from that, however, Massachusetts law and state regulations have provisions that require adoption agencies (whether they receive state funds or not) to observe nondiscrimination in their practice, including gender orientation. Catholic Charities of Boston was providing 31 percent of the special needs adoptions in the state. This service was offered through a contract with the Department of Social Service. Over a twenty-five-year span Catholic Charities had facilitated a small number of adoptions to gay couples, but in light of the intense debate in the state in 2004–5 about gay marriage, it was clear that the issue would take on greater prominence and the rationale the agency had used of minimal observance of the law would not be sustainable in the future. Charities made inquiry about the possibility of an exemption from the gender orientation clause but found no collaboration in either the legislative or executive branches of state government. Relief through the courts seemed unlikely at any level short of the U.S. Supreme Court, a long, costly battle with no certainty of success. In the end, the board of trustees of Catholic Charities made the decision to withdraw from providing adoption services. Again, the irony of the case was that the agency had been founded by Archbishop Williams to provide for adoptions. But by 2006, the situation in both church and state had changed dramatically.

Both of these cases involved more detail and more complexity than can be discussed here. The fundamental point they illustrate is that aspects of the American social system may pose severe challenges to Charities in the future that will bear upon the Catholic identity question in a way hardly imaginable fifty years ago.

But neither those challenges nor the more mundane issues of finance, staffing, quality of service, or role in the nonprofit world should cast a shadow on the future of Catholic Charities. For over a century it has found ways to be faithful to the prophets and the Gospels by serving those in need. The need continues and so will the ministry.

4

Catholic Schools

A Tradition of Responsiveness to Non-Dominant Cultures

Joseph M. O'Keefe
and Aubrey J. Scheopner

Introduction:
Bicultural Education and Catholic Schools

Throughout the history of Catholic education in the United States parochial schools have "provided the most widespread and sustained example of bilingualism and biculturalism" as these schools enrolled students from outside the dominant Protestant, Anglo-Saxon culture of the early United States.[1] European immigrants who arrived in U.S. cities were eager to establish Catholic schools because of their desire to hand on the faith according to cultural traditions, which included their own language and customs. Many immigrant groups founded native-language Catholic schools where instruction was in the language of students and subjects included study of the native language, cultural customs, and history. Though immigrant groups had varying levels of commitment to establishing parochial schools, "the commitment to bilingual and bicultural education was a prominent feature in the history of enrollment in Catholic schools."[2] The history of Catholic schools in the Archdiocese of Boston is no exception, though the story of native-language schools in the Boston area is unique.

Throughout the history of the Archdiocese of Boston over 450 Catholic schools have been established. These schools represent a combination of parish, private, and diocesan schools established and run by priests, religious communities, and the archdiocese. This chapter will highlight the growth of the sixty-nine native-language schools in the Archdiocese of Boston. To situate this history, the story of native-language Catholic schools across the United States will be discussed, examining the impact of immigration on the Catholic Church, the role of religious in Catholic schools, conflict over the Catholic Church and native-language schools, and the growth and decline of parochial schools. This background will set the stage for a parallel exploration of the history of Catholic and native-language schools in the Boston archdiocese, allowing for a deeper understanding of the role of native-language schools in the Boston area. Balancing breadth and depth, this chapter will provide an overview of major trends within this history as well as several in-depth examples by looking at specific religious communities and native-language schools. To better understand the growth of Catholic schools in the archdiocese, we created a table of all native-language Catholic schools established in the Archdiocese of Boston, including their establishment dates, locations, the religious communities that served the schools, and relevant closing dates. This listing is the only one of its kind, providing a comprehensive glimpse into the development, growth, and decline of native-language Catholic schools in the archdiocese. The table appears below on pages 101–111.

Native-language Catholic schools provided an environment where the cultural and linguistic backgrounds of students were acknowledged and respected. This sharply contrasted with public schools, which sought to strip immigrants of their cultural traditions and language to Americanize them as soon as possible. This approach also contrasts with typical education practices today, where language and cultural differences are often treated as deficiencies, making it difficult for young people to "sustain a clear image of themselves."[3] Language is an important component of identity, and in order for students to "invest their sense of self, their identity, in acquiring their new language and participating actively in their new culture, they must experience positive and affirming interactions with members of that culture. Nobody is more important in this process than the teacher."[4] Thus, providing opportunities for immigrants to engage in their native language builds confidence and positive self-perception, qualities necessary for productive citizenship. Culture is also "integral" to learning because it determines a child's learning preferences and communication styles. Educators must acknowledge the culture of their students, avoiding overgeneralizations that lead to stereotypes about students' abilities and intelligence. When native-language Catholic schools were established, efforts were made to find clergy and religious communities who were native to the ethnic group in order to provide teachers who were fluent in the native language of the students and who understood their cultural values and customs. These teachers were able to minimize the effect of "cultural discontinuities" or the "lack of congruence between home and school cultures" which cause numerous problems for immigrant students.[5] Conversely, separate schools could "effectively isolate" their students, barring them from important benefits of a more inclusive environment.[6] This was a major concern among the general public in the early United States, a concern that continues to impact education with fierce debates on how to best serve non-English-speaking students.

In the Boston archdiocese the first native-language Catholic school was Holy Trinity in Boston, a German-language school that was founded in 1844. Four years later St. Mary's, a French school, opened in Lawrence. In total, sixty-nine native-language schools were founded in the Archdiocese of Boston, but today only eight of these schools are still open and only one continues to emphasize native-language instruction for students (see the table on page 101). These schools changed with the times. No longer does the Boston area have a French Canadian community that seeks to instill French Canadian language, values, and customs. Today Catholic schools in the archdiocese serve an increasingly diverse student population. Twenty-eight percent of Boston's population is foreign born, and according to 2000 U.S. Census data, 75 percent of residents in Boston under the age of eighteen are African American, Asian American, or Latino.[7] The entire country is experiencing an influx of Latino immigrants, and enrollment of Latino Catholic children in parochial schools has been increasing since 1995.[8] Today 12 percent of Catholic school students identify themselves as Latino.[9] While this is promising, compared to the overall population of Latino Catholics in the United States, which is more than 30 million and comprises nearly half of all Catholics, it seems that more could be done by way of Catholic education for these immigrants, including providing culturally responsive education practices.

Catholic Schools across the United States

Catholics were a "scarcely tolerated" group in the early colonial period of the United States, often deprived of civic and political rights as citizens. Colonial Maryland, which was home to the largest concentration of Catholics, instituted several mandates suppressing Catholics, including requiring candidates for public office to take oaths against papal supremacy in 1716 and in the following year issuing fines for every Irish Catholic servant brought into the colony.[10] A Catholic priest found in the New York colony was subject to "perpetual imprisonment."[11] Catholics were barred from managing schools; thus, even though public schools were available to Catholic families, many refused to subject their children to these hostile, Protestant-controlled schools. Catholics accused public schools of maintaining "a subtle campaign to win the allegiance of Catholic children" while degrading their Catholic and ethnic cultures.[12] The Constitution of the United States brought reprieve from such practices, but anti-Catholic sentiment persisted and increased dramatically as immigration brought large numbers of Catholics to U.S. cities in the nineteenth century. The Catholic Church became a church of ethnic immigrants, who were intent on preserving their identities.

The Impact of Immigration
on the American Catholic Church

Massive waves of immigration, beginning in the early 1800s, changed the nation as a whole and the American Catholic Church in particular. Between 1840 and 1850 immigration into the United States tripled, due mainly to an influx of Irish and German immigrants who left their native countries to escape poor economic and political conditions.[13] Major cities were inundated with immigrants who settled in pockets creating "little Germanys" and "little Irelands." Starting in the 1880s, immigration would change with a wave of "new" immigrants from southern and eastern European countries, adding "little Italys" and "little Polands" to major cities across the country.[14] Over 50 percent of U.S. immigrants who arrived before World War I were Catholic.[15] For the first time in the United States, Catholics became a sizeable portion of the population that could no longer be ignored. Nonetheless, opposition remained. Earlier in the nineteenth century, Samuel F. B. Morse insisted that the immigration was a plot by Europe, claiming "there is good reason for believing that the despots of Europe are attempting, by the spread of Popery in this country, to subvert its free institutions."[16]

Early immigrants founded parishes that presented "something familiar, something of the culture they had left behind."[17] These parishes came to define whole communities, merging ethnic identity, religion, and neighborhood. This was especially true of national parishes, based on the country of origin of immigrants and founded to meet their linguistic needs. National parishes offered opportunities to worship together, hear sermons, and celebrate rituals in the native languages of parishioners. European devotional traditions were comforting to Catholic immigrants.[18] Some immigrants even argued that English was incompatible with Catholicism, arguing that it was "for all practical purposes a Protestant language."[19] Parishes also "became the conscious mechanism used to maintain a religious hold on non-English-speaking immigrants."[20] Many Catholic leaders feared that "too rapid assimilation would endanger the faith."[21] In every major city national parishes and native-language Catholic schools were founded because Catholic leaders feared that language barriers would alienate immigrants from the church, "resulting in a dangerous 'leakage' to other denominations."[22]

Catholic immigrants founded schools to provide their children with an education that included religious instruction. For both the Irish and non-English-speaking Catholics, parochial schools represented the means for preserving history, customs, and religious traditions. Unlike public schools, whose mission was to break immigrants from their European culture, language, and Catholic religion, parochial schools provided a more gradual acculturation process. Cardinal James Gibbons wrote of native-language schools, "Our Catholic schools afford a much easier pathway for the foreigner to enter the American life than is the case in the public school. There the child must enter at once upon the use of the English language — perhaps under the guidance of one who does not know the habits and customs of the immigrant child, and hence cannot enter in complete sympathy with his work."[23]

The first to establish native-language schools were the German Catholics in the 1830s and 1840s. With their motto "Language Saves the Faith," German immigrants were steadfast in establishing schools, maintaining more than any other ethnic population in the early years of immigration.[24] In fact, establishing schools took such precedence for German immigrants that construction plans for schools were often settled before those for the parish church. Schools were instrumental in passing on the faith, ensuring the future, and protecting against Protestantism and the loss of cultural identity and language. This driving force was not unique to German Catholics; German Lutherans were also quick to establish schools in the United States.

The impetus to open schools was not universal among all immigrant groups. At the opposite end of the spectrum were Italian immigrants, whose mass immigration into the United States began at the turn of the twentieth century. Italian immigrants were not interested in Catholic schools, and even when they did establish schools, retaining the Italian language was of little concern.[25] Indeed, many charged that Italians were not faithful Catholics, describing Italian males as those who attended church for three reasons: baptism, wedding, and funeral, or "when he [was] hatched, matched, and dispatched."[26] This "indifference" to Catholic schools and Catholicism perplexed leaders of the American Catholic Church. Many Italians, however, were suspicious of the clergy, having come from a country marked by strong anticlericalism. It was also difficult for Italian immigrants to adjust to the need to donate to the church because the clergy received salaries from the Italian government.[27] Italian immigrants maintained strong ties to their families and neighborhoods, which served to transmit culture and identity, thus replacing the need for parochial schools.[28]

Other ethnic groups — including Polish, French Canadian, Irish, and Slovak — fell in between the Germans and Italians in terms of their determination to establish their own native-language Catholic schools. Nationalism was strong among Polish immigrants, who were second to the Germans in founding native-language schools. Many Poles likened their religious and linguistic oppression to the suffering of Christ; thus national, cultural, and religious identity were intimately linked.[29] Polish immigrants were eager to start national parishes and native-language schools to preserve this identity. Nearly three of every four Polish parishes had a parochial school.[30] Similar to German and Polish immigrants, French Canadians were also intent on maintaining schools to preserve their culture, history, language, and religion.[31] Ethnic *suivance* was extremely important for these immigrants, as losing their language would not only mean a loss in cultural values, but also a loss of faith. The French language was closely tied to Catholic religious beliefs.[32] For French Canadians, a parish without a church was better than a parish without a school.

Irish Catholics were also interested in founding Catholic schools, but their reasons were not grounded in concerns over preserving cultural and linguistic traditions. Rather, "the concern for schools was predicated on the degree to which public schools had been overly influenced by Protestant or secular values."[33] Having arrived in this country before Polish and French Canadian immigrants, the Irish had endured many conflicts with public school supporters who were fervent in their endeavors to assimilate Irish immigrants to their "superior" Protestant ways. Irish aversion to public schools stemmed from imposed Protestant religious instruction and an onslaught of "other religious insults." Like the Irish Catholics, Slovaks were reluctant to send their children to public schools; when Slovak Catholic schools were unavailable, parents were more willing to send their children to other private institutions than send them to public schools. Slovak immigrants, similar to German, Polish, and French Canadians, sought to preserve their ethnic identity and religious traditions through parochial schools. By 1930 over half of Slovak Catholic parishes in the United States had their own parish schools.[34]

The European immigrant experience differed sharply from that of Latino Catholics, many of whom did not come to the United States; rather "the United States came to them."[35] This cemented Latino culture as inferior in the eyes of Americans, and even among the Catholic hierarchy "the Iberian Catholic heritage of Latino was denigrated as an impediment to full participation in the American Church."[36] American bishops imposed religious orders from the United States and Europe onto Latino communities, marginalizing native clergy. Unlike European Americans, Latinos were unable to resist efforts against their native identities, cultural customs, and traditions. Of the Spanish national parishes that existed, most lacked the resources to support Catholic schools. Many Latino communities did not have the option of attending Catholic schools since most lived in rural areas of the United States where Catholic schools were not readily available.

Conflict and Resistance to Catholic Schools

The rapid expansion of native-language schools did not come without conflict, both externally from the general public and from within the Catholic community. The increasing number of practicing Catholics in the United States spurned racism and hate. The Know-Nothings, a group of nativists who strove to stop immigration, especially of Irish Catholics who they saw as hostile to American values, proposed and even helped pass legislation depriving Catholics of some of their basic rights. A century and a half later, the Ku Klux Klan, another nativist group, pushed for a bill in the State of Oregon in 1922 to change the compulsory education law by requiring children to attend public schools. What struck fear for most citizens was that by sending their children to parochial schools, young Catholics would not benefit from public schools, whose mission was to assimilate immigrants.[37] Many worried about "the persistence of foreign nationalism and culture" in native-language parishes and schools.[38] National parishes and native-language schools were criticized for keeping immigrant groups separate from the rest of society, "retarding their assimilation."[39] When Bishop John Hughes in New York appealed for public funding of Catholic schools, a fierce battle raged as opponents accused the bishop of attempting to dismantle New York's free schools while Bishop Hughes charged that Catholic children subjected to these schools became ashamed of their religion "because in the school-books and from the teachers they hear of its professors only as 'papists,' and of the religion itself only as 'popery.' "[40] Others questioned the competence of religious teachers in these schools who had no formalized training. Increasing pressure mounted and by the 1920s legislators in many states began to pass laws mandating instruction in English and requiring private school teachers to meet state standards of teacher training. Between 1918 and 1923 over one hundred laws were enacted throughout state legislatures that directly impacted parochial schools.[41] From record keeping for attendance purposes to curricular mandates, many states sought control over private schools. Overwhelmingly the majority of state provisions were those requiring instruction in English.[42]

Nebraska serves as an example of states exercising further state control over Catholic and private schools through legislation. In 1921 the state legislature passed laws forbidding teachers in public schools from wearing religious garb and instituted mandatory inspections of private schools to ensure that all textbooks and instruction were not "subversive to American institutions and republican form of government or good citizenship."[43] Furthermore, it was mandated that all teachers, including public, private, and parochial school teachers, receive teacher certification and obtain United States citizenship. Most controversial, however, was a statute forbidding the use of all languages other than English in schools. According to the law, languages other than English could not be taught unless a child had successfully passed and met eighth-grade requirements as deemed by the state.[44] Advocates of the statute argued that the large foreign-born population in the state segregated themselves from the rest of society, hindering their assimilation into the United States and their ability to become productive citizens. The Supreme Court of Nebraska overturned the law, holding it unconstitutional and declaring that "imparting knowledge in a foreign language is not inherently immoral or inimical to the public welfare and not a legitimate subject for prohibitory legislation."[45] Since the statute held that the ancient or dead languages of Latin, Greek, and Hebrew were not prohibited under the law, but that German, French, Spanish, Italian, and other "alien speech" were banned, the Supreme Court argued, "Evidently the legislature has attempted materially to interfere with the calling of modern language teachers, with the opportunities of pupils to acquire knowledge, and with the power of parents to control the education of their own."[46]

At first, conflicts over native-language parishes and schools within the Catholic community were skirmishes between and even within ethnic groups. Irish Catholics dominated institutional authority in the American Catholic Church, and many other ethnic groups were not as willing as the Irish to adapt to American ways. Germans, in particular, felt their "place in the American church was being jeopardized by the growing influence of Irish-Americans."[47] German Catholics sent appeals to Rome reporting that the hierarchy was neglecting their needs, resulting in the loss of large numbers of Catholic immigrants to the faith. American bishops accused German Catholics of trying to "Germanize the Church" and charged that Germans were negatively affecting the "American Church's prestige, making it look ridiculous in the eyes of non-Catholic Americans."[48] The Irish were skeptical of the Italians for what they perceived to be their lack of commitment to the church. In turn Italians blamed the insensitivity of the Catholic hierarchy for low church attendance and their inability to attract Italian priests to the United States. The Irish were not always welcoming to incoming immigrant groups either. French Canadians were resented by the Irish for taking factory jobs and establishing a separate network of churches and parishes instead of attending their fledging congregations.[49]

Conflicts within the church were made worse when many in the Irish-dominated Catholic hierarchy began to worry that national parishes were keeping the Catholic community divided. By the latter half of the nineteenth century the Catholic Church began to take the stance that the best way to combat nativism and stop cruel persecutions of Catholics was to "adopt an assimilation policy."[50] Many Catholic leaders approved Canon 216 of the New Code of Canon Law, which barred the establishment of new national parishes.[51] When Bishop John Ireland of St. Paul endorsed Wisconsin's Bennett Law of 1890, requiring a minimum of sixteen weeks of English instruction in all schools, many German Catholics felt alienated. Some Catholic leaders even began to question the establishment of Catholic schools, favoring efforts to "develop cooperative plans with public school systems" to further assimilate Catholics into mainstream American society.[52] Concentrated efforts to "Americanize" ethnic Catholics took full force in the early 1900s, with Catholic bishops including John Ireland, James Gibbons of Maryland, and George Mundelein of Chicago, taking "a vocal and visible role in the process," asserting that the Catholic Church of the United States was 'The American Church.'[53] One of the reasons for this change of heart among Catholic leaders was a shift from foreign-born to American-born leaders within the Catholic hierarchy. For American-born Catholics, native language and customs were not as important as they were to their parents and grandparents, who emigrated from other countries. The new generation welcomed the Americanized curriculum. World War I also changed how American Catholics perceived preserving ethnic heritage, as the American public, including Catholic leaders, no longer accepted the notion "that immigrants could maintain native languages and cultures and still be loyal to their new nation."[54] During the war the task of "Americanizing" immigrants was extremely important as "the prospect of a polyglot, disunited America with citizens of conflicting loyalties trying to fight a major war horrified many thoughtful Americans."[55] This resulted in further speculation over the desirability of native-language Catholic schools. For example, in 1916 Chicago Archbishop George Mundelein took the extreme measure of removing all foreign-language textbooks from Catholic schools, announcing that "all foreign children would henceforth be taught solely from English texts."[56]

Religious Sisters in the United States

The establishment of native-language Catholic schools would not have been possible without the religious communities that provided teachers. European communities "viewed America as a vast field for missionary endeavor" and over 119 European orders and 8 Canadian communities established foundations in the United States between 1790 and 1920. In addition 38 American orders were founded during that time.[57] The number of female religious in the United States increased rapidly as pastors beseeched superiors for more sisters to work in the rapidly expanding Catholic school systems across U.S. cities. In 1822 there were about 200 sisters living in the United States, but by 1920 there were over 88,770.[58] Most native-language schools were taught by religious communities who were native to those countries and were "bilingual and thus well suited to teach students both foreign and new world language and culture in terms that the child could understand."[59] The French Canadian migrants fared better than most immigrant communities because New England bishops were successful in recruiting French-speaking Canadian clergy and religious to the United States. For other ethnic groups, recruiting enough religious from their native countries was challenging. Other religious communities also supplied native-language schools with teachers. For example, the sisters of Notre Dame de Namur had over 2,700 nuns in native-language schools across the country.[60]

The sisters who came to the United States faced harsh living conditions, sparse resources, inadequate classroom and living spaces, and sometimes hostile pastors. Sisters lived "under spartan conditions" as the growing nation struggled to accommodate their needs.[61] Annals from the sisters of Notre Dame de Namur report that the sisters in Dayton, Ohio, slept on the floor and did not have enough food when they first arrived in 1850. "Poverty of the strictest kind was theirs" as their income came from the annual penny collection.[62] When a group of the Notre Dame sisters arrived in Washington, D.C., they found themselves in the middle of a misunderstanding between the pastor and the St. Aloysius Relief Society. The Society had raised funds to provide a center for their work with the poor, but the pastor wanted the money to be distributed to the poor. When the Sisters of Notre Dame accepted donations from the St. Aloysius Society, they were received unkindly by the pastor, who refused to help the sisters in their efforts to establish a school. The house provided for the ladies "was far from finished," with no running water except in the kitchen, and no gas fixtures, heating, or fuel.[63] Schools were often without proper learning resources, including desks, textbooks, writing utensils, and other materials. The demand for religious outstripped the ability of communities to provide enough teachers. As a result, many classrooms were overcrowded.

Many religious communities struggled to fulfill their teaching duties with little or no training. In their haste to meet the growing demand for more teachers, most nuns were sent to teach "directly after the novitiate, if not before," thus lacking teacher training.[64] This was cause for alarm and criticism among the general public. By the 1920s pressures to improve teacher qualifications in Catholic schools led to their voluntary adherence to educational standards in efforts to avoid interference in their schools.[65] But the process of obtaining state certification posed major difficulties for religious orders. For example, the lack of uniform standards throughout the states made it difficult for orders to design teacher preparation programs. Prior to 1914 most Catholic men's colleges and universities "displayed little interest in training nuns and Catholic laywomen to become teachers."[66] But as the role of women expanded, many began to question the quality of women's education and became especially concerned when qualification requirements forced religious and laywomen to enter non-Catholic colleges. In 1907 over 1,500 women religious attended 220 non-Catholic colleges to receive proper training.[67] Attendance at secular colleges by these religious and laywomen was seen as a danger to their faith, their morals, and the charisms of their communities. The report of the Commission on Coeducation in Jesuit Schools in 1940 asserted that if women "are trained in secular institutions, then at best they will not have intelligent training in sound principles of Christian morality, at worst a considerable number will be imbued with communistic and atheistic ideas which will harm not only themselves but the whole new generation."[68] Furthermore, many of the women's colleges were normal schools or finishing schools that were not accredited and therefore could not supply its students with state certification to teach.[69] This put increasing pressure on Catholic colleges and universities to provide graduate courses for women needed to obtain state certification in an environment that would not jeopardize their faith.

Marquette was one of the first Catholic men's colleges to provide summer courses for nuns, and by 1916 Marquette's enrollment included 375 women.[70] Though not "signifying general permission for coeducation in Jesuit schools or other Catholic colleges and universities, Marquette's new policy set an influential precedent for the admission of women and undermined the existing Catholic rationale for single sex institutions."[71] By 1920 twenty-four different Catholic colleges and universities, including ten Jesuit institutions of higher education, were accepting both lay and religious women during summer sessions, and by 1924 women represented almost 45 percent of total enrollment in Catholic colleges and universities.[72] While allowing women to attend Catholic colleges was controversial, many viewed the move enthusiastically. Beginning in the 1920s and 1930s diocesan normal schools and teachers colleges were established to help relieve the burden of training from the orders. But many religious communities resisted these diocesan schools, concerned that "the mingling of religious from different orders threatened the transmission of a community's unique spirit and educational ideals."[73] As an alternative, many orders began to establish their own Catholic women's colleges or continued to send their sisters to nearby Catholic universities. The Academy of Notre Dame in Baltimore was the first example of a college established by its own order, in 1896. By 1917 communities had established Catholic women's colleges in Washington, D.C., New York, New England, and Pennsylvania.[74] Improvements in teaching standards and training were concentrated at the high school level. Young, inexperienced sisters began their careers in elementary schools, and those who showed promise were then encouraged to pursue further training and eventually would enter high school teaching.[75]

The Congregation of the Sisters of St. Felix of Cantalice, or the Felician Sisters, was one of the religious communities to migrate to the United States to meet the teaching needs of native-language schools, specifically Polish Catholic schools, and provides a specific example of the challenges religious communities faced. The community began as a socioreligious reform movement during Russia's oppressive rule over Poland during the late 1700s and 1800s. Sophia Truszkowska, later known as Blessed Mary Angela, entered religious life and began a charitable institute for orphaned children and the aged in 1851. Dedicated to the "instruction of the ignorant," she continued to provide education despite the decree abolishing all compulsory education in Warsaw, where her institute operated.[76] The small group of women became a formal religious community in 1856. Sophia's dedication to education laid the basis for the mission of the community. This attracted Polish priests in the United States who were looking for orders to run native-language schools.

Polish immigrants and priests were particularly concerned about maintaining their Polish heritage, as this would preserve not only their language and customs, but foremost their Catholic faith. German religious communities were recruited to teach in Polish schools, but immigrants wanted Polish orders to teach their children. Father Joseph Dąbrowski, a Polish priest in Wisconsin, appealed to the superior of the Felician Sisters in 1874, and five Sisters were sent to establish the first Felician mission in America; they founded the first Felician school in December 1874. Like many Catholic immigrants, the Felician Sisters were victims of racism and hate. Three months after their arrival a suspicious fire destroyed the school, and shortly after another fire halted their progress by destroying the temporary school location in a nearby church. When the Sisters first arrived none of them could speak English, but Father Dąbrowski reassured them that "the pioneer Sisters will learn English quickly because it is an easy language except for its orthography."[77] The school hired an American-born teacher, Mary McGreer, to teach English, and the Sisters sat in on the classes to learn English side-by-side with their students. "Thus, the curriculum incorporated from the beginning a bilingual program from which both the pupils and the Sisters benefited."[78] All main subjects, however, were taught in Polish, with the curriculum following public school standards so as not to "rate lower than the Protestants."[79] Another main concern among the community was teacher training for their members. Sister Mary Cajetan, who ran the first Felician school, noted that "one of the most numerous problems was the shortage of Sisters. Frequently, the young, inexperienced Sisters burdened with overcrowded classrooms, become fatally ill. Pastors lack understanding, so the newly invested, poorly educated postulants are sent as substitutes."[80]

The Felician Sisters eventually moved their headquarters to the more urban and centrally located Detroit, established a teaching institute for its members, and expanded their mission to staff schools in New York, Baltimore, and even Boston. Beginning in the 1920s the Sisters struggled to maintain their mission to preserve Polish cultural traditions in their schools as more of their students and even their members readily spoke and even favored the English language. A source of conflict among the Polish community, increasing acculturation has meant that most Felician schools no longer provide bilingual programs for their students.

Growth and Decline of Catholic Schools

Though the momentum in establishing national parishes and native-language schools may have subsided by the early 1900s due to Americanization movements, "The immigrant church was very much alive, and Catholicism continued to be a religion rooted in diverse ethnic traditions."[81] Despite the decline in native-language Catholic schools, the number of Catholic schools in the nation continued to increase as enrollment peaked to nearly 52 percent of Catholic children by the early 1960s.[82] Beginning in the mid-1940s, Catholic schools experienced unprecedented growth, enrolling nearly 5.6 million students in the 1965–66 school year.[83] Schools were established in suburban areas as many Catholics migrated to areas outside the city. Most parochial schools remained overcrowded; even in the 1950s the average class size was nearly forty-six.[84]

Starting in 1966, however, enrollment in Catholic schools began a steady decline due to financial strain as parishes discontinued their efforts to subsidize Catholic schools and as the numbers of religious to staff the schools decreased. Though the Second Vatican Council affirmed the importance of Catholic schools, many bishops began to question the efficacy of parochial schools, with religious communities such as the Marist Brothers refusing to accept assignments in Catholic schools and opting to serve the poor instead.[85] With declining numbers of Catholics in urban areas, over 260 inner-city elementary and secondary schools closed from 1966 through 1968.[86] In all, over 630 Catholic schools closed during that time. By 1987 only 27 percent of Catholic children were enrolled in Catholic schools.[87] By the late twentieth century Catholic schools were enrolling racially diverse students as new waves of immigrants from Latin America came into the United States and internal migration of African Americans from the South brought many into the cities that European Catholics had vacated for the suburbs. Catholic schools began to welcome African Americans, Latinos, Asians, and Native Americans. In the 1970s almost 11 percent of Catholic school students were minorities, and by 1980 that number doubled to almost 20 percent. Thus, Catholic schools continued in their tradition of "welcoming newcomers" and providing "multicultural education to new arrivals" resisting efforts to create a " 'melting pot' that might rob minority students of their identity, [and] try[ing] instead for a sensitive course between isolationism and assimilation."[88]

During the 1990s Catholic school enrollment increased, but in terms of overall growth Catholic schools failed to keep pace with increases of the student population. Since the turn of the century over eleven hundred schools have been forced to close, due to low enrollment and financial struggle.[89] Native-language schools are virtually nonexistent, as instead Catholic schools continue to enroll ethnically and racially diverse students. Minority students comprise one-quarter of parochial school enrollment. Twelve percent of Catholic school students are Hispanic, 8 percent are black, and almost 5 percent are Asian.[90] Ethnic groups, including Filipino, Mexican, Nicaraguan, Haitian, Vietnamese, and Korean immigrants as well as Puerto Ricans, are a growing presence in the church. Some of these groups, for example, Filipino Americans, are supportive of parochial schools, while others like Korean Catholics have focused on creating community centers and offering educational programs outside Catholic schools. One obstacle these groups face in establishing native-language parishes and schools is in recruiting native priests and teachers.[91]

It is in this context that we turn to the history of parochial schools in the Archdiocese of Boston. The history of Catholic schools in the archdiocese provides a parallel but unique story with regard to the nation as a whole due to a concentration of Irish immigrants. This had a significant impact on the structure of the archdiocese and the establishment of a Catholic school system. But there is a history here that is not Irish Catholic; many other ethnic groups immigrated to the Boston area and established native-language parishes and schools.

Growth (and Lack of Growth) of Catholic Schools in the Archdiocese of Boston

The growth of parochial schools in Boston "left much to be desired," wrote Harold Buetow in 1970.[92] Even in 1908, after massive waves of immigration, only one in every five Catholic children attended Catholic schools.[93] There are several reasons for this, including the concentration of Irish immigrants, low enthusiasm among Boston's bishops to establish schools, and impoverished conditions of parishioners. As with the history of parochial schools across the nation, the history of Catholic schools in the Archdiocese of Boston cannot be fully comprehended without an understanding of the immigrant experience and the role of native-language Catholic schools within the diocese.

The Impact of Immigration on the Catholic Church in the Archdiocese of Boston

Immigration into Boston began to have an impact in the early 1800s as throughout the area "little Irelands" and "little Germanys" began to take form. By the late 1860s and 1870s "little Canadas," "little Portugals," and "little Italys" were growing communities throughout the Boston area. In the mid-1890s Boston welcomed Poles, Lithuanians, and Syrians. Thus, like the rest of the nation, at the beginning of the nineteenth century most of the Boston area's immigrants came from northern and western Europe, while in the latter half of the century the Boston area became home to immigrants from southern and eastern Europe. Like in other major cities, immigration meant an increasing population of Catholics, which sparked racism and prejudice. As early as 1647 Roman Catholic priests were forbidden to enter the Massachusetts colony.[94] Irish and French Canadian Catholics in the nineteenth century were seen as unskilled laborers who had low standards of living and even lower morals.[95] The first Catholic school of the diocese, Mount Benedict, established in 1820, was burned down by a group of anti-Catholic rioters. "Nowhere was there a longer or deeper tradition of anti-Catholicism" than in Boston.[96] Immigration patterns, however, also differed from the rest of the country. Unlike the situation in many other cities, the Boston population consisted of a concentration of poor Irish immigrants. In the Boston area, Catholicism was synonymous with Irish Catholicism. German immigration into Boston was never great, and while there were French Catholics in the factory towns of Lowell, Lawrence, Waltham, and Salem, the archdiocese lacked ethnic diversity among its Catholic population, which set Boston apart from other major cities.[97]

One reason for the slow growth of Catholic schools in the Archdiocese of Boston is related to this lack of ethnic diversity. "In no other heavily Catholic city was the church so thoroughly dominated by a single ethnic group, the Irish."[98] This concentration of one immigrant group had an impact on the establishment of Catholic schools in two ways. First, the Irish were interested in becoming Americanized, much more so than many other ethnic Catholics. Irish Catholics spoke English, which meant they did not feel a strong desire to establish parochial schools to preserve their language. "Despite their obvious distaste for Yankees," many Irish wanted to assimilate into American society and used public schools to help facilitate that process.[99] Second, many Irish Catholics found teaching positions in public schools, making the public school system more appealing. By the early twentieth century almost 23 percent of Boston's public school teachers were either Irish immigrants or children of Irish Catholic immigrants, essentially creating Catholic schools within the public school system.[100] By the 1920s, Catholics were "in almost total control of the Boston public schools," holding positions on the school board as well as supplying a significant number of teachers. In fact, the character education curriculum implemented in Boston's public schools was written by "a devout Catholic," Edward Muldoon, and included Catholic religious heroes and heroines as models of good character.[101] The majority of Catholics, especially Irish Catholics, probably saw little difference between public and parochial schools.

The concentration of Irish immigrants in the Boston area also meant that many of the ethnic Catholics who were more committed to establishing

Catholic schools did not have political clout within the diocese. The German Catholics, who were the most zealous supporters of Catholic schools, were not numerous enough in New England to establish a system of parochial schools. The first German Catholic school was established in 1844 in Boston, but by 1891 only four other German Catholic schools existed, including three run by Holy Trinity parish and one in Lawrence (see the table on page 101). Holy Trinity established three grammar schools and a secondary school for girls in Roxbury. In addition, Holy Trinity ran an orphanage and even apartments for newly arrived immigrants. The parish and native-language school served immigrants from various German states, resulting in diversity even among the German community.[102] Differences in dialects and even customs were cause for dissension within the congregation. High German language courses were initiated in Holy Trinity's schools with the unification of Germany in 1871.[103] By the turn of the century, however, a trend toward stressing English began and was accelerated by World War I as parish schools limited instruction in German to prove loyalty to the United States. After the war, German language instruction was reinstated, but only a half-hour was dedicated to learning German.[104]

French and French Canadian immigrants supported the largest number of national parishes and native-language schools in the archdiocese (see the table on page 101). French Canadians migrated from the overpopulated Quebec province starting in the 1860s to settle in the factory and man-ufacturing towns of the Merrimack Valley. Lawrence became known as "Immigrant City" and Lowell as "Little Canada." In addition, cities like Lynn, Salem, and Waltham also became home to many French Canadi-ans. At first, French Canadians were quick to assimilate, abandoning their French names, language, customs, and even their Catholic faith.[105] Soon, however, "a movement aiming to prove that on the soil of the United States, and with all loyalty to the new fatherland...the French language, customs, and faith could be as well maintained as in Canada" led to ef-forts to protect French Canadian culture.[106] The main bulwark of this movement was the Catholic school. Franco-Americans "considered their schools to be flatly superior to public institutions" as they provided reli-gious, moral, and French-language instruction.[107] When these schools were first established in the early 1900s all instruction was in French as the sis-ters who served the schools could not speak English. The Sisters of the Congregation des Filles de Jesus of Bretagne came to St. Joseph's school in Waltham, but left seven years later "because they could not provide instruction in the English language."[108] This would change later in the twentieth century, when typically half of daily instruction was in French, with subjects like catechism, Bible study, French language, Canadian his-tory, art, and music taught in French. All announcements, prayers, and informal conversations between teachers, students, and parents were in French.[109] According to a local resident who attended a French school in the 1930s, every morning began with prayer and the singing of "My Country 'Tis of Thee" and "O Canada" all in French. Only the required subjects of reading, writing, arithmetic, American history, geography, civics, and hygiene were taught in English. These schools flourished throughout the 1920s, 1930s, and 1940s, "the golden age" of Franco-American Catholic schools.[110]

At the turn of the century "Irish and Catholic were no longer so nearly synonymous" in the Boston area as waves of new immigrants pored into Massachusetts.[111] The number of national parishes quickly increased as these new immigrants sought to establish their own native-language churches and parochial schools. Italian immigrants began to arrive shortly after the Portuguese. As with Italian immigrants across the nation, Italian Catholics in the archdiocese were "an unusually difficult problem for the Church."[112] Italian Catholics were the second-largest ethnic group in Boston, which also did not help the growth of Catholic schools since they were indifferent to establishing parochial schools. Differences in language, religious customs, and devotions led many Boston Italians to turn away from the Irish Catholic parishes and their schools. The Irish-dominated church was resistant to requests from Italian Catholics to establish their own parishes as many were suspicious of Italian Catholics' penchant for certain saints, their "colorful religious festivals, and what one Irish priest described as their 'superstitious emotionalism.' "[113] Italians were equally suspicious of Irish priests and bishops, as in their country "church leaders had generally come from the ranks of the aristocracy," often siding with ruling classes.[114] Still, Italians established eight parochial schools and eighteen national parishes in the archdiocese (see the table on page 101).

The Portuguese were part of the wave of newer Catholic ethnic groups to come to New England. Overpopulation, poverty, and mandatory military service requirements compelled many to immigrate to the United States. Seven Portuguese parishes were established between the 1870s and the 1960s. St. John the Baptist in Boston was the only Portuguese parish to have a Catholic school.

Polish immigrants arrived just after the turn of the twentieth century, settling in Boston, Lowell, Haverhill, and Salem.[115] Fifteen national parishes were established by the Poles in the archdiocese, eight of which had schools.

Lithuanians began arriving in the early 1880s, escaping famine, plummeting grain prices, and universal military conscription. At first, Lithuanians "commonly fraternized" with Polish immigrants, jointly establishing parishes and churches.[116] But in 1883 the Lithuanian nationalist movement drew a sharp distinction between Lithuanians and Poles, with Lithuanians "renounc[ing] every Polish association and every trace of Polonism."[117] Four Lithuanian Catholic schools were established in the archdiocese out of the eight national parishes that were maintained by Lithuanian immigrants. Despite their relatively small population, the proportion of Polish and Lithuanian parishes in the archdiocese that supported Catholic schools demonstrates their strong conviction with regard to parochial schools (see the table on page 101).

Boston's Bishops and the Impact of Poverty on Catholic Schools

The bishops of the Archdiocese of Boston varied in their level of support for Catholic schools. Some were quick to establish schools, while others were resistant to such efforts. Bishop Benedict Fenwick, the second bishop of the Boston archdiocese, was an ardent supporter of Catholic schools. At the time of his ordination, there was only one Catholic school in the diocese, run by the Ursuline sisters. According to his memoranda, upon his first visit to the Ursuline convent he was "greatly surprised that such a situation should have been selected for the establishment of a nunnery."[118] The sisters were living in confined conditions, resulting in declining health. Bishop Fenwick established a new site for the school in Charlestown and Mount Benedict became a boarding school, but one that few Catholic families could afford.[119] Most borders were wealthy Catholic and Protestant young ladies. Bishop Fenwick established several other schools, including one in the basement of the cathedral, and brought over several priests from Germany to meet the needs of German Catholics, who were adamant about getting a priest of their own in the Irish-dominated Catholic Church. Despite his support for Catholic schools some historians point out that Bishop Fenwick was more concerned with higher education, educating the elite, and building churches than in creating a system of parochial schools.[120]

Fenwick's successor, Bishop John Bernard Fitzpatrick, appointed in 1846, did not encourage or even favor the establishment of Catholic schools. Despite pressure from the First Provincial Council in 1829, which decreed the necessity of establishing parochial schools, Bishop Fitzpatrick "refused to use church moneys to duplicate public-funded agencies and facilities that he considered available to all American citizens equally."[121] Urging his parishioners to assimilate into American culture, Fitzpatrick believed that the highly regarded common schools in Boston could provide an adequate education for young Catholics that would gain them acceptance into American society. Horace Mann's common schools offered a "non-denominational but nevertheless Protestant Christianity" that Catholics could not accept.[122] Despite the Protestant orientation of Boston's common schools, Fitzpatrick maintained his support for relying on public schools, convinced that with time the situation would improve and traditional racism and prejudice would give way to better understanding.[123] Fitzpatrick set his sights on building churches, and "not just small, makeshift, temporary structures for transient parishioners — but large churches, *grand* churches."[124] This priority for building grandiose churches was a "psychological necessity," establishing economic respectability among "a people crushed economically and despised for both their religion and ethnic origins."[125] Over seventy churches were built during his time as bishop.

Archbishop John Joseph Williams, who followed Fitzpatrick, was just as leery of establishing a separate parochial school system. Interestingly, both

Bishop Fitzpatrick and Archbishop Williams were products of Boston's public schools, which could explain their hesitation to establish a parochial school system. The Second Baltimore Council of Bishops in 1866, the year Williams was consecrated the fourth bishop of Boston, noted "the dangers inherent in the public schools" and the Third Baltimore Council in 1884 demanded that parochial schools be established near every church.[126] Despite these proclamations, Williams was hesitant and took action only when Rome began questioning the absence of a Catholic school system in the Boston archdiocese and when several priests started condemning parents for not sending their children to Catholic schools. Williams's response was advocating the establishment of a parochial school system; however, his support was "in general enough terms that no clergyman felt compelled to begin immediately."[127] Still, between 1879 and 1884 the number of Catholic schools in the archdiocese more than doubled, from sixteen to thirty-five.[128] Williams even helped recruit French-speaking clerics and religious from Canada and France to staff native-language schools.[129]

The state of parochial schools in Boston improved near the turn of the twentieth century with the appointment of a new archbishop and a flood of immigration that brought "new" populations into Boston. With the ascent of Cardinal William Henry O'Connell in 1907 the Boston Catholic community had a strong supporter of Catholic schools. O'Connell's impetus for establishing schools came from church doctrine as well as his beliefs on human nature and "man's immense potential for self-destruction."[130] Children needed religious instruction to defend against this self-destructive nature, and public schools did not offer such salvation. O'Connell not only supported the construction of Catholic schools, but also began to develop an infrastructure, setting up committees to standardize curricula for Catholic schools within the diocese, outlining requirements for English, history, geography, arithmetic, physiology, and religious instruction for grades kindergarten through eight.[131] Economic prosperity, along with an increase in teaching communities within the archdiocese, made the growth of Catholic elementary and secondary schools possible.[132] The number of parochial schools more than doubled and enrollment grew by 60 percent.[133] Like other bishops, O'Connell supported native-language parishes as long as they were able to support themselves financially, but he was also concerned with Americanizing Catholic immigrants. O'Connell's responses to ethnicity have been described as reactive and subtle, replying to correspondences in English even when priests and laypersons wrote in a foreign language in which he was fluent.[134]

Many have argued that it was the poverty of Catholics in the Boston area that prevented the city from establishing a parochial school system. With a large concentration of Irish Catholics, devastated by famines in Ireland, many parishioners did not have expendable income to support their parishes, least of all Catholic schools. Bishop Fenwick, Bishop Fitzpatrick, and Archbishop Williams all believed that developing a parochial school system would put too much strain on their impoverished parishioners. Many

Catholics needed to send their children to work and could not afford to pay to send them to school. For example, payroll records from the Boston Manufacturing Company in Waltham during the 1850s and 1860s show that one-fifth to one-third of the company's employees were children who never graduated from grammar school.[135] When Archbishop Williams called for a parochial school system, many parish priests expressed doubt that their parishioners could afford to support such a system.[136] Others have argued that this logic does not hold up. While Boston Catholics were "poorer as a group than their coreligionists elsewhere," they were not so poor that they could not have afforded Catholic schools.[137] Instead, Boston's prelates prioritized building churches, spending parishioners' money to construct grand structures that stood out in Boston's neighborhoods. In 1900 at least 40 percent of the twenty-five parishes in Boston without parish schools "had built churches on a scale exceeding the parishioners' means."[138] Parishes waited on average twenty-eight years before establishing Catholic schools, whereas in other dioceses the school was often built first.[139]

Conflict and Resistance to Archdiocesan Schools

As in other cities across the nation, the development of national parishes and native-language Catholic schools sparked controversy both among Boston's general public and among Boston Catholic leaders. At first, many Catholic children attended public schools. In Lowell, several Catholic schools were "taken into the system of public schools" with an agreement that Catholic churches would accept funds in exchange for providing classrooms, as long as the teachers hired and school textbooks used were "satisfactory to both town supervisors and the Catholics."[140] This plan did not last long, however, ending in 1852 just as French Canadians began arriving in the city. Bishop Fitzpatrick was satisfied with how Catholic children were treated in Boston's common schools, despite "constant, prejudicial harassment" of students, with required readings of the Protestant Bible, singing of Protestant hymns, and recitation of the Protestant version of the Lord's Prayer.[141] Tensions escalated as Catholic parents threatened to take their children out of schools altogether in response to the Eliot School Controversy in 1859 when a Catholic student attending Eliot public school "was severely whipped" when he refused to read the Protestant form of the Ten Commandments. This led to a walkout of over four hundred students.[142] Bishop Fitzpatrick believed this response "would only allow 'the bigots' to win by default" and continued to urge his parishioners to keep their children in schools.[143] Despite his persistence, the number of Catholic schools increased, and with Archbishop Williams's announcement of a parochial school system, Boston's Protestant leaders "reacted in alarm," fearful of the "prospect that a whole new generation of immigrant children might grow to maturity without the painstaking guidance of Yankee headmasters and careful instruction of traditional New England schoolteachers, who could be counted on to steer them in the 'right' direction."[144] Native-language schools were particularly concerning to many Boston leaders. These schools and parishes resisted "all attempts to emphasize English at the expense of the native tongue."[145] According to many, this resistance stunted assimilation and "reinforced an 'us-them' way of looking at the world."[146]

Many Catholic parents who chose to send their children to parochial schools were forced to go to court in towns like Haverhill and Fitchburg as a result of growing concern over native-language schools. These Catholic schools were not recognized by these cities because instruction was not in English. Even non-native-language Catholic schools faced adversity; in Lawrence, a Catholic school run by the Sisters of Notre Dame de Namur failed to pass the city school board's approval.[147] The Sisters wrote in their annual, "The Lawrence school board did not approve of our school and made it compulsory for a child seeking employment to spend twenty weeks at the public school after leaving us, otherwise no child could obtain the certificate which was to be handed to the employer."[148] The issue was settled when the Sisters agreed to have their students take an exam. When the students passed, the school board approved of the school.

Opposition to parochial schools also prompted recommendations for state law. In 1888 a bill was introduced before the Massachusetts Legislature for the " 'inspection of private schools,' but in reality for the crippling, if not destruction, of Catholic schools."[149] A series of hearings was held in 1888 and again in 1889 when the bill was introduced a second time. Charles Eliot, the president of Harvard University, spoke at the first hearing against the bill, stating:

> I imagine that all the members of the Legislature will be apt to agree to the proposition that we desire to have the American school system made one for the whole State; that the breach between the Catholic population and the Protestant population is one that should be closed and not widened; that it is for the interest of the entire community that the breach which I say exists, or has widened greatly during the past ten years, between the Catholic population and the Protestant population in this State and in every other American community, should be closed or healed and not widened by legislation. Now, it seems to me that this proposed legislation, so far as it relates to the approval of private schools by public school authorities, tends very greatly to widen that breach, and it seems to me clear that this proposed legislation is therefore injurious and hostile to the interests of the entire community.[150]

The bill was defeated both times, but in 1921, the Massachusetts Legislature passed a state law approving private schools "only when the instruction in all the studies required by law is in English, and when satisfied that such instruction equals in thoroughness and efficiency, and in the progress made therein, that in the public schools in the same town; but they shall not withhold such approval on account of religious teaching."[151] According to the descriptions of typical school days in native-language schools, it seems that these native-language schools got around this bill by teaching all required subjects in English (reading, writing, arithmetic, American history, geography, civics, and hygiene), but providing all other instruction, including religious, foreign-language, and foreign history instruction in the native language of the students.

Conflict within the Boston Catholic community about Catholic schools focused on cultural differences as well as the necessity for a separate school system. At first, conflict between ethnic groups was minimal due to the heavy concentration of Irish Catholics. The coming of "new" Catholic ethnic groups, however, changed this atmosphere. Ethnic groups settled in previously Irish-dominated neighborhoods and often refused to attend Irish parishes and schools. Instead, these groups set out to establish their own national parishes and schools. This not only enraged many Irish Catholics, who could not understand why their churches were not good enough for these new immigrants, but also led to problems with parish boundary lines. For example, Portuguese immigrants, who were eager to establish their own national parish, were forced to share the old Free Will Baptist Church in the North End with an Italian congregation. Neither congregation could afford to support their own parish, so for two years the groups shared the church, renaming it the Church of St. John the Baptist.[152] Finally the Italian congregation raised enough money to establish its own church, giving the Portuguese parishioners sole possession of the building, where they quickly established a school, which was later closed when the church received a new pastor. Other conflicts arose between pastors, accused of stealing parishioners from their respective parishes. In Lawrence an Italian priest confessed to performing baptisms for Lithuanian parishioners in 1915 after complaints to Cardinal O'Connell.[153] The pastor was forced to return the offerings received for the baptisms to the local Lithuanian pastor. Similar charges were brought against a Polish pastor from Cambridge who also served Lithuanian parishioners.[154]

Even within ethnic groups there was conflict. For example, parishioners of Holy Trinity, who originated from different areas of Germany, formed two opposing groups, the High Germans and the Low Germans. Conflict arose over construction projects, including the building of a new church and later the rectory, with one group supporting construction efforts and the other opposing development projects. Two German pastors resigned from the parish as a result of "senseless" opposition among the congregation, leading Bishop Fitzpatrick to threaten closure of the church.[155] Lithuanians of St. Francis parish in Lawrence, dissatisfied with their Lithuanian priest, who had parishioners in fear of attending other parishes, began an effort to form their own independent church. Rev. Anthony Jusaitis was accused of refusing to marry couples when they would not agree to pay church dues in advance and condemning those who sought the sacraments from other parishes. Sacred Heart parish, an independent church, was established by those outraged with Jusaitis, and Cardinal O'Connell was forced to relieve Jusaitis of his duties to the archdiocese.[156]

As with the rest of the country, many in the Boston area Catholic community were divided about the Catholic school question. As alluded to earlier, when Archbishop Williams announced plans to develop a parochial school system, many in the Catholic community were concerned; they doubted whether parishes would be able to afford supporting parochial schools, and others believed that Catholic children could be educated in public schools with continued patience and appeals to the courts to alleviate discrimination in Boston's common schools.[157] As was the case across the nation, others also feared that sending their children to separate schools "would stigmatize Catholic schoolchildren and endanger peaceful relations with the Yankee community."[158] Pastor John O'Brien of Sacred Heart in East Cambridge supported the use of public schools and served on the Cambridge School Committee "as part of his public efforts to promote better relations between Catholics and the Protestant community."[159] Both Catholics and Protestants, however, criticized his efforts; Catholics "denounced him as a 'Protestant priest' and Protestants were critical of his 'Papist' teachings."[160] Others, known as the "Schoolmen," who were ardent supporters of establishing a separate system of parochial schools, forced Archbishop Williams into action when they began condemning parents for not sending their children to local Catholic schools. Father Scully "denounced from the altar those parishioners who continued to send their children to public schools, and on many occasions he denied such persons the sacraments."[161] Complaints about Father Scully gained national attention, adding fuel to the national debate of the appropriateness of Catholic schools and native-language Catholic schools.

Religious Sisters in the Boston Archdiocese

Over forty religious communities were recruited into the Boston area to serve its schools. Without the dedication of these religious men and women, Catholic schools would not have been possible. In 1870 there were twenty-seven nuns working in parochial schools throughout the archdiocese; by 1940 there were over twenty thousand.[162] Often living in subpar conditions, traveling between cities to work at multiple schools, and serving overcrowded schools, these religious made sacrifices to meet the needs of the growing Catholic population. For example, six sisters from the Sisters of Notre Dame de Namur traveled from Boston to St. Joseph's parochial school in Somerville each day by bus, which was "of the same make as that used for the conveyance of prisoners to the jail."[163] Some "little boys seeing them . . . ran after them, waiting to see their occupants alight at the jail."[164] Convents were often too small for the growing number of women who were needed to teach in the schools. Women religious were at the mercy of parish priests, who controlled the salaries and housing of the communities. If communities could not meet the demands of pastors, they could be dismissed. Sisters who staffed parochial schools, fearing such dismissal, "reluctantly accommodated unreasonable requests for more teachers, knowing that the young sisters were not being properly prepared for their work."[165]

The Sisters of St. Joseph and the Sisters of Notre Dame de Namur were two communities that served the majority of schools in the archdiocese, accounting for over 44 percent of all of Boston's religious women in 1920.[166] The Sisters of Notre Dame, as part of their vow, would not teach older boys and therefore often worked with the Xaverian Brothers to provide education for male students.[167] Over thirty different communities served in native-language schools (see the table on page 101). The Grey Nuns of the Cross (Sisters of Charity of Ottawa), the Sisters of St. Chretienne, the Sisters of the Assumption of the Blessed Virgin Mary, the Sisters of St. Anne, the Marist Brothers, the Sisters of the Holy Union of the Sacred Hearts, the Franciscan Sisters, and the Sisters of Jesus Crucified each ran more than four different native-language Catholic schools. The Felician Sisters served three schools: Holy Trinity School of St. Stanislaus parish in Lowell, Our Lady of Czestochowa in South Boston, and St. John the Baptist in Salem. All but the Sisters of Jesus Crucified, who served Lithuanian schools, the Felician Sisters, who served Polish schools, and the Franciscan Sisters, who served in Italian, Polish, and German schools, provided instruction in French-language schools.

The presence of religious caused such alarm for many Boston residents that the Sisters of Notre Dame de Namur never wore their religious habits while traveling until 1870.[168] "More than priests, women religious were singled out in Boston society as symbolic of the threat of the Catholic church."[169] In 1855 a petition was brought to the Massachusetts House of Representatives, then dominated by the Whig Party or the Know-Nothings, "praying for the enactment of such a law as would bring under the inspection of the civil authorities all such institutions as 'convents, nunneries, or by whatever name they may be designated.'"[170] A special committee, the Nunnery Committee, was formed to consider the issue, and it was ordered that the committee visit and examine nunneries and their institutions.[171] The Nunnery Committee visited three schools, Holy Cross in Worcester, a Catholic school in Roxbury, and another in Lowell, before outcries from the general public put a stop to the inspections. The visits were unannounced and came as a surprise to the unsuspecting Sisters who ran the parochial schools in Roxbury and Lowell. The Sisters of Notre Dame de Namur, who conducted the school in Roxbury, described the twenty-four men who came to inspect the house as "intruders": "without waiting to be conducted through the house, they rushed everywhere, opening every door, and peering into every closet."[172] What caused particular alarm, both among the Sisters and the general public, was that the Nunnery Committee visited the room of a sick child, questioned the students, and inspected the house for over an hour.

A main criticism of archdiocesan Catholic schools was the lack of teacher preparation for the Sisters. During the 1890s, pressures to improve teacher training were especially strong in Massachusetts with changes in public school policies: stricter requirements were put into place along with new hiring procedures on the basis of qualifications.[173] "The tension between the subordinate position of sisters in the ecclesiastical organization and their work as professional educators was nowhere clearer than in the matter of teacher training."[174] Pastors remained indifferent to increasing pressures, while the communities were increasingly concerned about their shortcomings in providing an adequate education to their members as well as the pupils they served. As the entire nation struggled with the issue of how to provide proper training for women serving these schools, Boston College began to feel pressure to enroll women. When Boston College announced plans for a school of education in 1919, Rev. Augustine Hickey, S.J., the diocesan supervisor of schools, saw this as an opportunity to provide quality training to sisters in the archdiocese.[175] A program was proposed including a twenty-lecture series on Saturday mornings. "Response exceeded all expectations," with over seven hundred sisters participating in the program.[176] Additional lecture series and summer programs were offered, but when Hickey and Rev. James Mellyn, S.J., dean of the School of Education, requested permission to expand the program and allow the sisters to attend classes at Boston College's main campus, the request was denied. When Cardinal O'Connell expressed interest in formal programs for the sisters at Boston College, Hickey and Mellyn advanced the issue once more, and in 1923 officials from Rome granted permission to open classes on the main campus to women.[177] The Graduate School of Education was restructured in 1926, allowing women to attend. Members of twelve different orders were enrolled as special students, including the Sisters of St. Francis, the Sisters of Charity of Halifax, the Religious of Christian Education, the Sisters of the Presentation of Mary, and the Marist Brothers, all of whom ran native-language schools in the diocese.

Parallel to the Felician Sisters, who had a significant impact on native-language schools in the United States, the Sisters of St. Chretienne were one of the religious communities that played a significant role in native-language schools in the Archdiocese of Boston. The Sisters of St. Chretienne served French-speaking native-language schools in the Boston archdiocese. This community was named after Nino, the apostle of Georgia, who in A.D. 300 saw the Virgin Mary in a dream and received her mission to evangelize the people of Georgia. Through her teaching and healing, Nino converted the entire population of Mtskheta, the ancient capital city of Georgia. She was known among the people as "the Christian" or "la Chrétienne" in French. She is invoked as the "Illuminator of Georgia and woman equal to the Apostles."[178] In 1807 the Congregation of the Infancy of Jesus and Mary, called the Sisters of St. Chretienne, was founded in France during the French Revolution by Superior Mère de Méjanès with the mission of teaching and nursing. The Sisters of St. Chretienne, along with other French communities, including the Religious of Christian Education who served in Waltham, arrived in the United States after the Article of the Educational Code in France (1903) forbade religious from teaching.[179] In 1902 all primary schools run by religious in France were closed, and over twenty thousand priests and nuns were expelled. Church property was seized and salaries of priests and nuns were withheld. As for the Sisters of St. Chretienne, over forty of their establishments were closed or confiscated between 1903 and 1907.[180] Superior General Mother Clemence, in an effort to ensure that the Sisters were not secularized, began to send the Sisters to other countries, including Belgium, Austria, England, and the United States. In 1903–4, forty-six Sisters arrived in the United States, and by 1925 over one hundred Sisters were serving in the United States. For these Sisters "to abandon one's country, culture, and life-style, and to set out for the unknown without the certitude of ever returning was indeed leaving everything in God's hands."[181]

The first group of Sisters arrived in New York in 1903 only to be expatriated; the priest who had invited the Sisters refused to receive them. The Grey Nuns of Montreal, however, welcomed the four Sisters and encouraged them to take over St. Joseph's school in Salem when the Grey Nuns were forced to withdraw from the school. The pastor of the parish obtained authorization from Archbishop Williams for the Sisters. Twenty-three more Sisters arrived from France and began teaching at St. Joseph's in 1914, with more than seventy students per class. Only one of the Sisters spoke English. In addition to the challenge of serving overcrowded schools, the Sisters faced adversity common to other religious communities. For example, the day following the completion of the Sister's new convent the great Salem fire that ripped through the city burned the new convent to the ground. The Sisters persevered, rebuilt the convent and school, and continued to teach the children of St. Joseph's parish until 1925. "Teaching methods were different; so were customs. Their faith was tested, their patience tried. But these ladies were courageous and very determined."[182]

In all, the Sisters of St. Chretienne served nine schools throughout the Archdiocese of Boston. In Salem, the Sisters served not only in St. Joseph's school, but in St. Anne's and St. Chretienne Academy as well. The opening of St. Chretienne Academy was stalled with the influenza outbreak in 1918, with over six thousand cases in Salem. Schools in the city were closed, and the Sisters opened the academy as an emergency hospital. The city was thankful for their assistance and expressed their gratitude by never again charging the Sisters for water.[183] The Sisters also ran an elementary and a secondary school in Amesbury at Sacred Heart parish. Like the Sisters in Salem, they too offered their services to help the sick during the influenza outbreak of 1918. The Sisters also served St. Aloysius parish in Newburyport, though the conditions there were less than ideal: "the living conditions were unbearable with unfinished rooms on the third floor of the school where the Sisters suffered especially from the cold."[184] The parish pastor would not communicate with the Sisters, and though the parishioners loved the Sisters, another community was invited to replace them in 1923. In Shirley the Sisters who served St. Anthony's school also experienced less than ideal conditions, though their relationship with the parish pastor was much better. The living conditions were poor, with the bedrooms in the unfinished attic of the school.[185] St. Stanislaus School in Ipswich was run by the Sisters, with double-grade classrooms in the basement of the church. The Sisters also served Ecole St. Pierre school in Waltham.

Throughout the Depression, their schools experienced an increase in enrollment and they continued to serve the poor and sick. But, as with the entire country, the 1960s "brought turmoil and change" as religious communities lost many members and school enrollments fell. The Sisters of St. Chretienne were not spared as several of their schools were forced to close, including the Academy of St. Chretienne, St. Anne's, and Sacred Heart. In 2007 the Sisters of St. Chretienne celebrated their bicentennial. They maintain a convent in Wrentham and a retirement residence in Marlboro. Most of their efforts are concentrated in third world countries, including the Democratic Republic of the Congo, Rwanda, and Tanzania.

Growth and Decline of Catholic Schools in the Archdiocese of Boston

As in the national story of parochial schools, World War I efforts to Americanize immigrants in Boston led to a decline in growth of native-language parishes and schools. Prior to World War I sixty-three national parishes and thirty-seven native-language schools were established, but during the war years of 1914–18 only eight native parishes and four native-language schools were founded (see the table on page 101). In the ten years following the war ten native-language parishes and eleven schools opened. As the population of Catholics increasingly became a population of native-born Americans, the impetus to maintain cultural identities was not as strong as with foreign-born Catholics. During the Great Depression and up until the beginning of World War II six native-language Catholic schools were founded at a time of growth within the diocese. After World War II between 1945 and 1965, there was a dramatic increase in school openings in the archdiocese. By 1957 the Boston archdiocese became the largest Catholic school system in New England.[186] There were over 350 Catholic schools within the archdiocese in 1956 with a total enrollment of over 151,500 students.[187] In 1956 only fifty-nine of these schools were native-language schools. Mirroring trends across the nation, 1965 marked the peak year for archdiocesan schools. Native-language parish schools continued to decline, with only six schools established between 1947 and 1965. In fact, beginning in the late 1960s many native-language schools closed. By 1977 thirty-two of the sixty-nine native-language schools had closed, and in 1987 forty-one had shut their doors. Declining enrollments throughout the diocese were to blame for many school closures, with enrollment down to only 53,925 students in 1990.[188] Today only eight native-language schools remain in the archdiocese, most of which have ceased offering bilingual and bicultural education.

National Parishes and
Native-Language Schools Today

In the Boston archdiocese there are currently nineteen active national parishes out of the ninety-four that were established in the diocese to provide Mass and sacraments in the native languages of parishioners (see the table on page 101). Of these parishes, five are Polish, four Portuguese, four Italian, two Lithuanian, one French, and one Haitian. In addition, one is an Italian and Brazilian parish. The German national parish established in 1844, Holy Trinity, also continues to provide services and sacraments in German. Aside from these national parishes, many other parishes offer liturgy and sacrament services in foreign languages. For example, St. Peter's in Dorchester, which originally was as an Irish parish, now serves Hispanic, Haitian, Vietnamese, and Cape Verdean parishioners. Every week services are offered in English and Portuguese. Fifty-two parishes in the Archdiocese of Boston offer services in foreign languages, including Spanish (31 parishes), Portuguese (8), Brazilian (6), Vietnamese (4), Italian (4), Creole (4), Polish (3), Haitian (2), Cambodian (2), Lithuanian (2), Chinese (1), Nigerian (1), and French-Creole (1).[189]

Unfortunately, most native-language Catholic schools in the Boston archdiocese have closed. Of the sixty-nine native-language schools established in the Archdiocese, eight are still operating, only one of which continues to offer a traditional dual-language program. The Armenian Sister's Academy in Lexington, one of only three schools in the United States run by the Congregation of the Armenian Catholic Sisters, was founded in Watertown in 1982 as St. Stephen's nursery school. With increasing demand, grades were added and the school was forced to move for need of more space. Property was purchased from the Grey Nuns in Lexington, where today the school serves preschool through eighth-grade students. One-quarter of the school's families are Armenian, one-quarter are non-Armenian, while half are mixed with one Armenian parent and one non-Armenian. Most families do not speak Armenian at home, but all students know and speak Armenian as the school provides a bilingual program in preschool and kindergarten and classes are taught in Armenian from first through eighth grade, including Armenian history, language, religion, music, art, and physical education. All other subjects are taught in English. Currently the school is struggling with enrollment, with only one hundred students attending the school.

Though native-language schools have become rare, the archdiocese continues to provide culturally responsive educational opportunities, welcoming an increasingly diverse student body. According to the National Center for Education Statistics' *Private School Universe Survey* of 2003–4, many schools throughout the archdiocese are now serving an ethnically diverse student population. For example, at the time of the survey St. Angela's elementary school in Mattapan served an all-black student body. In Somerville, St. Catherine of Genoa School also had a majority of black students, with 113 of its students identifying themselves as black, 17 as Hispanic, and

69 as white. Other Catholic schools in the archdiocese serve a majority of Hispanic students. St. Patrick's elementary school in Roxbury had 160 Hispanic students and 88 black students enrolled in the school while St. Mary/Immaculate Conception School in Lawrence served 204 Hispanic students, 25 American Indian or Alaskan Indian, 3 Asian, 14 black, and 5 white students. St. Jude in Waltham served students from several distinct cultures, with 14 Asian students, 60 black, 40 Hispanic, and 115 white students. Secondary schools within the archdiocese are also beginning to welcome a more ethnically diverse student body. North Cambridge Catholic High School served 12 Asian, 113 black, 113 Hispanic, and 20 white students, and Trinity Catholic High School in Newton had 5 American Indian or Alaskan Indian students, 4 Asian, 106 black, 28 Hispanic, and 99 white students.[190] While these categorizations are limited, they do provide a glimpse into current trends experienced in schools across the Archdiocese of Boston. Black students include not only African Americans, but Haitian Americans and immigrants from African countries who may not speak English and often do not have the same language backgrounds. Therefore, those schools with a majority of black students may be serving students with at least three different language backgrounds. Many of these students come from families where English is not the native language and require other learning and social services. Catholic schools in the archdiocese have continued in their long tradition of serving culturally diverse students, responding to these current demographic trends by welcoming these students and providing them with every opportunity their resources allow.

Conclusion

The history of Catholic schools in Boston cannot be understood without consideration of the role of native-language schools. Indeed, national parishes and native-language schools provided immigrants the means necessary to maintain their faith and culture while assimilating successfully into American culture. As Rev. Robert H. Lord and his colleagues so aptly stated in their history of the Archdiocese of Boston: "What other church could have maintained its unity and authority and exerted a salutary discipline over these tens of millions of newcomers, drawn from forty different nations, as did the Catholic Church in the United States?"[191]

While native-language schools certainly had their drawbacks, and there was reason for concern in terms of the divisive nature of these schools, it seems that the key component of these schools is worth retaining: providing culturally responsive education for students. While many opposed ethnic schools for delaying assimilation and negatively impacting loyalty to the United States, those who fought for the establishment of these schools saw this differently. In 1919, on the twenty-fifth anniversary of St. Joseph's French parish (Ecole St. Pierre) in Waltham, a book commemorating the parish's history concludes with an appeal to patriotism for both France and the United States:

> Situated on the banks of the Charles River, this is the land upon which we have pitched our tent and where our families have established themselves. It is our home; it is our country. Under the star spangled flag we enjoy the free exercise of our religion. With our clergy, our schools, and our national societies we hope that our children and grandchildren will preserve the language of their mother country, her traditions, and the faith of her ancestors.[192]

Thus, many wanted to keep their faith and maintain their language, but were also grateful for the freedoms granted in the United States and expressed great loyalty to this country. By providing culturally responsive education for students, these native-language Catholic schools fostered not only maintenance of ethnic cultures, but assimilation into the United States.

Today "monolingual and monocultural students are the exception rather than the rule," with over 50 percent of the school population coming from non-native-English-speaking backgrounds.[193] When schools force students to abandon their language and culture while in the classroom, children also abandon part of their identities, which in turn impacts their ability to "participate actively and confidently in classroom instruction."[194] Current research illustrates linguistic, cognitive, and affective advantages for students when they develop literacy skills in more than one language and "continue biliterate development at least through elementary school."[195] Students benefit academically when they are able to maintain their heritage language while they learn English. When students are allowed to participate in instruction in their own language they develop conceptual and academic knowledge that can transfer across languages. Language plays a crucial role in student success in school, including not only their performance in reading and writing, but also other subjects like mathematics, social studies, and science, where language skills are necessary for understanding teacher instruction, reading subject texts, and writing and explaining answers to questions about the subject. When students are cut off from their native language and not allowed to study these subjects in their native languages, their progress can suffer. Students should learn the language particular to these contexts and develop skills necessary to learn independently, but they should also be supported through their native language to ensure that the concepts are understood. In other words, language should not get in the way of understanding basic skills.[196]

When children are allowed to use their native languages in schools, this not only develops native-language skills, but abilities in English as well.[197] Teachers should actively affirm children's linguistic and cultural identities by providing opportunities for students to engage and even learn in their native languages and English. Instead of viewing children's cultural and linguistic diversity as a problem, schools need to recognize the linguistic, cultural, and intellectual resources children bring to their schools and to society and realize this does not pose a threat to assimilation and patriotism.

Despite the history of native-language Catholic schools meeting the needs of immigrants, it seems that many of today's Boston Catholic schools are not seeking to provide these types of opportunities for their students. Ethnic diversity among schools is certainly one reason for this; most schools enroll students from a variety of cultural backgrounds and must strive to accommodate the needs of all learners. Providing instruction in French certainly is not going to help a class of students where some speak Spanish, others speak Creole, and a few speak English as their first language. However, it also seems that given the influx of immigrants from Spanish- and French-speaking countries, Catholic schools could provide services similar to those that native-language schools once did. As the U.S. bishops wrote: "Historically, the Church in the United States has been an 'immigrant Church' whose outstanding record of care for countless European immigrants remains unmatched. Today that same tradition must inspire in the Church's approach to recent Hispanic immigrants a similar authority, compassion, and decisiveness."[198]

National Parishes and Native-Language Schools in the Archdiocese of Boston[1]

German

1844–present	HOLY TRINITY (Boston)
1844–1962	HOLY TRINITY SCHOOL (Boston) Sisters of Notre Dame de Namur ǀ Franciscan Sisters
1874–1927	HOLY TRINITY GRAMMAR SCHOOL (South Boston) Sisters of Notre Dame de Namur
1891–1966	HOLY TRINITY GRAMMAR SCHOOL (Roxbury) Sisters of Notre Dame de Namur
1933–1966	HOLY TRINITY SECONDARY SCHOOL – GIRLS (Roxbury) Franciscan Sisters
1867–2005	ST. FRANCIS DE SALES (Roxbury)[2]

---

1. Numerous sources were consulted, including archival material from the Archdiocese of Boston, annual reports on archdiocesan schools, materials from orders that served the schools (including the Sisters of St. Joseph, the Sisters of Notre Dame de Namur, and the Sisters of St. Chretienne), secondary sources, school websites, and the Kenedy, Hoffman, and Sadlier Catholic directories: *Official Catholic Directory Anno Domini* (New York: P. J. Kenedy and Sons, 1889–2006); *Sadlier's Catholic Directory, Almanac and Ordo, 1864–1886* (New York: Sadlier, 1864–1886); *Hoffman's Catholic Directory, Almanac and Clergy List, 1886–1889* (Milwaukee: Hoffman Bros., 1886–89).While efforts were made to make this list as comprehensive as possible, it is still incomplete and not entirely accurate. For example, some of the reported establishment dates for schools conflict, it was not always clear when a school closed or merged with another school, and since we took the approach of looking at the official Catholic directories every five years starting in 1861 there could be some schools that are missing. National associations are as they appeared in official Catholic directories and the archdiocesan documents.

2. Secondary sources list as German, but never listed as German in official Catholic directories.

| 1887–1994 | **ASSUMPTION OF THE BLESSED VIRGIN MARY** (Lawrence) |
| 1888–1971 | ASSUMPTION OF THE BLESSED VIRGIN MARY SCHOOL (Lawrence)[3]
Sisters of St. Dominic |

| 1893–unknown | **ST. JOSEPH CHAPEL** (Roxbury)[4] |

French

| 1868–1911 | **ST. JOSEPH** (Lowell)[5] |

1868–1993	**ST. JEAN BAPTISTE** (Lowell)
1883–1992	ST. JOSEPH / ST. JEAN THE BAPTISTE SCHOOL (Lowell) Sisters of Charity of Ottawa (Grey Nuns of the Cross) | Oblate Fathers
1892–1969	ST. JOSEPH COLLEGE – BOYS ELEMENTARY (Lowell) Marist Brothers
1892–1966	ST. JOSEPH COLLEGE – BOYS SECONDARY (Lowell)[6] Marist Brothers
1928–1989	ST. JOSEPH SECONDARY (Lowell)[7] Sisters of Charity of Ottawa (Grey Nuns of the Cross)

| 1870–2004 | **ST. MARY** (Marlboro) |
| 1881–1970 | ST. MARY / ST. ANTHONY SCHOOL (Marlboro)
Sisters of St. Anne |

1871–1991	**ST. ANNE** (Lawrence)
1886–1991	ST. ANNE AND ST. JOSEPH ELEMENTARY (Lawrence)[8] Sisters of Good Shepherd | Marist Brothers | Sisters of the Immaculate Heart of Mary
1893–1970	ST. ANNE SECONDARY – GIRLS (Lawrence) Marist Brothers

1873–2004	**ST. JOSEPH** (Salem)[9]
1893–present	ST. JOSEPH ELEMENTARY (Salem)[10] Sisters of Charity of Ottawa | Sisters of Ste. Chretiénne | Sisters of l'Assumption
1925–1981	ST. JOSEPH SECONDARY (Salem) Sisters of the Assumption of the Blessed Virgin Mary

---

3. Lost German association in 1910.
4. Listed only in the 1893 official Catholic directory.
5. Becomes a shrine in 1956.
6. Closed in 1910, reopened in 1920; merged with St. Joseph High School – Girls in 1966.
7. Began as girls school; St. Joseph High School and St. Louis Academy merged to become Greater Lowell High School in 1989.
8. Separate schools for boys and girls.
9. Was a French/Spanish parish when closed.
10. Still open under St. James parish; lost French association in 2004.

1876–1998	**ST. JOSEPH** (Haverhill)[11]
1885–present	ST. JOSEPH SCHOOL (Haverhill)[12] Sisters of Charity of Ottawa (Grey Nuns) I Brothers of the Sacred Heart I Marist Brothers
1880–present	**NOTRE DAME DES VICTOIRES** / Our Lady of Victories (Boston)[13]
1886–1997	**ST. JEAN THE BAPTISTE** / St. John the Baptist (Lynn)[14]
1893–1992	ST. JEAN THE BAPTISTE ELEMENTARY (Lynn)[15] Sisters of St. Anne
1917–1967	ST. JEAN THE BAPTISTE SECONDARY (Lynn)[16] Sisters of St. Anne
1890–present	**ST. ZEPHERIN** (Wayland)[17]
1891–2004	**SACRED HEART** (Brockton)
1900–2006	SACRED HEART ELEMENTARY (Brockton)[18] Sisters of the Assumption I Sisters of the Assumption of the Blessed Virgin Mary
1891–1972	ST. ANN ACADEMY (Marlboro)[19] Sisters of St. Anne
1892–1998	**NOTRE DAME DE PITIÉ / OUR LADY OF PITY** (Cambridge)[20]
1896–1974	NOTRE DAME DE PITIÉ / OUR LADY OF PITY ELEMENTARY (Cambridge) Sisters of the Holy Union of the Sacred Hearts
1931–1972	NOTRE DAME DE PITIÉ / OUR LADY OF PITY SECONDARY (Cambridge) Sisters of the Holy Union of the Sacred Hearts
1894–2004	**ST. PETER SCHOOL / ECOLE ST. PIERRE** (Waltham)
1895–1970	ST. PETER SCHOOL / ECOLE ST. PIERRE SCHOOL (Waltham) Sisters des Dilles de Jesus of Bretagne I Sisters of Ste. Chretiénne
1901–present	**ST. ANNE** (Salem)
1907–1976	ST. ANNE SCHOOL (Salem) Sisters of Ste. Chretiénne

11. Merged with St. George, St. Michael, and St. Rita to form All Saints parish.
12. Still open under All Saints parish.
13. Lost French association in 2006.
14. Acquired French association in 1918.
15. Acquired French association in 1918.
16. Acquired French association in 1918.
17. Lost French association in 1961.
18. Merged with St. Edwards and St. Casimir Schools to form Trinity Catholic Academy in 2007.
19. Lost French association in 1912.
20. Becomes a Haitian chaplaincy in 1998.

1902–1999   **ST. ALOYSIUS / ST. LOUIS DE GONZAGUE** (Newburyport)[21]
  1907–1974   ST. ALOYSIUS / ST. LOUIS DE GONZAGUE SCHOOL
(Newburyport)[22]
Sisters of Ste. Chretiénne I Sisters of Joan of Arc

1903–1998   **SACRED HEART** (Amesbury)[23]
  1903–1976   SACRED HEART ELEMENTARY (Amesbury)[24]
Sisters of Holy Childhood I Sisters of Ste. Chretiénne
  1921–1946   SACRED HEART SECONDARY (Amesbury)[25]
Sisters of Ste. Chretiénne

1904–2004   **ST. LOUIS DE FRANCE** (Lowell)[26]
  1907–present   ST. LOUIS DE FRANCE (K1–8)[27]
Sisters of the Assumption of the Blessed Virgin Mary
  1918–1989   ST. LOUIS ACADEMY SECONDARY – GIRLS (Lowell)[28]
Sisters of the Assumption of the Blessed Virgin Mary

1905–present   **ST. ANTHONY / ST. ANTHONY OF PADUA** (Shirley)[29]
  1908–1969   ST. ANTHONY / ST. ANTHONY OF PADUA SCHOOL (Shirley)[30]
Sisters of Ste. Chretiénne I Sisters of Joan of Arc I Sisters of the
Holy Union of the Sacred Hearts

1905–2005   **SACRED HEART** (Lawrence)
  1899–2005   SACRED HEART SCHOOL (Lawrence)
Marist Brothers I Sisters of Good Shepherd I Sisters of the Holy
Union of the Sacred Hearts
  1928–1979   SACRED HEART SECONDARY (Lawrence)
Sisters of the Holy Union of the Sacred Hearts

1907–1999   **OUR LADY OF THE ASSUMPTION** (Chelsea)
  1912–1999   OUR LADY OF THE ASSUMPTION (Chelsea)
Sisters of the Holy Union of the Sacred Hearts

1908–2004   **NOTRE DAME DE LOURDES / OUR LADY OF LOURDES**
(Lowell)
  1909–1977   NOTRE DAME DE LOURDES / OUR LADY OF LOURDES SCHOOL
(Lowell)
Sisters of Charity of Ottawa (Grey Nuns of the Cross)

---

21. Name changed to St. Louis de Gonzague in 1955.
22. Name changed to St. Louis de Gonzague in 1955.
23. Merged with St. Joseph to form Holy Family parish, but church remained open until 2007.
24. Acquired French association in 1917.
25. Closed sometime prior to 1946.
26. Altered to include territory of St. Jean Baptiste parish in 1993.
27. Now under St. Marguerite d'Youville parish in Dracut.
28. Began as girls school; St. Joseph High School and St. Louis Academy merged to become Greater Lowell High School in 1989.
29. Never officially French.
30. Never officially French.

1910–1997	**ST. STANISLAUS** (Ipswich)[31]
1926–1978	St. Stanislaus (Ipswich) Sisters of Ste. Chretiénne
1911–1997	**ST. JOHN THE EVANGELIST** (Newton)
1925–1983	St. John the Evangelist School (Newton)[32] Sisters of St. Anne
1912–2000	**ST. JOSEPH** (Everett)[33]
1928–1968	St. Joseph School (Everett) Sisters of the Assumption of the Blessed Virgin Mary
1918–1972	Academy of Ste. Chretiénne – Secondary (Salem)[34] Sisters of Ste. Chretiénne
1918–1990	**ST. ALPHONSE** (Beverly)[35]
1928–1938	St. Alphonse School (Beverly) Sisters of St. Anne
1922–2004	**STE. JEANNE D'ARC** (Lowell)[36]
1910–present	Ste. Jeanne d'Arc Elementary (Lowell)[37] Sisters of Charity of Ottawa (Grey Nuns of the Cross)
1927–2000	**CHRIST, KING** (Hudson)[38]
1929–1934	Christ, King School (Hudson) Sisters of St. Anne
1928–2001	**STE. THERESE** (Dracut)[39]
1954–1978	Ste. Therese School (Dracut) Sisters of the Assumption
1930–2000	Jeanne d'Arc Academy – Elementary (Milton)[40] Religious of Christian Education
1931–2006	**STE. MARIE** (Lowell)[41]
1954–1978	Ste. Marie / Sancta Maria School (Lowell) Sisters of the Assumption of the Blessed Virgin Mary

---

31. Merged with Sacred Heart and St. Joseph to become Our Lady of Hope parish.
32. Lost French association in 1947.
33. Lost French association in 1976.
34. School not attached to a parish.
35. Lost French association in 1969.
36. Never officially French.
37. Never officially French.
38. Lost French association in 1947.
39. Merged with Our Lady of Assumption to form Ste. Marguerite d'Youville in 2001.
40. Never officially French; school not attached to a parish.
41. Existed as a mission for twenty-five years before gained parish status.

1936–2000	**ST. THERESE** (Methuen)[42]
1939–1971	St. Therese Elementary (Methuen)[43] Sister Servants of the Immaculate Heart of Mary
1945–1952	St. Therese Secondary (Methuen)[44] Sister Servants of the Immaculate Heart of Mary
1963–present	Franco-American School (Lowell)[45] Sisters of Charity of Ottawa (Grey Nuns of the Cross)

Italian

1873–present	**ST. LEONARD OF PORT MAURICE** (North Boston)[46]
1902–1983	St. Anthony (North Boston) Franciscan Sisters of the Immaculate Conception
1888–2004	**SACRED HEART** (North Boston)
1895–present	St. John School (North Boston)[47] Sisters of St. Joseph
1892–1985	**ST. LAZARUS** (East Boston)[48]
1925–1991	St. Lazarus School (East Boston)[49] Sisters of St. Joseph
1903–1998	**ST. ANTHONY** (Lawrence)[50]
1904–2004	**HOLY ROSARY** (Lawrence)[51]
1909–1991	Holy Rosary Elementary (Lawrence) Holy Rosary Congregation of Pious Sisters | Venerini Sisters | Sisters of Notre Dame
1904–1969	**OUR LADY OF POMPEII** (Boston)
1905–2004	**OUR LADY OF MT. CARMEL** (East Boston)
1931–1974	Our Lady of Mt. Carmel School (East Boston)[52] Franciscan Sisters of the Immaculate Conception

---

42. Merged with St. Augustine to become Our Lady of Good Counsel in Quincy; listed as French on archdiocesan website.

43. Listed as French on archdiocesan website, but never listed as French in official Catholic directories.

44. Listed as French on archdiocesan website, but never listed as French in official Catholic directories.

45. Began as an orphanage in 1908; school not attached to a parish.

46. Lost Italian association in 1992.

47. Lost Italian association in 2004.

48. Merged with St. Joseph to form St. Joseph–St. Lazarus parish.

49. Lost Italian association in 1985.

50. Closed in 1965 and reopened in 1986 as Maronite parish.

51. Merged with St. Francis, Holy Trinity, and SS. Peter and Paul to form Corpus Christi parish.

52. Merged with Our Lady of the Assumption, Most Holy Redeemer, and Sacred Heart parish schools.

1906–present	ST. ANTHONY / ST. ANTHONY OF PADUA (Revere)[53]

1907–present	ST. TARCISIUS (Framingham)
1959–present	ST. TARCISIUS PRE-K–8 SCHOOL (Framingham)[54] Sisters of St. Joseph

1915–present	ST. ANTHONY (Somerville)[55]
1959–2006	ST. ANTHONY SCHOOL (Somerville) Sisters of Notre Dame de Namur

1917–present	ST. FRANCIS OF ASSISI (Cambridge)
1926–1969	ST. FRANCIS OF ASSISI (Cambridge) Franciscan Sisters

1918–2003	ST. MARY (Salem)

1921–2004	ST. ANN (Marlboro)[56]

1922–present	CHURCH OF THE SACRED HEART (Waltham)[57]

1922–present	HOLY FAMILY (Lynn)

1927–present	ST. ANTHONY (Everett)

1932–1998	ST. RITA (Haverhill)[58]

1972–2004	ST. PETER (Malden)[59]

Polish

1893–present	OUR LADY OF CZESTOCHOWA / CZENSTOCHOWA (South Boston)
1908–present	ST. MARY SCHOOL (South Boston) Felician Sisters

1903–present	ST. JOHN THE BAPTIST (Salem)
1908–1978	ST. JOHN THE BAPTIST SCHOOL (Salem) Felician Sisters of St. Francis

1904–present	HOLY TRINITY (Lowell)
1907–2004	ST. STANISLAUS (Lowell) Felician Sisters

53. Merged with St. Theresa and St. John Vianney in 2001. All three parishes were closed and St. Anthony of Padua formed.
54. School closed in 1970, reopened in 1980.
55. 2004 becomes Brazilian parish; 2007 listed as Italian/Brazilian.
56. First established as a mission.
57. Lost Italian association in 2006.
58. Existed first as an Italian mission; merged with St. George, St. Joseph, and St. Michael to form All Saints parish.
59. First established as a mission in 1924.

1905–present	**ST. STANISLAUS** (Chelsea)
1912–1991	ST. STANISLAUS SCHOOL (Chelsea) Franciscan Sisters
1905–2004	**HOLY TRINITY** (Lawrence)[60]
1907–2004	HOLY TRINITY SCHOOL (Lawrence) Felician Sisters | Franciscan Sisters of St. Joseph
1906–present	**ST. MICHAEL** (Lynn)
1919–1981	ST. MICHAEL (Lynn) Franciscan Sisters of St. Joseph
1907–1995	**ST. HEDWIG** (Cambridge)
1914–1956	ST. HEDWIG SCHOOL (Cambridge) Sisters of the Holy Family of Nazareth
1908–1997	**SACRED HEART** (Ipswich)[61]
1912–1999	**ST. CASIMIR** (Maynard)
1910–1998	**ST. MICHAEL** (Haverhill)[62]
1913–present	**ST. ADALBERT** (Hyde Park)[63]
1914–2002	**OUR LADY OF OSTROBRAMA** (Brockton)
1918–1997	**ST. PETER** (Norwood)
1927–1997	**ST. JOSEPH** (Peabody)[64]
1933–1976	ST. JOSEPH SCHOOL (Peabody)[65] Franciscan Sisters
1933–1968	**OUR LADY OF OSTROBRAMA** (Boston)

Lithuanian

1896–1914	**ST. JOSEPH** (South Boston)
1898–present	**ST. ROCCO / SS. ROCCO AND CASIMIR / ST. CASIMIR** (Brockton)[66]

60. Merged with St. Francis, Holy Rosary, and SS. Peter and Paul to form Corpus Christi parish.

61. Merged with St. Joseph and St. Stanislaus to become Our Lady of Hope parish.

62. Merged with St. George, St. Joseph, and St. Rita to form All Saints parish.

63. Lost Polish association in 2006.

64. Archdiocese website listed as Polish, but never listed as Polish in official Catholic directories.

65. Archdiocese website listed as Polish, but never listed as Polish in official Catholic directories.

66. 1954 becomes SS. Rocco and Casimir; 1975 becomes St. Casimir.

1945–2006	ST. ROCCO / ST. CASIMIR (Brockton)[67]
	Sisters of Jesus Crucified
1903–2002	**ST. FRANCIS OF ASSISI** (Lawrence)
1958–1979	ST. FRANCIS ELEMENTARY (Lawrence)
	Sisters of Jesus Crucified
1904–present	**ST. PETER** (South Boston)[68]
1945–2006	ST. PETER (South Boston)
	Sisters of Jesus Crucified
1908–2000	**ST. JOSEPH** (Lowell)
1910–2005	**IMMACULATE CONCEPTION** (Cambridge)
1910–1970	IMMACULATE CONCEPTION SCHOOL (Cambridge)
	Sisters of Jesus Crucified and the Sorrowful Mother
1912–2004	**ST. GEORGE** (Norwood)
1914–1998	**ST. GEORGE** (Haverhill)[69]

Portuguese

1889–present	**OUR LADY OF GOOD VOYAGE** (Gloucester)
1901–present	**ST. ANTHONY** (Lowell)
1902–present	**ST. ANTHONY** (Cambridge)
1907–2004	**SS. PETER AND PAUL** (Lawrence)[70]
1921–1999	**ST. JOHN THE BAPTIST** (East Boston)[71]
1883–1889	ST. JOHN THE BAPTIST (East Boston)
	Sisters of the Third Order of St. Dominic
1965–present	**OUR LADY OF FATIMA** (Peabody)
1965–1976	**PORTUGUESE CATHOLIC MISSION** (Peabody)

Maronite

1893–1999	**OUR LADY OF THE CEDARS OF MT. LEBANON** (Boston)

---

67. Merged with St. Edwards and Sacred Heart to form Trinity Catholic Academy.
68. Church and parish built by laymen in 1895.
69. Existed as a Lithuanian mission until 1961; merged with St. Joseph, St. Michael, and St. Rita to form All Saints parish.
70. Existed as a mission until 1976; merged with St. Francis, Holy Rosary, and Holy Trinity to form Corpus Christi parish.
71. Parish formed in 1872, but not given official parish status until 1921.

1933–1998	**ST. THERESA** (Brockton)
1986–1998	**ST. ANTHONY** (Lawrence)[72]

Spanish _____

1990–2004	**NUESTRA SEÑORA DEL CARMEN** (Lowell)
1993–2004	**ASUNCIÓN DE LA VIRGEN MARÍA** (Lawrence)[73]

Ukranian Catholic _____

1918–1998	**ST. JOHN** (Salem)
1953–1966	**SACRED HEART OF JESUS** (Jamaica Plain)

Armenian _____

1920–1998	**HOLY CROSS** (Cambridge)
1982–present	ARMENIAN SISTERS' ACADEMY / ST. STEPHEN'S SCHOOL (Lexington)[74] Congregation of Armenian Catholic Sisters

Melchite-Greek _____

1902–1998	**ST. JOSEPH** (Lawrence)[75]
1908–1998	**ANNUNCIATION CATHEDRAL** (Roslindale)

Ukranian-Greek _____

1940–1997	**CHRIST THE KING** (Jamaica Plain)

Montello _____

1897–2003	**ST. EDWARD** (Brockton)[76]
1953–2006	ST. EDWARD (Brockton)[77] Sisters of Charity of Nazareth

Syro-Melchite _____

1911–1967	**OUR LADY OF THE ANNUNCIATION** (Boston)[78]

---

72. This parish listed twice; began as an Italian parish which closed in 1965; parish reopened in 1986 as Maronite parish.

73. Merged with St. Mary of the Assumption in 2004.

74. Founded in Watertown and moved to Lexington; school not attached to a parish.

75. 1902–1923 listed as Melchite-Greek; 1923–1956 listed as Syrian; 1956–1998 listed as Melchite.

76. Merged with St. Nicholas to become St. Edith Stein parish in 2003.

77. Lost Montello association in 1990; merged with St. Casimir and Sacred Heart to form Trinity Catholic Academy in 2006.

78. First listed as Syro-Melchite; 1950 becomes Melchite Byzantine.

Campello

1902–2004   **ST. MARGARET** (Brockton)[79]

Haitian chaplaincy

1998–present   **OUR LADY OF PITY** (Cambridge)

Italian/Brazilian

1915–present   **ST. ANTHONY** (Somerville)[80]

---

79. Lost Campello association in 1991.
80. Parish listed three times; 1915–2004 listed as Italian; 2004–2007 listed as Brazilian; 2007 listed as Italian/Brazilian.

"I Am a Catholic Just as I Am a Dweller on the Planet"

John Boyle O'Reilly, Louise Imogen Guiney, and a Model of Exceptionalist Catholic Literature in Boston

LIBBY MacDONALD BISCHOF

On Saturday afternoon, June 20, 1896, at two o'clock in the afternoon, 150 singers from the St. Cecilia and Apollo Clubs, accompanied by 50 members of the Boston Symphony Orchestra and directed by B. J. Lang, sang a Jubilee Overture welcoming the hundreds of people gathered at the edges of the Back Bay Fens for the presentation of the John Boyle O'Reilly Memorial monument to the city of Boston.[1] Sculpted by the prominent artist Daniel Chester French, the monument features, on one side, a bust of O'Reilly with "Poet, Patriot, Orator" inscribed beneath, and on the other, allegorical figures of Patriotism, Hibernia (Ireland), and Poetry. The pedestal of the memorial includes numerous Celtic engravings — among them a cross, harp, and traditional Celtic knots. The monument was the product of six years of fundraising by a memorial committee of twenty-four who canvassed subscriptions from "the rich and poor alike who loved O'Reilly while living, and forgot not his memory when dead." The monument, according to Mr. A. Shuman, chairman of the executive committee, would "stand as a reminder to future generations that our free land recognizes the worth of her people, no matter under what sky they may first see the light, if they be but true to her."[2]

Many distinguished guests from Boston and elsewhere attended the unveiling of the monument. In addition to O'Reilly's wife and their four daughters, the audience included Vice President Adlai Stevenson and his family; John Walcott, governor of Massachusetts; Josiah Quincy, mayor of Boston; the most Rev. John J. Williams, archbishop of Boston; William Lloyd Garrison; Thomas Bailey Aldrich; Julia Ward Howe; Annie T. Fields; Sarah Orne Jewett; Arlo Bates; Louise Chandler Moulton; fellow Catholic authors and editors Katherine E. Conway; George Parsons Lathrop; Patrick Donahoe; and Jeffrey James Roche; as well as numerous Massachusetts senators and representatives, alderman, city-councilors, naval officers, judges, lawyers, Catholic and Protestant clergy, and prominent Irish Americans.[3] Spectators gathered for the unveiling, performed by O'Reilly's youngest daughter Blanid, as well as speeches by executives of the Memorial committee; readings of poems by O'Reilly and one written in his honor by his successor as editor of the *Pilot,* James Jeffrey Roche; the crowning of the statue with a laurel wreath by the poet Louise Chandler Moulton; impromptu remarks by Vice President Stevenson, and a stirring eulogy given by Rev. Dr. Elmer H. Capen, a Universalist minister and president of Tufts College. O'Reilly was a highly respected and well-loved literary and political figure, and the number of prominent individuals present at the dedication of his memorial monument was testament to his popularity and the uniting effect he had among peoples of diverse occupations, races, and creeds in Boston and beyond.

Of O'Reilly's untimely death in August 1890 Capen recalled in his eulogy that "in many of the chief cities of the nation men, without distinction of race or creed, gathered in great companies, and eloquent lips broke forth in eulogy. High and low, rich and poor, scholars and unlettered, men vied with each other in casting their laurel wreaths upon his bier and dropping their tears upon his sepulchre."[4] In describing the outpouring of grief and sympathy upon O'Reilly's death, Capen highlighted O'Reilly's nearly universal appeal. Those who gathered to eulogize him six years prior, "without distinction of race or creed," gathered once again to mourn the era's most prominent Irish Catholic American.[5] The *Boston Daily Globe* reported that at the close of President Capen's remarks, "the multitude arose, waved hats and handkerchiefs and cheered the speaker for fully five minutes."[6] Such heartfelt recognition by the citizens of Boston was unprecedented for an Irish immigrant in this era, and O'Reilly's lavish monument in the newly developed Back Bay and his memorial ceremony were both testaments to his international prominence in literary, religious, and political circles. Perhaps more than any other figure, O'Reilly, with his "superb physique, his exquisite culture, his fine poetic sensibility, his friendly cordiality, his wit and pathos . . . his enthusiasm of humanity" successfully reconciled (and at times united) Catholic and Protestant Boston, making space for himself, and others who would follow, in both worlds.[7] O'Reilly's nearly twenty-year tenure as editor of the *Pilot,* the nation's most prominent Catholic weekly newspaper, marked the fullest flowering of the Catholic literary impulse in Boston.

Introduction

This essay explores the possibility of a golden age of Catholic literature in turn-of-the-century Boston, focusing largely on O'Reilly and the circle of Catholic authors he published in the *Pilot* during the 1880s, especially Louise Imogen Guiney, but also James Jeffrey Roche and Katherine E. Conway. Robert H. Lord observed in the third volume of the *History of the Archdiocese of Boston,* "Catholic writers were numerous here in the days of Archbishop Williams — to the point where there was much talk of the dawning of an important Catholic literary movement. In the field of scholarship it must be admitted that the output was disappointing.... In the field of *belles-lettres* the Catholic output was much more creditable."[8] In 1944 Lord wrote retrospectively of the *possibility* of an important Catholic literary movement centered in Boston, a movement that never fully materialized. Other scholars have echoed this theme of possibility and failure. Paula Kane described the authors I focus on here as "prophets of a cultural renaissance that never really materialized in the 1880s and 1890s," while Donna Merwick, in her study of Boston priests, highlighted the accomplishments of O'Reilly's circle by arguing that "Catholic writers in Boston in the 1890s did have some of the range and humanity for which critics have searched vainly among Catholic writers until the appearance of Flannery O'Connor."[9]

The supposed failure of these authors to realize an undefined and perhaps indefinable "cultural renaissance" is less significant, however, than the way these men and women served as "prophets" and worked to bring about a golden age of Catholic literature in Boston by providing alternative definitions as to what it meant to be a Catholic writer in the 1880s and 1890s. Authors like O'Reilly and Guiney did not readily and automatically conform to a particular vision or formula — institutional or otherwise — of what it meant to be a Catholic author at the end of the nineteenth century.[10] While most Catholic authors of the era addressed particularly Catholic subject matter and provided moral lessons within their work, Boston Catholics such as O'Reilly, Guiney, Roche, and the novelist Mary Agnes Tickner felt it was enough to simply be Catholic and to let the religion naturally pervade one's work rather than subscribing to a particular formula prescribed either by Catholic hierarchy or by the burgeoning Catholic presses and journals. By not limiting themselves to specific subject matter and by mixing in larger literary circles, "exceptionalist"[11] Boston Catholic authors such as Guiney and O'Reilly provided an alternative model to aspiring Catholic writers. As O'Reilly's circle fought "to maintain a free intellectuality and creative gentility among Catholic Bostonians,"[12] they demonstrated to Boston's dominant Protestant literary establishment that their Catholic beliefs and participation in church activities need not hinder or overwhelm either the quality of their literary production or its appeal to audiences beyond a Catholic subculture. Although institutional mandates eventually won out in Boston and elsewhere as the church of the twentieth century began to "mobilize its resources to control and shape its own myth, by authorizing and encouraging an approved version and carefully excluding those works which did not conform to that version,"[13] at the turn of the century an alternative to following an institutional prescription as to what constituted acceptable Catholic literature was presented by Boston's exceptionalists. Although their exceptionalist model was largely suppressed in the early decades of the twentieth century, the attitudes of O'Reilly's circle have been resurrected in more recent years as the debate about what makes literature particularly Catholic continues. The failure of this circle to extend their influence beyond the decades of the

1880s and 1890s deserves to be more than a footnote in Boston's Catholic history, for their failure was a highly significant and complicated one that tells us much about the centralization of the Catholic Church in Boston as well as the fading of Boston as the center of literature and culture in the United States.

The success and growth of Catholic literature in Boston, as well as the varying definitions of what made a work Catholic, had a great deal to do with the leadership of the archdiocese. When Archbishop Williams led the archdiocese, Kane says he "wishfully promoted whatever literary talent was available," and in her work on Catholic subculture in Boston in the early decades of the twentieth century, she argues that "Williams' unassuming personality nurtured lay cultural activity without threat of heavy-handed church interference but stopped well short of organizing Catholic intellectuals and artists into a movement."[14] When Archbishop O'Connell took over control of the Archdiocese, however, he attempted to centralize control of everything related to the church, including literary production. He made the *Pilot* the official vehicle of the archdiocese in 1908 and expressed in a chancery office circular of the same year that works by Catholic authors would only be considered "Catholic" if they were stamped with "some mark of ecclesiastical approval."[15] The exceptionalist style and practices of O'Reilly's circle were no longer acceptable in an administration that wished to strictly control what parishioners were reading.

The varied definitions of what made both authors and their literature particularly Catholic was a subject of debate within the Catholic hierarchy and in such Catholic periodicals of the era as the Paulist publication the *Catholic World,* published in New York; *Donahoe's Magazine,* published in Boston; the *Sacred Heart Review,* published in Cambridge, Massachusetts; the *Catholic Reading Circle Review,* published in Worcester; and the *American Catholic Quarterly Review,* published in Philadelphia. Each publication included Catholic fiction and poetry within its pages and promoted Catholic authors and Catholic presses. These publications also took it upon themselves to help develop an informed Catholic readership by promoting Catholic Reading Circles and including extensive book reviews and biographical pieces on Catholic authors. As Paul Messbarger has argued in his study of American Catholic literature at the turn of the century, much of the Catholic fiction produced by and for Americans in this era was self-consciously didactic and retained a parochial purpose. Catholic authors were encouraged to focus on such religious themes and subjects as doctrine, moral conduct, and devotional life, and to write for a specifically Catholic audience.[16] Ultimately, this focus and approach limited the success of many Catholic authors by diminishing the appeal of such works to larger non-Catholic audiences. Debates over what makes literature particularly Catholic continue to the present day and will be addressed more fully in the conclusion of this chapter.

Another topic of Catholic literary debate at the turn of the century that carried into the twentieth century was the role of Catholic converts in the production and the wider appeal of Catholic literature.[17] In Boston, converts historically played an important part in the promotion and dissemination of Catholic literature, dating back to the 1844 conversions of Orestes Brownson and Isaac Hecker. Brownson edited a quarterly review while Hecker, the founder of the Paulist order, began publishing the *Catholic World* in 1865.[18] George Parsons Lathrop, author and one-time associate editor of the *Atlantic Monthly*, converted in 1891 with his wife, Rose Hawthorne Lathrop, a poet, and did much, before his untimely death in 1898, to champion Catholicism and Catholic literature in both mainstream and Catholic periodicals.[19]

Debates about what constitutes Catholic literature as well as who can produce and claim it are relevant beyond the context of a specifically Catholic history. Rather, we must look at the way debates about Catholic literature and Catholicism played out in the larger literary canon, on the streets of Boston, and in the personal lives of Catholic authors. One little-studied aspect of Boston Catholic authors in this era is the way such men and women mediated their faith, their society, their literary careers, and their literary subject matter. The cases of Catholic authors John Boyle O'Reilly and Louise Imogen Guiney demonstrate some of the difficulties of being a Catholic writer in Boston at the turn of the century. Faced with both nativist prejudice from Protestant citizens and organizations such as the American Protective Association (APA) as well as the varied pressures of being under the watchful eyes of the Catholic hierarchy and Catholic citizens, both O'Reilly and Guiney nevertheless exemplify authors who were considered successful in the larger world of Boston letters at the turn of the century and who remained true to their faith. O'Reilly was a founding member of the literary and art social clubs the Papyrus Club (1872) and the St. Botolph Club (1880) and also played an active role in the Boston Press Club. Guiney was very friendly with a young and innovative circle of Bohemian authors and artists and was an instrumental part of such small Bohemian magazines as the *Knight Errant* and the *Chap-Book* as well as an influential poetry editor for the small press Copeland and Day.[20] Both O'Reilly and Guiney, in addition to writing for the *Pilot* and other Catholic serials, published in prominent literary magazines with national audiences, such as the *Atlantic Monthly, Harper's Weekly,* and the *Century.* Both also served as informal Irish Catholic ambassadors to the largely Protestant Boston literary scene, and as such helped to gain a wider acceptance for both Irish Catholics and Catholic literature in Boston.

For the ideal of a "golden age" of Catholic literature to really succeed in Boston, good literature needed to be made widely available to the Catholic reading public, and parishioners needed to be encouraged to read, study, and discuss such literature. In an archdiocese that became increasingly ethnically diverse as the century came to a close, language and socioeconomic barriers certainly hindered the spread of this literature, but in the 1880s a variety of methods to ensure Catholic literary consumption began in Boston and spread to other dioceses throughout the country.[21] The Catholic Reading

Circle movement and the organization of Catholic summer schools both helped to build an audience for Catholic literature. In addition, as Catholic colleges such as Boston College and Holy Cross began to increase their enrollments, students also contributed to the Catholic literary canon with such ventures as the *Boston College Stylus,* begun in 1882, and the *Holy Cross Purple,* begun in 1894. No publication, however, did more to promote Catholic literature in Boston than the *Pilot* under the editorship of John Boyle O'Reilly.

John Boyle O'Reilly and the *Pilot*

The Divine Faith, implanted in his soul in childhood, flourished there undyingly, pervaded his whole being with its blessed influences, furnished his noblest ideals of thought and conduct. Even when not explicitly adverted to, Faith's sweet and holy inspirations were there to shape his thought and direct his life. — Cardinal James Gibbons, Baltimore[22]

O'Reilly has long been credited with facilitating Catholic and Irish immigrant progress in America in an era rampant with nativist prejudices and unfounded Protestant fears of a "papist" takeover. Katherine Conway, poet, journalist, and O'Reilly's protégée at the *Pilot,* later wrote of his faith and influence: "A sincere Catholic, his great influence, used lavishly in forwarding the interests of younger Catholics destined to special careers, and in lifting up the lowly without regard to any claim but their need, was for twenty years a valuable factor in Catholic progress in America."[23] O'Reilly, born June 28, 1844, in County Meath, Ireland, first arrived in Boston in 1870, having escaped a long sentence of British penal servitude in Australia resulting from his youthful involvement in the Fenian Irish Nationalist movement.[24] He quickly became a popular journalist in Boston, writing for and later editing the *Pilot,* and "came to hold a well-nigh unique position in this community, hailed not only as the greatest of Irish-Americans, but as one of the few men of whom all Bostonians, regardless of race or creed, were unanimously proud."[25] As an Irish immigrant and fervent patriot of both his home and adopted nations, O'Reilly did far more than simply assimilate into Boston society. His literary talents, his interest in "manly" sports such as boxing, and his skillful oratory endeared him to a diverse body of citizens, and he was often called upon to make speeches or read his poetry at commemorative events throughout the United States. In his short life of forty-six years, O'Reilly published four books of poetry: *Songs from the Southern Seas and Other Poems* (1873), *Songs, Legends and Ballads* (1878), *The Statues in the Block* (1881), and *In Bohemia* (1886); one novel, *Moondyne* (1879); and a treatise on sport, *The Ethics of Boxing and Manly Sport* (1888). These publications, his public lectures, and his active participation in Boston literary and art clubs such as the Papyrus Club, the Press Club, and the St. Botolph Club as well as Catholic organizations such as the Catholic Union (which he helped Archbishop Williams found in 1873) assured O'Reilly's prominence in both Catholic and Protestant circles. His greatest service to Boston Catholic literature, however, was his editorship of the *Pilot* and his showcasing of young Catholic talent in its pages.

O'Reilly began reporting and writing for the *Pilot* in the spring of 1870; his first report was a critical eyewitness account of the failed Fenian invasion of Canada. The weekly newspaper, owned by Patrick Donahoe, an eminent Irish Catholic publisher, was the nation's most popular Catholic weekly, and was directed especially at Irish Catholic immigrants. First called the *Jesuit* or the *Catholic Sentinel,* the paper had been founded in Boston by Bishop Benedict Fenwick in September 1829 as a vehicle to "explain, diffuse, and defend the principles of the One, Holy, Catholic, and Apostolic Church."[26] In 1834 Bishop Fenwick turned over the publication to a layman, Donahoe, who later became editor and sole proprietor and renamed the newspaper the *Boston Pilot* in 1836. By 1858 the title was shortened to the *Pilot.* Under Donahoe's editorship the paper had a national circulation nearing 100,000, "with a larger and abler staff of writers and correspondents than any other Catholic or Irish-American weekly."[27] It was Donahoe who first hired O'Reilly as a reporter, and when Donahoe fell into financial ruin as a result of the Great Fire of 1872 in Boston's business district, which destroyed his buildings, O'Reilly and Archbishop Williams bought out his interest in the *Pilot* in order to pay off his creditors.[28] It is not entirely clear exactly when O'Reilly took over editorship of the *Pilot* from Donahoe, but it was certainly prior to the buyout. O'Reilly reported to his Irish aunt in September 1874: "My position in Boston — which is the chief city in this country for literature and general culture — is quite good. I am chief editor of the *Pilot* — which is the most influential Catholic paper in America, probably the world."[29]

Much of the *Pilot*'s overall literary, religious, and political influence can be credited to O'Reilly's editorship. After he and Archbishop Williams assumed control of the paper in 1876, "The *Pilot* entered upon a halcyon period of its history. Few journals of that time could have surpassed it for literary excellence, for dignity, sincerity, fairness, and true liberality, or for devotion to the highest ideals in religious, civic, and social life."[30] Under O'Reilly's tenure, the "working man's paper" introduced more literature to its largely Irish Catholic audience, 80 percent of whom were, O'Reilly observed in an August 1878 editorial, "in the truest sense 'honest, horny-fisted sons of toil.' "[31] O'Reilly struck an admirable balance of Catholic and secular subject matter in the pages of the *Pilot.* Although he commented frequently on political happenings and unrest in America and Ireland, he also included columns that would appeal to a wide variety of readers such as: "Latest Irish News," which gave brief snippets of news from each of Ireland's counties; "Boston and Vicinity," where local parish news, announcements of importance to Boston Catholics, as well as new theater performances and social club news were printed; "The Sporting World," which included box scores, articles on sport, and announcements of interest to both athletes and spectators in Boston; "Our Boys and Girls," which contained stories, puzzles, parables, and poems for children; and occasionally also "Catholic College News," and "Catholic News." By including such a diverse body of news material, O'Reilly attempted to ensure that his readers would be well-informed Catholic and American citizens — without losing ties to Ireland. He always insisted to his Irish American compatriots that, "We can do Ireland more good by our Americanism than by our Irishism."[32] Any reader of the *Pilot* would have been well-versed in major Catholic issues of the day, such as the debate over parochial schools, and at the same time given a working knowledge of local, national, and international politics.

O'Reilly also included numerous weekly columns dealing with literary and cultural matters such as "New Books," which recommended and reviewed both religious and secular titles to readers, and "The Magazines," which reprinted excerpts of interest to Catholics from religious magazines like the *Catholic World,* the *Catholic Review,* and the *American Catholic Quarterly,* as well as secular magazines like *Atlantic Monthly, Lippincott's Magazine,* and *Harper's Weekly.* O'Reilly also promoted other Catholic periodicals. In 1889 he wrote that "if the *Pilot* were asked to indicate the high-water mark of American Catholic intellectual achievement, it would touch *The American Catholic Quarterly Review,* satisfied that the standard will not be overpassed in any sectarian or secular comparison" and further emphasized to his readers that "American Catholics should be proud to be represented by this magnificent publication."[33] The influential O'Reilly effectively urged his readers to patronize other Catholic publications, thus furthering the growth and dissemination of Catholic literature. O'Reilly also included in the pages of the *Pilot* the interesting weekly feature "Rich Words from Many Writers," where readers of the *Pilot* sent in edifying quotations from their favorite authors, both Catholic and secular. On any given week, this column included quotations from such varied literary figures as Dante, Shakespeare, Milton, Mark Twain, Virgil, Longfellow, Oliver Wendell Holmes, Theodore Parker, Alexander Pope, and O'Reilly himself. By including all these columns related to literature — both Catholic and secular — O'Reilly ensured that his "workingman" readership and their families, a majority of them Irish immigrants, would be able to further educate themselves and expand their cultural knowledge base. Such edification served the dual purpose of helping Irish immigrants to combat popular stereotypes as uneducated, unskilled, and violent drunkards and promoting Catholic literature.

In addition to these weekly columns, and most important to Catholic literature in Boston in the 1880s and 1890s, O'Reilly also published his own poems, as well as the stories, poems, and lyrics of Boston Catholic writers such as Katherine Conway, James Jeffrey Roche, Louise Imogen Guiney, and Mary Elizabeth Blake, among others. While O'Reilly was editor, each issue of the *Pilot* included a serialized story or novel and four or five poems. With few exceptions, the top of the left-hand column on the front page of every issue featured a poem, highlighting the importance placed on literature within the newspaper.[34] Under O'Reilly's tenure as editor the paper also reprinted many poems and articles by and about non-Catholic authors — many of whom were O'Reilly's literary companions in Boston, among them Oliver Wendell Holmes, Annie Adams Fields, and Wendell Phillips. He also printed the work of Walt Whitman, Henry James, James Whitcomb Riley, William Butler Yeats, Mathew Arnold, Henry Wadsworth Longfellow, and Alfred Lord Tennyson. In the "New Books" column of every issue, O'Reilly was as likely to announce the publication of Thomas Wentworth Higginson's *Short Studies of American Authors,* Annie Adams Fields's *Under the Olive,* or Emile Zola's *Nana* as he was Catholic titles such as *The Life of Our Lord and Savior Jesus Christ and of His Blessed Mother, The Miracle at Lourdes,* or *A Catholic Child's History.*[35] By giving Catholic authors exposure alongside the better-known authors of the day, O'Reilly effectively elevated the status of Catholic literature for his readers. And, by exposing his Catholic readers to all sorts of literature, not exclusively Catholic, he implied that good literature was elevating and educational in and of itself, and that Catholic readers could and should read both inside and outside of the faith.

O'Reilly did not privilege the secular literature, however. He continually championed the Catholic press and other Catholic newspapers and journals in the pages of the *Pilot* and consequently rejected complaints that the Catholic press was "poorly patronized." The remedy to poor patronization, according to O'Reilly, was to "give the people a good paper, and they must take it."[36] Including a wide variety of good literature was one way O'Reilly made a good paper for his readers. And, as Katherine Conway wrote, "By his dignified and widely generous management he made a paper at whose quality not even the most bigoted anti-Catholic could sneer."[37] O'Reilly's editorials and the quality of his paper were both so well respected by other editors and journalists in the city that he was elected president of the Boston Press Club in 1879. In his presidential address he told the members of the press club that "freedom and purity of the press are the test of national virtue and independence," and he held fast to this belief as long as he was editor of the *Pilot.*[38]

In addition to including a good deal of literature in the pages of the *Pilot,* O'Reilly regularly covered Boston's literary scene in the *Pilot* because he considered Boston to be the center of American letters and because he was an important part of it. When O'Reilly included full reports of Papyrus Club activities in the paper, especially the "Ladies Night" he instituted when he was elected president of the literary club in 1879, he demonstrated to his readers that Catholics could fully be accepted into the vibrant world of Boston letters. In his accounts of Papyrus Club meetings published in the *Pilot,* O'Reilly always included the names of prominent author guests who attended, including Mark Twain, William Dean Howells, Thomas Bailey Aldrich, and others.[39] That O'Reilly was often called upon to read his poetry at these meetings and that his name was mentioned frequently in the same lines as other famous American authors certainly highlighted his literary esteem to the readers of the *Pilot.* O'Reilly's distinction in Boston letters elevated the position of the *Pilot,* and his presidency of the Papyrus Club (1879–80) as well as his active participation in club activities throughout his life introduced Catholic literature to many writers, artists, and patrons who might otherwise have ignored it. In his diary, the Boston author and playwright T. R. Sullivan, who first met O'Reilly through the Papyrus Club, recorded in 1891 that he went to a reading of Catholic authors in the hall of Boston College, a reading that was arranged by O'Reilly the spring before he died. Sullivan was not a Catholic and had no desire to be one, but he attended such events because of his friendship with O'Reilly.[40] O'Reilly, as a cultural ambassador, freely moved in both Protestant and Catholic circles and did much to foster interaction between the two groups. Thomas Wentworth Higginson, memorializing O'Reilly at the Tremont Temple, said that his particular mission was the reconciliation of the "Roman Catholic Irishman and the Protestant American" in the city of Boston, and O'Reilly went about this work "as if he had been born with that mission stamped upon his forehead, and as if a hundred vicar-generals had anointed and ordained him for the work."[41]

One important reason O'Reilly was able to maintain the freedom and purity of the press in regard to the *Pilot* was the free reign given to him by Archbishop Williams. When he and Williams assumed control of the paper in 1876, O'Reilly promised to "conduct the *Pilot* as becomes an Irishman, a Catholic, and a gentlemen," and as Williams proclaimed after O'Reilly's passing, "He kept his word."[42] Although the *Pilot* was considered the official voice of Irish Catholics in Boston, the paper was not the official organ of the archdiocese until 1908. Williams did not impose institutional Catholic mandates on the *Pilot,* and in that way the newspaper remained very much a representative of the Catholic exceptionalist style O'Reilly championed. His paper was not Catholic because of an institutional imprimatur from the archbishop; it was Catholic because O'Reilly himself was a faithful Catholic and wrote for a Catholic audience in a fair and free spirit without external demands. In this way he and his writers were able to freely report on the political, social, intellectual, *and* religious issues important to their Irish-Catholic readership, keeping faithful always to the tagline that ran below the title of the newspaper in every issue: "Be just, and fear not, let all ends thou aim'st at be thy God's, thy Country's, and Truth's."

O'Reilly's faith left a lasting impression on his Protestant friends, and many admired him for it. His close friend the Hon. E. A. Moseley of Washington wrote that "his childlike faith in the teachings of his youth,... his beautiful trust and repose in his religion, his Church, and his God" was what he admired most about O'Reilly. Moseley also noted that O'Reilly's literary associations never weakened his faith because "with him it was a fixed fact, a never faltering attitude of his mind, and when, by his literary associations, he was thrown with men who were doubters, agnostics, and disbelievers, his faith was as sublime, his conviction as unshaken, and his devotion as constant as when he learned the lesson at his mother's knee."[43] The Unitarian Reverend Elmer Capen acknowledged O'Reilly "occupied a peculiar place

among literary men in an age that is sometimes called agnostic and irrever-
ent. His religion was an ever present reality, pervading his whole being, not
as is often the case . . . something to be kept in the background of one's life
and to be apologized for to his friends."[44] The strength of O'Reilly's faith
only improved his ability to mix in numerous diverse social circles, and his
conviction certainly endeared him to many who previously shunned other
Irish Catholics. When assimilating into Boston's literary culture, O'Reilly
never abandoned his faith, or played down his Catholicism. If he was going
to be accepted, he wanted to be known as a Catholic. He was unabashedly
proud of his heritage and identified with all who were oppressed, as well
as individuals who had fought valiantly for what they believed to be true
and just. Because of his legendary and nearly universal appeal, O'Reilly is
often viewed by historians, as he was by his contemporaries, as an atypical
and exceptional figure. Although his personality was larger than life and his
influence greater than many others, his acceptance and esteem in the larger
community of Boston authors, as well what he did to promote both Catholic
and non-Catholic literature in the pages of the *Pilot,* cannot be dismissed as
just an anomaly. As numerous as his abilities were and as charming as he
was, the particular climate of Boston and the Catholic leadership of the era
had much to do with his successes.

Despite many accounts of the strength of O'Reilly's faith from his contemporaries, O'Reilly was sometimes called upon by other Catholic publications
to defend his own literary choices. In 1878, following the publication of his
serial *Moondyne Joe* in the pages of the *Pilot* (later just *Moondyne* when
published by Roberts Brothers in 1880), J. A. McMaster, editor of the Catholic publication the *Freeman's Journal* of New York, criticized the "pagan"
and "anti-Christian" qualities of the work, finding it unfit for a Catholic
audience. *Moondyne,* a story of British penal colonies in Western Australia
that focused on the prisoner Joseph Wyville (named Moondyne by Aus-
tralian aborigines), was loosely based on some of O'Reilly's own formative
experiences as a political prisoner, and he dedicated the book "to all who
are in prison." O'Reilly's novel, like much of his other work, championed
social reforms based on brotherhood, redemption, and forgiveness, moving
beyond distinctions of class and creed. Although romantic and adventurous, the novel seriously addressed the plight of prisoners and the pressing
need for prison reform. In *Moondyne,* O'Reilly wrote that the penal colony
constituted "the purest democracy on earth" because there was "no caste
there. They have found bottom, where all stand equal. No envy there, no
rivalry, no greed nor ambition, and no escape from companionship."[45] Despite McMaster's criticisms of the novel as unfit for Catholics, the book was
well received by many critics. *The Literary World* called the book "one of
the most powerful books of the year," and found within its pages, "a sweet
strain of true Roman Catholic piety . . . here and there."[46]

Despite strong critical reviews in secular publications, O'Reilly was hurt
by McMaster's Catholic criticism and defended his literary choices in the

pages of the *Pilot*. O'Reilly countered McMaster's criticisms with the editorial "Is Moondyne a Bad Book?" and revealed some of his own ideas about what made a piece of literature fit for Catholic readers.[47] "To demand of a Catholic author that his chief character shall be a Catholic is absurd. A novelist must study types as they exist.... There is not, could not be, an anti-Christian word in 'Moondyne.' If there were, it should not stand for one moment."[48] O'Reilly's defense of his work reveals the perspective of an exceptionalist Catholic author. Unlike McMaster, an "ultra Catholic," O'Reilly believed that Catholic authors did not necessarily have to feature "Catholic" characters, and that instead, Catholic novelists, like *all* novelists, must study "types as they exist" in real life. Given O'Reilly's own dedication to his faith, expressed by Cardinal Gibbons at the opening of this section, O'Reilly's work could never be anti-Christian because "the Divine Faith... pervaded his whole being with its blessed influences." Although Messbarger described O'Reilly's editorial as "unorthodox," it should instead be seen as typical of O'Reilly's feelings about how Catholic authors *should* write.[49] He did not need to write about Catholic "types," or focus solely on Catholic "characters." It was the man wielding the pen that mattered, not what he wrote. O'Reilly was a Catholic "type," and thus his characters did not have to be. As he later wrote to a non-Catholic friend, "I am a Catholic just as I am a dweller on the planet, and a lover of yellow sunlight, and flowers in the grass, and the sound of birds. Man never made anything so like God's work as the magnificent, sacrificial, devotional faith of the hoary but young Catholic Church. There is no other church; they are all just way stations."[50] *Moondyne* demonstrated the exceptionalist model of Catholic literature to other young Catholic writers in Boston and beyond. As far as O'Reilly was concerned, a Catholic writer could focus on all types of people in the world as long as the author remained true to the church. Furthermore, the novel's emphasis on brotherhood, social reform, forgiveness, and redemption reflected the larger mission of Christians and thus broadened the appeal of the novel to those outside of the Catholic faith.

Because of his strong patriotism and his belief in justice, equality, and brotherhood, O'Reilly's poetry and speeches also appealed to those outside of Irish and Catholic circles, as evidenced in the great variety of occasions he was called to speak at. O'Reilly was chosen as the poet of the Grand Army of the Republic reunion in Detroit in 1881, where his poem "America" was praised by General Grant as the "grandest poem" he had ever heard.[51] He read his poem "The Exile of the Gael" at the 150th anniversary of the Irish Charitable Society in 1887 and read a dedication poem at the opening banquet of Catholic University in Washington, D.C., in 1889. He eulogized close friends such as the abolitionist Wendell Phillips and read poetry to factory workers, Catholic Reading Circles, and fellow writers of all creeds at the Papyrus Club.

In December 1888, O'Reilly was invited to read his poem "Crispus Attucks, Negro Patriot — Killed in Boston, March 5, 1770" to the Massachusetts Colored League at the A.M.E. Church on Charles Street in Beacon Hill, saying, upon his introduction to the congregation, that "the colored men have their future in their own hands."[52] O'Reilly had written the poem for the unveiling of the memorial dedicated to Crispus Attucks and the other victims of the Boston massacre on the Boston Common the previous month, and like so many of his poems, "Crispus Attucks," the last stanza excerpted below, underscored the idea of a brotherhood of man regardless of class, race, or creed. Presenting Attucks as a hero and a patriot, he wrote:

> And so, must we come to the learning of Boston's lesson today;
> The moral that Crispus Attucks taught in the old heroic way;
> God made mankind to be one in blood, as one in spirit and thought;
> And so great a boon, by a brave man's death, is never dearly bought![53]

O'Reilly saw Crispus Attucks as a key sacrifice in the struggle for America's ultimate freedom from England and wrote, "His breast was the first one rent apart that liberty's stream might flow; / For our freedom now and forever, his head was the first laid low." In writing "our freedom" and by praising "this Negro slave with an unfamiliar name," O'Reilly refashioned the story of American democratic origins to include the historically disenfranchised African American *and* the new immigrant. In 1888, as evidenced in "Crispus Attucks," O'Reilly saw an America where all races and creeds should share a common vision of freedom:

> Indian and Negro, Saxon and Celt, Teuton and Latin and Gaul —
> Mere surface shadow and sunshine; while the sounding unifies all!
> One love, one hope, one duty theirs! No matter the time or ken,
> There never was a separate heart-beat in all the races of men!

O'Reilly did not express his vision solely in his poetry. Close to Wendell Phillips and other prominent abolitionists, O'Reilly supported Boston's African American community, especially in its struggles for increased freedom and equality. Unlike his predecessors at the *Pilot,* O'Reilly was sympathetic to the plight of African Americans during the Jim Crow era and saw much in common between the struggles of Irish and African American workers. As historian Mark Schneider observed, "More than any other Irish-American of his day, John Boyle O'Reilly expressed" possibilities of a "commonality of interest" between Boston's Irish and African American citizens.[54] Such possibilities of a united front faded quickly after his death, but as John Betts noted, during O'Reilly's lifetime, "many Negroes came to look upon him with respect, affection, and even love."[55] The "Crispus Attucks" poem for the Boston Massacre memorial was well received by the audience, and the next year O'Reilly was called upon to memorialize another symbolic act of the patriotic mythology of the United States.

The invitation to write and deliver a poem for the dedication of the Pilgrim Monument in Plymouth held on August 1, 1889, was, perhaps, the most notable sign of O'Reilly's acceptance by Boston's Protestant community. By all accounts, O'Reilly's poem, delivered to the throngs of spectators at the unveiling of the monument, was very well received, despite earlier criticism regarding the choice of an Irish Catholic immigrant rather than a native Bostonian or Puritan descendant as official poet of the celebration. As the *Boston Daily Globe* reported, "Without any question this poem will pass at once into the standard text book among accepted American classics. John Boyle O'Reilly has thus given another striking proof of the breadth and universality of his genius."[56] An excerpt from the poem "The Pilgrim Fathers" displays O'Reilly's brand of universal patriotism and egalitarianism.

> Here struck the seed — the Pilgrim's roofless town,
> Where equal rights and equal bonds were set,
> Where all the people equal-franchised met;
> Where doom was writ of privilege and Crown;
> Where human breath blew all the idols down;
> Where crests were naught, where vulture flags were furled,
> And common men began to own the world.[57]

His vision of common men owning the world, and his delight at the "writ of privilege and Crown" surely rang true for many Irish nationalists, who, like O'Reilly, were advocating home rule. If the Pilgrims had broken from England two centuries prior, Ireland could do the same. At the same time, the poem praised the Pilgrims for founding a "Kingdom not of Kings, but of men," thus overseeing the "making of the world again." He praised the religious devotion of the Pilgrims, but even more their doing away with nobility and royalty, celebrating instead "civil" rights. The 1889 dedication of the monument at Plymouth Rock, from today's perspective, overlooked many of the complications and historical implications of the Pilgrims' landing, but in choosing O'Reilly as the poet laureate of the occasion, the committee showed how far Puritan tolerance had come in two centuries. As Lord noted of O'Reilly's performance at Plymouth in the *History of the Archdiocese of Boston,* "He, the recently arrived Irish refugee, showed the fullest understanding of what was the finest in the early Anglo-American tradition: he the uncompromising Catholic, was able to pay such a just and glowing tribute to the Pilgrim Fathers as warmed and won the hearts of Protestant New Englanders."[58]

O'Reilly had a vision of universal brotherhood rare in his era and imparted this vision in his published works, as editor of the *Pilot,* and in the many public appearances he made throughout his short life of forty-six years. When in August 1890 he died unexpectedly of heart failure after an overdose of a sleeping draught at his summer home in Hull, Massachusetts, his friends and fellow Bostonians were shocked. Cardinal Gibbons of Baltimore, the leader of the church in America, called his death "a public calamity — not only a loss to the country, but a loss to the Church, and to humanity in general."[59] The hundreds of letters of condolence and appreciation from all over the world that poured into the editorial desk of the *Pilot* echoed this statement and the profound sense of loss felt by so many. Priests, politicians, fellow editors, Catholic societies, friends, and loyal readers wrote to express their condolences to Mary Boyle O'Reilly and to celebrate O'Reilly's many talents and accomplishments. The leading men and women of Boston letters also wrote in to the *Pilot.* Julia Ward Howe called his death "a loss to the world of letters and to the community," while Oliver Wendell Holmes wrote, "We have been proud of him as an adopted citizen, feeling always that his native land could ill spare so noble a son;... he was a true and courageous lover of his country and of his fellow men."[60] Numerous friends and admirers wrote memorial verse for O'Reilly, including the young Catholic writers he championed in the pages of the *Pilot* — James Jeffrey Roche, Louise Imogen Guiney, Mary Elizabeth Blake, Katherine Conway, and others. Coverage of O'Reilly's death filled nearly all of the columns of the August 16 and August 23 issues of the newspaper, and James Jeffrey Roche, the new editor, wrote to his readers, "We make no apology to our readers for almost filling the present number of the *Pilot* with some of the many tributes from men and journals of every class and creed and race. . . . Such widespread and spontaneous expressions of love and admiration could have been evoked by the death of no other private citizen in all the country, nor, indeed, in all the world."[61]

The August 23 issue featured messages of condolence as well as reprints of memorial poetry and articles of appreciation from numerous newspapers. All noted his universal appeal, his poetic gift, his patriotism toward Ireland and America and the hole left in many communities by his death. The Rev. John Talbot Smith in the *Catholic Review,* however, most aptly expressed the loss to the Catholic community. Of O'Reilly's unique position he wrote:

> He held one position before the American public with respect to his faith and the cause of Ireland which was unique. He was the interpreter of both to the American people, and in this point his loss will be most deeply felt. We do not know any man at the present moment who wields such influence with cultured non-Catholics. . . . He proved to them by his own behavior that Catholicity did not make a man a boor, an enigma, a mere clod-hopper. They were quite willing to follow him, Irish and Catholic though he was, because they saw his manly nature, felt his culture, and were certain of his sincerity in patriotism and religion.[62]

O'Reilly was so successful during his two decades in Boston because he was able to interpret his religion and his homeland to those who had previously held negative stereotypes about both. The strength of his personality and the sincerity of his beliefs endeared him to Catholics and non-Catholics alike. When he died, the golden age of Catholic literature in Boston began to slowly fade. Although Roche, Conway, Guiney, and others worked to continue the exceptionalist legacy of O'Reilly, they unfortunately, as Merwick claimed, "never honed to a fine point their argument that belief should be integrated with contemporary life on the basis of one's own judgment."[63] Many of them did, however, continue to write as exceptionalists throughout their lives, as they worked to honor O'Reilly's legacy.

The *Pilot* after O'Reilly:
James Jeffrey Roche and Katherine E. Conway

O'Reilly's work at the *Pilot* was immediately taken up in August 1890 by his two chief editorial assistants and staff writers James Jeffrey Roche and Katherine Conway, who were respected members of Boston's literary community in their own right. Roche assumed the position of chief editor, a position he held for fifteen years, and Conway became associate editor.[64] Conway became managing editor in 1905, a position she held until 1908 when the *Pilot* became the official organ of the archdiocese under the auspices of Cardinal O'Connell. From the beginning, Roche and Conway faced the challenge of continuing a paper that had been nearly synonymous with its editor. Roche, Irish born and raised in Canada, came to Boston in 1866, worked in the mercantile world for a bit, and wrote verse and prose on the side; he became associate editor of the *Pilot* in 1883.[65] Conway was a native of Rochester, New York, and in 1883 came to Boston from Buffalo, where she was assistant editor of the Buffalo *Catholic Union and Times*, at the invitation of O'Reilly, who admired her poetry. Together, Roche and Conway aimed to produce a paper every bit as good as the one they had inherited.

After assuming the position of editor, Roche began to work on a memorial of his close friend and mentor, and his *Life of John Boyle O'Reilly* was published in 1891. In the preface Roche told his readers "the following pages have been written in the scant leisure of a busy life made doubly so by the loss which called them forth" and endeavored to present a "faithful picture of John Boyle O'Reilly as he was in public and private."[66] Conway, who also edited an 1891 appreciation of her former boss — *Watchwords from John Boyle O'Reilly* — gave Roche's biography a favorable review in a memorial article on O'Reilly she wrote for the *Catholic World*. After summarizing the high points of O'Reilly's life and emphasizing his strong Catholic principles, she concluded by admitting that O'Reilly "had no peer; he left no heir-apparent to his own peculiar place and work; but his memory and example are vital forces still, and the sacrificial seed he sowed so lavishly must bear befitting harvest."[67] In her closing lines, Conway accepted the fact that neither she nor Roche could ever fully replace O'Reilly, but that it was their duty to carry on his legacy to the best of their collective abilities, especially within the pages of the *Pilot*.

In addition to assuming the mantle of leadership of the *Pilot*, Roche became, by default, "Boston's foremost Catholic journalist, poet, and prose writer, the idol of the Catholic intellectual group, and a social favorite with the Catholics and Protestants alike."[68] Like O'Reilly before him, Roche was an active member and favorite among other literary men at the Papyrus and St. Botolph Clubs, though many noted his lack of charisma when compared with O'Reilly. Roche's verse and prose tended to be lighthearted and adventurous, and he was often lauded for his skill with ballads. Louise Imogen Guiney gave an apt description of his appeal: "Mr. Roche is, first, a scrivener and chronicler, utterly impersonal, full of joy in deeds, a discerner

between the expedient and the everlasting right, wholly fitted to throw into
enduring song some of the simple heroisms of our American annals. We bid
fair to have in him an admirable ballad-writer."[69] While he worked at the
Pilot under O'Reilly, Roche wrote poems for the *Atlantic Monthly, Harper's
Weekly,* and the *Century* as well as a published volume *Songs and Satires*
(1886). In addition to his appreciation of O'Reilly, while editing the *Pilot*
Roche managed to publish three novels: *Her Majesty the King: A Romance
of the Harem* (1898), *The Story of the Filibusters* (1891), a popular adventure story, and *The Sorrows of Sap'ed* (1904). He also published more
collected verse, including *Ballads of Blue Water and Other Poems* (1895)
and *The V-a-s-e and Other Bric-a-Brac* (1900). Roche was often praised for
his sense of humor, and his published work had a broad appeal as evidenced
by the fond praise he received from some young Boston College students in
the pages of the college literary magazine, the *Stylus,* who wrote: "He is
essentially a poet of the plain people. He does not profess to disclose in his
poems great wells of hidden truth; he is more concerned with the life of the
people. He sings his song, whether it be a stirring tale of war or a cheery
note of love and hope, in simple strains that cannot fail to reach their mark,
the human heart."[70] The student editors of the *Stylus* paid close attention
to prominent Catholic writers of the day, especially in their native city, and
looked to them for inspiration in their own literary work. Roche's manly
verse celebrating naval battles, Civil War heroes, and international adventure was well loved by his readers of all creeds, as were his simple love poems
and his memorial appreciations. Roche, a faithful Catholic who edited the
nation's most important Catholic weekly, was an exceptionalist because he
did not feel the need to write particularly Catholic verse or novels. He occasionally wrote Catholic verse, such as his poem "The Way of the World,"
but he relied upon an independent Catholic audience, like the students of
Boston College, to recognize his own faithfulness, and to keep that in mind
when reading his prose.

One of the many challenges Roche had to face as editor of the *Pilot* was a
decided shift in his reading audience. As Roger Lane has argued, "The *Pilot*
under Boyle O'Reilly had been largely oriented toward the old country";
however, "many of the old formulas were no longer useful in appealing to a
new and more Americanized generation." As a result, Roche had to guide the
paper through a period of transition, "and in areas outside the controversial
realm of politics, he began to change the tone and content of his paper."[71]
Under Roche, the paper lost some of its initial "Irishness" and increasingly
became the "responsible voice for all American Catholics." This shift was
necessary in a decade that saw increasing numbers of Italian and French
Canadian Catholics moving into the city. In the pages of his newspaper,
Roche increasingly engaged with political issues important to Americans
(not just Irish Americans) including immigration, labor problems, America's
imperial expansion (which Roche did not support), and the ascendancy of
Theodore Roosevelt. Ultimately, Lane argued that Roche's tenure as editor
was a failure as the *Pilot* ceased to be the most influential voice in the Irish

American community, replaced by the dominance of ward politicians such as Martin Lomasney, John F. Fitzgerald, James Michael Curley, and others.[72] Roche left the *Pilot* in December 1904 to assume a consulship at Genoa, Italy, a position given to him by President Roosevelt, and died four years later, in Berne, Switzerland, while filling another consulate post. The *Boston Daily Globe* remembered him as a "poet, wit, historian and diplomat," and in the same article Katherine Conway, his successor at the *Pilot,* recalled, "Mr. Roche's strong points in journalism were literary criticism and the short editorial paragraphs, but he was above all things a literary man."[73] When Roche left Boston, Conway was left to serve O'Reilly's legacy at the *Pilot* alone, writing for an increasingly middle-class Catholic audience and contending with the policies of a new archbishop.

Of all the Boston exceptionalists of the 1890s, Katherine Conway's work was the most unabashedly Catholic in subject matter. While working for the *Pilot* she published a popular book of devotional poetry, *A Dream of Lilies* (1893), as well as a variety of nonfiction books published by the *Pilot* press as part of the "Family Sitting Room" series that addressed the proper moral conduct of young women. The series included: "Making Friends and Keeping Them," "A Lady and Her Letters," "Questions of Honor in Christian Life," and "Bettering Ourselves." As James Kenneally noted in his *History of American Catholic Women,* "The underlying theme of her writings, especially apparent in her nonfiction, was a reinforcement of the traditional role of women."[74] When from time to time the *Boston Daily Globe* ran a series on women's issues such as education, work, and suffrage, Conway was asked to provide lengthy comment on such timely questions as "Where Shall the Line Be Drawn in the Employment of Women?" "Has American Freedom Made American Women Less Womanly," "Have American Women Really More Rights than Other Women?" and "Is it a Disadvantage to be a Woman?"[75] Given her unflagging support of the traditional roles of wife and mother in her responses to such topics, Conway's own personal life was a bit of an enigma: she championed motherhood as a crucial role for Catholic women and shied away from suffrage, but she never married and held an independent journalistic position rare in her day. She was president of the New England Women's Press Club from 1890 to 1913, a member of the Boston Author's Club, and on the board of trustees of the Boston Public Library as well as the board of Prison Commissioners of Massachusetts.[76] Nonetheless, Conway always maintained that her activities, "whether in literature, journalism or in extension work" were always "serving the Church."[77]

Conway's most significant contribution to the spread of Catholic literature was her championing of the Catholic Reading Circle movement and active participation in the Catholic Summer School movement. Conway was president of the John Boyle O'Reilly Reading Circle, founded in 1889, and did much to promote Catholic Reading Circles throughout the country. The *Catholic World* frequently reported on the activities of Reading Circles in their "Columbian Reading Union" column and praised the success of the circles in the Boston area, particularly the John Boyle O'Reilly circle Conway

fronted. Reading Circles tended to meet monthly with members either reading and discussing a common text, listening to prepared papers and lectures,
or soliciting prominent Catholic literary workers, like Conway, to speak to
the group. In 1892 Conway reported of her Reading Circle that "the literary
gleanings prove that every day reading is gradually reaching a higher standard, and the selections from poetry, history, and biography indicated that
the Reading Circle is helping more and more every year to render enjoyable
only the highest and best in all literature."[78] Conway also spoke to national
audiences about the religious, educational, and cultural benefits of belong-
ing to Reading Circles, delivering lectures like "The Literature of Moral
Loveliness" to the Catholic Summer School in New London, Connecticut,
in 1892, or "The Catholic Summer School and the Reading Circles" to the
World's Congress of Religions held concurrently in 1893 with the World's
Columbian Exhibition in Chicago. In January 1895 she read a paper on
Catholic literature to the Phillips Literary Association in Medford, and the
Boston Daily Globe reported that Conway "condemned the modern novel
and 'yellow-covered' literature in general for its immoral influence," telling
her audience, however, that "the Catholic standard in literature had always
been high." She then praised such notable non-Catholics as Dickens, Thack-
eray, Tennyson, Longfellow, and Holmes "as writers whose influence was for
the highest in life."[79] Although Conway was less of an exceptionalist than
O'Reilly, Roche, or Guiney, it is clear that O'Reilly's promotion of good secular literature as being suitable for Catholic audiences had remained with
her. Conway was much in demand as a speaker in Reading Circles throughout New England and was also the first Catholic invited to speak at the
Women's Educational and Industrial Union on Boylston Street.

Conway, more so than either O'Reilly or Roche, was singled out for
her contributions to a particularly Catholic literature in both secular and
Catholic publications. In 1893 *Publisher's Weekly* called Conway "one of
the noblest workers in the Catholic journalistic field,"[80] while in 1901, Mary
Gilmore wrote a lengthy appreciation of Conway in *Dominicana: A Magazine of Catholic Literature,* where she informed her readers that "in the
present day's galaxy of famous Catholic women of the younger generation, Katherine E. Conway, poet, novelist, essayist, critic, and editor shines
forth . . . commanding the recognition, respect, admiration, and enthusiastic
tribute of the intellectual and artistic world in general as well as Catholic
circles in particular."[81] Throughout Gilmore's article Conway's industry and
womanly qualities were praised effusively, but in Catholic terms, Gilmore
could pay Conway no higher compliment than to say that her eight published books "stand to Miss Conway's credit in every sense of the word,"
which was the "highest tribute of praise that can be given an author in the
present day of degenerate, impious, and immoral literature."[82] In 1907 Conway received national recognition for her contributions to Catholic literature
and culture when she was presented with Notre Dame University's Laetare
Medal, an award given annually to a talented and exceptional member of
the Catholic laity. Conway was only the fifth woman to receive the honor,

and the medal was presented to her by the Rev. John W. Cavanaugh, the president of Notre Dame, at Boston College in May 1907.[83] *Rosary Magazine* reported the news with great excitement and noticed "much rejoicing among the Catholic literary folk of Boston" when the medal was awarded to their "most prominent member."[84] The *Rosary* praised Conway by saying, "She is, however, first, last, and always, a Catholic journalist and litterateur as her constant work on the *Pilot* and her other literary work testify. This is why the Catholic literary colony of Boston is feeling very proud these days."[85] Despite her numerous personal trials and physical ailments, Conway remained a devoted Catholic worker. Although she was dismissed as editor of the *Pilot* when O'Connell bought the publication for the archdiocese in 1908, she continued to write and went on to serve Catholicism by teaching at St. Mary's College in South Bend, Indiana, in 1911–12, before returning to Boston to edit John Fitzgerald's weekly, the *Republic* until its demise in 1926. Throughout her career Conway brought much national attention to the Catholic literary movement in Boston, carrying on O'Reilly's legacy as best she could despite the more conservative administrative changes brought on by O'Connell. Although in the first decade of the twentieth century Conway was the best-known Catholic woman author in Boston, at the turn of the century, one of her contemporaries, Louise Imogen Guiney held that distinction.

The Many Challenges of Being a Catholic Writer in Boston: Louise Imogen Guiney

The young Irish Catholic poet Louise Imogen Guiney first appeared in the pages of the *Pilot* in 1880, at the age of nineteen, just one year after her graduation from the Elmhurst School of the Convent of the Sacred Heart in Providence, Rhode Island. O'Reilly, a friend of Guiney's Irish-born father, included some early examples of her poetry in the pages of his weekly, thus encouraging the development of her literary career. When Guiney is remembered today in the larger literary canon, it is as a poet of minor importance at the tail end of the nineteenth century, somewhere in the gray area between Emily Dickinson and Edna St. Vincent Millay. Her place in Catholic literature is more prominent; Lord referred to her as "our nearest approach to a major poet," and Messbarger named her as "perhaps the one literary genius among nineteenth century American Catholic writers."[86] But her place in American Catholic literature was, for some historians, compromised when she moved to England in 1901.[87] In the 1880s and 1890s, however, Guiney stood at the center of Boston's vibrant literary culture. She was the support structure and grounding influence for her group of literary and artistic friends, who included the novelist Alice Brown, the publisher and photographer F. Holland Day, the architects Ralph Adams Cram and Bertram Grosvenor Goodhue, the poet Bliss Carman, and the painter

Thomas Buford Meteyard, among many others. She was, in addition, a favorite among her Anglo-Protestant literary elders such as Louise Chandler Moulton (whom she called "Godmam"), Annie Adams Fields, Sarah Orne Jewett, and Oliver Wendell Holmes, who often referred to Guiney as his "little golden guinea." The literary critic Van Wyck Brooks, alluding to Guiney's father's status as the first Irish-born general in the Civil War, asserted that "Miss Guiney's spirit rode forth in her father's stirrups. None of this was lost on the city of the Puritans. The Bostonians knew a soldier, as they knew a poet."[88] Guiney embraced her heritage as the daughter of one of Boston's prominent Irish Catholic figures.[89] She was always conscious of representing her ethnicity as well as her religion, and at time, her responsibilities as a Catholic limited her abilities to fully participate in all of the activities of her Bohemian group of literary and artistic friends. Despite personal and financial hardships, Guiney mediated between her varied identities throughout the 1880s and 1890s.

Guiney served as an important link between established Bostonian authors and the younger Bohemian artists she called her "dear boys," and also, like O'Reilly, between the city's prominent Catholic and Protestant authors. As Samuel Maxfield Parrish noted, "Miss Guiney was, in two ways, a pivotal figure in Boston's nineties. Thoroughly Irish, and an ardent Roman Catholic, she won ready and warm acceptance from literary lions in the other half of Boston."[90] In addition to mediating between the literati of Catholic and Protestant circles in Boston and abroad, Guiney was a pivotal figure in the lives of her closest friends and "succeeded better than anyone else of her generation linking the two halves of cultural Boston."[91] By maintaining a close relationship with Moulton, as well as the famous nineteenth-century salon hostess Annie Adams Fields, Guiney was able to bring her young friends into the company of more established scholars and authors, thus furthering their development while providing the older generation with a new audience.[92] She was always ready to proof work sent to her by friends and wrote letters of encouragement to her elders, contemporaries, and younger writers, both Catholic and not. Her friend the architect Ralph Adams Cram, in his 1936 autobiography, called her "the most vital and creative personal influence in the lives of all of us who gathered together at this time. In herself she seemed to concentrate and make operative all the best qualities of the great days of English letters."[93] This, coming from Cram, was no small praise, for in the 1880s and 1890s he and Guiney mixed with a circle of well-known poets, artists, and publishers. Like O'Reilly, Guiney proved by mixing with larger literary circles that Catholic writers in Boston could maintain their faith *and* be popular with secular and religious audiences alike.

Beginning in the mid-1880s, Guiney's poems graced the pages of many prominent newspapers and magazines like the *Atlantic Monthly, Harper's Weekly,* the *Pilot,* the *Catholic World,* the *Boston Evening Transcript,* and the *Century.* In addition, she published three collections of poetry and essays: *Songs at the Start* (1884), *Goose Quill Papers* (1885), and *The White Sail and Other Poems* (1887). Her book dedications aptly show how Guiney moved in both Catholic and secular literary circles. She dedicated *Songs at the Start,* her first book of poetry, to John Boyle O'Reilly, who had mentored Guiney after her father's death, and she dedicated *Goose Quill Papers,* a book of essays, to another mentor, Oliver Wendell Holmes. As Guiney began to gain the attention of literary circles throughout the 1880s, some of the Catholic hierarchy in Boston made sure that she did not stray too far from the fold. Father Robert Fulton, president of Boston College, wrote an impassioned letter to Guiney in 1888 when she was twenty-four. Fondly recalling when he first met her as a young girl, Fulton went on to praise her talents and her early successes as a poet, but not without a caveat. He wrote, "I wonder (again) — if the little girl I knew to be so pious, now growing into a famous woman, in the culture of the intellectual part, improves equally the moral and religious part. There are difficulties: it is right I should suppose they are surmounted. Then what a complete and lovely character will be recognized by those who love her!"[94] Fulton's reminder to Guiney, to improve "equally the moral and religious part," was not lost on the poet, who struggled to remain true to her Catholic faith while holding true to her calling as a writer of poetry and prose. Fulton reminded Guiney she was, above all else, first and foremost a Catholic. No matter how much fame and recognition her poetry and prose won her, she was never to privilege the intellectual above the moral and religious. Catholic authors in turn-of-the-century Boston, as evidenced by Guiney, and O'Reilly before her, were always conscious of their audiences — both Catholic and not. On paper and in person, Catholic authors in Boston were seen by many as representatives of the faith. This was a difficult position to be in and, at times, caused Guiney much frustration.

In May 1892, four years after Fulton expressed his concern at Guiney's increasing literary celebrity, Guiney expressed the difficulties inherent in remaining true to both her faith and her work in an eight-page letter to her closest confidant, the publisher and photographer F. Holland Day.[95] In her lengthy effusive letter, full of regret and impassioned belief, she revealed a great deal about her own desires and her willingness to suppress them in order to follow the rules of the church. Guiney spelled out the complications inherent in her own religious practice and personal beliefs. Her lengthy response was occasioned by a simple request, made by Day, that Guiney attend a service with him at the Anglican Church of the Advent in the Beacon Hill section of Boston (she made *many* similar requests encouraging Day to attend various Catholic services and celebrations with her). In her return response to this seemingly simple invitation, Guiney begged and pleaded with Day to understand her precarious position, namely, that if someone, regardless of his or her own religion, should *see* her attend another service, it would reflect poorly on both her own reputation and the position of Catholicism in Boston as a whole. It was not that Guiney did not wish to attend — she appreciated, even *adored,* "the Plain song" and was friendly with the rector, the Rev. W. H. Van Allen, but she was also fully aware of the expectations and the hierarchy of her Catholicism. It was better for her not to make an appearance, to avoid undue gossip in a city already in a troubled relationship with the Catholic faith, and so, she explained:

> If you were of the Pope's own, you would know what enormous stress is always laid upon the edification and encouragement of others. At every turn, it is your duty to do not only what is right and innocent, but to look out that you afford no occasion of scandal, of gossip, of doubt, (even ever so slight) in them. This lays an awful burden upon people like me, constitutionally reckless, so long as I am conscious of *intending* the virtuous thing. ... I have to look out for the *possible* brother or sister who might be wrongly impressed.

Momentarily speaking of her faith as a "burden" in terms of the constant stress she felt while out in public to behave as a paragon of Catholic moral piety, she confessed to Day the difficulties of maintaining this persona when she, herself, had a tendency to be "constitutionally reckless," although she quickly changed her tone, professing, in a striking and rather touching way, the sacrifices she was willing to make for her religion. At twenty-eight years old, Guiney was sure of her beliefs and reminded Day:

> I was born into the church; I once did a tremendous amount of thinking, and fell under the influence of the modern air, and slid a long way into youthful agnosticism, but fought my fight alone, and said not a word of it to anybody; and by some immense Providence, still, I hope, active in perfecting what it long since began, I am back on my own deck, with sea legs a thousand times stronger and steadier, and with the most joyous and complete mental relish.

At the end of her missive Guiney explained that it was only in Boston that she felt it necessary to remain constantly aware of the Catholic public opinion in regards to her actions, writing "in England, where my action can affect nobody, I do as I please in everything." Guiney, as "one of the Pope's own" in Boston, was concerned with public opinion and religious and social conventions in a way that Day neither was nor could be. Concerned also that another writer might see her attending an Anglican service, Guiney was quite adamant about the potential catastrophe of being possibly mistaken for anything other than a Catholic author. Guiney's open and honest letter to her best friend reveals the precarious position of Catholic writers in Boston society at the turn of the century. Guiney not only worried about the typical concerns of any writer — getting published, book sales, and critical reviews — she also had to worry about her Catholic *and* secular audience, both as readers and as observers of her actions in the city. Guiney's mature acceptance of her Catholic responsibilities in the specific context of turn-of-the-century Boston is most evident at the end of her letter when she wrote of the overall dangers of her attending a service at the Church of the Advent. If a fellow author or Catholic citizen, in Guiney's words, "were to infer that I was tired of an unpopular and antiquated religion, and had vague softenings and coquetries towards what is (AD 1892) considered charmingly exclusive and elegant, it would be my fault entirely that I had given him cause, and that I had given Catholicism, in his estimation, so much the more discredit." Guiney had, over the course of her youth, internalized this behavior and its necessity for the greater good of Catholicism in Boston, and it was the greater good she was more concerned with than her own desires, closing to Day, "Am I clear? This is not my individual way of looking at the thing; but I prefer the family way, the authoritative way, in moral matters, to my own."[96]

As scrupulous as Guiney was in terms of her public behavior in Boston, she was still subject to nativist prejudices. As Guiney was not able to support herself and her mother on writing alone, in 1894 she was appointed the postmistress of the Auburndale, Massachusetts, Post Office by President Cleveland.[97] The salary of a postmistress was largely dependent on how many stamps were sold, and it soon became clear that in terms of stamp sales, Guiney was being boycotted by some of Auburndale's citizens, at the behest of the American Protective Association (APA). The APA, a somewhat secret society, was founded by Henry Bowers of Iowa in 1887 with the purpose of distributing anti-Catholic literature and prohibiting Catholics from holding political offices nationwide. The boycott against Guiney was extensively covered in the press, and the *Boston Daily Globe* reported in 1895 that "it is well known that certain conservative people in the district objected to buying stamps of Miss Guiney because she happened to be Catholic and treated her to a mild type of boycotting."[98] The boycott ultimately backfired, however, as her literary friends rallied around her, and stamp orders poured into her office from around the country. The increase in orders resulted in a $700 raise in Guiney's salary, and allowed her to take a well-deserved vacation in the summer of 1895 — a walking tour of the English countryside with her friend Alice Brown.

The combination of anti-Catholic sentiments and the long hours spent working at the post office took their toll on Guiney's physical and emotional well-being. Although at first reluctant to admit her feelings about being persecuted and the effect of the persecution on her literary work, in April 1895, Guiney wrote a clear expression of her frustrations to her friend Dora Sigerson in Dublin. "The fuss about my office, I regret to say, absurd as it seems, was no myth, and gave me great worry. Auburndale is a town populated with retired missionaries, and bigots of small intellectual caliber." She confessed that she was being persecuted "thanks purely to my being a Catholic: i.e., one likely at any moment to give over the government mail, and the safe keys, to the Pope! And the salary ran down in consequence, and I was so like a fish swimming in the wind, with the stress and novelty and difficulty of a business life, and the utter impossibility of getting the mood or the time for the one thing I had been doing all my life."[99] Guiney was clearly hurt by the prejudices and the insinuation that her religion made her incapable of performing as an impartial civil servant. She frequently wrote to other friends that the work completely drained her, leaving no time to write.

On July 5, 1897, Guiney resigned as postmistress and happily wrote to the Reverend Van Allen, "I am so pleased, I cannot refrain from dancing: though dancing was never in my line." She continued, "I am even as I was four years agone, only with the po'try carefully drained out, and some character, let us hope, screwed in."[100] Certainly her facing of adversity strengthened her character, but her tenure at the post office did nothing to improve her literary production. The "utter impossibility" of getting in the mood or finding the time for writing prose and poetry took its toll on Guiney's literary career, and though she published a few more volumes of poetry — *England and Yesterday* (1898), *The Martyr's Idyl and Shorter Poems* (1899), and *Happy Ending* (1909), a collection of her previous verse, she wrote on numerous occasions that the muse had left her. She next took up a position cataloguing at the Boston Public Library, where she no longer had to deal directly with the public. Although Guiney was happier at the library than she had been at the post office, her experience at the post office had spoiled Boston for her. As she confessed to Sigerson in 1899, her greatest wish was to "emigrate to some hamlet that smells strong of the Middle Ages, and put cotton-wool in my ears, and swing out clear from this very smart century altogether."[101] Guiney's affinity for eras long past — especially for the Middle Ages — was everywhere evident in the poetry she had written throughout the 1880s and 1890s, and the only place she felt she might find peace was in England. Guiney achieved her greatest wish when she moved in 1901 to Oxford, England, where she remained, except for a few visits home, for the rest of her life.

Guiney occasionally wrote verse once she moved to England, but by and large she turned to the true passion of her life, the study and resuscitation of authors such as Blessed Edmund Campion, William Henry Hazlitt, Henry Vaughan, and James Clarence Mangan. She spent her days researching in the Bodelian Library, discovering all she could about the Recusant poets. She wrote to a Boston friend, Charlotte Maxwell, in 1903 that "I can't go home... much as I long for the faces of my friends. The pace at which everything goes there, the noises, the publicity.... I am not equal to face them now; and I fall back, as on and into, a mossy bank, to the peace, the utter simplicity, the anonymity, of my life in England, and feel that I cannot give it up, and more, that I have actually some right to it."[102] After her tumultuous career in Boston, Guiney claimed the right to a simple life of her own design in England. In England, she was no longer in the public eye; newspapers were not reporting on post office boycotts, and she did not have to check her public behavior for fear of offending Catholics and non-Catholics alike. Her faith only grew in England as did her admiration for the English Catholic Church. In 1906 she and her housemate, Harriet Anderson, began a series of evening lectures at their Oxford house, focusing on "Catholic questions of the hour," in order to "increase community of feeling among local Catholics, further intelligent interest in Catholic ideals, and get a rather centrifugal congregation together."[103] Guiney took the best of what she had learned from Boston's literary Catholic community in turn-of-the-century Boston and applied it on her own terms in England. Nourished by the supportive Catholic community she helped to create, Guiney was able to continue her literary work once again. She never forgot her home, however, and continued to engage in issues important to Catholic literature on both sides of the Atlantic, continuing, until her death in 1920, to write for American magazines, both Catholic and secular.

Guiney furthered the acceptance of Catholic literature throughout her life primarily by the strength of her work and her poetic gift. Much of her poetry was not overtly Catholic, but she did occasionally address Catholic themes. One of the most poignant of Guiney's poems with respect to both her faith and her love for nature is "An Outdoor Litany," which appeared in her collection *The Martyrs' Idyl and Shorter Poems*. The first stanza of the poem celebrates the beauty of the natural world around her — the sea kelp, the sycamore, the tanager, the mink, the wind and the rain, and ends with a plaintive plea:

> ...I cry to Thee
> Whose heart
> Remembers each of these: Thou art
> My God who hast forgotten me.

Guiney recognizes in this poem that all that is beautiful in nature belongs to and is nourished and given strength by God, and in a moment of crisis of faith she asks in the second stanza for the same nourishment, to not be afraid of neglect:

> So too,
> Am I not Thine?
> Arise, undo
> This fear Thou hast forgotten me.

In the final stanza she proffers her beliefs and asks for help to endure the possibility that she has been forgotten.

> I ask no triumph, ask no joy,
> Save leave to live, in law's employ.
> As to a weed, to me but give
> Thy sap! Lest aye inoperative
> Here in the Pit my strength shall be:
> And still
> Help me endure the Pit, until
> Thou wilt not have forgotten me.[104]

In this poem Guiney placed herself firmly in the natural world and confessed a sense of doubt that likely would have resounded with many of her contemporary readers. Her sincerity of faith evident, she only asked for the same as any weed would receive, nourishment to continue on, and the strength to arise from the pit. Throughout her life, Guiney never cared if her work was overlooked or forgotten, as long as her commitment to the church and her faith were perceived clearly by both casual readers and critics. Such intentions are unmistakable in "An Outdoor Litany," but much of her other verse was far less overtly "Catholic." Her fidelity, which only strengthened as she aged, did not always aid her critical reception. Although Guiney knew in her heart that she remained true to her faith when writing, there were instances in her life where she feared her faith as put forth in her poetry and prose was ignored or misunderstood.

In critical reviews of her work by contemporaries, some of Guiney's fears about her religion being ignored, misconstrued, or misunderstood by the reading public came to light. When Guiney published her third book of poems, *A Roadside Harp* (1893), her close friend, the poet Bliss Carman, wrote an appreciation of Guiney's work in the *Chap-Book,* a small literary and aesthetic magazine published by their mutual friends Herbert Stone and Ingalls Kimball to which they both frequently contributed verses. Carman was a great admirer of Guiney's work, and of her poetic influences he wrote:

> There are, it seems to me, two characteristics in Miss Guiney's work, either one of which would render her most worthy of distinction as a poet. The first is this pagan quality of joy, which she must inherit from our New England saint, Emerson; the second is a rich and anything but modern quality of style entirely her own, yet one whose seeds must have been sown by those robust and individual poets of the Elizabethan times.[105]

In describing the quality of Guiney's verse as "pagan" multiple times within the article, Carman inadvertently offended his friend's Catholic sensibilities. Although she never conveyed her disappointment directly to Carman, Guiney was hurt by this descriptive, as she lamented to the Reverend W. H. Van Allen nearly two years after the appreciation first appeared.[106] Van Allen, well aware of Guiney's strong Catholic faith, had apparently wondered at her being described as "pagan," and so she responded, "No! I can't answer for Bliss Carman's restoring me to the ranks of "paganism," which I think is a word he used erroneously for natural religion. Bliss is an old friend of mine, and I am much attached to him, and admire him...but I never quarreled with his saying that, though it hurt me, and complimented me not, as it was meant to do." As Carman was not a Catholic poet, he did not understand Guiney's precarious position in Boston's literary world. She was loathe to be presented as anything but faithful to her religion because she did not want to disappoint representatives of the Catholic hierarchy like Fulton and did not want to discredit a religion already struggling for acceptance. As much of Guiney's early work was not transparently Catholic to many readers, she often wished her faith could more clearly shine through her verse, as she confessed to Van Allen:

> It has always troubled me mightily to be so inarticulate, or, at best, merely allusive, on any subject I deeply feel. I am sure I can conceive of no beauty, even in the material world, quite apart from Divine Grace: but who can guess that from the hedonistic stuff I write? Once in a while, someone who has strong faith, sees by instinct through said "Paganism," and knows I am founded, in fact, upon exactly its opposite: like you!! And you may judge whether I must not feel pretty grateful to such an interpreter. I know of nothing else so comforting and heartening in the world![107]

Such sympathetic readings of Guiney's work surely occurred when she appeared in the pages of Catholic publications, but it is rare to find mentions of Guiney's Catholicism in popular publications and reviews of her work. Only after her death, when appreciations of her life and work began to appear, was Guiney's Catholicism brought to the forefront of discussions about her work.

After Guiney's death, perhaps seeking to articulate a corrective to Carman's unintended slight, her close friend the novelist Alice Brown published a memorial appreciation and study of Guiney's work that recognized *both* the natural "pagan" qualities of her verse and her staunch belief in Catholicism. "Christian in belief, she was pagan in her listening nerves. Being Christian, she was, as in her life, all devotion, all pure obedience, rapt celebrant of the story of the Birth and the Cross.... There was, too, the voice of Erda, the Earth, crooning from the root of caverns in abysses of time past."[108] Here Brown gets closest to the core of Guiney's own life. She was always, above all, "all devotion" — devotion to her faith, to her family, to her literary calling, and most of all, to her friends. Her early verse, written in her twenties, may have had some of the "pagan" qualities Carman and Brown celebrated, but Guiney did make a choice regarding her literary production. She effectively stopped writing verse after the publication of her collected works *Happy Ending* in 1909 and instead focused on her historical studies of the Recusant (Catholic) poets of seventeenth-century England. She ultimately chose her faith over her poetic muse. Brown lamented Guiney's choice, writing "if she could have besought her Lord, in moments of a child's resistless longing, to give even the gifts that are not solely to His glory, her song might have a fuller sweep, a wilder melody. Out of earthly hungers the music of earth is made. As she grew in spiritual aspiration, her verse attuned itself more and more to the echoes of a harmony heavenly if austere."[109] As Brown explained, Guiney could have achieved more popularity as a poet if she had heeded only the pagan qualities of her muse. Guiney, her faith deepening as she aged, eschewed wider popularity and instead worked on the subjects nearer to her heart and her Catholic faith. She chose, as Father Fulton urged her early in her life, to improve the moral and religious part.

Guiney's intentions were often more lucid in prose than poetry, and she served and promoted quality Catholic literature by continuing to write for specifically Catholic publications throughout her career. As a young woman her poems frequently appeared in the *Pilot*, but as she matured and her literary fame grew, she was regularly asked to write for the *Catholic World* in addition to contributing short essays to *Donahoe's Magazine*, the *American Catholic Quarterly Review*, the Jesuit magazine *America*, and the Catholic weekly *Ave Maria* published by the University of Notre Dame. Guiney also occasionally wrote for international Catholic journals such as the *Dublin Review* and the *London Tablet*, in addition to penning entries for *The Catholic Encyclopedia*.[110] The range of Guiney's published work and her broad appeal demonstrated the potential for acceptance as a Catholic author of high-quality work. Guiney did not deny the particular challenges of being a Catholic writer, but she rarely addressed the subject in print. One exception was her 1909 article "On Catholic Writers and Their Handicaps," published in the *Catholic World*. Guiney was compelled to write this article as a rejoinder to "The Young Catholic Writer," an article written by the Rev. John Talbot Smith and published by another Catholic periodical, *St. John's Quarterly* of Syracuse, New York.

Smith, lamenting the lack of a powerful Catholic press and the constant overlooking of talented Catholic writers in America, called the popular press biased and advised the "young Catholic writer" to "keep the fact of his faith in the background until he has won his place in public favor" and to "avoid all Catholic gatherings, associations and movements." Only when the "young Catholic writer," having heeded such suggestions, had become popular among secular individuals, won critical acclaim, and was published widely could he then express "the inmost notions of a religious nature" and "send out Catholic books of artistic worth."[111] Guiney, though careful to convey Smith's good intentions, vehemently disagreed with his advice and opinions. She did not feel that a failure of a Catholic literary movement was the result of Catholic presses, the Catholic reading public, the ecclesiastical hierarchy, or that Catholic writers were ignored *because* they were Catholic, but rather:

> The American Catholic, like the vast bulk of his Protestant compatriots, is in a chronic tearing hurry. People read, if they read at all, only light magazines and vapid novels: and he — well, he is people! He fails to read Catholic books, not because these are Catholic, but because they are likely to stir up serious thoughts, and are by that token a bore. We are all external, superficial, in this brilliant semi-civilization of ours: we fight shy of solid religious literature, not as Catholics but as Americans.[112]

Guiney argued that the lack of acceptance of Catholic literature lamented by Smith was evidence of larger modern societal problems and not the fault of overworked Catholic readers. She also contended that the "acrobatic ethics" of "de-Catholicizing and re-Catholicizing" that Smith suggested would only harm the "young Catholic writer" warning that the "one little trick" of masking Catholicity "will have been the end of soundness in his moral na-ture" and "the end of soundness in his art."[113] Instead, Guiney argued that there was no better era in which to be an aspiring Catholic writer as "the tone of our lesser American Catholic publications is coming up visibly" and secular magazines "are more hospitable than ever to our scholars and apol-ogists."[114] Being Catholic would not stop a young writer from achieving public acclaim in the early twentieth century, for, as Guiney argued, "great books, as we know, have a rude fashion of forcing their way everywhere." According to Guiney, mediocrity and a lack of a seriousness of purpose would do more harm to the aspiring writer and the progression of Catholic literature than any public criticism or publisher's prejudice ever could.

At the end of her piece, Guiney added her own series of caveats to the young Catholic writer. She likened the decision to enter into the writing profession to the entering of a religious order, calling writing "a terribly responsible vocation," which "should have its dissuasive or corroborative novitiates, slow, severe, with endless fasts, vigils, and penances, and confes-sion of faults in chapter."[115] Writing was a trying process, and after much soul-searching and careful consideration authors should be sure that they were offering their best work to the public. This was not the first time Guiney offered such advice to aspiring Catholic writers. Ten years earlier she wrote to Coletta Ryan, a young Boston Catholic poet who had sent Guiney her work, and urged her to "just work your golden gift as faithfully as you can, in Heaven's eye; be merciless with it until it shines forth as your best and utmost; but hold back *the Book* until you are sure by your own greater calm and simplicity and your own conscious preference of them that your poetic apprenticeship is over."[116] Guiney was frustrated with individuals who did not take the vocation of writing seriously, and in the above it is clear that she felt that both Ryan and Catholic literature would be best served with only the "best and utmost" examples of an author's work. Guiney urged young writers and the American Catholic reading public to look to her adopted home, England, as a shining beacon of "a more spiritual society" where writers "write as they do because they live as they do."[117] Guiney, like O'Reilly before her, lived openly as a Catholic, and both authors felt that their living as Catholics — not their subject matter or critical reception — made them "Catholic authors." If Catholic literature was to succeed, as Guiney argued that it ultimately would, young writers must never apologize for or hide their true beliefs. That would only set Catholics further back.

Conclusion: Lessons from the Exceptionalists

When Louise Imogen Guiney wrote "Catholic Authors and Their Handicaps," she was writing from an exceptionalist view that had passed out of fashion, especially in Boston. Whereas she urged young Catholic writers to produce literature of the highest quality for a diverse audience without compromising their faith, thus promoting Catholic literature by the strength of their talent, others in her native city were taking a very different position. On January 16, 1909, the *Pilot,* now fully under the auspices of the Archdiocese of Boston, ran a lengthy front-page article on "The Future of Catholic Literature." The article was intended for both Catholic authors and Catholic readers and argued that if Catholic literature was to succeed, the only way forward was an active and involved readership. After admonishing Catholic authors for not seeking a wide enough audience among fellow Catholics and for too much moralizing, the rest of the article was directed toward the reader. In order for Catholic literature to flourish, it was the duty of the Catholic reader "to repeat and repeat continuously our praises of Catholic writers," to "push our writers just as the frivolous world pushes its own, and force the public to recognize that the style and interest of our class can stand comparison side by side with anything the non-Catholic public admires." Catholic readers were not only encouraged to purchase the works of Catholic authors, but to take their patronage one step further and to "do all in his power to advertise them by conversation and otherwise," never speaking ill of Catholic authors, and never putting them "in an inferior light when comparing them with non-Catholic works of no greater talent." The *Pilot* told its readers that the patronage of Catholic authors was their duty, and to abandon the Catholic author was "nothing short of a betrayal of the interests of his Faith." Without such support, "the Catholic author, though he be a very Shakespeare, will die if the Catholic people abandon him; he has no other audience."[118] Instead of promoting good literature accepted by Catholic and secular presses on the strength of literary merits, the *Pilot* instead urged Catholics to patronize literature deemed Catholic by the church hierarchy, arguing that the *only* audience a Catholic author could and should both write for and count on was a Catholic one.

This sort of article would never have been printed in O'Reilly's *Pilot,* and its tone and content exemplify how much the church had changed under the leadership of Archbishop William Henry O'Connell. O'Reilly, independent of any edicts from Archbishop Williams, printed Catholic and secular literature of merit and recommended a wide variety of literature to his readers. O'Reilly supported intellectual freedom and trusted his audience to choose their reading material. He promoted Catholic authors because they were talented, and urged his readers to patronize their novels, essays, and collections of poetry because they exemplified good literature *and* were written by Catholics, not just because they were Catholic. O'Connell, however, desired more intellectual control over Boston Catholics, including over what lay audiences were reading. He wanted every family in every parish within the archdiocese to carry a subscription to the *Pilot* and discouraged independent parish publications such as the *Sacred Heart Review.*[119] Such attitudes foreclosed any possibility of a vibrant and continuing golden age of Catholic literature in Boston and fostered the Catholic subculture Kane details in *Separatism and Subculture: Boston Catholicism 1900–1920.*

Explanations of why the exceptionalist attitude held by O'Reilly, Guiney, and others at the turn of the century failed to materialize into a golden age of Catholic literature in Boston are neither simple nor straightforward. It would be easy to say that those who championed and produced quality literature penned by faithful Catholic authors simply died or moved away, or to place blame squarely on the shoulders of O'Connell and his leadership style, but these explanations only partly account for the failure. The failure of the Catholic intellectual renaissance in Boston also reflects the decline of Boston as the center of literature in the United States during the same era.

Donna Merwick described O'Reilly and his circle as writers who "stood always on the fringe of the congregation looking out, as it were, at the snowfall rather than at the preacher."[120] In many ways, that was true, but we should not just dismiss them as a Catholic intellectual fringe that never fit in with contemporary definitions of Catholic authors because they needed the world around them for inspiration. They needed no formulas or directives from the church hierarchy about what defined Catholic literature. Rather, they relied upon the internalization of the strength of their own faith to define their literary productions as "Catholic," because they could not be otherwise. In late nineteenth-century Boston, before the turn of the American church toward Rome and before Pope Pius X's 1907 anti-modernist encyclical *Pascendi Dominici Gregis,* the definition of what made Catholic literature "Catholic" was closer to today's views. The Boston exceptionalists of the 1880s and 1890s believed that Catholic literature did not have to always be instructive for the faithful, promoting church and institutional values, nor necessarily always include Catholic main characters.

Scholars are still struggling to find a workable definition of what makes literature "Catholic," and such a definition remains, as it did in the nineteenth century, a subject of debate among historians, literary critics, the church, and Catholic audiences, as well as among the authors themselves. While some still wish to maintain a narrower vision of Catholic literature by including in their definitions and studies only authors who were practicing Roman Catholics, or works "that center on Catholic belief and spirituality," other scholars have worked to broaden the definitions of Catholic literature, and, in doing so, have also broadened the appeal of such literature for a readership outside the church.[121] In her study of post–Vatican II Catholic literature in the United States, Anita Gandolfo broadly defines fiction as Catholic "insofar as it is informed by the experience of being a Catholic in the United States" and not wholly dependent upon church teachings and practices or the author's own beliefs.[122] In her recent work Jeana DelRosso, rather than settling for a specific definition of what constitutes Catholic literature, instead proposes the idea of a "continuum of Catholic literature." As DelRosso defines it:

> At one end of this continuum of Catholic literature will reside the traditional, conservative literature that appropriated and often promotes Catholic teaching — including the rules, obligations, and practices that are distinctly Catholic.... At the other end of the continuum of Catholic literature will be placed the unremittingly anti-Catholic texts that seek alternatives to meaning-making but cannot forget (or forgive?) the impact of Catholicism on individuals.... The middle ground of the continuum consists of texts that foreground Catholicism — and perspectives on the religion — to varying degrees... the use of Catholicism in the text ranges from the crux of a story to the backdrop for a plot, and the attitude toward religion fluctuates as well.[123]

DelRosso's continuum is a decisively modern and practical definition of Catholic literature, necessary, as she argues, because "Catholics define themselves in the same way: they embody varying investments in and attitudes toward Catholicism."[124] The inclusive nature of DelRosso's continuum recalls the Boston exceptionalists of the turn of the century.

In their own way, O'Reilly's circle was modern in the sense that they could envision a Catholic literature that encompassed many types of engagement with the Catholic faith. In their continuum there was room for the poets, the journalists, the converts, the immigrants, and all those who labored to proffer their literary gifts in service of their faith. Guiney's exceptionalism allowed her to find redeeming Catholic tendencies and evidence of true faith among people whom other more conservative Catholics would have otherwise eschewed or ignored, as evidenced by her 1899 article "Aubrey Beardsley: A Reconstruction," which appeared in the *Catholic World*. In the 1880s and 1890s, the creation of a Catholic subculture in Boston, separate and distinct from the rest of the city, was not the overriding goal or vision. Instead, as O'Reilly proved to his readers, assimilation was possible without relinquishing faith or heritage. As Guiney pointed out to her fellow Catholic readers in 1909, "the remedy for our too low intellectual status in this country lies in our own hands."[125] In Boston, Catholic authors in the years when Williams was archbishop did seek to remedy their intellectual status by producing solid literature for a wide audience. At the same time, they also sought to expose increasing numbers of their fellow Catholics to good sacred and secular literature by promoting it in the pages of the *Pilot* and by championing membership in Catholic Reading Circles. Boston's exceptionalist Catholic writers at the turn of the century teach us much about the challenges of remaining faithful in an increasingly secular world.

People of Faith, People of Color

Two Hundred Years of Diversity
in the Archdiocese of Boston

William C. Leonard

On any given weekend in the Archdiocese of Boston, Mass is celebrated in over fifteen different languages in dozens of churches. Parishes are home to Haitians, Brazilians, Dominicans, Cape Verdeans, Vietnamese, and Nigerians to name only a few of the different ethnic and racial groups found in the archdiocese today. They are a testament to its growing diversity and a reflection of the archdiocese's past. As the archdiocese celebrates its bicentennial and looks to the future, it is important to remember that Catholics from different parts of the world have made the church what it is today, and they will be a crucial component of its future. It is estimated that in a few years a majority of the nation's Catholics will be Hispanics and that white Catholics, descendants of various European ethnic groups, will be a minority.[1] While this fact is not as pronounced in Boston compared to other areas of the country, there is no mistaking the city's Catholic population is now less white than it ever has been.

In 2000 the National Conference of Catholic Bishops estimated that Hispanics accounted for over 71 percent of the growth of the church in the United States in the last forty years and that they are the fastest-growing ethnic group in the country.[2] This is true for Boston as well. Immigration is the driving force behind this shift. This is similar to what happened in the United States in the nineteenth and early twentieth centuries when people from many predominately Catholic countries like Ireland, Italy, parts of Germany, and eastern Europe arrived. In 1924 the United States severely curtailed immigration from southern and eastern Europe. At the same time migration from Central and South America and the Caribbean increased. Since the 1950s, emigration from these regions has intensified. By the 1980s and the 1990s legal emigration from heavily Catholic Mexico and Central and South American countries greatly increased the nation's overall Catholic population. Likewise, emigration from the Philippines, Vietnam, Cambodia, and parts of Africa have also been on the rise, contributing to the growing cultural, ethnic, and racial diversity of the American church, both here in the archdiocese and around the country.[3]

In 2000 the percentage of Catholics "who belong to specific racial and ethnic minority groups roughly approaches that of the U.S. Census," according to the Center for Applied Research in the Apostolate at Georgetown University. It found that overall 78 percent of Catholics are white, 16 percent are Hispanic/Latino, 3 percent black, 2 percent Asian, and 1 percent Native American. Racial and ethnic diversity across the country varies by region, with urban areas tending to be more diverse than nonurban areas. For historical reasons and patterns of immigration, different Catholic populations are concentrated in various regions. For example, African American Catholics are found in greater numbers in Louisiana and Maryland, 15 percent and 13 percent respectively, than the overall 3 percent statistic would suggest. Likewise, Asian Catholics are concentrated on the West Coast, and Hispanics are more numerous in the Southwest, particularly California and Texas.

One measure of the increased diversity among Catholics is the number of Masses each Sunday that are conducted in a language other than English. In 2000 approximately 20 percent of parishes reported celebrating two non-English Masses each week; that language is increasingly Spanish.[4] In Boston, over thirty-five parishes currently offer Mass in Spanish, according to the Office of Hispanic Apostolate.

This essay will examine the racial diversity found within the archdiocese, primarily on the parish level, over the last two hundred years. It will present a broad overview of non-European Catholics by focusing on the presence of different racial and minority groups that have shaped the archdiocese both historically and currently. The presence of African Americans, Hispanics, Brazilians, Africans, and Asians will be explored. These people are not meant to represent the entire experience and history of non-European Catholics, but they will help us in understanding the larger issues and experiences of non-white Catholics in the archdiocese. It is also important to note that there is much diversity within each of these geographical groupings. For example, the histories and experiences of Nigerians and Ugandans differ, even though both are African.

Prior to the 1960s, "Boston Catholicism" was synonymous with Irish American Catholicism in the minds of many. Irish Americans have been a majority in the archdiocese since its founding in the late eighteenth century. Over time, the Irish and their descendants came to dominate the priesthood and the episcopacy. To this day they represent a significant portion of the laity, priests, and hierarchy, although that is starting to change, particularly among the laity. To simply describe the history of Boston's Catholics as the history of Irish Americans would be inaccurate and would not help in understanding the church's past and, more importantly, its future. During the nineteenth century, diversity usually referred to the various white European ethnic groups who came to Boston. First the Irish and French Catholics arrived in Boston and vied for influence. The Irish soon won out. Later it was the Germans who challenged the Irish-dominated church and who brought new customs, including such novelties as Christmas trees and cards. They yearned for German-speaking priests and a parish of their own, which they eventually got when Holy Trinity Church was established in the 1840s.[5]

The pattern of providing priests for parishioners from their own ethnic background (and usually a parish) was replicated numerous times for many other groups. This policy of accommodation, usually in the form of separate Masses and then distinct parishes, was controversial from the beginning. Some felt immigrants should quickly learn English and meld into the larger Catholic community, which usually meant the larger white native-born community, which in Boston meant Irish Americans. Others disagreed, fearing the newly arrived immigrants would lose their faith without such efforts. Eventually the idea of accommodation won out and the example was set. We see this pattern later with the French from Quebec and Italian Catholics (among other groups) who migrated to the archdiocese during the later nineteenth and early twentieth centuries.[6]

The church's early diversity was not limited to ethnic Europeans, but included those from Africa, usually via the French Caribbean. How the church treated those of African descent, had, and has, ramifications for how the church has dealt with groups of newer and more racially diverse immigrants coming to the archdiocese over the last sixty years. The history of racial minorities in the church is generally one of struggle and the desire to be accepted within the larger white Catholic community. They have struggled for acceptance, attention, and parishes to call their own for much of that history.[7]

While the church in Boston was relatively small and its people largely poor, little was done by way of accommodation for racial minorities until the twentieth century. The change occurred when some black Catholics demanded recognition as a separate group, and the church began to view them as another ethnicity in need of their own apostolate, with nuns and priests to work exclusively among them. Eventually they received a "national" parish of their own. For many different reasons this policy was largely abandoned by the 1960s. What emerged has been a hybrid approach toward black Catholics and the increasing number of new immigrants coming to Boston from Central and South America, the Caribbean, Asia, and Africa since then.

Catholics were few in number when Mass was first publicly celebrated in November 1788.[8] One early church historian estimates there were no more than fifteen hundred Catholics in all of New England.[9] The church was growing, however, and blacks were an important part of this growth. Initially the French formed the nucleus of the small Catholic community in the city. They had commercial ties to the Caribbean, where contact with black Catholics provided opportunities for migration.[10] Blacks, mostly from the Caribbean, were present, according to sacramental records. The church grew and prospered during the 1790s and early 1800s under the effective French leadership of Father Francis Matignon, one of Boston's first priests, who was joined by the future first bishop of Boston, John Cheverus, in 1796.[11]

Black Catholics had connections to the French Caribbean. In 1778 Boston's town selectmen warned a "French Negro" barber not to open on Sundays.[12] Black Catholics are found in the 1790 federal census. The census lists Rev. Louis de Rousselet (an early French priest in Boston) as living with a black man. Cheverus, the future bishop of Boston, arrived from the Caribbean in 1796 with a black woman from Guadeloupe.[13] The sacramental registers list many individuals with French-sounding names.[14] Migration to Boston from the West Indies was fueled by revolutions throughout the French Caribbean, particularly in Haiti.[15] In many ways black Catholic migration was the first wave of Catholic immigration to postcolonial Boston.[16]

Between 1790 and 1810, 139 blacks were baptized, the majority (93) between 1795 and 1805. Twenty-six percent of Catholics baptized in 1800 were black![17] This situation, however, did not last long. By the late 1810s and early 1820s, the proportion of black Catholics declined in relation to the overall number of both blacks and Catholics. In total, between 1790 and 1827 there were 211 black baptisms (190 of them before 1820) out of approximately 2,500 total baptisms.[18] If we use baptisms as one measure of birth rate the black Catholic population could have been as high as 300, based on a birth rate of 55 per 1,000.[19] Marriage and death rates suggest a similar finding. Thus, black Catholics comprised almost 25 percent of the black population and over 30 percent of the Catholic population at the turn of the nineteenth century.[20]

Because of the rise in Catholic population, there was a need to build a place of worship larger than the small Huguenot chapel on School Street. The construction of Holy Cross Church on Franklin Street in 1803 provided larger accommodations.[21] Inside there was a gallery above the vestibule, with room for about twenty pews, reserved for the "exclusive" use by "people of colour," according to early church records. Segregation did not appear to dampen their enthusiasm, and many blacks immediately rented pews.[22] Blacks, for the most part, did not hold positions of authority within the church with one exception. Thomas Haney, a black man also described as Irish, was superintendent of Holy Cross's catechism classes. This fact suggests that those of mixed racial background could hold important positions. Reference to blacks in the church's correspondence and nonsacramental records is nonexistent. They did not serve as church wardens or on the organizing committees that planned the purchase of the land for the building of Holy Cross even though many of them apparently contributed significantly to the project. The sacramental and city records suggest a close community of black Catholics existed in the city. Black Catholics lived near each other, served as godparents to each other's children, and were witnesses at each other's weddings.[23]

During the middle of the nineteenth century the black population remained steady, and overall there is little evidence of their presence or activities. Two nineteenth-century individuals are worth noting. James Augustine Healy was a priest and chancellor of the archdiocese during the

middle of the nineteenth century. Healy was biracial but never publicly identified himself as such. While his superiors knew of his background, Boston's
black and white Catholics did not. Robert Ruffin was from a prominent
Boston black family and converted to Catholicism. He also was a leading
organizer of the nineteenth-century black Catholic movement that resulted
in a number of congresses which drew black Catholics from around the
country.[24]

The archdiocese started taking a greater interest in the community, particularly after the Third Plenary Council of Baltimore in 1884 and the Vatican's
insistence that their needs be addressed.[25] Daniel Rudd, editor of the black
Catholic newspaper the *American Catholic Tribune* (published between 1887
and 1899), noted in 1889 that there was a large community of black Catholics in Massachusetts. In 1889 there were at least six hundred black Catholics
in Boston alone according to the *Philadelphia Sentinel*. The newspaper attributed the increase in the number of black Catholics in Boston and the nation
to "colorphobia" found in white Protestant churches throughout the North
and in Boston particularly.[26] Agents promoting subscriptions to the *American
Catholic Tribune* found "large and attentive audiences," of Catholics and
non-Catholics alike when they visited Massachusetts cities in March 1888.
Catholics gave enthusiastic welcomes in Boston, East Boston, Cambridge,
Salem, and Lawrence to the newspaper's agents.[27]

By the end of the nineteenth century American Catholicism adapted
itself to its increasing ethnic diversity by establishing national parishes to
meet the needs of immigrants from eastern and southern Europe. Following
this course of action seemed perfectly standard for many African American Catholics and the American hierarchy, even though most blacks were
native-born and almost all spoke English. Just prior to the death of Archbishop John Williams (Boston's fourth bishop and first archbishop), black
Catholics expressed interest in a parish. A 1906 article in the *Pilot* argued
for a separate church and noted "it is quite true...that Negro Catholics
have been made at home in any Catholic Church which they have chosen
to attend, and that they have attended in fair numbers from time to time,
especially the Cathedral, the Immaculate Conception and St. Joseph's West
End....But for all that they prefer a church to themselves." Some black
Catholics felt a church would "develop the sense of parish responsibility in
Negro Catholics and simplify the work of the priests in reaching those who
are or should be of the Church; that a spiritual home, so to speak, will draw
many by the strong bond of blood who might otherwise be estranged." The
author of the *Pilot* article described a harmonious atmosphere for blacks in
Boston's Catholic churches but failed to recognize that some black Catholics
felt the *need* for a black parish.[28]

Williams's successor, William O'Connell, was unknown to African Americans at first but he soon reached out to the black community just as he did
to ethnic Europeans.[29] His approach was to find a religious order specially
dedicated to African Americans, which he felt would do a better job reaching the population than his own diocesan priests. The group he turned to

was the Sisters of the Blessed Sacrament. The order was founded by Katherine Drexel and devoted to work among the Indians and "Colored" in the United States.[30] In August 1914, the Sisters arrived in Boston where they set up a "social service center" that administered to the sick, instructed the "ignorant," and provided "food and clothing for the poor, besides conducting a sodality and sewing circle for colored women."[31] When the Sisters arrived "they found the colored Catholics struggling under discouragements." Their mission, located at 21 Worcester Square in the South End, was a place where black Catholics were welcomed. O'Connell instructed them to work with Father Garrett J. Barry, pastor of St. Philip's Church in the South End/Lower Roxbury area in whose care O'Connell had earlier placed the city's black Catholics. St. Philip's was only a few blocks from the Sisters' mission.[32]

Most black Catholics preferred to attend nearby St. Philip's (and not the Sisters' Mission), where the pastor estimated there were about 350 black parishioners.[33] In 1913 Mother Mary Katherine Drexel wrote Cardinal O'Connell that a local black Catholic, representing "one of the best elements of Colored Catholics" claimed that there were between 900 and 1,000 "practical [practicing]" Catholics in Boston. Mother Drexel noted that blacks wanted their own church, a priest, and a school where they could meet socially, but that they did not want to be segregated or barred from attending their local parish.[34] Black Catholics also appear to have been numerous enough in Cambridgeport that the nuns contemplated opening a Sunday school to meet the needs of the one hundred or so Catholics there.[35]

Black Catholics met and formulated a plan in April 1917. They deferentially petitioned Cardinal O'Connell, focusing on the benefits a parish would have: "We the undersigned, members of the colored Catholic Congregation of Boston and greater Boston," they wrote, "have come together as a body to draw up this petition to ask your Eminence if you will please give us a church and a spiritual director and also the good sisters to take charge of our children."[36] Their request went without reply.

In 1920 they were compelled to write the cardinal again, reframing their argument: "We take pleasure in writing you on behalf of the colored Catholics of Boston. Like all other races we desire to have our own Church." They told O'Connell that they were "greatly in need of a church and priest to take charge of Negro work in Boston." They noted, "Irish Parishes are interested in the Irish question whilst we are deeply interested in the Negro question. There is no way for us to be useful and of assistance to our people unless we take a personal interest in our Church and we cannot take that amount of interest necessary into that of another." Fifty-three men signed this petition, many of the same as in 1917.[37] They again received no reply. The petitioners turned to Rome for help. O'Connell was able to effectively put off the issue.[38] Black Catholics would have to wait for O'Connell's successor, Richard Cushing to act upon their request.

Cushing's involvement with the African American Catholic community began in the 1930s. He had been assigned to African American religious instruction of the adults at the Sisters' convent.[39] The need for a permanent priest was crucial since his work was part time, however. Blessed Sacrament sister Mary Charles suggested that the number of blacks was increasing and that much work needed to be done, chiefly among Cape Verdeans who, she said, made up a large portion of the black Catholic population in Boston.[40] Cape Verdeans immigrated to New England during the late nineteenth century, usually settling in New Bedford. Some soon migrated to the Boston area. While Cape Verdeans saw themselves as Portuguese immigrants (Cape Verde was a Portuguese colony until 1975), the larger white society and the church saw them as black due to their darker complexion and mixed-race ancestry.[41]

By the fall of 1938 priests from St. Joseph's Society of the Sacred Heart (known as Josephites) were working with the Sisters of the Blessed Sacrament. African Americans are at the heart of the Josephite mission. Father Thomas McNamara served as chaplain for the Sisters initially.[42] The number of people attending Mass at the Convent went from 65 the first Sunday to 138 on the fourth Sunday after his arrival.[43] McNamara left the next year and was succeeded by Father Richard R. Early, who said Mass every Sunday at 9:00 a.m. for the Sisters and the black Catholic community.[44]

Cushing succeeded O'Connell as archbishop in September 1944. The black population was ecstatic; the *Chronicle* (Boston's black newspaper) proclaimed "Jubilation throughout the Negro Community of the Commonwealth."[45] The black community felt they finally had a strong friend in the archbishop of Boston. They were not disappointed; Cushing was an articulate spokesman on behalf of minorities. Most importantly, Cushing would soon make the dream of many African American Catholics for a parish of their own a reality.

The parish, to be called St. Richard's, became a reality when the archdiocese received a generous financial gift of $50,000 from a local priest, Rev. Maurice O'Connor. Father Edward V. Casserly, the superior general of the Josephites, wrote Father Early: "In connection with the proposed venture, the Archbishop suggests that you contact some respectable colored Catholic laymen without telling them of our plan and hopes. . . . They should be made to see the opportunity of starting a parish for the special care of the colored and be brought to the point where they will present a petition to His Excellency, asking for such an establishment." Casserly wanted "to forestall any charge of segregation." He also urged Cushing to issue a statement "assuring the people that they are still welcome to attend, as they choose, any Catholic church besides that which is created especially for them."[46]

African Americans debated the need for a separate parish. Opposition came mainly from people who saw an all-black church as another form of racial segregation. The Reverend William L. Clayton, of the Union Baptist Church in Malden, Massachusetts, accused Cushing of setting up a "Jim Crow for Colored."[47] Clayton's opposition prompted Henry E. Quarles, Sr., a leading member of the local black Catholic community, to reply. Quarles argued that just like Irish, French, and Italian Catholics before them, blacks wanted and needed their own parish.[48] Other local black Catholics also defended the parish's creation.[49]

A former Protestant church was eventually purchased at Warren and Buena Vista Streets in Lower Roxbury in May 1945.[50] Cushing released a statement stressing that the church was dedicated to the service of the "colored people of the area and the Archdiocese, insofar as they wish to avail themselves of it and in accordance with the oft expressed wish of many devout Catholics of our colored Community." Cushing said the church "will have the status of a national parish" along the same lines as "the Italians, French, Syrians, and other groups." He took issue with the notion the Catholic Church in Boston promoted discrimination.[51] Ernest Sylvanus, a local African American Catholic, opposed the parish, challenging Cushing's rationale behind it: "Let the French, Italians and Syrians have their separate centers; they are of foreign origin with foreign languages and customs."[52]

Opposition notwithstanding, the dedication of the church was set for March 30, 1946.[53] At the ceremony, Cushing noted, "Except for the Cathedral, I undoubtedly will be at this Church more often than any other." The same day the *Pilot* noted there was "one Negro student at St. John's Seminary, Brighton, and the Archbishop looks forward to the day when more colored boys with vocations will enter so that the Negro people will have their own priests to minister to them."[54] Whether Cushing supported a black clergy exclusively for African American Catholics is uncertain. When Father Paul R. Francis, a native of Honduras, was assigned to St. Francis de Sales in Roxbury, some black Catholics wrote Cushing and "accused him of trying to give them a segregated clergy." In 1959 the pastor of St. Richard's reported that white parishioners at St. Francis de Sales would not receive communion from Francis. Father Coyne described the situation at St. Francis as "Good Old Boston's Catholicism."[55]

Parish life at St. Richard's was similar to that of other Catholic churches. There were communion breakfasts, religious societies, novenas, and sodalities. A Boy Scout and Girl Scout troop were formed in association with the Sisters of the Blessed Sacrament, who were quite active with children of all ages. In 1957 St. Richard's "became the first and only church or organization in all of South Boston and Roxbury to sponsor the entire scout program." Members of the Sisters of the Blessed Sacrament provided the religious education for the parish. St. Richard's was usually staffed by two Josephites. Three Masses were held on Sundays at 7:30, 9:30, and 11:30 in the morning, according to advertisements in the *Chronicle*.[56]

St. Richard's made considerable progress over the years; estimated parish membership was as high as two thousand in 1956.[57] Many black Catholics also remained members of their local parishes, even if they attended St. Richard's on Sundays or were members of its organizations such as the Holy Name Society.[58] In short, many chose not to avail themselves of its services, religious or social. Both St. Phillips and the Sisters' mission held services and continued sponsoring events.[59] It seems that by the late 1950s and early 1960s, many other Catholic churches in the area were becoming increasingly diverse and drawing blacks.[60]

Cushing expressed doubts about the parish by 1956. The new pastor, Father Samuel Mathews, noted Cushing's concerns: "Your Excellency noted also in your last letter to me that from a recent observation at the Cathedral that a lot of Colored are moving into that area. I think that is true of all the parishes in this section of the city." Mathews explained the situation: "Many of the Colored Catholics even here in Boston are de-sgregation [*sic*] conscious and for that reason prefer to attend church in the parishes in which they live."[61] Cushing tried to distance himself from St. Richard's in his reply. "I am thinking of organizing an apostolate of our own diocesan priests to work among them in the South End area of the diocese," Cushing explained. "I think the negroes [*sic*] are too scattered to be handled by your setup at St. Richard's." Cushing referenced the *Brown v. Board of Education* decision: "Furthermore in the light of the recent Supreme Court decision, I think we should do more and more to incorporate the colored people in the parish in which they live."[62] Cushing waited until 1961 to act and declared St. Richard's a chapel of ease under the direction of the nearby territorial parish and appointed the Josephites assistants to St. Joseph's.[63] By the spring of 1962, the Josephites were withdrawn from Boston. The parish closed in 1964.[64]

After St. Richard's closed, its parishioners joined nearby parishes. Many of these churches were becoming increasingly frequented by people of color throughout the 1960s and 1970s. The transition to surrounding parishes like St. Patrick's, St. John's, or St. Paul's in Roxbury; St. Francis de Sales or St. Philip's in the South End/Lower Roxbury area; or the cathedral in the South End was, for the most part, fairly smooth because these parishes already had African American parishioners or other people of color in them. While upset over St. Richard's demise, most of its congregation found that these new parishes had sympathetic and supportive archdiocesan priests from the 1960s onward. By the 1970s, the overwhelming majority of black Catholics were attending church with other African Americans or blacks from the Caribbean or Cape Verdeans.[65]

As Cushing's health declined many priests and lay Catholics assumed Rome would appoint a bishop of Irish descent, possibly even one of the city's auxiliary bishops. Many were surprised when Humberto Sousa Medeiros, the bishop of Brownsville, Texas, a Portuguese American born in the Azores who grew up in Fall River, Massachusetts, was named to replace Cushing in May 1970. Medeiros was seen as an outsider by the majority of Boston's white Catholics. Reaction was mixed. Many of the city's Irish priests and laity saw Medeiros's appointment "as a threat to their historical prerogatives," according to J. Anthony Lukas. Derogatory remarks ranging from "that little Portogee" to the "spic Archbishop" were heard throughout Boston.

As the day approached when Medeiros was to be officially installed, the chancery received a number of death threats against Medeiros. A cross was burned on the chancery lawn and a pipe bomb was discovered in the chancery doorway.[66] Many of Boston's Catholics were enthusiastic at Medeiros's arrival, however, especially the city's growing population of Hispanics (particularly Puerto Ricans) and other groups such as Haitians, Cape Verdeans, and African Americans. Many of them saw in Medeiros a gentle caring man, dedicated to the poor and racial equality.[67]

Medeiros was cautious regarding racial matters, diversity, and problems of urban poverty to the disappointment of more progressive elements within the church. A year after his arrival, all sixteen members of the Commission on Human Rights (CHR) threatened to resign if Medeiros did not become more outspoken on race and poverty. In October 1971, Archbishop Medeiros established the Office for Urban Apostolates in an "effort to coordinate church work in the area's cities as it relates to racism, violence, housing, the elderly, and the like."[68] The office was a forerunner of a number of apostolates directed toward racial and ethnic minorities established during the 1980s and 1990s.

His most pressing and daunting challenge was the issue of school desegregation. In early March 1972 the *Pilot*, of which Medeiros was the publisher, editorialized on the issue but seemed to waiver on what should be done to integrate the city's schools. In the end the paper concluded that busing "is good when it solves a transportation problem; it is even better when it offers a service to the underprivileged and the deprived." That same month, Rev. Paul Rynne, executive director of the CHR, testified before the state legislature on behalf of Archbishop Medeiros supporting the racial imbalance law. In the end Medeiros could do little to ease tensions.[69]

The city's racial problems prompted the archdiocese to look within its own institutions to see whether more could be done to attract minorities to the church, particularly to the priesthood. The archdiocese had one African American priest during the 1960s, Harold Furblur, and he eventually left the priesthood in 1971. As racial tensions flared in January 1973, the rector of St. John's Seminary requested that a faculty committee research the question: "Can the seminary play a role in recruiting candidates for the priesthood from minority groups?" The seminary was most interested in recruiting black and Spanish-speaking Catholics, evidence of an increasing Hispanic population and need. In a frank assessment of their own limitations, the seminary members concluded that it would be all but impossible to do so. They argued "against the Seminary taking an immediate and direct role in recruiting from minority groups," noting "that there is little or no chance for success in recruitment at this time." Those contacted observed that "cultural barriers" played an important role in limiting minority vocations, particularly "celibacy, militancy, [and] a lack of interest in the institutional Church." They concluded that "if an applicant demonstrates the cultural characteristics of his own minority groups, it would probably be most wise to send him elsewhere for seminary training, i.e. to a seminary that caters to the particular minority group ... or at least to a bilingual or bicultural seminary." Accepting them at St. John's might actually do them more harm than good, they argued: "To introduce these young men into the cultural milieu of St. John's Seminary might well harm their vocations." Finally, "Applications from those diverse groups would have to be handled very delicately, since culturally they may not fit into our seminary system in any positive way." Nowhere in the report does it ask or suggest that the "cultural milieu" be changed at the seminary. The problems were in the applicants, not the seminary.[70]

Nonetheless, four years later, two men, Perard A. C. Monestime, a Haitian American, and Russell Winston Martin Best Jr., an African American, were admitted to the seminary. Monestime was ordained in 1985 and Best, a year later. Father Monestime was assigned to St. Angela's in Mattapan to work with the growing Haitian American community there. Father Best was assigned to St. John–St. Hugh's in Roxbury, where he had been a deacon. The next year he was transferred to St. Patrick's parish in Roxbury, home to a diverse community of Catholics.[71]

Throughout the 1970s the *Pilot* began printing articles concerning African American Catholics, along with features about members of other racial minority groups. Many of these questioned the church's commitment to its black members and other racial minorities. In June 1975 the *Pilot* ran a lengthy story on John Boyle O'Reilly, calling the Irish American an "Apostle of Racial Equality." O'Reilly, editor of the *Pilot* for many years after the Civil War, promoted racial tolerance and acceptance. The March 26, 1976, *Pilot* recalled Bishop James Augustine Healy's history and connection with Boston.[72]

By the end of the decade, race relations in Boston were entering a less volatile phase for the most part. Busing as an issue died down. In 1983 Raymond Flynn, an outspoken opponent of busing during the 1970s, was elected mayor of Boston with a promise of supporting equal opportunity for all of Boston's citizens, black and white. That same year, Cardinal Medeiros, died, after suffering from numerous aliments for years. Bernard F. Law, bishop of Springfield–Cape Giradeau, succeeded him in early 1984. In 1988 Archbishop Law supported (as did the *Pilot*) Mayor Flynn's efforts to desegregate Boston's public housing by having priests read a pastoral letter supporting integration and condemning racial bigotry. The letter stated, in part: "First, discrimination of any kind, based on race, creed, or national origin, is contrary to the clear teaching of the Catholic Church.... No person should be excluded from housing, public or private, because of color."[73]

The number of Catholics of color increased during the 1980s when immigrants began arriving in large numbers from the Caribbean, Central, and South America, adding to the church's diversity. By the 1980s predominantly black and Hispanic parishes were found in Roxbury and parts of the South End, Dorchester, and Mattapan. They included St. Joseph's, St. Patrick's, St. John–St. Hugh's, and St. Mary of the Angels all in Roxbury; St. Philip's, St. Francis de Sales, and to a lesser extent the Cathedral, in the South End/Lower Roxbury area; St. Kevin's, St. Matthew's, and St. Leo's in Dorchester; and St. Angela's in Mattapan. Over the years many of these churches have come to have a vibrant and active parish life, centering on diverse communities of African Americans, and those from Cape Verde, Haiti, and Puerto Rico, among others. This was the clearest sign that the face of Boston Catholicism was changing. Within some of these parishes an emphasis on the black experience has been promoted. Many marked Black History Month, celebrated the lives of Martin Luther King and Bishop James Healy, and sponsored workshops on bettering race relations in Boston.[74]

Lay people began taking a more active role within their parishes and the archdiocese as people of color found themselves a majority in a number of parishes. The Black Catholic Coordinating Committee of the archdiocese was formed in the early 1980s under Cardinal Medeiros. Black Catholics from Boston attended the 1982 Afro-American Culture and Worship workshop sponsored by the National Office for Black Catholics founded in 1970. One goal of the workshop was to foster interracial cooperation and to "allow 'people of color' to contribute to the Church as a whole, making it possible for everyone to rejoice in the rich variety of God's creation." In October 1982, lay people from Roxbury, Dorchester, and Jamaica Plain gathered to identify, affirm, and empower lay leadership in minority parishes.[75]

In preparation for the spring 1987 Congress of Black Catholics, the first since the late nineteenth century, Robert Gittens, chairman of the Black Catholic Coordinating Committee for the archdiocese, called for a local Day of Reflection among the city's black Catholics on October 25, 1986. In December, black Catholics met again and heard Rev. Edward K. Braxton, pastor of a church in Chicago, give a talk entitled "The Hour of Awakening: Black Catholics in Boston" in preparation for the congress. He noted that there were at least twenty-five thousand black Catholics (from many different ethnic backgrounds) in Greater Boston and lauded them for their efforts on behalf of racial and social justice.[76]

Gittens, Rev. Russell Best, and Cardinal Law led Boston's delegation to the gathering in May. Fifteen thousand delegates from 110 dioceses attended the meeting. Father Walter Waldron, pastor of St. Patrick's in Roxbury, "cited 'the bond of unity' among the Congress delegates and the 'spirit of hope that the church would become far more open and hospitable for black people.'" He noted there was still work to be done: "The Broader church has not yet had to pay too much attention to Black Catholics.... Black music, Black culture, Black expression and Black spirituality remain on the fringes of the Church even today, and the role of the Congress was to bring that to our attention."[77]

Father Best credits Cardinal Law with many of the positive changes in Boston's black Catholic community and the wider Catholic community, particularly the clergy. Shortly after returning from the Congress, the cardinal met with the delegates and asked them, "What would you like?" Father Best and the others told him they wanted two things: an Office of Black Catholics and a black bishop. Cardinal Law immediately said, "O.K. Office of Black Catholics, we'll do that." He also said he was working on getting a black bishop for Boston but that it would take time. Law immediately started a search for a director for the new office.[78]

In January 1988 Cardinal Law appointed Greer G. Gordon director of the Office for Black Catholics. Gordon was personally recruited by Law, had a master's degree in theology from Notre Dame, and was the author of a number of theological articles and pastoral studies. Cardinal Law celebrated Mass at the Cathedral on the last Sunday in February 1988 to mark Black History Month and Gordon's appointment. Robert Gittens, chairman of the black Catholic advisory committee, noted that Gordon's appointment was "a tremendous step forward in the Archdiocese of Boston." Over one thousand people attended the Mass at the Cathedral. At the service Law said, "We have come not only to celebrate history, but to make history." Cardinal Law acknowledged that "even Catholics have placed obstacles in the way through their blindness and prejudice," but black people have "clung to the word of God."[79]

By the late 1980s it was clear to many that the archdiocesan demographics were changing, particularly in Boston and other large urban areas. Immigration was the reason. The archdiocese responded in 1990 by establishing an office to serve ethnic parishioners and newcomers filling the pews in many Catholic parishes. The office estimated there were twenty-seven different national groups in the archdiocese. That same year, the archdiocese began celebrating National Migration Week, honoring recent immigrants and the ethnic and cultural diversity they have brought to the church. In 1992 posters for the event called on Catholics to "Make room" and to "open your mind, open your heart, open your arms" to the increasing number of immigrants, which, according to archdiocesan estimates, made up about 10 percent of the Catholic population. Catholics representing many of the city's ethnic and racial groups joined Cardinal Law for Mass at the Cathedral on the Feast of the Epiphany. They did so again in 1993, drawing people from five continents and as many as fifty countries, many of them from Puerto Rico, and refugees from Rwanda, Croatia, and Haiti.[80]

Although relative newcomers compared to black Catholics, Hispanics, it is estimated, will be the single largest group of Catholics in the nation and in Boston within twenty years. In 2004 the archdiocese approximated "that about 300,000 of the 2 million Catholics in the Archdiocese of Boston are Spanish speaking."[81] Hispanics, first from Puerto Rico, began arriving in New England during the 1940s and 1950s, working in agriculture and industry.[82] In Boston, Puerto Ricans primarily settled in the South End, and before long the Cathedral of the Holy Cross became a primarily Spanish-speaking parish with people from the neighborhood. On Easter in 1957 the first Mass specifically for Spanish-speaking parishioners was held.[83] The church, under Cardinal Cushing, reached out in other ways. A year later Cardinal Cushing formed the Society of St. James Apostle, which sends priests to Latin America, where they learned Spanish and worked among the community. Upon their return to Boston these priests began administering to the growing Hispanic population.[84] At the same time, a Hispanic ministry was organized and dedicated to this growing community. The Cardinal Cushing Center for the Spanish Speaking has operated near the cathedral for decades. In 1980 young Hispanic Catholics formed a group called Catholic Youth in Action. One of their first events was to travel to the Dominican Republic to help build a school and community center in Los Alcarrizos.[85]

The Hispanic community consists of more than a dozen nationalities. In the archdiocese, a small number of Cubans followed Puerto Ricans during the 1950s and 1960s. Dominicans soon joined them during the 1960s. The 1970s and 1980s saw an influx of people from Central America fleeing civil war, poverty, and unemployment. Beginning in the 1990s Colombians, Ecuadorians, Venezuelans, and Peruvians added to the complexity.[86] As early as 1988 there were reportedly 150,000 Spanish-speaking Catholics in the archdiocese.

That same year hundreds of Catholics from Puerto Rico welcomed Bishop Roberto Octavio Gonzalez as an auxiliary bishop of Boston. Gonzalez, who grew up in Puerto Rico, was given special responsibility to care for the spiritual needs of the archdiocese's Spanish-speaking Catholics. Gonzalez welcomed them in Spanish, which he called "God's language." He acknowledged that the Hispanic population of Boston was a mixed group with people not only from Puerto Rico but also from the Dominican Republic, Central America, and Mexico.[87] In 1995 Gonzalez was chosen by Pope John Paul II as the bishop of Corpus Christi, Texas.[88]

When he left Boston, there were thirty-three parishes in the archdiocese with a growing Hispanic population, many in the city but also in other areas north and west of the city. He noted that there were "five Hispanic priests, 12 deacons, and 12 nuns in the archdiocese." These numbers reflect the growing Hispanic population, which doubled between 1985 and 1995 in Massachusetts, amounting to approximately 342,000 people during the ten-year period. During Gonzalez's time in Boston, Hispanic parishes were also founded in both Lowell and Lawrence.[89] By the late 1990s it became apparent that the composition of the archdiocese was changing rapidly. The Hispanic population of Boston increased 64 percent between 1980 and 1990; the number of Bostonians who reported Irish ancestry decreased to only 22 percent during the same period.[90]

This increased attention given to Hispanic Catholics throughout the 1980s was not just a reflection of their growing numbers but also a recognition by the church that some of these newcomers were leaving. At a meeting in Rome called by Pope John Paul II, American cardinals reported that sixty thousand Hispanic Catholics were leaving the church for Protestant evangelical groups each year.[91] Upon his departure in 1995, Bishop Gonzalez recommended another auxiliary bishop be named to care for the archdiocese's growing Hispanic population. A year later Pope John Paul II appointed the Rev. Emilio S. Allue, a native of Spain, to the position. One area of concern for both Allue and Cardinal Law was how few Hispanics were found in the archdiocese's schools. Out of a total enrollment of over 54,000 students in 1996, only 2,280 students were Hispanic.[92] These numbers don't show the whole picture, however. These students could usually be found in urban areas like Boston, particularly in the South End and Roxbury.

Cathedral High School is a good reflection of the changing face of Catholicism. Opened in 1927, Cathedral High has educated the children of immigrants. Over the years Irish, African Americans, Puerto Ricans, Dominicans, and Vietnamese have attended the school. By 1995 it was estimated that "of the school's 250 students...more than 240 are people of color." Almost 40 percent were from Southeast Asia, and the majority lived in Roxbury and Dorchester. Cathedral High has worked hard for this kind of diversity. Many of the students receive financial aid. Diversity is celebrated at the school.[93]

The archdiocese has relied on lay leaders to help serve the pastoral needs in the community. It "opened the Instituto de Formación de Laicos (IFL) Archdiocesan Institute for Ministry ([AI] — Spanish track)," which offers a two-year program aimed at those who wish to work among Hispanics. Boston College has a similar program through its Institute of Religious Education and Pastoral Ministry.[94] The worries have remained.

By 2000, the archdiocese estimated there were almost five hundred thousand Hispanics living within its boundaries. Many of them, however, had either stopped attending church or had left the church altogether. Leaders were worried that their efforts were "hamstrung by a shortage of Spanish-speaking priests" according to a report in the *Boston Globe*. A study done by the National Conference of Catholic Bishops conducted in 2000 found that the number of Hispanic seminarians was drastically declining. While there was one priest for every twelve hundred Catholics in the United States, there was only one Spanish-speaking priest for every ten thousand Latinos. The archdiocese has recruited priests from Central and South America to fill the need. Many non-Spanish-speaking priests have learned the language, which has been much appreciated. A shortage remains, however. As of June 2003 there were only fourteen Latinos studying in all of New England's seminaries. The church in Boston decided to launch *La Vida Católica,* a Spanish-language newspaper, in the hopes of stopping the flow of Hispanics out of the church. The archdiocese was one of the last major dioceses to do so. The paper's executive director and assistant editor, Antonio M. Enrique, told the *Boston Globe* that "we want to help those already attending church in their development, and we want to reach out to the biggest part of the community, which is not attending church even though sociologically they are Catholics." The monthly newspaper was to be distributed free of charge to parishes that have Mass in Spanish. In 2000 it was sent to thirty-six parishes throughout the archdiocese. The bishop's report also noted that many Hispanic Catholics felt marginalized by the church, which has on occasion discounted their popular devotions.[95]

Simply saying Mass in Spanish is not enough to stem the tide of Hispanics leaving the church. What began as a trickle seems to have accelerated in the last fifteen years. While a majority of immigrants from Central and South America arrive as Catholics, the "percentage of Latino Catholics drops from

72 percent in the first generation to 61 and 52 percent among the second and third generations, respectively," according to studies conducted by the Cushwa Center for the Study of American Catholicism at Notre Dame. Latinos seem to be drawn to Evangelical churches, where they can worship in their own language, where there is a sense of community, active involvement, and, importantly, services for immigrants. Many Latinos are looking for a closer and more personal relationship with God.[96]

The increased immigration from Central America has continued unabated since 2000, according to Census Bureau figures released in 2006. In fact, while many native-born are leaving Massachusetts, the influx of immigrants has helped keep the state's population level at 6.4 million. The census reports that "14.4 percent of the state's population was foreign-born in 2005, up from about 12.2 percent in 2000." The largest increase came from Latin America. "The census found that 321,321 people living in Massachusetts last year were born in Latin America. The figure represents 37 percent of the total immigrant population in 2005 and amounted to a 40.7 percent increase over 2000." In addition to the large number of Latin Americans, "the second largest-growing immigrant group came from Africa" during the same period. Asians and those from the Caribbean make up the third- and fourth-largest group of immigrants, respectively. Those coming from Europe actually decreased between 2000 and 2005. The Census Bureau noted that the majority of all immigrants were "moving to Boston, Cambridge, Somerville, Lynn, Lowell, Lawrence, Quincy, and Brockton."[97]

One of the most diverse neighborhoods in Boston by the early 1990s was East Boston. Physically not connected to the downtown, East Boston has been the home to many different ethnic groups over the years: Irish, then Jews, and in the twentieth century Italian Catholics. As white Catholics began leaving the city for the suburbs after World War II, East Boston retained its ethnic flavor, but even here things started to change. By the 1990s one in four residents of East Boston was either Hispanic, Asian, or black. While the 1980 census showed the neighborhood was 96 percent white, in 1990 it was 18 percent Hispanic, 4 percent Asian, and 2 percent black. While not all these newcomers were Catholic, it is clear the Catholic population was growing and that parishes are often the first to recognize the change.

This demographic shift can be clearly seen in Most Holy Redeemer Church in East Boston. It was once primarily an Italian parish, but by the 1990s the majority of its parishioners were not Italian Catholics. By 1991 Mass was celebrated in Spanish, Portuguese, and Vietnamese.[98] In 2001 Most Holy Redeemer Church could boast that it was one of the fastest-growing parishes in the archdiocese, thanks to the increasing Hispanic population. The Rev. Robert R. Hennessey estimated that thirty-two thousand people come for the four Spanish-language Masses every weekend. The first Spanish Mass was held in 1983 for about fifty people, mostly from Mexico. By 1990 the number of Hispanics surpassed the number of Brazilians and Vietnamese in the parish. In 2001 the largest Hispanic groups came from El Salvador, Guatemala, and Peru.

The influx of new immigrants did not always sit well with older parishioners. The Rev. Bernard McLaughlin, who was pastor from 1983 to 1995, remembers a longtime Italian parishioner who said that she had "no use" for him now that the new immigrants were his first priority. The church's mission has remained the same, however: to help new immigrants adjust to American life and sustain their faith. According to Hennessey, Latinos "are coming to revitalize it." The church has an active community center, and parishioners often turn to the parish priests for help with immigration problems. They also help one another find jobs or places to live.[99]

Portuguese-speaking Catholics make up the second-largest-growing immigrant population in the archdiocese today, as they have for the last fifteen to twenty years. The Portuguese-speaking Catholic community consists primarily of Brazilians but also includes people from the Azores and the Cape Verde Islands who speak a version of Portuguese called *Crioulo*. As noted above, Cape Verdeans and their descendants were a significant portion of the community attending the Sisters of the Blessed Sacrament's Mission during the 1930s, according to Sister Mary Charles.

People from the Azores, and later from Cape Verde, which is located off the coast of Africa, began immigrating to Massachusetts at least as far back as the 1830s. Settling primarily in the southeastern part of the state around Fall River and New Bedford they worked in the whaling and fishing industries in the nineteenth and early twentieth centuries.[100] Today in Boston the Cape Verdean community resides primarily in Dorchester and Roxbury. St. Patrick's Church in Roxbury is the spiritual home to many of them. When St. Patrick's celebrated its 150th anniversary in 1986, Cardinal Law commented on what he saw at the church: "That's why I say this is the future of the church; not one little group over there, and one little group over there. But all of us together living our faith." Described as one of the few trilingual parishes in Boston, St. Patrick's "has remained an immigrant church." Then and now Mass is celebrated in English, Spanish, and Portuguese.

A second wave of Cape Verdeans began arriving during the 1970s, joining the black and Hispanic parishioners already there.[101] Cape Verdeans have often been described as a minority within a minority, not African American but not viewed as white either.[102] Some identify themselves as African. This reality has had an impact upon the community. Paulo De Barros, a program coordinator who worked at the Teen Center at St. Peter's School on Bowdoin Street summed it up this way: "We aren't accepted being black because I am Cape Verdean and my culture is different and I am lighter. We know we are from Africa but we are from Cape Verde. We are not accepted in the white culture because we are dark and speak Portuguese. We are caught in the middle of blacks and whites." St. Patrick's Church has had Mass in Portuguese for the community every weekend since the 1980s. Cape Verdeans also call nearby St. Peter's home, helping to serve the more than 25,000 Cape Verdeans estimated in Boston.[103]

In 1992 the archdiocese estimated there were 150,000 Brazilians living in the five counties that make up the archdiocese. Those working with the community believed that Brazilian Catholics even outnumbered the archdiocese's Spanish-speaking Catholic population at the time. Brazilians were not just living in East Boston but were also present in Allston-Brighton, Somerville, and the Framingham and Marlborough area. Sister Barbara Ciccolini, a member of the Sisters of Notre Dame de Namur, worked extensively with the Brazilian community. She estimated there were approximately 11,000 Brazilians in Allston-Brighton and 12,000 in Somerville by the early 1990s. In total, the Brazilian community was affiliated with at least nine different parishes throughout the archdiocese. according to Sister Barbara.[104] Those numbers could be inflated, however. According to the Census Bureau, Boston's Brazilian population (defined as those born in Brazil) was only 5,454 in 2005, a 17 percent increase since 2000. Whatever the actual number, it is clear that the Brazilian immigrant population is growing and adding to the diversity found in the archdiocese. While the number of Brazilians is increasing, overall the city's foreign-born population actually decreased during the first half of the present decade by 5 percent. This decrease reflects a move to nearby suburbs of Boston, the western suburbs, and the Merrimack Valley.[105]

One of those Brazilian parishes is Immaculate Conception Church in Marlborough, Massachusetts. In 1993 the Office for Ethnic Apostolates for the archdiocese estimated that Marlborough had the state's highest proportion of Brazilian residents. As many as eight thousand Brazilians called Marlborough home, out of a total population of thirty-five thousand, almost 23 percent. According to several people, the city has done a good job integrating the Brazilians. Brother Michael Galvin from the Office of Ethnic Apostolates noted that there is an "outstanding degree of integration, interaction, and acceptance" in the city. Due to their increased numbers, Immaculate Conception began celebrating Mass in Portuguese in the evening.[106]

Dorchester is a good example of the growing Catholic diversity due to migration. Immigration to the neighborhood has changed this section of Boston. "In 1980, the neighborhood was two-thirds white, most of that of Irish descent. Today whites are a third," noted the *Boston Globe,* drawing on 2000 census data. The Boston Redevelopment Authority divides Dorchester between North and South. Census numbers for the year 2000 "show North Dorchester 36 percent white, 24 percent black, 14 percent Hispanic, 13 percent Asian, and the rest mixed or other races. South Dorchester was 30 percent white, 42 percent black, 10 percent Hispanic, and 10 percent Asian."[107]

By the early 1990s, particularly at parishes like St. Peter's Church, known as "The Rock," the archdiocese's diversity is readily apparent. Once home to many Irish and Italian American families, the parish (and the neighborhood) was transformed in the 1990s. By 1992 the three principal language groups at St. Peter's were Vietnamese, Spanish, and English. The Rev. Daniel Finn noted, "This is a parish that didn't change for 100 years and then changed rapidly in seven years." Few whites remained at the parish, which by the early 1990s became home to African Americans, Puerto Ricans, Dominicans, Vietnamese, Cape Verdeans, and Haitians. Nearly half of Dorchester's white population left during the 1980s and the parish became ethnically mixed by the early 1980s. There were tensions in the parish between the different communities. Carmen Torres, a parishioner at St. Peter's, noted, "There was a time when the Americans would not say hello to us, when we sat next to them they would move to another pew." In addition to the Spanish-speaking population at the church, Vietnamese began coming to the parish during the 1980s. When the Rev. Diem Van Nguyen arrived in 1986, he began saying Mass weekly in Vietnamese, attracting about seventy worshipers. By 1992 the Vietnamese liturgy drew nine hundred people. The growth was not without difficulty. Attempts to truly integrate the parish have met with mixed results. "There already are trilingual prayer services and other activities at St. Peter's. But some parishioners and clergy wonder whether this will be enough to integrate the parish." One of the newer realities for urban parishes these days is the fact that many people who attend services do not live within the parish boundaries. Like many other ethnic groups before them, the Vietnamese community will eventually move to the suburbs and leave the parish behind, according to Father Nguyen. Similarly, the Vietnamese will find it difficult to leave St. Peter's behind. Tien Lai Kim, an active parishioner at the church, noted, "We are looking for a place with a backyard and a playground for our kids. But we still want to stay close to the Vietnamese community. We teach our culture. That is how we understand one another. I understand how Americans think. And I have a chance to tell the Americans and Spanish how we are. Inside we are brothers."[108]

By 2001 St. Peter's was offering daily services in Vietnamese to meet the growing needs of that community, drawing Vietnamese Catholics from all over Dorchester and beyond with sixty people attending the 6:00 p.m. weekday Masses and over five hundred on Sundays. Vietnamese Catholics have also found a home at St. William's Church in the Savin Hill section of Dorchester. "Church attendance was solid; it was a good-sized parish," the Rev. Dan Riley noted in 2001, "but nine or ten years ago, you could see a major increase due to the Vietnamese population, and it's held steady." He noted that half of those attending services are Asian and that they are steady churchgoers. "They come at the rate that [white] Catholics used to go in the 1950s and 1960s." Over four hundred people attended the Vietnamese-language Mass each Sunday at St. Williams. There are challenges to integrating the different ethnic groups. St. William's sponsored multicultural services and a parish picnic, which draws about eight hundred people each fall.[109]

Another group of Asians, Cambodians, have been coming to the United States since the 1980s. Many have settled in Chelsea, Lowell, and Lawrence. In 1996 the United States Catholic Conference on Migration and Refugee Services estimated there were at least 160,000 Cambodians in the United States, most of whom were not Catholic. The conference estimated there were approximately 150 baptized Cambodian Catholics in the archdiocese and that the population was growing here and in other American cities. In Lawrence, the Asian Center of Merrimack Valley opened in 1987 under the Sisters of Charity to meet the needs of the Asian community there by providing food, shelter, counseling, and immigrant services to the community regardless of religion. Similarly, the St. Julie Asian Center opened in Lowell in 1985 under the Sisters of Notre Dame de Namur. The center became the heart of the Cambodian community, estimated at almost thirty thousand people. This center provided computer services to its clients along with the more traditional offerings such as English as a second language. The Migration and Refugees Services Bureau noted, "The reality for the future is that many Catholic Cambodians will disappear if no one ministers to them." Ethnic apostolates have been established at St. Rose of Lima in Chelsea and St. Patrick's in Lowell, helping to fill the pews once occupied by previous generations of immigrants.[110] Quincy, just south of Boston, has seen a large influx of immigrants from Asia during the late 1980s, including Cambodians, creating what Alexander Reid of the *Boston Globe* called "an Asian melting pot." Between 1980 and 1990, the Asian population rose from 330 to over 5,000. A large majority of the immigrants were of Chinese ancestry, but the city also included an increasing number of Vietnamese and Koreans among others.[111]

Chinese Catholics have been present since the early 1990s. While Chinese Catholics are spread throughout the archdiocese, St. James the Greater in Boston's Chinatown serves as a focal point for the community, attracting people from the neighborhood and the suburbs. The lower chapel, used for services, "is decorated with hand embroidered banners paying homage to Our Lady of China and embellished with the Chinese characters for the word 'love.'" Services and religious education are offered in Mandarin, Taiwanese, and Fujianese. Many parishioners want a cultural connection, which they find lacking in their hometown Catholic church. One immigrant who lived in the suburbs noted that she and her husband did not feel "part of the suburban churches. When you're an immigrant, you can feel lost in this country. Part of the reason we come here is because of the community feel."[112]

Another group of Asian Catholics who feel particularly connected to their parish is Koreans. Catholicism in Korea was a lay initiative from the beginning, and this feature arrived with the immigrants beginning in the 1950s.[113] The Korean Catholic community of the greater Boston area traces its roots back to the early 1970s when several professionals, most of them doctors, decided to stay in the Boston area after attending school here. This group, led by Henry Cho, M.D., found a visiting Korean priest named John Won, who was assigned to St. Agatha's parish in Milton, Massachusetts. The community celebrated its first Mass together in 1976 and has stayed close ever since. The group searched for a home parish throughout the 1980s and 1990s, finally settling on St. Philip Neri in Waban, a village of Newton, Massachusetts. They have been there since 1996, but they will, however, need to find a new home due to the parish's closure in the recent parish re-configuration. The community worships in Korean and attracts people from New Hampshire and Rhode Island. The parish and community help to encourage their cultural identity and have served as a social and immigrant aid center.[114]

St. Mary of the Angels in Roxbury's Egleston Square is another parish with a diverse population. In 1992 the outgoing pastor of St. Mary's was Rev. John Roussin, known to the neighborhood simply as Father Jack. He had been at the parish for sixteen years. The church building, founded in 1907, had seen better days. The church was in physical disrepair. For his first Sunday at the church in 1976 only eight people attended Mass. By 1992 the church had three Sunday Masses with one in Spanish and anywhere between seventy-five and two hundred worshipers. Hispanics made up the largest portion of the parish but included people from forty-four different countries, according to Father Jack, who taught himself Spanish while working in Boston's South End. He also went on to learn Portuguese and Haitian Creole.[115] Haitians soon became a significant portion of parishioners at St. Mary of the Angels and at a number of other parishes in Boston.

Haitians, fleeing turmoil and revolution, have been making Boston their home for over two hundred years. This continues today. The current Haitian Catholic community in the archdiocese has its roots in the turmoil which has engulfed Haiti for the last several decades. Leaving behind persecution, political upheaval, and poverty, Haitians began arriving in Boston during the late 1950s; the number increased dramatically during the 1980s and the 1990s, contributing greatly to the church's diversity. During the 1950s Haitian professionals began fleeing the dictatorship of François "Papa Doc" Duvalier. The number leaving Haiti and coming to Boston increased during the reign of his son. By the early 1980s "20,000 Haitians were living in the city," according to one estimate.

Compared to many of the early migrants, these immigrants tended to be less educated and poorer. The Haitian Apostolate was established to serve the needs of the community along with an innovative social services agency.[116] In 1978 local community leaders founded the Haitian Multi-Service Center in an effort to help recent immigrants with learning English. In 1984 the center became affiliated with Catholic Charities of the Archdiocese of Boston and began to expand its services to meet the growing needs of an increasing population. In addition to English-language programs, the center provides counseling, HIV prevention, education, and job training. By 2000 there were about forty-four thousand Haitians living in the Greater Boston area.[117]

Father Gabriel Michel is the parochial vicar of St. Angela's Church in Mattapan and coordinator of the Haitian Apostolate for the archdiocese. St. Angela's has an active and growing Haitian population. In 2004 Rev. John Morin estimated that about 75 percent, almost twelve hundred people, are Haitian or of Haitian descent at the parish. The community is not just limited to St. Angela's, however. A Haitian youth event in June 2006 drew young people from five other parishes to the parish: Christ the King, Brockton; St. Mary's Church, Lynn; St. Ann, Somerville; Immaculate Conception, Everett; and St. Matthew, Dorchester.[118]

In 2001 Haitians from all over the area came to St. Matthew's in Dorchester to say goodbye to Monsignor Leandre Jeannot, "who was indeed revered as one of the fathers of this city's burgeoning Haitian community and its only spiritual leader." Having fled Haiti in 1959, Monsignor Jeannot came to St. Leo's in 1972 after being ordained in 1970. Jeannot worked hard to bring French Creole to parishes throughout Boston. For a while his parish was the only one to do so.

Haiti celebrated its bicentennial in 2004, and Boston's Haitian community was understandably proud. To help mark this occasion, Archbishop Seán O'Malley offered Mass in Creole at the cathedral for the community, a first for the archdiocese. Haitian flags decorated the cathedral and Haiti's national anthem was sung. Many community leaders credited O'Malley's predecessor, Cardinal Law, with turning a corner "in their [Haitians'] relationship with the church in 2002." Law attended the annual fundraising dinner for the Multi-Service Center. The Mass was considered the "next step." According to Pierre Imbert, executive director of the center, "The archbishop's message clearly showed that we as Haitians belong to the church here in Boston. The church as a whole understands the challenges we face as a community of immigrants."[119] O'Malley marked Haitian Independence Day once again in 2006 with a Mass.[120]

While immigration and the increase in diversity were first felt on the parish level, the institutional hierarchy was forced to take action. The archdiocese responded to the growing wave of immigrants and the increased diversity in 1990 by establishing the Office for Ethnic Apostolates. That year the office estimated there were twenty-seven different national groups in the archdiocese. The office, along with Black Catholic Ministries and the Hispanic Apostolate, is how the church is reaching out to these communities.

The church no longer erects true national parishes it has done in the past. Parishes designated for a particular ethnic/racial group are now called personal parishes; they can be part-territorial parishes. Catholics have options for where they attend. Integration into established territorial parishes is now the norm. Following the civil rights movement, the Second Vatican Council, and a shift in immigration patterns, church officials began "to rethink their willingness to encourage ethnic groups to worship separately from one another." Some studies have called into questions the effectiveness of this approach. Some ethnic groups are encouraged to worship together in the archdiocese. In 2004 the *Boston Globe* reported, based upon information from the archdiocese, that 67 out of 357 parishes (these numbers are before the recent parish reconfigurations and closings) "have sizable ethnic communities" offering liturgies in languages including Cantonese, Haitian Creole, Korean, Portuguese, and Spanish.[121]

The newest groups coming to the archdiocese include those from Africa. In October 1997 the archdiocese opened the African Pastoral Center in Roxbury to meet the growing needs of the large increase in immigrants from Nigeria, Cameroon, and Rwanda. Rev. Joseph Cogo, then director of the ethnic apostolate for the archdiocese, said, "These immigrants have certainly added a tremendous amount of diversity to the archdiocese, and we want to make sure that they feel welcome as Catholics." He noted that there were between two thousand and three thousand Nigerian Roman Catholics in Massachusetts. The immigrant influx was breathing new life into these old parishes according to Cogo. "They are providing many churches with a brighter future."[122]

At St. John–St. Hugh church in Roxbury (now St. Katherine Drexel) the Nigerian Catholic community has found a home. They have brought their traditions, just as other ethnic Catholics have done over the years. The traditions are present in the "fabric woven with the intricate patterns, rich textures, and vibrant colors of the Igbo and Yoruba people of Africa." Their Sunday Mass, which draws upward of two hundred people each week, is a mixture of "Catholic and African ritual, when dozens of women dance and sing their way down the center aisle, moving slowly and gracefully toward the altar. There, as a priest sprinkles holy water on their heads, they sway from side to side, like a river rippling in bright shades of fuchsia, emerald, and turquoise." The church serves as an "anchor" for the community as it does for many other newly arrived immigrants who are remaking the face of Boston Catholicism.

St. Katherine Drexel is also home to an active black Catholic worshiping community. After having coalesced around St. Phillip's/St. Francis de Sales since the 1980s, this community was merged with African Americans and Nigerians from St. John–St. Hugh during the recent parish reconfiguration. A new name was needed for the church. St. Katherine Drexel was chosen in acknowledgment of the Sisters of the Blessed Sacrament's history with the community and the archdiocese.

By 2003 the Office of Ethnic Apostolates had grown to represent thirty-six different ethnic groups. "Immigrants from Portuguese- and Spanish-speaking countries now constitute more than 350,000 of the two million Catholics in the Archdiocese and account for the highest proportion of the new growth," said Rev. Christopher Coyne, then spokesman for the archdiocese. One study estimated that about 40 percent of legal immigrants to the United States identified themselves as Catholic, a figure much higher than for the native-born population. According to the study's author, Guillermina Jasso, "The bottom line is that there is a strong contingent of Catholic immigration to the U.S." She noted, "these are fresh people for the American church, with a diversity of background, language, and culture. The challenge for the Catholic Church is to maintain and invigorate its traditional ecumenical mission while taking people who are different and emphasizing what they have in common."[123]

The diversity is not limited to Boston's neighborhoods alone or to nearby cities. One example is St. Joseph's Church in Salem, Massachusetts. Originally founded in 1873, the parish was opened to meet the needs of the ever-growing French Canadian population, which began arriving after the Civil War. Today, Mass is no longer celebrated in French. Typical of many ethnic parishes, St. Joseph's changed over the years as the population shifted. In 1948 a book commemorating the parish's seventy-fifth anniversary was written in French; by the time of the one hundredth anniversary celebration the commemorative volume was in English. The last French Mass was celebrated in the early 1990s. By the late 1980s the parish began offering Mass in Spanish. During the 1990s the parish served people from many different backgrounds, including African, Asian, Irish, Haitian, and Hispanic.

The number of Hispanic families continued to grow in Salem. By 1994 according to the youth minister at the time, Andrea Lausier, there were between 150 and 175 Hispanic families who called St. Joseph's home. It was not easy for them. Unlike the French Canadians before them, who brought priests and religious women with them, the Hispanics "are struggling in their homes and amongst themselves" according to Robert St. Pierre, who grew up in the parish.[124] While St. Joseph's began as a national parish serving the needs of the French Canadian community, that has ceased to be its primary mission. The Rev. Lawrence Rondeau, pastor of St. Joseph's, noted in 2004 that Hispanics made up about half of the nine hundred families at the parish.

In many ways it became a traditional territorial parish serving the needs of many Hispanics, primarily from the Dominican Republic, as they moved in during the 1980s and 1990s. They seem to be enthusiastic parishioners, filling the church at the 4:00 p.m. Sunday Mass with five hundred people. Having Mass said in Spanish and listening to music with a Latin beat are particularly important to many in the community. One parishioner told a reporter for the *Globe*, "The music was my favorite part. It made things special." Another young member of St. Joseph's noted, "Praying in Spanish is the only way I feel better." St. Joseph's also has an elementary school, the only one left in a city that used to have five parish schools. The school serves a diverse population. In 2005 the school had an enrollment of 21 percent minority, mostly Hispanics who live in Salem and are its largest minority group.[125]

Another example can be found at Christ the King parish in Brockton, Massachusetts. Christ the King was founded in 2004 with the merger of Sacred Heart and St. Colman of Cloyne, both of which were established in 1891. Sacred Heart first served Brockton's French community and then its Haitian community. Sacred Heart had been losing members for years, however, and plans were laid to merge it with St. Colman's, which attracted twice as many churchgoers on the weekends. The new church has an active Haitian ministry under the direction of Rev. Garcia Breneville, a native of Haiti.[126] How integrated the Haitian community actually is within the new parish is open to question. Many of the special celebrations, like those during Holy Week, have bilingual elements. The Haitian community celebrates

Mass in Creole at 1:00 p.m. on Sundays. Part of the weekly bulletin is in Creole as well.[127]

Conclusions

While it is true that the Irish and other European Americans have been the dominant presence in the archdiocese over the last two hundred years, that reality obscures the fact that racial minorities have been an important part of this history. More importantly they will be a significant presence into the foreseeable future, particularly in urban areas. African Americans in the archdiocese have served as a mirror that reflects the church's troubled and complex past with people of color. As the church in Boston becomes even more racially and culturally diverse, these challenges will only increase. How the institutional church and the laity of all backgrounds respond will affect the overall growth, vibrancy, and relevancy of Catholics in the Greater Boston area. Issues such as the clergy shortage will have a major impact on the institutional church's ability to reach out to some of the oldest and newest Catholics. The Boston archdiocese has always been an immigrant church. How native-born Catholics have treated these newcomers has been at times disappointing at best. Periodic attempts to deal with the increasing diversity have had mixed results. Overall, European Catholics of different ethnic backgrounds have become American Catholics. Our understanding of that term will have to change due to the demographic shift under way in Boston and across the country. The continued racial diversity coming from Central and South America, Asia, the Caribbean, and Africa has challenged the church in even more complex ways. It will require more effort on the part of all Catholics in the archdiocese if these groups are to be fully welcomed, retained, and integrated within the church.

As Cardinal O'Malley stated in December 2003 to priests assembled at Boston College, "Special regard must be given to the new immigrants who have cultural needs, linguistic and otherwise."[128] How the parish reconfiguration will ultimately affect immigrants is still to be seen. A number of the closed or merged parishes have sizable immigrant populations and are concentrated in urban areas, the very same areas that have been hardest hit by the reconfiguration. The archdiocese's immigrant population has needs beyond language. The many cultural complexities within all of the communities must be addressed by clergy and laity alike, particularly in newly blended parishes. In some parishes, Mass is offered in two or three different languages to different nationalities. The level of interaction between native-born and recent arrivals varies from parish to parish. As some immigrants leave urban areas they will encounter less diverse parishes in the suburbs. Truly integrated parishes remain more a hope than a reality. This along with their enculturation will be an ongoing struggle, as it has always been. New immigrants bring their vibrancy, hope, and faith with them, as they always have. It will be up to everyone to make sure their faith can be maintained.

The Role of Women in the Archdiocese of Boston, 1808–2008

Carol Hurd Green

Imagine a collage of photographs and line drawings: a young Irish woman, traveling alone, tired and cold, disembarking in the port of Boston; four sisters, called to New England to teach, facing the hostility of anti-Catholic crowds; rows of women in starched cornettes arrayed in Cathedral pews under the eye of the cardinal on his throne; girls in white dresses as far as the photographer's eye can see along an East Boston street on a May morning; young women of the Young Ladies Charitable Association visiting the aged sick poor; Italian and Portuguese immigrant women bent over their sewing in a North End room; Mary Dahill Cushing, softly pleased, comfortable in her neat print dress, holding a picture of her son; a group of sisters, their habits covered by white cloths, caring for those ill with cholera; nursing sisters under the tents on the Carney hospital lawn, caring for the war wounded; tired mothers coming from early Mass in a struggling mill town; Boston-born Mary Josephine Rogers sending new Maryknoll sisters to China; African American Sisters of the Blessed Sacrament with the St. Richard's Drum and Bugle Corps; middle-class women behind their tables of fine work in Mechanics Hall at an orphans' fair; the O'Neil family, ten daughters, in the Easter Parade; young women in caps and gowns carrying a daisy chain; Corita Kent's gas tank mural on the Southeast Expressway; Catholic Interracial Council members, women and men, black and white, marching in South Boston on St. Patrick's Day 1965; women, guests, and volunteers at Rosie's Place; over four hundred women gathered at Boston College in 2004, "Envisioning the Church Women Want"; further hundreds of women gathered in a diocesan convention to explore their faith....

These are a very small fragment of the images that tumble from the stories of two hundred years of Catholic women's lives in the Diocese of Boston. Not chronological, they represent an attempt to suggest the breadth of Catholic women's work and vocations, the significant presence of women religious, the development of an apostolate of hospitality, and the ongoing commitment to justice and to the poor. For many reasons — the anonymity of most women's lives, the traditional position of women within a hierarchical church, and the vocational decision by women religious to subdue the individual within the collective mission of serving and saving souls — there are many gaps here, important or interesting stories that remain untold.

To find the names and deeds of women in the histories and repositories of the Catholic Church in Boston, one reads between the lines and searches footnotes and indexes, hoping for a woman's name. A few representative (and remarkable) figures do appear with some frequency: among them, Sister Ann Alexis, "the servant of the poor," who founded and guided both St. Vincent's Orphan Asylum and Carney Hospital; Katherine E. Conway, the first woman editor of the *Pilot;* Martha Moore Avery, convert from socialism and cofounder and street corner orator for the Catholic Truth Society; and, in a different idiom, the iconic twentieth-century figure of Rose Fitzgerald Kennedy. But the stories of most Catholic women are subsumed in the collectivity of institutions and organizations, domestic lives and parishes.[1]

With the significant development of women's scholarship in the 1970s, the paradigm of invisibility began to shift. Important new scholarship since then — especially for Boston Catholic women's history the work of Mary Oates, C.S.J. — uses women's work and life histories as the starting point for understanding the Catholic experience. Oates documents the wide-ranging work that women, religious and lay, have done to develop and sustain the church in Boston; she also documents the massive debt the church owes to the "free help" of sisters in the schools and in the practice of charity.[2] Oates's work and that of scholars such as James Kenneally, Karen Kennelly, and Paula Kane also allows us to see significant thematic continuities in the lives of Catholic women — religious and lay — in both their daily labors and as voices of wisdom, offering thoughtful reflection and important writing on matters of spirituality, theology, and social justice.[3]

Women Lay and Religious: The Catholic Laywoman

The phrase "Catholic laywoman" is imprecise, suggesting more what she was not (a vowed woman) than the many things she is. But it provides an umbrella under which to gather the many roles of women who were baptized into and lived the Catholic faith outside of a religious order. The documents of Vatican II defined women religious as members of the laity, a change important in the consciousness of religious women. Until the post–Vatican II years, however, the lives of religious and laywomen ran typically on separate lines, and class issues sometimes led to differing interpretations of poverty and responsibility. The transformative incidents of the 1960s and the 1970s brought laywomen and religious women in closer contact, as they worked together for peace and justice. The conventional division of religious and lay remains useful for historical understanding, however.

There are occasional tantalizing glimpses of individual laywomen in pre-nineteenth-century Boston. The first to gain public attention was Goodwife Ann (Goody) Glover, an "elderly Irish widow" who was hanged as a witch on November 16, 1688; accused of causing the strange behaviors of her employer's daughters, she had "refused to renounce her Catholic faith."[4]

A century later, in 1788, the year of the formation of the first Catholic congregation in Boston, Marie Margaret Price was one of the "prime mover(s) in finally obtaining a priest for the Catholics" there.[5] Mary Connell Lobb (1734–1816), widowed, remarried, and the mother of three, was, historian Robert Lord says, "truly one of the pioneers." An active member of the first congregation and a member of a family that owned "both land and slaves," she appears very early in church records, listed with Margaret Price as witness to baptisms performed by the Abbè de la Poterie, the first priest resident in Boston. She also served as hostess to Father Francis Anthony Matignon, the "second founder" of the Boston church. She and "a Mrs. Doyle" (Anne Doyle, 1728–1814) were influential enough to negotiate a hostile dispute between Irish Catholics and French Catholics over the use of a chapel. Lobb's will left a considerable gift "in trust...solely for the use and relief of the Roman Catholic Church in Boston."[6]

Coming to Boston

Throughout the nineteenth century, the dominant motif of Boston Catholic women's stories was the movement from the known to the unknown. Large numbers of immigrants, primarily from Ireland, refugees from famine and poverty, flooded into New England and, unable economically to move on, stayed and embarked on the struggle to survive. Because of traditional family structures that limited the possibilities of marriage at home, more Irish women (than those of other nationalities) traveled to America alone.[7] Although there were more male than female Irish immigrants to the United States before the famine years, over the course of the nineteenth century more than 4 million women — more than half the total — came. As Bronwen Walter notes, they retained strong ties with relatives at home, providing remittances, seeking jobs for relatives and encouraging them to come to America.[8]

The greatest number of single Irish women in the post-famine generation "went into service" (80 percent of paid household labor in New York City in the 1850s were Irish), permitting middle-class women the advantage of genteel leisure expected by the cult of domesticity. Colleen McDannell suggests, however, that those in service benefited, too: the work was cleaner than factory work, and women had an opportunity to see a more comfortable way of life to which they could aspire.[9]

Although the second generation of women workers (coming in the wake of New England farm girls) in the Lowell mills were also disproportionately Irish, the history suggests that domestic service was viewed more favorably; its provision of housing and food allowed more opportunity to save money for sending remittances to those at home, or for building a dowry in the hope of eventual marriage. The pattern persisted: Walter notes that in 1920 in six states "with large Irish-born populations, 81 percent of Irish-born women were in service." But another pattern was stronger: women encouraged the generation of their daughters to seek education and move into more desirable occupations. Hasia Diner cites a 1913 study by sociologist E. A. Ross showing a decline from 54 to 16 percent between the first and second generations of Irish women employed as servants and waitresses.[10] In the 1920s and 1930s the proportion of second-generation Irish women teaching in city schools grew sharply, a pattern that persisted in Boston and New York well beyond the mid-twentieth century. Even though the Baltimore Council of 1884 had mandated the education of Catholic children in parochial schools, in Boston the percentage of children in public schools remained large, offering opportunities women were eager to take.[11]

"Maternity, Sweet Sound": Catholic Motherhood

The story of the founding of Catholic charitable institutions from the mid-nineteenth to the mid-twentieth century should be told, therefore, not only as the story of the women religious, but also of mothers and of their children. The hundreds of Catholic orphans brought in increasing numbers every year to be cared for by the Sisters of Charity at St. Vincent's Orphan Asylum (opened 1834) and the street children sent by civil authorities to the Home for Destitute Catholic Children (founded by laymen, 1864; turned over to Sisters of Charity, 1867) may be seen as the legacy of women whose lives were storm-tossed by illness (tuberculosis and other diseases of poverty, the cholera epidemics of 1832, the lack of medical care), by widowhood and desertion — frequent when work was scarce and too hard and families large — and by their struggle to survive in a hostile climate.

Similarly, the many, mostly young women who found their way to the House of the Good Shepherd (founded 1849; moved to the Brigham estate on Huntington Avenue in Boston 1870) — or were committed there by the courts (in 1902 of 175 admitted, 79 were from the city courts) provide a view into the risks faced by abandoned and poor women, into their very limited options, and into the shame visited on the "fallen" women.[12] Some of the "children" (as all Good Shepherd residents were called) presented difficult challenges to the consecrated virginity of the Good Shepherd Sisters, and the house regimen was often very difficult for young women, but the refuge and the imposed order within its walls were often a way to survival. (Not all were Catholic, and the Religious of the Good Shepherd hoped not only for moral improvement and employability but also for conversion.)

Domestic Expectations

The late nineteenth century in America were years of what women's historians have defined as the "cult of true womanhood," when "domestic ideology hailed the mother as the center of the home" and — in its Catholic translation — "the foundation of Catholicism."[13] Colleen McDannell opens her very useful study of Catholic domesticity between 1860 and 1960 with a quotation from "Maternal Affection," which appeared in the May 1887 issue of the *Catholic Home Journal*; she considers the social imperative to domesticity in three phases. The first occurred between 1860 and 1920, the years of the "cult of true womanhood."[14] The cultural expectation that the woman was to be the "angel in the house" was differently valenced for Catholic women, given the church's pronouncements; it was an impossible ideal for those caught in poverty.

The second, overlapping, era, from 1880 to 1940, is marked by the impact of immigration and the diversification of women's burdens; in Boston the *Sacred Heart Review,* as well as sermons and Catholic advice books, emphasized the sacredness of the home and women's responsibility to maintain it in the face of both external and domestic challenges. From 1940 to 1960, McDannell notes that "Catholic culture" emphasized the threat to the family of modern secular values and "reassert[ed] the patriarchal nature of Catholicism as a balance to suburban domestic life."[15]

In the years since the 1960s and 1970s, as women's workplace participation and access to education have risen dramatically, as women have claimed the right to make decisions about their lives, the role of motherhood has taken on another kind of centrality. Discussions of work/life conflicts are frequent; marriage and childbearing increasingly come later and Catholic families are smaller; the challenges of childcare are frequently daunting. Nonetheless, the commitment to family and children retains a strong emotional hold.[16]

The mid-twentieth century offered some striking models of motherhood for Boston Catholics. Rose Fitzgerald Kennedy was a unique and deeply admired emblem of Catholic motherhood: the successful lives and tragic deaths of her children, her complex marriage, her enthusiastic campaigning for her sons, her absolute fidelity to the church, and her strength in suffering made her a figure of mythical — and rather intimidating — proportions. On a more homely level, and an emblem of Catholic domesticity, mid-twentieth-century Boston Catholics enjoyed the testament to Catholic family life provided by the Easter parade appearance of the O'Neil family from Blessed Sacrament parish in Jamaica Plain. Six daughters and a son when the family first marched in the parade in 1946, the family grew to include ten daughters and a second son. Every year Julia O'Neil designed and sewed identical outfits for the girls: eight girls in "beautiful turquoise coats and hats" and then ten in 1952 in "warm gray sharkskin wool jackets with peplum and flared skirts." *Life* magazine ran a feature on the family in April 1952 (the year they were invited to march in the New York City Easter parade); the issue cover has a seductive photograph of another iconic mid-century woman, Marilyn Monroe.[17]

Organizing for the Faith; the "Fair Ladies"

Sharp divisions persisted between Catholic and Protestant at the century's end, and the 1890s brought a resurgence of virulent anti-Catholicism. But there were changes: with growing Catholic political and economic power in Boston women saw the possibility of a new public image. The struggling immigrant mother was not gone, as the records of hospitals and asylums make clear. But the class status of many Catholic Bostonians was shifting; they were becoming "lace curtain," concerned with demonstrating their gentility and success and anxious to gain respect from judgmental non-Catholics.

From 1832 on, when Bishop Fenwick called together a group of women to provide support for the work of the newly arrived Sisters of Charity, Catholic laywomen reached out to their less fortunate sisters, forming guilds and leagues to support charitable institutions, inhabiting and extending the sisters' apostolate of hospitality by adding their support to it. Throughout the nineteenth century a phenomenon of Catholic women's culture was the fundraising events conducted for charity, especially the "fair." The records of institutions conducted by the Sisters of Charity (and others) are rich in accounts of these striking examples of collaboration between sisters and laywomen. Women and children did the work (the curriculum of St. Vincent's Orphan Asylum included two two-hour periods weekly for children to work on goods for the fair, and the sisters also sewed), and parish women spent many hours at their tables. Held in very large venues (the sites included Horticultural Hall and Mechanics Hall) some fairs lasted for as much as ten days. Men attended and presided, offering witticisms on the "fair ladies," though also making donations. The first fair, hoping to raise money for a building for St. Vincent's Orphan Asylum, occurred on the heels of its founding in October 1833 and earned $2,000. Profits from two more (in 1839 and 1841), augmented by some small legacies, enabled a down payment on a much-needed building. By 1845, when overcrowding in the asylum meant the Sisters had to move again, a fourth fair made only $750 (the weather was bad), but a fifth fair, in 1850, resulted in "the handsome sum of $3,500." That paid the debts on the current building and provided the beginning of a fund for the next: their present residence had already "become full to over-flowing." The fair accompanying the well-attended 1882 Sisters of Charity Golden Jubilee was very successful. Laywomen (including, unusually, several single women) from nineteen Boston parishes presided over tables; the most successful at the Saturday's children's festival were conducted by Miss S. A. Curran from Immaculate Conception, Boston ($292.62), and Miss Madeline Walker from St. Joseph's in Roxbury ($292.50).[18]

Other institutions also depended on the volunteer work of laywomen; the work not only provided the opportunity for generosity to others but also (at a time when work outside the home was frowned on for Catholic middle-class women) could provide the satisfaction of work well done. The Working Girls' Home (later St. Helena's), opened with the enthusiastic support of Archbishop Williams in 1888, was the beneficiary of "our ladies." Thanking actual and potential benefactors at an 1893 event sponsored by the Working Girls' Friends Society (who had been "indefatigable in their labors for the cause"), Williams summoned a poignant image of the home's residents: "She has to find a lodging, and as her purse is light, it must be a poor one. It is easier for those who are not in need of work to find it than those who are hunting for it to obtain it. But suppose the girl does find work. It must be at very low wages; and how can she half pay her way and clothe herself decently . . . ? And when this sum is not sufficient how is she to manage to pay her board? Then again she may become ill. . . . All this time she is surrounded . . . by temptations to seek means of living which are not honorable." By 1891 a second, larger home was needed: since 1888 they "had received 1250 girls . . . but were compelled to refuse 2837 applicants." While praising all of their lay benefactors, Williams also noted in passing that the ability to conduct the house was assisted by having "no salaries to pay"; he had invited the Grey Nuns early on to run the house, and they had agreed.[19]

The Young Ladies Charitable Association came into being in 1891, when Elizabeth Powers, a recent graduate of Sacred Heart at Kenwood, sought and gained the support of Archbishop Williams to "band together young girls for the care of the sick poor in their homes." Distraught at the condition of an elderly blind and destitute woman whom she had visited at a priest's suggestion, Powers realized that there were many such suffering aged in the city and determined to try to alleviate their distress. In the course of their work the young women encountered many aged suffering from tuberculosis; Powers and her companions worked to open a nonsectarian Free Home for Consumptives in Dorchester. Williams bought the house (coincidentally, Powers's childhood home); the young ladies put their energies into raising money to support it. Mother Augustine, Williams's biographer, remembers with pleasure that "the Young Ladies" were everywhere and they were indefatigable. They held a "Kirmess," which netted $4,000 and was the first of a series of "original and delightful entertainments" that "became a feature of social life" in Boston. The association formed several branches in Boston and the suburbs, caring for sick in their homes and sending the most serious cases to the home in Boston. By 1903 there were a thousand members and it was estimated that they had cared for ten thousand patients.[20]

In addition to their volunteer work for hospitals and asylums, the records show that some women, like Mary Lobb in the early years, left generous bequests. Convert Florence Lyman, a "daughter of the old Puritan stock, though a convert to the Catholic Faith," was a particularly generous benefactor of the House of the Good Shepherd. Involved with the House since its foundation, she gave "generously of her personal service, her influence, and her money"; when the superior became "discouraged by the then prevailing bigotry," Lyman introduced her to wealthy friends. She also held three fundraising fairs in her home, and at her death in 1907 left to the Good Shepherd House a generous bequest of $50,000.[21]

The League of Catholic Women

The League of Catholic Women (LCW), founded in 1910, went some steps beyond the charitable associations and guilds in its ambition. One of a number of gender-specific Catholic social, cultural, and literary organizations founded by Catholics in the late nineteenth and early twentieth centuries, the League is the best known and most enduring of the women's organizations.

It began with two women converts. (A phenomenon of late nineteenth- and early twentieth-century Catholicism was the increasing number of converts, many of them women, and many from distinguished families.)[22] In 1910 Pauline Willis brought to her friend Elizabeth Dwight the news of an English Catholic women's league that was designed to anticipate and respond to modernism's threats to the faith and to consolidate the work of women's Catholic associations. Dwight gained Cardinal O'Connell's approval for a comparable Boston league and served as its president for seven years. (As with all organizations led by women, O'Connell supervised it very carefully; he mandated that every lay organization must have a chaplain, appointed by him.) Membership lists and press accounts of League activities into the 1920s suggest that members were primarily of Irish ancestry; an occasional Italian surname appears by the teens.[23]

The League, like the Reading Circles organized by Katherine Conway and poet Mary Elizabeth Blake, and the Catholic Summer School, for which Conway was a regular lecturer, acknowledged women's intellectual interests. The stated purpose of the LCW was to "unite Catholic women for the promotion of spiritual, cultural, and educational work"; it would also meet the obligations of charity. A regular lecture series, featuring contemporary as well as religious topics, was an ambitious undertaking; the League brought in such well-known speakers as novelist and convert Monsignor Robert Hugh Benson and, especially in the years after World War I, expanded the lectures to address broader social and economic questions. Although the League worried about membership, and eventually had to sell the Arlington Street house that served as its headquarters, the members committed both to the lectures and to charitable concerns. In 1951 Monsignor John Tracy Ellis came to speak about the history of the American church; among the historians who spoke in the 1970s were Thomas O'Connor from Boston College and Historic Deerfield director Donald Friary. From the beginning, the lectures, along with whist parties and other entertainments, had served the dual purpose of supporting Catholics' intellectual lives and providing the League with funds for its other activities.[24]

Paralleling the endeavors of progressive Protestant reformers but with the focus on preservation of the faith, in 1915 the League hired social worker May Burke to assist them in the work they had undertaken with young women on probation. When they realized that they had not paid enough attention to the plight of poor Italian immigrant women, the League formed a Committee for Italian Social Service and began sewing classes for women in the North and West Ends of Boston. In addition to volunteers, they engaged a professional cloth cutter and a social worker, Miss Pellegrini, to conduct and oversee classes.[25]

The League also became involved in debates over social issues. A long-time (1919–32) League president (and friend of Cardinal O'Connell), Lillian Slattery represented O'Connell's adamant opposition in the 1920s to the proposed federal child labor amendment before the recently formed National Council of Catholic Women (NCCW — part of the National Catholic Welfare Conference, which O'Connell had also opposed). NCCW supported the law, and Slattery tangled sharply with NCCW secretary Agnes Regan. O'Connell was decidedly unsympathetic to such progressive legislation: for him, and for Lillian Slattery and many other Catholics, passage of the child labor law was an unwarranted intrusion of the state into the rights of the family.[26]

What League minutes call the "perennial Birth Prevention bill" was a persistent concern: with strong support and direction from church leaders, League members were determined to prevent the legalization of birth control in Massachusetts. In this as in other social matters touching on Catholic principles, the League strove to maintain its original mission. At its height in the 1940s, it continued to seek both to grow its membership and to add breadth to its members' sense of Catholic citizenship.

Redefinitions: Professional Lives

From the mid-nineteenth through the mid-twentieth centuries, Catholic women primarily entered professional life as teachers. As Mary Oates demonstrates in her remarkable survey of Catholic working women between 1850 and 1950, however, there was considerably more variety in women's occupations over that time.[27] It is also true that until the late twentieth century it was unusual to find Catholic women in any numbers outside teaching, and to a lesser extent nursing and social work.[28] An important exception was the large number of women with careers in journalism and literature, as Libby Bischof has described in her essay outlining the work of Katherine E. Conway, Louise Imogen Guiney, and other women writers.

Women's Scholarship in Theology

Since the latter years of the twentieth century, however, the concept of the Catholic woman writer has taken on an important new meaning as women theologians and scholars have produced transformative and influential texts. As theologian Mary Ann Hinsdale, I.H.M., points out, the church as a whole has been the beneficiary of an increasing number of women who have chosen to study, write about, and teach theology and to seek positions in various forms of ministry. In her 2004 Madeleva lecture, *Women Shaping Theology*, Hinsdale uses the narrative of her own life as Catholic woman, scholar, and teacher to illuminate the changing role of women in the U.S. Catholic Church.[29]

Since the late 1960s, Boston has been the site of major work by Catholic theologians concerned with women's issues: Mary Daly, Lisa Sowle Cahill, Shawn Copeland, and Mary Ann Hinsdale at Boston College and Elisabeth Schüssler Fiorenza at Harvard. Mary Daly's work has been revolutionary from the beginning; her two early volumes, *The Church and the Second Sex* (1968, 1975) and *Beyond God the Father* (1973, 1985) radically altered the conventional understanding of the theological and historical position of women in the Roman Catholic Church. In the breadth of their scholarship and their insistence on the destructive ramifications of patriarchy the books made arguments that were much debated, but could not be disregarded. In many subsequent books, written from a post-Christian perspective, she has challenged the conventions of language and of literary and philosophical forms to create a new understanding of women's mind and spirit. A longtime member of the Boston College theology faculty (now retired), Daly has been broadly influential, both in the United States and abroad.[30]

In her reflections on the "embodiment" of theological and ethical issues, ethicist Lisa Sowle Cahill has made invaluable contributions to the ongoing dialogue on a Catholic feminist theology. Her work on sexual and gender ethics has engaged her with questions of central moral importance: the debates over reproductive issues and the controversies surrounding stem-cell research among the most visible. Cahill has been widely honored (she has received eight honorary degrees), and has served frequently as a consultant to the U.S. bishops: in their preparations for the Synod on the Laity, a pastoral document on AIDS, on marriage and family, and on Catholic universities.[31]

Systematic theologian M. Shawn Copeland, the first African American woman to serve as president of the Catholic Theological Society of America, and a founding scholar of black Catholic theology, returned to Boston College (where she had completed her doctorate in theology) in the 1990s. She has also been director of the Institute for Black Catholic Studies held annually at Xavier University in New Orleans. In an article in *Taking Down Harps,* Copeland illuminates the history and methodology of black Catholic theology: "The term...irrupted in the United States in the mid-1960s, to account for black people's social ferment, spiritual urgency, and unyielding 350-year struggle to win and realize their freedom, to create for themselves before God a future full of hope.... Black theology distinguished Sacred Scripture as the word of God from Sacred Scripture as an ideology wielded for the religious, cultural, and social benefit of white Protestant and Catholic churches and their membership. It directly linked the struggle of black people for freedom and liberation to the message of the gospel."[32]

Elisabeth Schüssler Fiorenza, the Krister Stendahl Professor of Divinity at Harvard, has formed a theological language that opens the epistemological and social questions regarding women's full participation in the faith. Her work in biblical interpretation and in feminist theology has been widely translated and is internationally influential, beginning with the methodologically pathbreaking *In Memory of Her: A Feminist Theological Reconstruction of Christian Origins* (1983, 1992). Schüssler Fiorenza and other Catholic scholars who interrogate the tradition from a feminist viewpoint, along with the numbers of women enrolled in theology and ministry studies at Boston College, the Weston School of Theology, the Harvard Divinity School, and elsewhere have significantly altered Catholic and women's intellectual landscape.

Women and the Labor Movement

Women's writing careers demonstrate one kind of continuity in the choices that women made, or could make, as professionals. Another kind of continuity comes with women familiar with the hardworking lives of many women and determined to make those lives better.

As Hasia Diner and other historians of Irish women in America demonstrate, many women worked in industry, as did members of other immigrant populations — but not in such large proportions. With the development of the labor movement in the United States, a sense of justice rooted in the Irish colonial experience, in the labor encyclicals of Pope Leo XIII, and in their own experience as workers drew a number of Catholic women to embrace the cause of worker's rights. Several rose to prominence in the unions. Probably the best known are Mary Harris "Mother" Jones (1830–1930), the fearless organizer of western miners, and Margaret Haley (1861–1939), who fought for teachers' rights through the Chicago Teachers Federation. In New England, Mary Kenney O'Sullivan (1864–1943) continued in Boston a career of organizing women workers that she began in Chicago in the late 1880s, where she organized a women bookbinders union, gaining the support of Jane Addams, and also founded a boarding club for working women. The first salaried woman organizer of the American Federation of Labor (AFL), Mary Kenney was sent to Boston by AFL head Samuel Gompers to organize women in the rubber, shoemaking, and garment worker industries. There she met and married (1894) Boston labor journalist and union activist John O'Sullivan; they had three surviving children. After her husband's accidental death in 1902, she continued her labor activism, becoming cofounder of the National Women's Trade Union League (NWTUL), a collaboration of working women and their professional and middle-class supporters, and actively supported such major labor actions as the Lawrence, Massachusetts, "Bread and Roses" Strike. O'Sullivan was also a supporter of women's suffrage, in contrast to the determined antisuffrage position of Cardinal O'Connell and other Catholics, and as a member of the Women's International League for Peace and Freedom she opposed U.S. entry into World War I.[33]

In the next generation, Julia Parker O'Connor (1890–1972), the daughter of Irish Catholic immigrants to Massachusetts, was one of a small committee that gained telephone company recognition in 1913 for the new Boston Telephone Workers Union. The new job of telephone operator had become women's work, and in April 1919, as union president, O'Connor led a six-day strike that paralyzed regional telephone service and succeeded in gaining better wages for the operators. O'Connor remained active in the labor movement and in Democratic politics, employed from 1939 until her 1957 retirement as an organizer for the AFL.[34]

Best known for her passionate support of women's suffrage, Margaret Lilian Foley (1875–1957) was also a labor organizer. From a working-class Dorchester family, Foley organized women workers in the hat factory where she was employed and served on the board of the WTUL. As an outspoken and sometimes confrontational working-class Catholic woman, Foley met opposition both from Catholics and from the Protestant middle-class leaders of the suffrage movement.[35] Leaders such as O'Sullivan, O'Connor, and Foley provide a reminder of the large numbers of women working in tiring and often demeaning jobs for whom they sought better lives.

Public Lives: Politics and the Law

Catholic women, like most American women, began to expand their professional ambitions in the 1950s, as postwar prosperity allowed families more often to send daughters to college. The proportion of Catholic women in schoolteaching remained high; a very small number of Catholic laywomen had moved into college teaching (especially in Catholic women's colleges) during the 1930s.[36]

Two Massachusetts Catholic women reached out early beyond the classroom. At the turn of the twentieth century, Julia Harrington Duff (1859–1932), a former Charlestown teacher, wife of a physician, and a mother, was elected to the Boston School Committee, the first Catholic woman to hold that position. An 1878 graduate of the Normal School in Boston, she had been one of nine Irish Catholics in a class of fifty-eight. The proportion of Irish Catholics at the Normal School (over one-third by 1898) was growing, but the number hired for the city schools was diminishing, passed over by the Yankee school establishment in favor of Yankee women graduates of private colleges. That "tapped her store of resentment" against Yankee Protestant control of the schools, "and aroused her sense of justice."[37]

Duff believed in "Boston girls for Boston schools." Between 1901 and 1904 (when she was forced to leave the School Committee because of accusations against her brother, a school principal, possibly fueled by her opponents in the Protestant Public School Association), her primary goal was to win position and respect for Irish Catholics in the schools. Although her plan for a teachers college was not realized, the Normal School did add a voluntary third year for better teacher training, and began to admit men — both argued for by Duff. As Polly Kaufman notes, "For Duff the Boston schools were the place where her own children were being educated and she wanted to make sure their teachers gave them all the respect she believed the Harringtons and the Duffs deserved."[38]

In 1902 a second Catholic woman gained election to the School Committee: Mary Dierkes (1870–1950) was a young woman of German descent, a lifetime member of the Jungfrauen Sodalitet at the national German parish of Holy Trinity Church in the South End, and, rare in the circles of Catholic influence, a single woman. She had studied music in Europe, but returned to Boston in 1895 to take responsibility for her family during her parents' final illnesses. A supporter of Duff's positions on the normal school and local hiring, in her second year on the committee she became chair of the music committee; she ended a dispute over music textbooks and began a new experimental program for teaching music.[39]

Once the forces of progressive reform succeeded in their long-held goal of bringing professional management to the schools, the size and influence of the School Committee decreased. After Duff and Dierkes (end of term 1905), no Catholic woman served on the School Committee until 1950. Of the Catholic women who have served in the years since 1950, the most controversial was undoubtedly Louise Day Hicks (1916–2003), who served three terms on both the School Committee and the Boston City Council, and one term in Congress. In the 1960s she fiercely denied the (accurate) charge brought by concerned citizens, black and white, that the Boston schools were segregated by race. As founder of ROAR (Restore Our Alienated Rights) Hicks led the forces of opposition to court-mandated desegregation in the 1970s. She became a heroine to the forces of reaction, many of them Catholic South Boston women (as she was) who feared and fought against the busing of their children to schools outside their neighborhood. In a sad and terrible period in Boston and Catholic history, they also sought to intimidate the black children who were being bused into South Boston.[40]

Hicks was one of the most successful Catholic women in Massachusetts politics. There have been others, although primarily in municipal offices and on school boards; only three women have held statewide office, and only one (Shannon O'Brien, state treasurer from 1999 to 2003, the first woman elected to statewide office except for lieutenant governor, and Democratic nominee for governor in 2002) was raised as a Catholic. After Hicks and until the 2007 election of Nikki Tsongas, the only congresswoman from Massachusetts was Margaret Heckler (1931–). A Catholic and a Republican, Heckler was a graduate of Albertus Magnus College and the Boston College Law School (1956). She entered politics as a governor's councilor in 1962. She ran successfully for Congress in 1966 against Joseph Martin, an eighty-two-year-old longtime Massachusetts politician and former Speaker of the House, and served seven terms, losing in 1982 to Barney Frank. Heckler served from 1983 to 1985 as secretary of health and human services in the Reagan administration and as ambassador to Ireland from 1985 to 1989. Generally a moderate Republican, she was a supporter of the Equal Rights Amendment; subsequent to her retirement she was a speaker for pro-life groups.[41]

The study of law has become a favored option for women, and women's enrollment in law schools since the 1990s has burgeoned; in New England, law firms formerly unwelcoming to Catholic practitioners have opened their ranks to Catholic women and men, as have the faculties of prestigious law schools. Legal scholar and Learned Hand Professor of Law at Harvard Law School Mary Ann Glendon is "the highest ranking woman in the Catholic Church." Recipient in 2005 of the National Humanities Medal, in 2008 she assumed the post of U.S. ambassador to the Vatican, appointed by President George W. Bush. The first woman to be president of the Pontifical Academy of Social Sciences (appointed 2004 by Pope John Paul II) and a member of the Pontifical Council of the Laity, in 2005 she was the Vatican representative to the U.N. Conference on Women in Beijing, the first instance of a woman leading a papal delegation. Glendon holds traditional stances on matters of Catholic theology and morals; she is also an international human rights advocate. Her admiration for Eleanor Roosevelt's role in bringing about the Universal Declaration of Human Rights led to her 2001 book, *A World Made New: Eleanor Roosevelt and the Universal Declaration of Human Rights.* In a collection of essays called *Why I Am Still a Catholic* (1998), Glendon remembers feeling "liberated by Catholicism" when she was growing up in a small western Massachusetts town; seeing the church as a "woman's place," she particularly praises Pope John Paul II for having made it that.[42]

Women Religious

During the late nineteenth and early twentieth centuries, as Mary Oates has observed, hundreds of young women entered religious life and found opportunities for a more autonomous professional life than many of their lay contemporaries. The first order of sisters to come to New England were Ursulines. Founded by St. Angela Merici in Brescia, Italy, in 1535, with the then revolutionary idea that the sisters were not to be hidden in cloister but to serve in their community, by 1639 the order had come to North America. Recruited by Bishop Jean-Louis Cheverus from their Montreal house to open an academy for girls in Boston, a small group of Ursulines made the stagecoach journey to Boston in 1819. The drama of their victimization by a fierce anti-Catholic mob and the burning of their Charlestown convent in 1834 powerfully illustrates the risks that sisters faced as they ventured "on faith" into new worlds, in this case to an environment deeply suspicious of Catholics, very different in class expectations and in ethnic composition and sensibilities from the one for which their training had prepared them.[43]

Although the brilliant but difficult superior of the Charlestown academy, Mother Mary St. George (Mary Ann Moffat), returned to Canada in 1835 and subsequently disappeared from traceable history, a small number of Ursuline sisters tried to re-establish their school and convent in Boston after the Charlestown tragedy.[44] Their efforts proved unsuccessful, however, and they, too, returned to Canada. In 1946 Archbishop Richard Cushing invited them to return, and the Ursuline Academy in Dedham, Massachusetts (staffed primarily by lay faculty but still under Ursuline direction), continues to educate young women.

In early May 1832, at the invitation of Bishop Fenwick, three members of the Sisters of Charity — Sister Ann Alexis Shorb, Sister Loyola Ritchies, and Sister Blandina Davaux — came from their founding house in Emmitsburg, Maryland, to Boston. No woman has ever held authority equivalent to that of Bishops Cheverus, Fenwick, Fitzpatrick, and their successors. Nonetheless, as several commentators note, the known face of the church in Boston well into the twentieth century was that of Catholic women, especially that of the sisters — and most notably the daughters of St. Elizabeth Ann Seton (1774–1821, canonized 1975), the Sisters (later the Daughters) of Charity.[45]

Although they did not meet until Cheverus visited her in Emmitsburg. Maryland, in November 1810, the Boston bishop and Mother Seton had deep mutual respect, fortified by a long correspondence and by Seton's gratitude to Cheverus for his spiritual direction and support for her conversion. In 1805 her friend and mentor in the faith Antonio Filicchi had asked Cheverus to respond to her " 'scruples and anxietys [sic], for instruction, comfort, advice." In response, Cheverus assured her that she was "never for a moment a strong protestant. . . . I believe you are always a good Catholic. The doubts which arise in your mind do not destroy your faith, they only disturb your mind. . . . I would therefore advise your joining the Catholic Church as soon as possible, and when doubts arise, say only: I believe, O Lord, help thou my unbelief." On the reverse of the letter, Seton noted, "Bishop Cheverus first answer to an earnest entreaty for his advice — Entered the church immediately afterward."[46] Their correspondence, and Mother Seton's confidence in Cheverus's advice, continued throughout her life.

A free school for girls in the basement of their small Hamilton Street house and the opening in October 1833 of an asylum for orphaned girls were the beginning of an unparalleled history of devotion and care in Boston. In May 1882 the *Pilot* ran a lengthy account of the Sisters' fiftieth anniversary. The occasion brought an audience of eight thousand to Mechanics Hall and the audience was full of titled dignitaries from state and church. Archbishop John Williams paid tribute to the "noble" and "pious work so well inaugurated 50 years ago . . . work done in the silence of a religious home, by women the most retired and most modest to be found in this world." To remind the congregation of how much had changed, Bishop James A. Healy (of Portland) recalled the sisters' first public appearance, on June 25, 1832: "Here was a sight for Boston to look at. Three hundred children — and, remember, this was the whole Catholic population in children at that time — 300 walking in procession. . . . And all Boston turned out to look at them."[47]

Following the liberating rule of St. Vincent de Paul ("the parish church is their chapel, the streets are their cloister"), they harbored hundreds of orphans, cared for the sick in the Carney Hospital and at St. Mary's Infant Asylum and Lying-In Hospital and, Healy continued, "for seven years past have struggled through difficulties and privations . . . caring for those abandoned waifs of society that we call foundlings . . . received 3849 such infants; they have cared for 475 mothers. Most of these little ones die in infancy owing to the previous neglect which they have suffered, but they die under a care more tender than that which their natural mothers would have given them." They were a source of wonder, the angels in the city's house.

As Paula Kane has shown, under the ambitious leadership of Cardinal William O'Connell, early twentieth-century Catholic Boston developed a separate culture within the city, building schools, hospitals, charitable institutions, and organizations for laymen and women that established the authority of the hierarchy, satisfied the obligation of charity, and resisted the forces of Protestantism and secularism. The direction was set earlier, however, both as a result of the rapid growth of the Catholic population in the latter half of the nineteenth century and as a response to the virulence and persistence of anti-Catholic prejudice. From the time of the arrival of the Sisters of Charity and through the long episcopate of Archbishop John Williams (1866–1907), Catholic institutions proliferated, demonstrating women's skills as institution builders. Many religious orders responded to Williams's invitations to open new houses; they staffed homes for orphans, for destitute children, for working girls and for working boys, hospitals of several kinds, and, particularly, schools. The many institutions of the Sisters of Charity set the pattern.

As Bishop Healy noted, until 1857 the Sisters ran one institution, the St. Vincent's Orphan Asylum, although the free school continued for some years after its 1832 founding. (It was eventually turned over to the teaching order of the Sisters of Notre Dame de Namur.) Bishop Fenwick brought the first child to the Sisters, and he continued central to the work. At the incorporation of the asylum in 1843, he became president of the board of directors (composed of prominent Boston laymen), a role held also by his successors.[48]

By the 1840s, with the rapidly expanding immigrant population and especially in the wake of the cholera epidemic of 1852, the asylum population (only girls and only "full orphans," i.e., with no living parent) was growing steadily; the Sisters had constantly to balance their work of rescue with a search for adequate quarters. After nine years of hard work, of making do, and of persistent fund seeking, the asylum moved to adequate quarters (1841); they were soon crowded out, however. In 1857 children and sisters were able to move into a larger home at Shawmut and Camden Streets, which would be the home of St. Vincent's for some decades to come. The twelfth annual report (1855) of the board of directors lists eighty-one orphans and eight sisters; "twelve children have been placed in families, and there was one death." An 1864 report notes, that "in the past year about 325 Orphans have been cared for and protected within its walls." In 1870 there were 225 children, with 108 admitted that year. An 1869 debt of $13,000 had been reduced to $3,550, "through the liberality of the public, and the untiring energy of Sister Ann Alexis and her able assistants." By 1875 they had cared for, boarded, clothed, and educated 2,644 girls; the Asylum then held "some 230 girls."[49] Throughout, under the direction of the legendary Sister Ann Alexis (1805–75), the small number of sisters worked without wages; to keep the work going they depended on contributions begged from parishes that had turned children over to them, a few legacies, and especially the profits from the fairs that were an outstanding feature of Boston Catholic life.

Thirty-eight years after her arrival in Boston, and for some years after, Ann Alexis continued her remarkable life of administration and care of the ill and the poor. Model of Catholic fidelity, Ann Alexis was praised by a Boston reporter, interviewing her shortly before her death, as a "most remarkable lady, whose reputation as an able, efficient and untiring worker in the noble field of charity is widespread." Memorialized by her order for her "untiring energy, and unabating zeal,... humility, modesty, and patience," they also credited her for "the wonderful decrease of prejudice, and the consequent rapid progress of Catholicity" in Boston.[50]

Nursing

The birth of professional nursing came with Florence Nightingale and her work in the Crimean War. From experience, she came to insist that nurses must be trained rather than accepting the assumption that the ability to nurse was a natural part of women's endowment. The earliest nurses in the American Catholic hospitals were sisters of the founding order; their degree of formal training was at best uneven, but it is clear from the records that the Sisters of Charity, particularly those in authority, sought professional training. As medical care became professionalized, the sister-nurse became problematic. As the work of the Sisters at Carney, St. Elizabeth's, Holy Ghost, and other Catholic hospitals shows, they were dedicated and apparently indefatigable; nevertheless there was work that their status as consecrated women forbade, particularly in gynecological and maternity care.[51] Crucially, the professionalization of nursing and the need for Catholic hospitals to be professionally competitive demanded more, and hospitals, including Catholic hospitals, began to open schools of nursing in the years after the Civil War.[52] With the recognition that skilled nursing required more than just a good woman's touch, the process of professionalization began and opportunities opened.

Carney Hospital

By the 1860s, the needs of the Boston Catholic population and the Sisters of Charity's commitment and institutional expertise had led them to other important ventures, notably Carney Hospital, which was under their direction from its founding until 1996. Catholic philanthropist Andrew Carney (1794–1864) presented land and buildings on Dorchester Heights to Sister Ann Alexis and her Sisters to be used as a hospital; the first patient was admitted in June 1863. Unfortunately, Carney died before signing a codicil to his will that would have provided an endowment for the hospital; his bequest was generous ($75,000) but not enough to pay the cost of building a hospital. Thus Carney Hospital's history is one of long (and ongoing) struggles to fund it at the level of care and professionalism to which the sisters were committed. Despite the constant story of funding anxiety, however, Carney Hospital soon became an indispensable institution for its community.

Sister Ann Alexis remained as the hospital's director and superior until 1868; she had opened the hospital with a staff of five sisters. She was succeeded by Sister Aloysia Reed, whose brief tenure was marked by more financial difficulties but also by the building of an additional house on the South Boston property. Becoming superior in 1869, Sister Simplicia Rigney, an "excellent business woman with tremendous executive ability," managed to pay off $90,000 in debt and sustain operating expenses of $25,000 a year. A believer in "the importance of progress and medical achievement" and a trained and talented nurse, she strove to develop the professional medical staff.[53]

During the tenure of Sister Gonzaga McCormick as superior and hospital director (1890–1910), Carney inaugurated an outpatient care department, which continued to treat thousands of the area's needy ill. She was more than equal to the challenges of building a modern hospital: a doctor who had been on the Carney staff remembered her admiringly as "frank, outspoken, and so far as I could judge knew no fear. Her first interest beyond her religion was the Carney Hospital."[54] She faced challenges: an unfriendly legislative committee, evaluating Carney's request for its annual state appropriation of $10,000, visited in 1892, during a time of resurgent anti-Catholicism. The committee chairman warned her: "Sister, we are going to give you a close examination today; we have heard such hard things about the institution, but I guess you can stand it." She could: It was a "very trying ordeal.... The Committee inspected everything and everybody asking the ... patients if they were kindly treated, if anything was ever said to them about religion.... Thank God everything passed off well." She took strong stands on administrative issues, facing down the house officers who had threatened to resign over the appointment of a resident surgeon. Later, reflecting the tensions over hospital hierarchies and status, the medical staff threatened to[55] quit over her decision to place a sister in charge of the new nursing school; she accepted their resignations.[56]

Sister Gonzaga's sharpest challenge may have been Cardinal William O'Connell's determination to assert his authority over the hospital. On acceding to the episcopate in 1907, O'Connell had undertaken a fierce review of diocesan institutions and — especially with institutions run by women — sought to consolidate Catholic institutions under central authority. When he expressed his wish to be named president and treasurer of Carney, however, Sister Gonzaga pointed out that the administration of their houses was "under the Jurisdiction of our Superior General, as declared by the Supreme Pontiff again and again. Hence we could not, without infringing on his authority, elect your Grace President of our Corporation." Offering to send the cardinal an explanatory copy of "our 'Privileges and Indulgences,'" she concluded graciously but firmly with "the hope and assurance that you will always find the children of St. Vincent most obedient and loyal to your Grace and devoted to the interests of Your diocese."[57]

Naming the various institutions led and staffed by the Sisters of Charity provides the narrative of need in late nineteenth-century Boston. The Home for Destitute Catholic Children, to which social workers from across the city consigned the children of the streets, came under their direction in 1867 at Archbishop Williams's request. Inevitably, the abandoned and neglected babies who were the tragedy of the poor were also brought to the Sisters. St. Ann's Infant Asylum and Lying-In Hospital was incorporated in 1870 and remained within Carney for six years before a separate building was constructed. During that period, it cared for 1,465 infants and 328 unmarried mothers (to the dismay of Carney's widow, who had his body moved from the hospital site, thus depriving the sisters of an annual fee that they received for the care of the grave).[58]

Carney Hospital remained the property and the responsibility of the sisters for 133 years. In January 1997, a letter from Sister Louise Gallahue, provincial of the Daughters of Charity, to Friends of Carney Hospital, announced "with sadness that we will no longer sponsor Carney Hospital and Labouré College."[59] She had been assured that the new directors would maintain the sisters' "mission of serving the sick poor in Dorchester and the surrounding area." Remembering the "more than 300 Daughters of Charity" who had served at Carney, she reminded her readers that Carney had been unique in its blend of the " 'high tech' of the downtown teaching hospitals with the 'high touch' of the smaller community hospitals. It has reached out to the neighborhoods to meet the needs of the people where they live."[60]

The Home for Destitute Catholic Children eventually became Nazareth, a home for children in need of care either from poverty or from mental or emotional difficulties; it served sixty thousand children before closing in 1985. The *Boston Globe* ran an editorial, "More Than Foster Care," regretting its closing and that of three other Catholic residential centers for children and disagreeing with the state's position that foster family care would be preferable for children.[61] The increasing involvement of the state in child care may have been inevitable, but it is clear that it challenged the traditional belief of the church that "the poor belong to us."

St. Elizabeth's Hospital

St. Elizabeth's, the second major Catholic hospital in Boston, originated in 1868 through the efforts of "five pious ladies" (Ann McElroy, Ann Dolan, Margaret McNarney, Elizabeth A. Earling, and Anna Doherty) who organized a small hospital to provide care for "sick women and also to afford shelter, at reasonable rates, to retired or feeble women who had grown old in domestic service." The founders and their supporters sought incorporation in 1872; the document of incorporation specified that this would be a hospital for women. As the early history notes, within the first ten years the hospital extended "its service to practically every form of human ailment, while support from the charitable public seemed assured." With this success, the hospital decided to open its services to both men and women. In 1884 Archbishop John Williams invited the Franciscan Sisters of Allegany, New York, to take responsibility for care at St. Elizabeth's. The original founders became Third Order Franciscans and continued their service; in addition two Franciscan sisters, Mother Rose and Mother Bridget, came from New York to supervise the work of the hospital. Here (unlike Carney), the cardinal became hospital president; the directors were well-known Catholic laymen. From its original location in the South End of Boston, the hospital moved in search of space to develop; finally, in November 1912, Cardinal O'Connell broke ground for the hospital in Brighton, where — very greatly expanded — it remains. Reverend Mother Rose, "with certain of the sisters attached to the hospital corps," was in attendance at the groundbreaking. At the completion of the fundraising campaign of early 1914, she had been superior of the community and treasurer for thirty years, the only woman whose name appears in records of trustee meetings.[62]

The anonymous historian of the hospital emphasizes the care it offered for "women afflicted with ailments or diseases peculiar to their sex." Gynecological care was difficult to find in the general hospitals of the city (especially for the poor women whom St. Elizabeth's sought to serve); an 1893 report emphasized the founding of the gynecological department and noted that "many physicians prefer to send their gynaecological cases requiring operation to St. Elizabeth's Hospital." Logically, it also came into demand as a "Lying-in-Hospital," a service not then typically offered at general hospitals. The history also notes that its Obstetrical Department had "done much in establishing Caesarian section as a safe and suitable procedure." An outpatient gynecological department performed large numbers of operations, "which have not failed to draw upon us the eyes of the medical world as well as of suffering womanhood."

Although Carney and St. Elizabeth's hospitals provided the most visible care to the inhabitants of Boston, they were not alone. The Sisters of Charity of Montreal (known because of their habits as the Grey Nuns), founded by Marguerite d'Youville in 1738, opened Mary Immaculate Health/Care Services in Lawrence, Massachusetts, in 1868. More central to the history of Catholic health care, the order opened Holy Ghost Hospital as a hospital for incurables in Cambridge in 1895. The Grey Nuns took not only the usual vows of poverty, chastity, and obedience, but also a vow to serve "suffering humanity"; Holy Ghost Hospital (later named Youville) demonstrated that commitment into the late twentieth century. In 1986 the Grey Nuns restructured their U.S. States health care facilities as Covenant Health Systems. Subsequently, Youville Hospital became a rehabilitation and assisted living facility, as did the site of their former provincial house in Lexington, Massachusetts.

While hospital and charitable care was a major contribution of the religious to Boston's welfare for many years, only a small percentage of the hundreds of sisters were engaged in this area. Examining "Catholic Churchwomen in Boston" between 1870 and 1940, Mary Oates presents comparative data: of the 221 sisters in Boston in 1870, 27 worked in 4 hospitals and 54 in 6 asylums/homes while 102 taught in 11 parochial schools and 18 in 4 academies and boarding schools. In 1940 the distribution was slanted even more clearly toward education; of 4,164, sisters over half (2,606) were in (155) parish schools and 341 in (18) academies. The number of hospitals had grown from 4 to 6; 131 sisters worked in them. There was a more than fourfold increase in asylums and homes, from 6 to 27; they employed 383 sisters. With the increasing professionalization of medicine and the imperative for Catholic hospitals to maintain their reputation for care, there was need for more professional education than most sisters had time to undertake or orders had funds to finance; necessarily, the number of lay staff increased and nurses' training schools opened, first in general hospitals such as Massachusetts General and later in Catholic hospitals. Workloads remained herculean. In 1947 Cardinal Richard Cushing, having observed that no Catholic college had a baccalaureate nursing program, asked that Boston College open one. Initially sited in downtown Boston, the Boston College School of Nursing moved in 1950 to the Chestnut Hill campus.[63]

Higher Education

At the end of the nineteenth century women religious in many areas undertook a new mission — founding colleges for women. The colleges were a natural outgrowth of their work in the schools, but also, Mary Oates notes, a way to "right an injustice to their sex." In addition, the colleges would allow women religious to "move into a prestigious male-dominated profession and assume leadership roles."[64]

Emmanuel College

The first Catholic college for women in Boston was Emmanuel College, established on the Fenway by the Sisters of Notre Dame de Namur in 1919 in the tradition of Trinity College. The SNDdeNs had come to Boston in 1849: in addition to the many schools under their direction, they conducted a successful academy, sited on the Fenway in Boston from 1850 on. Under the leadership of Sister Helen Madeleine, they sought Cardinal William O'Connell's permission to open a college. Unlike other order-founded colleges, it was not to be a training school for the sisters; rather, they explained, it rose in "response to an urgent demand in Boston for a Catholic institution devoted to the needs of young women . . . who desire to pursue courses of advanced study in a Catholic college near their homes."[65] The cardinal agreed, with the understanding that he would maintain considerable oversight of the new institution. He did.[66]

Emmanuel's traditional liberal arts curriculum followed that of Trinity College, which drew in turn on the curricula of the earlier but still relatively new women's colleges — Mt. Holyoke, Vassar, Wellesley, Bryn Mawr, and Radcliffe. The goal was to transmit the "intellectual heritage and moral heritage of Western culture" within the context of church teachings and to ensure that the graduates would be "unquestionably" qualified. That required a strong faculty, in the sciences as well as in the humanities, at a time when graduate education for women religious was very rare. Thus, well before the sister formation movement of the 1950s, some Notre Dame sisters pursued graduate degrees. Sister Mary Edwina received an M.S. in physics from the Massachusetts Institute of Technology in 1929; she was the first woman religious to study there.

In addition to the sister faculty, diocesan priests (eleven in 1938) taught philosophy and religion, and lay persons joined the faculty in the late 1920s. Pay for the lay faculty was low (as it was in all of the women's Catholic colleges); Genevieve Steffy Donaldson, an early faculty member who was also an Emmanuel graduate, recalled, "We were not considered faculty. We did not attend faculty meetings. In fact we did not know when they took place." Primarily (though not all) women, many of the lay faculty at Emmanuel and at similar colleges understood their teaching as an apostolate and valued the sisters' devotion to the education of women; so they stayed despite low wages and few benefits. (It appears that some lay faculty donated their services.) As was true for all Catholic institutions, the sisters' salaries were returned to the college — a major fact in the history of their survival.[67] In the aftermath of Vatican II, however, and the shrinking number of available religious faculty, lay faculty had to be hired at competitive wages, costs went up, and many colleges founded by women religious had to close.

Emmanuel enrollment had risen rose from twenty-nine in 1919 to over three hundred in 1929. The college maintained enrollment in the three hundreds during the Depression years (with pastors sometime subsidizing parishioners' tuition) and was a popular choice for Boston-area Catholic women into the 1960s. With its urban setting, over the years Emmanuel attracted a student body of greater diversity than other local Catholic women's colleges, and its history demonstrates a concern for social justice. In 1934, not long after the opening of the first Catholic Worker house in New York, Dorothy Day was invited to speak. The students raised an honorarium from their one-dollar-a-year sodality dues and sent a collection of bedding and clothes to the Worker. In the 1960s students participated in the civil rights and antiwar movements and supported Cesar Chavez and the farmworkers' movement. By Friel's account they seem to have been more active than some of their colleagues in other Catholic colleges — perhaps reflecting the prophetic model provided by sociologist and Emmanuel faculty member Marie August Neal, SNDdeN. In the late 1970s Emmanuel also played a significant role in the burgeoning women's movement by offering a gathering place for an important conference. It included what proved to be a revolutionary panel on "Women and Their Bodies"; five of the eight panelists were cofounders of the Boston Women's Health Collective, the writers of the very influential *Our Bodies, Ourselves*.[68] In 1976 Emmanuel hosted a Women and the Church conference: urban minister Kip Tiernan, the founder of Rosie's Place, the first drop-in shelter for women in the United States, challenged the attendees: "If the system takes precedence over people we would do well to confront that system. Jesus did. Of course there are risks; there will always be risks. He took the ultimate one. What risks are we willing to take?"[69]

Emmanuel had added many new programs to its liberal arts curriculum over the years, but — like many women's Catholic colleges — it experienced a drop-off in enrollments beginning in the 1950s that accelerated in the 1960s and 1970s. Tuition dependent, seeking to maintain their historic commitment to educating women of limited means, affected by the loss of the donated services of women religious faculty in the wake of changes in the church after Vatican II, with limited endowments and limited alumnae giving, these colleges had to find innovative ways to survive.[70] Emmanuel responded by tuition increases and by developing programs to attract non-traditional women students. Like many comparable colleges, it established continuing education and graduate programs in health care, business administration, and education.[71] It also inaugurated a successful program in campus ministry. In the 1990s, under the leadership of Janet Eisner, SNDdeN, Emmanuel joined the consortium of the Colleges of the Fenway, an innovative plan to share resources and costs among six Boston colleges. Eisner also presided over ambitious campus expansion, including a new library and a modern science building supported by Merck Pharmaceuticals and used both by students and by Merck. Despite the innovative planning, Emmanuel continued to be affected by the national downturn in the enrollment of young women in single-sex colleges; an added significant blow to recruitment was the decision by Boston College (and other men's Catholic colleges) in 1969 and 1970 to admit women. Emmanuel remained a single-sex college through the 1990s; in the fall of 2000 Janet Eisner announced that Emmanuel would admit male undergraduates. Enrollments have risen subsequently.

Regis College

Founded by the Sisters of St. Joseph, Regis College had its origins in the same convictions and sense of need that lay behind other colleges founded by women religious: to provide young Catholic women with an education within their means that would make them good citizens and mothers and also equip them with usable skills. Recognizing a growing demand, Mother Domitilla, C.S.J., the "indomitable Domitilla," approached Cardinal O'Connell with the Sisters' plan for a college. Their abilities as educators were well proven: the order staffed large numbers of parochial schools and a successful academy (Mount St. Joseph Academy, founded in 1885). The

Demmon Morrison estate, on a beautiful 160-acre tract of land in the very Yankee town of Weston, had just come up for sale. The order was able to purchase the property (although there were Weston residents who were not pleased) and Regis College (named for Mother Mary Regis, the first superior of the order in Boston) opened in 1927 as a residential college for women. The *Pilot* welcomed it as the newest jewel in the crown of Boston Catholic institutions, helping to fulfill Cardinal O'Connell's vision of a city "where from every hilltop that sacred sign [of the cross] teaches its mighty lesson of patience and hope."[72] The article also notes that the faculty, all Sisters of St. Joseph, had college and university degrees; under Sister Domitilla's direction, sisters had been sent to Emmanuel and on to Catholic University to prepare for the opening of the college.[73]

The curriculum was traditional, but with opportunities in music and the arts (the order had its own symphony orchestra in the 1940s, with eighty members at its height); the residential option and the beautiful campus were also attractions. Pre-professional courses — home economics and business in addition to education — broadened the curriculum; the college also strove to offer strong science courses. By the time of Regis's sixtieth anniversary in 2007, programs to grant bachelors' degrees to nurses, continuing education programs, and expanding arts opportunities for the community had been in place for some time; increasingly, programs to prepare health care professionals had become a significant segment of the college's offerings. For reasons similar to those at Emmanuel, enrollment was a problem, however. Led since 2004 by its first lay president (Mary Jane England, M.D., a 1959 graduate), in the fall of 2008 Regis enrolled men at the undergraduate level for the first time. Admissions figures have risen in the first year of coeducation.

A significant part of Regis's history — the Lay Apostolate program founded and directed by English professor Sister John Sullivan, C.S.J. — was path-breaking. Originating in a "mission unit" begun by Sister John, Regis sent Marie McCormick ('50) to Guam in 1950, and from 1953 until Sister John's retirement, the program sent a total of over 250 young women graduates to teach and to establish schools in underserved areas of the United States, Latin America, and elsewhere. The papal mandate for "Catholic Action … the participation of the laity in the apostolate of the hierarchy" underlay the program's ideals: it invited young women to volunteer for a year or more to share in the teaching ministry of the church. Few of the students had teacher training or experience, but they had Sister John's faith that they could learn to teach, and, as the program went on, the experience of earlier volunteers to prove she was right. Between 1953 and 1966 Regis graduates worked in ten states (most in the South and the Southwest although a number went over several years to a frontier region of Alaska), seven countries in Latin America and three in the Caribbean, and as far away as Micronesia and Taiwan. In the early years of the program, when expectations for young Catholic women were still quite circumscribed, the Lay Apostolate provided the perfect combination of service and adventure.

Three other Catholic colleges for women opened in the Boston archdiocese in the second half of the twentieth century, none of which remain. Cardinal Cushing College in Brookline was established by the Holy Cross Sisters in 1952 and closed in 1972. The Sisters of St. Joseph opened two branches of Aquinas College, a two-year college offering business and preprofessional training to young women; Aquinas closed in 1999.[74] The last founded of the Catholic colleges for women in Boston, the more ambitious Newton College of the Sacred Heart (later known as Newton College), was opened in 1946 by the Religious of the Sacred Heart (R.S.C.J.) on land in Newton adjacent to their academy. The Sacred Heart tradition of academic education for young women within a rigorously Catholic setting and the order's prestigious social reputation were already well established: the R.S.C.J.s had opened academies across the United States since their arrival in 1849. Several Sacred Heart colleges were also in operation, notably Manhattanville just outside New York City.[75] Among many famous graduates of Sacred Heart schools were Rose Fitzgerald Kennedy and her daughter, Eunice Kennedy Shriver. Congresswoman Margaret Heckler was a Manhattanville graduate. Rose Fitzgerald had hoped to go to Wellesley College after her graduation from Dorchester high school, but Cardinal O'Connell reacted fiercely to the idea of the mayor's daughter attending a Protestant college. Honey Fitz capitulated, and Rose Fitzgerald enrolled at the Convent of the Sacred Heart in New York in the fall of 1907. In her second year, her father enrolled her in the even stricter Academy of the Sacred Heart near Aachen in the Netherlands, but she returned to graduate from the New York academy.[76]

Eleanor Kenny, R.S.C.J., in 1944 head of the Newton Country Day School of the Sacred Heart, remembered Newton College's beginnings: "I was startled by a sound. *'Adjutorium nostrum in nomine Domini'* came ringing up from the floor below. The voice was unmistakable." Cardinal Richard Cushing had burst in to tell her that the nearby "Schrafft property is being given to me. I will give it to you, and if you buy the Harriman estate [adjacent to the School] you can open a college in the finest location on the East coast. But the offer is only for a week. I must have my answer by then." She was cautious, but Cushing was determined and his enthusiasm eventually carried the day. It turned out that Cardinal Cushing was mistaken; the Schrafft estate had to be purchased. He donated $75,000; the order provided the balance. Newton College of the Sacred Heart welcomed its first students, a class of thirty-five, in the fall of 1946. The cardinal remained very supportive, and he also engaged the generosity of other prominent Catholic donors.[77]

The educational tradition of the Sacred Heart order permitted the recruitment of a well-trained faculty; the college also became known for its arts education. Ahead of its time, it encouraged interdisciplinary learning, encouraged students' involvement in social action, and supported such new programs as the Center for Women and Politics.[78] With the debts accruing from building a college, however — the number of campus buildings grew from the original three to ten by 1970 — Newton was more vulnerable than the older Regis and Emmanuel to the forces arrayed against Catholic women's colleges. It was forced to cease operation in June 1974 and merged with Boston College. Newton College students began to enroll at Boston College in 1974–75, furthering the process of women's undergraduate education that had begun with the founding of the School of Nursing in 1947 and the School of Education in 1952.[79] Earlier, women had attended classes in the city at Boston College Intown and the School of Social Work, and women — many of them sisters from local schools — pursued graduate study as early as the 1920s.[80] In 1970 the university became fully coeducational, and in 2006 Boston College announced that, with that year's commencement, the number of women alumnae exceeded that of men.

The impact of the thousands of graduates of Catholic colleges for women on the culture and economy of Boston and beyond is incalculable, as is their influence on the lives of families and of the church. Taught most often by women, in institutions led by women, these graduates have experienced women's efficacy, and it has had a positive effect.[81]

Women and a City in Crisis

Boston in the 1960s and 1970s was seriously troubled. The struggle over urban renewal and the displacement of the poor was a particular challenge for women. Importantly, and for a long period of time, Boston was marked by egregious failures of racial justice — institutional and individual. Longstanding economic inequalities, the denial of opportunities to African Americans, and the segregation of neighborhoods and schools became visible during the school busing crisis, especially in the lives of women. Mothers lined the streets to watch with anxiety as black and white children boarded buses and, in white areas of the city, to react with fury as black children got off the bus to go to school. When Cardinal Medeiros announced a strict policy limiting transfers from public schools to Catholic schools he was besieged by protests: mothers staged prayer marches, women knelt in the street, defiantly chanting the Hail Mary; he was attacked by those who felt "the church had failed her own." Some pastors disregarded the policy and allowed the transfers.[82]

The problems were not new: there had been a generally unassimilated African American population in the city since the eighteenth century, augmented by immigrants from Caribbean nations (often Catholic) and from Cape Verde and by the internal migrations of the 1930s and 1940s. The nineteenth-century Boston church had been distinguished by the presence of two distinguished African American priests, Rev. Sherwood Healy and Bishop James Healy, but concerns of racial equality were not an important subject of diocesan concern until the middle of the twentieth century.[83]

Cardinal Cushing spoke out on the sin of racism; he acceded, too, to requests from black Catholics for a church analogous to those provided for ethnic communities. When St. Richard's parish in Roxbury opened in

1946, the response was mixed: for many struggling to remove barriers a church for black Catholics seemed a reassertion of them. It became a vital community, however, enriched until the 1960s by a Mission Center directed by the African American Blessed Sacrament Sisters. Their founder, Mother (St.) Katherine Drexel, convinced that "Boston has the nucleus of a splendid work among their Colored people," sent three sisters to Boston in 1913; they opened St. Joseph's Mission in the South End.[84] The Mission was transformational for young people, as several interviewees in the Black Catholics Oral History Project attest. The sisters formed a choir and an award-winning Drum and Bugle corps; they also conducted family visits and provided after-school classes. Gertrude Townsend gives them credit for her success: "I did so well in teaching, working with the community and the children because of the background I got from attending the Blessed Sacrament Mission."[85] By 1956, however, Cardinal Cushing was questioning the future of St. Richard's; the Josephite fathers who had staffed it left in 1962, and the last Mass was said on December 13, 1964. The Oral History text notes sadly that the Blessed Sacrament Mission Center's property was taken by eminent domain in 1967; they then moved to St. Paul's parish in Dorchester. Some blacks attended other parishes in Roxbury and the South End, but the movement of economically more secure Catholics out of the city and into the suburbs decimated city parishes and resulted in primarily white suburban parishes. The accompanying need to build and staff schools in the growing suburbs had taken many teaching sisters out of the city.

The reactions of anger, violence, and "white flight" that met the 1974 federal mandate to desegregate Boston's schools exposed long-existing fault lines. Black parents and some white supporters had attempted for some years to right the racial imbalance in the schools and to ensure that the schools in the black areas of the city had the same resources as those in the white areas. Finally it had come to a federal order: black children from Roxbury were being bused into predominantly Catholic, Irish, and white neighborhoods — South Boston, Charlestown, Dorchester, and other, smaller sections of the city, and, despite the efforts of several individual laypersons and priests and strong statements on racial justice by Archbishop Medeiros, the level of racial antagonism in the white communities and among their supporters was fiercely destructive; it took a toll on the city and the church for many years.

There had been efforts for racial peace by Boston Catholics in the 1960s: a large group of Bostonians had gone to Washington for the 1963 march, carrying the banner of the Archdiocese of Boston; Robert Drinan, S.J., then dean of the Boston College law school, encouraged Catholic antiracist activism, and lay and religious joined demonstrations and marches, including the march at Selma. Members of the Boston Catholic Interracial Council (CIC, founded in New York in 1934 by John LaFarge, S.J.) had written to Cardinal Cushing in 1965, warning of a " 'crisis of faith' " among African American Catholics because of the attitude of white Catholics. "It is hard enough to be denied justice...but when that denial comes from fellow Catholics it is almost unbearable."[86] The CIC and others worked against resistance from parishioners and sometimes from pastors to educate Catholics in parishes and to give public witness to racial justice; in 1965 a racially mixed CIC group of women and men, including nuns and priests who had been at Selma, marched in the annual St. Patrick's Day parade in South Boston, to the loud displeasure of many parade watchers. The same year, women of the CIC attending a speech by Martin Luther King Jr. on Boston Common "arranged for African American members to hold white babies, and white members to hold African American babies."[87] As incidents of racial violence and hatred escalated over the following decade and the rifts among Boston Catholics widened, many Catholics, lay and religious, recognized the need to act. Two significant endeavors, the Association of Urban Sisters and the St. Philip's/Warwick House parish in the South End, importantly engaged the work of women.

In 1965, and with the establishment of a diocesan Commission on Human Rights, sisters joined eagerly in a renewed urban apostolate. Sixty-five sisters received permission to live in the city during the summer, to work with community and education programs. In 1968 a group of sisters who had been meeting with the Boston CIC decided to form the Association of Urban Sisters (AUS; an Association of Urban Priests had begun a few years earlier), with a focus on providing education programs for children in the city. Many of the sisters had previously taught in the city and had been caught up in the need to staff Catholic schools in growing white suburban neighborhoods. Approximately 70 sisters met first in late summer 1968; by fall their number was up to 160. A large number were members of the diocesan Sisters of St. Joseph, but several other orders were represented too: the Religious of the Sacred Heart, Sisters of Notre Dame de Namur, Sisters of Providence, and others. One of the founders was Caroline Putnam, R.S.C.J., an art faculty member at Newton College of the Sacred Heart (who would direct a closed-circuit TV initiative for AUS). Her parents (Caroline and Roger Putnam) had been generous supporters of education programs for black students.

Noted Catholic educator Patricia Goler (1929–94) agreed to become executive director of the AUS educational programs and guided their core education program, which worked with teacher training and curriculum development in five Boston Catholic schools. A 1950 graduate of Regis College, Goler had been the first black student there and the recipient of the Resident Scholarship for Colored Students, a scholarship given by the Putnams.[88] Goler received master's and doctorate degrees in history from Boston College and became a faculty member at Lowell State College (later the University of Lowell). Her significant work on school improvement and urban issues led to her appointment to the Archdiocesan Commission on Human Rights and the Archdiocesan school board; she was also one of the first two women appointed to the Boston College board of trustees. In a talk at Regis in the 1980s, Goler reflected on the changes she had experienced, from the sense of alienation within the church experienced by African Americans in her youth, through her work with AUS, in schools and parishes and through archdiocesan organizations, she "was never alone . . . I got and gave support. Sometimes it would seem that we moved too slowly; other times we appeared to move too hastily. Always, we had a common goal — the promotion of social justice in and by the institutional church."[89]

Sisters in AUS valued the support of others who shared their passion; they also brought sizable numbers of children into summer schools and programs. By the third year, as programs under other sponsorship were available, the number of sisters had begun to dwindle. The remaining members realized that they had become essentially a support group for each other, and the organization disbanded in 1973. In the years of its existence, however, the AUS had done very significant work for children in the city and had importantly been workers for reconciliation in a city torn by racial disputes.[90]

Prophetic Women

The history of two hundred years is replete with the stories of women who took risks in defense of and in advocacy for the faith. As a tentative conclusion, one can celebrate three contemporary women who are truly prophets: Dorothy Day, Sister Marie Augusta Neal, and Kip Tiernan, who came to her work through the urban ministry of St. Philip's parish/Warwick House.

In an attempt to reach across the gulf between city and suburban parishes, experiments in partnership between white suburban churches and churches in Roxbury and the South End had some successes. St. Philip's parish, known as Warwick House, was one of them from the late 1960s into the 1980s. Roxbury parishioners welcomed parishioners from Sacred Heart parish in Lexington and others who sought to combine their commitment to peace and justice with their faith. St. Philip's Church had fallen to the forces of urban renewal, and the parish had relocated in a house on Warwick Street in lower Roxbury. The priests resident there included members of the Milwaukee Fourteen, participants in the raid on the Milwaukee draft board, one of several such actions of nonviolent resistance to the ongoing war in Vietnam.[91] Among the women was former Sister of St. Joseph Anne Walsh, a member of the Defense Committee and also a part of the movement. She participated with the New York Eight in raids on draft boards in the Bronx and Queens in August 1969; she was also interrogated threateningly by police in February 1970 when she was in Philadelphia to support three draft board raids by members of the East Coast Conspiracy to Save Lives. Community leader, longtime passionate activist for justice, and Orchard Park resident Cynthia Harris and Lexington resident Miriam Donovan, who contributed long hours to draft counseling and to the support of young men threatened with being called to an unjust war, were among those for whom Warwick House was a place of community engagement and spiritual nourishment.

It was at Warwick House that Kip Tiernan came into her vocation when she joined the urban team ministry, "having decided that as a public relations consultant and advertising writer, my needs were not being met." It was during her years at Warwick House that she founded Rosie's Place, the first drop-in center and emergency shelter for women in the United States (1974). She recalls the times in *Urban Meditations:* "The explosive '60s and '70s created a new hope for disillusioned Christians, with the fresh breeze created by Pope John XXIII.... Although the 'inner city,' as Roxbury was called, was a war zone ready to happen, the beginning of the Civil Rights movement, coupled later with the antiwar movement, created a powerful moment in history." Tiernan and others, especially Fran Froelich, a former Sister of Providence who became Tiernan's partner in the founding of the "economic ministry" of the Poor People's United Fund, responded with new forms of the apostolate of hospitality that had characterized Catholic women's work, but also with rage at injustice and insistence on action for change. After Rosie's Place, she began the Greater Boston Food Bank, and, as she continued to seek alternatives for the marginalized, the Boston Women's Fund, Community Works, Health Care for the Homeless, and the Ethical Policy Institute. Tiernan and Froelich, and many others, have continued to speak out in rage, in anger, and in love and work against homelessness, economic inequality, violence, and the other sins against justice that continue to be a large part of the lives of the poor.[92]

Kip Tiernan frequently cites the importance to her of two other prophetic women's voices, those of Dorothy Day (1897–1980), founder of the Catholic Worker movement, and of Sister Marie Augusta Neal (1921–2004). Day began the conversation about the obligation of the church to the poor and the obligation of Catholics to change the injustices in which they lived. Like Seton, a convert and a mother, from the time of her conversion in 1927 Dorothy Day lived in voluntary poverty and in hospitality to the poor and suffering; she has inspired countless others through her actions and through her writing. Central to her Catholicism is the doctrine of the Mystical Body, the belief that all the members of the church belong to one body with Christ as its head. For Day — but also for many other women seeking their place in the church — this is the model of living for and in community.[93] There have been Catholic Worker houses in Boston since the early days of the movement; in 1966 Kathy McKenna founded Haley House in Boston's South End as a Worker house, which continues in 2008 to invite the poor for food and shelter and to provide the opportunity for thoughtful conversation about the theology of social change and for communal action to bring it about.

In Boston, other prophetic women's voices have called for justice.[94] Harvard-trained sociologist, activist, and longtime Emmanuel College faculty member Marie Augusta Neal had an immeasurably important impact on the discernment and profound changes among American sisters after Vatican II. Working with the Conference of Major Women Superiors (later the Leadership Conference of Women Religious), she devised the National Sisters Survey, a very long questionnaire that embodied the spirit of the Vatican II Decree on the Renewal of the Religious Life and, according to Mary Jo Weaver, helped to explain a key issue for the future: the "relation between religious belief and support for structural change."[95] Administered in 1967 to 139,000 American sisters (with a phenomenal 88 percent response), it opened an enormous conversation that led both to a greater understanding of what religious life might become, and also to many reassessments of vocations to the religious life. Some criticized it for asking "leading questions," such as those about participation in public protests. Forty years later, however, sisters recall the passionate attention they gave to the document, and the powerful and critical questions and discussions it created.[96]

Maria Augusta Neal understood the deep differences in the mission of religious women that had come with the mid-twentieth century. "In the nineteenth century...we brought the poor, the aged, the sick, the little children into our schools, homes, hospitals, and institutions and cared for them with a deep compassion....We approached the rich to subsidize our work and we loved them for their generous response....We faced two separate worlds. The poor whom we serviced as loving mothers, the rich whom we thanked...as our betters. We relieved pressing problems of the immigrant and outcast. We gave psychic support to the generous donor who was pleased that the good sister appreciated his gift."

But in so doing, "We built up huge establishments that so serviced the pressing needs of the society which created...these poverty patterns that ...our works, became indispensable to the *status quo*....We did this so intensely we never stopped to ask why these poor were poor, why these needy suffered."[97] She knew what must be done: those who benefit by society's inequities must commit to a "theology of letting go": "We have our hands on the resources of the world and we tighten our grasp as the poor reach out in their new liberation to take what is rightfully theirs. We need at this time to develop a theology of letting go so that as the poor reach out to take health, education, and welfare services we teach the graspers how to let go so the people can develop more human structures. It is this that the will of God affirms."[98]

Since 1974 the Paulist Center in Boston has given the Isaac Hecker Award to women and men who most represent the gifts of generosity and faith. The list includes Dorothy Day, Sister Marie August Neal, and Kip Tiernan — but also other prophetic women who have made the Archdiocese of Boston a more faithful place: Sisters Barbara Scanlan and Barbara Whelan, founders of Bridge Over Troubled Waters; Sister Rose Marie Cummins, who established Centro Presente to reach out to Central American immigrants and refugees; Sister Carole Rossi, founder in 1978 of the East Boston Ecumenical Community Council; Sister Lena Deevy, whose direction of the Irish Immigration Center expanded its work to serve all groups in need. Saying the names brings a reminder that behind each woman's names are hundreds more, unnamed, who have tried to keep the faith over two hundred years.

8

Changing Patterns of Parish Life

WILLIAM T. SCHMIDT

Growing up in Boston during the 1950s and 1960s, if someone asked you where you came from, you might readily respond "I'm from Gatey" or "I'm from St. Col's" or "I'm from M.P.B." Invariably the questioner would understand that you were from the neighborhood of Gate of Heaven parish, South Boston, or St. Columbkille parish, Brighton, or Most Precious Blood parish, Hyde Park. Catholic parishes defined the Boston neighborhoods and even non-Catholics were apt to identify their neighborhoods by reference to the Catholic church at the center of that particular neighborhood. My father grew up in South Boston. When he spoke of his teenage years as a member of the "Rosary Gang," it sounded remarkably pious to me until I learned that his group of friends hung out in the general vicinity of the former Holy Rosary Church on West Sixth Street. The parish was not only the center of the spiritual lives of Boston Catholics of that generation; it was also the center of their intellectual, philanthropic, and social lives.

The parish was the place where Catholics went dutifully to line up for Confession on Saturday afternoon in preparation for reception of Holy Communion at Sunday Mass. The parish was the place where Catholics went to celebrate the defining moments of their lives: baptisms, weddings, and funerals. The parish was the place where a family could go to get help with the fuel bill so that an empty oil tank could be filled in time for winter. Lay parishioners who were members of the Society of St. Vincent de Paul would respond readily and unobtrusively to the plight of any family in need. The parish was also the place where Catholics went for Scout meetings, CYO dances, adult socials, and parish bazaars. Roman Catholics are part of a Universal Church, but they experience church directly at the level of the parish. From generation to generation, Catholics have considered their parish to be a natural extension of their home and family.

For Roman Catholics, a particular church headed by a bishop is called a "diocese," but because a diocese is ordinarily quite large, a diocese consists of smaller units called "parishes." A diocese is actually a communion of parishes.[1] The term "parish" comes from the Greek word *parokein*, which describes "those living near or beside one another." A parish was seen as a community of Christians living in the same neighborhood. The Greek term had a secondary meaning of resident aliens or settled foreigners, which denotes the parish as the place where Christians related daily to those they

201

lived beside in this world, while also sharing with them membership in a community whose true homeland is in heaven, as pilgrims on their life journey.[2] Local Christian communities came to describe themselves in the very early years of church history as *parokia,* and the term was used in official church documents as early as the fourth century. While parishes continued to develop their particular identity throughout the Christian centuries, the sixth-century *Pastoral Rule* of Pope Gregory the Great was tremendously influential on parish life during the Middle Ages, establishing the expectation that every bishop, and by extension every pastor, should be "a man of personal holiness committed to preaching and the care of souls."[3]

> It took the cataclysm of the Protestant Reformation to shock the Church into a full-scale evaluation of parish life at the Council of Trent (1543–65). The Council made a valiant attempt to reform parish life and parochial structures, reaffirming the care of souls as the preeminent mission of the parish, but it placed particular emphasis upon the *benefice,* that is the office of the pastor and his right to receive the income of any endowment assigned to the parish. The Council of Trent emphasized the sacred responsibility of pastors for the spiritual well-being of their people.[4]

> The Council made preaching and catechetical instruction on every Sunday and holy day an obligation for parish priests, and also required them to provide sacramental and moral education for their people. It insisted that pastors maintain residence in the parish entrusted to them. Bishops were asked for the spiritual good of souls to assign the faithful within their diocese to clear and distinct parishes so that all the people will have pastors who will know them and from whom they may receive the sacraments.[5]

> Veering away from the original understanding of parish, however, the laity was relegated to a passive role, its main duty being unquestioning obedience to Church authority and its principal rights being the availability of the Sacraments and pastoral care. The impact of the council, praiseworthy in terms of what had preceded it, was a preoccupation with the parish as a juridico-geographical district of the apostolate, and not as the people of God or as a pilgrim community in which the Church is actualized.[6]

The Council of Trent, placing its emphasis upon the geographical territory of the parish along with the rights and responsibilities of pastors, dominated the Catholic understanding of parishes right down to the deliberations of Vatican Council II, which ushered in a renewed ecclesiology. This new ecclesiology referred to church less in terms of its institutional structure and more in terms of its primary identity as a community of the faithful that constitutes the People of God.[7] This shift in ecclesiology would focus attention on the parish as the community where priests and people assume their distinct and essential roles as members of the People of God. The contemporary definition of parish is "a community of the faithful established on a stable basis within a particular Church."[8] This reflects an understanding of the parish as a voluntary association of those who freely choose to affiliate with a particular parish. Catholics no longer consider parish membership to be determined by their residence within a geographical territory.[9] The automobile has provided a mobility for American Catholics to join the parish that they prefer.[10]

A Pilgrim People

The word "parish" in the New Testament scriptures denotes a sense of transience. The members of the earliest Christian communities saw themselves as pilgrims who did not claim citizenship in this world as they looked toward their true homeland in heaven.[11] The sense of parish as a community of pilgrims certainly resonates with New England as the land of the pilgrims. The parish has been a key component of New England society right from the beginning of the colonial period. The classic icon of the New England village places the traditional white-clapboard church with its weathervane-topped steeple as the focal point of a town common. The Pilgrim fathers who gathered as a body politic on the deck of the *Mayflower* on November 11, 1620, adopted the Mayflower Compact as a civil agreement to govern their lives as charter members of the Plymouth Colony. The strict Separatists among the settlers, however, were definitely more focused on the foundation of the first parish of Plymouth Colony that finally afforded them the freedom to worship God within the framework of their Separatist Puritan ideals. Their preeminent goal at the end of their long pilgrimage from England to Holland to the New World was an independent and self-governed parish within a protective civil order.

The foundation of the Massachusetts Bay Colony at Boston ten years later was centered in a similar way on the establishment of a parish, but this time in accord with the slightly less rigorous demands of the Puritan adherents who had not formally separated themselves from the Church of England. Sharing the Separatist motivation to purify the established Church of England of its papist traditions and practices, the Pilgrims and the Puritans were determined to establish their parishes as self-governed congregations without deference to the hierarchy of bishops that was continued by royal decree within the Church of England. The Pilgrim and Puritan founders of Plymouth and Boston established their parishes according to the Calvinistic ideal of the self-contained and internally governed community that posited full autonomy and authority within the local congregation, which enjoyed the right to call and dismiss its ministers as deemed expedient. While dissenters such as Roger Williams and Anne Hutchinson, coupled with the later establishment of the Anglican Church within the Massachusetts Bay Colony, brought some diminution of this unanimity of religious practice, the Congregational parish stood at the center of community life in Massachusetts well into the nineteenth century. The Pilgrims and Puritans gave way to successive generations of New England Yankees who influenced every sector of society within the Commonwealth of Massachusetts for three hundred years.

A Hidden Presence

It is not surprising that the lives of the earliest Roman Catholic residents of Massachusetts were greatly influenced by the traditions and practices of the Protestant majority that worshiped in the Congregational manner. The first Catholics in Massachusetts maintained a necessarily quiet, if not invisible presence within the wider community. From the time of the foundation of the colony right up until the period following the American Revolution, it was a civil offense for anyone to adhere to the tenets and discipline of the Roman Catholic Church. The prohibition of papist priests within the colony was treated with particular importance. The first-time offender might suffer exile, but a repeat offender might well risk the death penalty.[12] Probably in no other section of the country was there a longer or deeper tradition of anti-Catholicism. Not until 1820 could Catholics hold public office. This antagonism harkened back to the Reformation and more immediately to the exclusionary Puritan theology.[13] While there had been a Roman Catholic presence in Maine as early as 1604 and French Jesuits had carried on a fruitful mission to the Native Americans of northern New England throughout the seventeenth century, the Catholic presence in New England during the eighteenth century was minuscule, and it was an understandably hidden presence. Catholics did not need to add the rancor of their anti-Catholic Protestant neighbors to the other challenges of establishing new lives in a New World.

The Roman Catholics of eighteenth-century New England were scattered over a wide area and rarely had contact with a Catholic priest. They utilized the services of Protestant clergymen at the times of weddings and funerals and sometimes participated in Protestant worship services. Some, especially in rural areas, were gradually weaned away from their traditional Catholic practice to Protestant congregations.[14] Others held staunchly to their Catholic faith and patiently waited for the time when the sacramental ministrations of a priest would be available to them. There was little prospect, however, that this would happen at any point in the near future. The widely dispersed Catholic population of New England came more and more to equate the experience of church in America with the readily accessible Congregational parishes. That experience would in turn impact the manner in which later Catholic parishes in New England were established and maintained during the nineteenth century. The earliest Catholic parishes, in a nod to New England custom, developed most often from lay initiative and depended upon the commitment of the laity for their ongoing maintenance and continued growth.

Independence from Great Britain marked a watershed moment for the Roman Catholics in Massachusetts, who could finally emerge from the shadow of the Pilgrims and begin to establish a visible presence. The assistance that the Catholic nations of France and Spain extended to the American colonies during their War of Independence encouraged a gradual retrenchment from a longstanding and deeply rooted spirit of intolerance toward Catholics within most of the thirteen colonies. Maryland and Pennsylvania were the notable exceptions as freedom of religious practice for Catholics had been guaranteed in their colonial charters. During the War of Independence General George Washington made a strategic effort to quash the flames of anti-Catholic bigotry by his prohibition of the Guy Fawkes Day demonstrations, which afforded the Protestant majority within the colonies the opportunity to vent their anti-papist sentiments with the traditional burning of a straw-stuffed effigy of the pope. Washington knew that the rebellious colonies could ill afford to offend their new Catholic allies or their predominantly Catholic neighbor to the north and thus encouraged a process of gradual, somewhat begrudging tolerance of Catholics. This nascent spirit of tolerance continued after the War of Independence was successfully concluded.

As Boston became a regular port of call for French and Spanish warships and merchant ships during the years following the War of Independence, it was incumbent upon its citizens to welcome the representatives of the Catholic sovereigns who had come to the assistance of the American colonies during their time of need. French and Spanish naval officers, government officials, and merchants were feted at civic receptions and the homes of the leading families of Boston during the years following American Independence. Part of this hospitality demanded a reluctant willingness to allow for these Catholic visitors to avail themselves of the sacramental ministrations of Catholic priests during the time of their sojourn in Boston.

The first recorded Roman Catholic Mass in Boston took place on October 19, 1788, celebrated by a somewhat mysterious cleric who identified himself as L'Abbé Claude de la Poterie. He arrived as chaplain to a French fleet that anchored in Boston for a month of civic and private receptions between August 28 and September 28, 1788. When the French fleet sailed out of Boston Harbor at the end of September, L'Abbé de la Poterie remained behind as a deserter, which did not seem to be a matter of great concern to the commander of the French fleet! While L'Abbé initially saw little prospect of establishing a stable Catholic community in Boston that could support a full-time priest, he was convinced by a French merchant, M. Baury de Bellerive, to celebrate Sunday Mass for the small Catholic community on the last two Sundays of October in 1788. The Masses were celebrated at M. Baury's residence, which was quite close to the present-day Church of St. Joseph in the West End. The positive response of the Catholic community to this opportunity for Sunday Mass encouraged L'Abbé to stay in Boston. M. Baury was later commended by Father John Carroll, then the apostolic prefect of the American Missions, for his assistance in "promoting and encouraging the introduction of the divine service in Boston."[15]

L'Abbé de la Poterie proved to be instrumental in securing the provision of a former French Huguenot church at 18 School Street for the use of the small community of Spanish, French, and Irish Catholics in Boston. The first public Mass in Boston was celebrated on November 2, 1788, which would later be observed as the foundation date of Boston's Church of the Holy

Cross. Father Carroll extended a formal appointment and canonical faculties to L'Abbé de la Poterie with some relief that he was finally able to respond to the repeated requests of the small and scattered Catholic community of New England for the services of a priest. This approbation from Father Carroll unleashed a whirlwind of activity on the part of L'Abbé to properly restore the new house of worship that had fallen into some disrepair to make it a more appropriate venue for the Catholic liturgy. As part of this effort, L'Abbé convened a meeting of the Catholic congregation to solicit their support.

Two wardens were chosen from the community to assist with the management of the church property and finances. One of these wardens was M. Baury and the other was either Patrick Campbell or John Magner as representative of the Irish community. This was the beginning of a longstanding tradition of a lay vestry at the parish of the Holy Cross. This custom of lay participation in parish governance had already become an accepted practice in France and Germany and was becoming more accepted in England and Ireland.[16]

It seems that L'Abbé managed to overextend his improvements and provisions for the nascent Church of the Holy Cross and was soon enveloped in a bitter dispute with impatient creditors and embarrassed parishioners. Warning signals reached Father Carroll in Maryland that all was not well with the pastoral leadership of the Boston community, and after some unsatisfactory correspondence and a personal visit of L'Abbé to meet with Father Carroll, it was determined that L'Abbé would be relieved of his pastoral appointment to Boston effective May 20, 1789. It was shortly thereafter that Father Carroll learned from the archbishop of Paris that L'Abbé de la Poterie had only recently assumed his present name and had been earlier suspended from priestly ministry in France "in consequence of impropriety of conduct" and had actually initiated his ministry in Boston without valid priestly faculties. After some bitter complaining and scheming against Father Carroll, L'Abbé de la Poterie finally departed Boston, leaving the Catholic community once again without the services of a Catholic priest.[17]

The Catholic community in Boston took the initiative to recruit the services of another French émigré priest, Father Louis de Rousselet, and prevailed upon Father Carroll to transfer Father Rousselet from Philadelphia to the pastoral care of the Boston congregation. Boston's second resident priest arrived during early September 1789 and restored normal services at the School Street Church. There was to be little normalcy, however, in Boston's Catholic community during the ensuing months. L'Abbé de la Poterie returned to Boston from Quebec City in December to reassert his claim to the pastoral leadership of the Boston Catholic community, an action that would eventually lead to a schism within the community.

The division of the Boston Catholics over their loyalty to the two French priests intensified with the long-awaited and oft-delayed arrival in Boston of Father John Thayer, a Boston-born convert to Catholicism who had lingered long months in Europe following his ordination to priesthood and his assignment by Bishop Carroll to the pastoral care of the Catholic community in

Boston. The return of Father Thayer to Boston as a former Congregational minister of some repute generated a virulent campaign of anti-Catholic rhetoric in the Boston newspapers and in the pulpit pronouncements of Protestant preachers. Father Thayer's haughty and overbearing personality only exacerbated the division within the Catholic community. Protestant Boston looked on with bemusement as the tiny Catholic community at the Church of the Holy Cross was torn asunder by months of bitter rivalry among the three Catholic clerics.

The eventual departure of L'Abbé de la Poterie from Boston for the last time focused the dispute more squarely along ethnic lines as the French community supported the continued pastorate of Father Rousselet, while the growing Irish community preferred the English-speaking Father Thayer as its pastor. The public scandal of this bitter rivalry between the two priests and their respective factions impelled the newly consecrated Bishop John Carroll to remove both priests from Boston. The fledgling parish of the Holy Cross in Boston was left in an uproar, bitterly divided and once again without a priest.

"Where Two or Three Are Gathered in My Name"

A daunting pastoral challenge greeted Father Francis Anthony Matignon when he arrived in Boston on August 20, 1792, to assume responsibility for the pastoral care of the Catholics of Boston. It would demand the wisdom of Solomon and the patience of a saint to restore order and harmony to the parish of the Holy Cross — and just such a pastor was provided. Father Matignon was described as a "tactful healer of schism, gentle remover of prejudice, zealous pastor of souls, prudent administrator of pitifully meager church revenue, and builder of our first church,"[18] and it seemed that the Lord had finally provided the priest who was needed to set the Catholic Church of Boston on a solid foundation. Father Matignon had been forced to flee France for the safe refuge of England during the worst excesses of the French Revolution. He then accepted Bishop John Carroll's invitation to undertake a transatlantic journey that would bring him to Boston and the pastoral care of its struggling Catholic community. His humility, sincerity, and generosity quickly endeared him to Catholics and non-Catholics alike over the course of his twenty-six-year tenure as the head and heart of the Catholic community in Boston.

The arrival of Father Jean Lefebvre de Cheverus in 1796 to provide assistance to Father Matignon completed the pastoral team that would transform the Catholic Church of Boston from a struggling, humiliated congregation into a church with a hopeful future. Father Cheverus had first come to know and appreciate Father Matignon in Paris as a revered confessor during the time of his seminary studies. Cheverus followed Matignon across the English Channel to the safe sanctuary of French émigré priests in England. Four years later he followed him across the Atlantic Ocean to the Church of the

Holy Cross in Boston. Reunited in Boston, the two priests labored together harmoniously for twenty-two years as the true founders of the Catholic Church in Boston. The revered remembrance of the communal life of Fathers Matignon and Cheverus at the tiny rectory of the Holy Cross Church on Franklin Street is certainly evocative of the ideal of the primitive church described in the Acts of the Apostles: "they devoted themselves to the teaching of the apostles and to the communal life, to the breaking of the bread and to the prayers" (Acts 2:42). The simplicity of their lives, their mutual support, and their pastoral zeal would instill a sense of confidence and well-being in the Catholic community of Boston. The laity, who had become greatly concerned by the erratic behavior of L'Abbé de la Poterie and the division of loyalties among three rival pastors, finally came to entrust the pastoral care of their parish to revered shepherds who were deemed worthy of their confidence.

Thus began a period of welcome stability within the Catholic Church of Boston, a church that was singularly blessed by the pastoral solicitude of the two French émigré priests. Father Cheverus provided a zealous ministry to the Native American converts of the original French Jesuit missioners in Maine, while also attending to the far-flung Catholic communities that lived in relative isolation throughout the New England region. Father Matignon attended to the daily schedule of the parish in Boston and especially to the planning and construction of a proper Catholic church on Franklin Street, which was dedicated on September 29, 1803, by Bishop Carroll. This Church of the Holy Cross, whose architectural design was the gift of the noted federalist architect Charles Bulfinch, would serve as the first Cathedral for the Diocese of Boston from 1808 to 1860. The courageous and faithful ministration of Father Matignon and Father Cheverus to the victims of the contagious fevers that inflicted heavy death tolls upon the city of Boston during the late 1790s raised the image of Catholic priests appreciably in the eyes of Yankee Boston. The Catholic community basked in the glow of this growing appreciation of the esteemed caliber of its spiritual leaders within the wider community. "All exaggeration apart, when the town resumed its normal life the Catholics of Boston, with their clergy, found themselves already far removed from the odium and persecution of their previous history. They were an organized unit, under the saintly guidance of priests who had gained the respect, and to a large extent even the admiration, of their fellow citizens."[19]

While their earlier experience with L'Abbé de la Poterie might have made the lay leaders of the parish somewhat wary about investing much trust in their clerics for the supervision of the fiscal and temporal concerns of the Catholic community, there was a gradual growth in confidence at the turn of the century that the careful and prudent Father Matignon was providing a responsible stewardship for the limited resources of the Catholic community. While he continued to work in partnership with the wardens of the Holy Cross parish, there was every indication within the lay leadership that the temporal affairs of the parish were in good hands. The civil law in effect at this time required that property held in public trust, such as churches, be administered by the duly elected members of a vestry. Both Father Matignon and Father Cheverus respected this provision of the law. Certainly there was evident in the relationship of the pastors and trustees a deepening sense of mutual cooperation and trust. The pastors respected the role of the laity in the administration of the parish, while the laity also deferred to the advice and consent of their pastors. While conflicts between lay trustees, pastors, and bishops were emerging as major concerns within other Catholic congregations in the United States, there was a period of relative harmony and mutual trust between the clergy and laity of Boston, which was reflective of the high esteem of the laity for the integrity and devotion of their priests.[20]

April 8, 1808, marked the foundation date of the Diocese of Boston as Pope Pius VII published the brief, *Ex debito pastoralis offici*, raising the Diocese of Baltimore to the dignity of an archdiocese with Boston as one of its four suffragan sees. The new Diocese of Boston claimed one parish church, the newly designated Cathedral of the Holy Cross on Franklin Street. Three priests served the scattered Catholic population of the new diocese, which encompassed the entire territory of the six New England states. Father Cheverus had argued forcefully during the preceding years that New England was not yet able to sustain itself as a diocese and should instead be constituted as part of the jurisdiction of a new Diocese of New York. He accepted the appointment as first bishop of Boston with studied reluctance.

The diocese gained its second church on July 17, 1808, as Father Cheverus dedicated the Church of St. Patrick in Damariscotta, Maine, which stands today as the oldest Catholic Church in New England.[21] A third church would follow eleven years year later when Bishop Cheverus dedicated the cemetery chapel of St. Augustine in South Boston on July 4, 1819. Here he provided the final resting place for his beloved confrere, Father Francis Matignon, who had passed away on September 19, 1818, the fortieth anniversary of his ordination. St. Augustine cemetery chapel stands today as the oldest Catholic church within the current territory of the Archdiocese of Boston. Enlarged by Bishop Fenwick, it served as the worship site for the Catholics of South Boston until the dedication of St. Peter and St. Paul Church on lower Broadway in 1845.

What was the experience of the Catholics within the Diocese of Boston during the time of Cheverus and Matignon? First of all, most of the Catholics did not see themselves as being members of a local parish. The Church of the Holy Cross in Boston provided the pastoral care for the six states of the New England region. It was not a regular occurrence for most New England Catholics to travel to their parish church in Boston for services. Most Catholics did not see a priest on a regular basis. The native Americans at Old Town and Point Pleasant in Maine, along with small Catholic communities in Maine, New Hampshire, and Massachusetts might receive a visit from a priest once or twice a year. For the rest of the time, the Catholics would do the best they could to maintain their Catholic faith and practice in the absence of priestly service. As reported by the Catholic community at Damariscotta, Bishop Cheverus prepared the lay leadership of the community to coordinate Catholic devotions when a priest was not available. Aware that the faith of this group could not survive in such an isolated atmosphere unless faithfully practiced, Cheverus directed pointed epistles to each community concerning their Sunday obligation when a priest was not available:

> Have charity for all men, pray for the salvation of all, do good to everyone, according to your power, whatever may be his religious persuasion, but never forget that you belong to the Roman Catholic Church of Jesus Christ, and that it is unlawful for you to attend the public worship of any other persuasion. Obey, like dutiful children, the laws of your mother the Holy Church; keep the days of fasting & abstinence, etc.
>
> Every day, say your prayers on your knees, morning & night with attention and devotion.
>
> Every Sunday meet all together, if possible, read in the morning the prayers & instructions for Mass with at least one chapter in the poor man's catechism, & in the afternoon some of the prayers appointed for Sundays with another chapter in the same book.
>
> Moreover let everyone of you learn & recite every Sunday something out of your Christian Doctrine, so that you may know the whole of it perfectly & never forget it. Take care to be well prepared for confession and for receiving the Blessed Sacrament, against the next time that you will have a Catholic priest with you.[22]

The spiritual welfare of the scattered Catholic communities of New England was thus dependent upon lay leaders who implemented the program established by Father Cheverus for the community during the major portion of the year when a priest was not available to provide the sacraments.

The death of Father Matignon in 1818 presaged the return of Bishop Cheverus to France after years of vacillation between his love for France and family and his devotion to his fledgling Diocese of Boston. It finally took a royal edict to uproot him from Boston to take possession of his new diocese in France. Bishop Cheverus set sail for France on September 26, 1823, after taking leave of his devastated flock in Boston. After a brief tenure as bishop of Montauban, Cheverus came to the end of his life journey as cardinal archbishop of Bordeaux, but he always held a special place in his heart for his little flock in Boston.

The personal goodness and pastoral solicitude of Bishop Cheverus left a lasting mark on the city of Boston, which had taken the French émigré priest to its heart. Dr. Annabelle Melville, in her definitive biography of Bishop John Lefebvre de Cheverus, described his impact in this epitaph: "The power of one man in his own time should not be underestimated. And if the influence he exerts is direct enough, flowing unimpeded from a pure heart and a zealous soul, he does, in the end, change history."[23] Bishop John Cheverus and Father Francis Matignon established the Catholic Church in Boston upon a firm foundation.

A Proliferation of Parishes

When Bishop Benedict Fenwick arrived in Boston as the second bishop of the young diocese just before Christmas in 1825, he observed in his journal that he had inherited a diocese, which although comprising all six New England states, contained only eight churches, "all of which with the exception of the Cathedral scarcely deserve the name."[24] It would be the mission of Bishop Fenwick to construct upon the foundation of Matignon and Cheverus the parish infrastructure that would be needed by a steadily growing Catholic community. Cheverus and Matignon experienced their ministry as pastors of a very large parish, which encompassed New England. Fenwick arrived in Boston with a well-considered sense of his particular mission as a bishop for a church that was just beginning to experience the first significant waves of Catholic immigration from Ireland and Germany. The diocese desperately needed churches to accommodate the new arrivals. Fenwick attended immediately to a long-postponed enlargement of the Cathedral of the Holy Cross on Franklin Street and the completion of the Church of St. Mary in Salem. He also initiated building projects for St. Mary's Church in Charlestown, St. Patrick Church on the border of Roxbury and the South End, and the Church of St. Patrick in Lowell, as well as two churches named for St. John, one in East Cambridge (now Sacred Heart) and one in the North End of Boston (now St. Stephen) and three more churches named St. Mary — in the North End of Boston, Waltham, and Quincy.[25]

> The vital element in the development of American Catholicism was the parish. Between 1780 and 1820 many parish communities were organized across America. Perhaps as many as 124 Catholic parishes dotted the landscape in 1820, and each one represented a community of Catholics. In the vast majority of these communities laymen were involved in the government of the parish as members of a board of trustees. The principal reason for such a trustee system was the new spirit of democracy that was rising across the land. In Catholic parishes it meant that laymen wanted to have more control over their parish churches.[26]

As the number of churches grew, so did the number of lay vestries attached to those churches.

Some of Bishop Fenwick's most difficult moments in Boston were connected to the emergence in his new diocese of the trustee issues that had plagued other dioceses in the country much earlier. Father Fenwick had already been personally engaged in one such situation in Charleston, South Carolina, with the trustees of an Irish parish who refused to accept a French archbishop's appointment of a French pastor and asserted their demand for the appointment of an Irish pastor. Father Benedict Fenwick, S.J., was dispatched by Archbishop Marechal to deal with the controversy in Charleston, which demanded all of his personal powers of persuasion and diplomacy. Bishop Fenwick thus arrived in Boston already somewhat wary of lay trustees holding title to church property and exerting control over church finances as well as the appointment of pastors. He moved immediately toward implementing a diocesan policy that all parish property should be held in the name of the bishop. There were a number of instances that would test his patience during his twenty-year tenure as bishop. His resolve would be reflected in the stipulation of the First Provincial Council of Baltimore in 1829 that bishops should hold the title to church property and that the right to appoint pastors, claimed by some trustees, was to be reserved to the bishop.

The parishioners of St. Mary's parish in the North End created quite a stir in Boston in 1834 as the parish divided into two hostile parties supportive of two different priests who were serving as its co-pastors. This division erupted into a near riot during a Sunday evening Vespers service when a number of parishioners vented with loud protestation their unwillingness to accept the bishop's transfer of one of the co-pastors. This demonstration impelled Bishop Fenwick to place the parish under interdict, effectively closing the church for two weeks. The bishop eventually transferred the remaining co-pastor and appointed the recently ordained Father (later Bishop) John Fitzpatrick as pastor to restore some order to the parish.[27] Bishop Fenwick recognized the need to encourage lay initiative in the establishment and maintenance of parishes, but he also recognized the importance of the legitimate prerogative of the bishop and pastor to exert ultimate authority in parochial matters.

This was a time when most parishes were established through lay initiative, as the Catholic community in a particular locale purchased the property, made plans for the construction of a church, and then petitioned the bishop for a priest to serve as pastor. The initiating agent in the new industrial city of Lowell, however, was actually a non-Catholic, Mr. Kirk Boott of the Boston Associates, who had constructed and operated the first textile mills in Lowell. He was concerned with the incessant, often-times violent quarreling of rival Irish factions in Lowell which regularly disrupted the work camps. The inhabitants of the shantytown called "The Acre" were primarily migrants from Cork and its environs, while the nearby "Half Acre" was home to those who came from Connaught or the West Country of Ireland.[28] Boott recognized the potential for a Catholic parish to become a stabilizing force in Lowell as it provided for the spiritual needs of the burgeoning Catholic community in the so-called paddy camps. Boott entered into negotiations with Bishop Fenwick to provide company-owned land for the construction of a Catholic Church midway between the two rival camps. St. Patrick Church was dedicated by Bishop Fenwick on July 3, 1831. Wary of establishing more parishes with trustee issues, Fenwick insisted that the title for the property be placed in his name.

St. Patrick Parish Lowell would later prove to be a vexing venue for Fenwick in his determination to maintain episcopal control over pastoral appointments in the face of sometimes monumental opposition from the laity. In 1836 Fenwick appointed Father David McCool as pastor, described by archdiocesan historians as "an unfortunate man suffering from mental derangement." His personal issues were exacerbated by a quite public display of an intemperate affection for alcohol.[29] Nevertheless, Father McCool enjoyed the deep affection of many members of his flock and Fenwick's decision to replace him as pastor was met with such dissatisfaction that some parishioners locked the doors of the church to prevent the new pastor from taking possession. Not to be deterred, the redoubtable Father James McDermott managed an unceremonious climb through a window and unfastened the church doors to begin his tenure as pastor. The parishioners finally relented and accepted their new pastor, but one can only imagine the reaction of Bishop Fenwick when he heard reports of this rather unorthodox installation of a duly appointed pastor.

Bishop Fenwick also received the first petition for the establishment of a national parish as German immigrants began to arrive in Boston in significant numbers around the same time as Bishop Fenwick. Three brothers, Melchior, Sebastian, and Mathias Kramer came to Boston as clockmakers in 1827 and began to organize the German Catholic community as early as 1829. The Germans found Bishop Fenwick to be a solicitous friend as he welcomed them to worship at the Holy Cross Cathedral and personally provided some preaching in their native tongue. Fenwick was receptive to the petition of the Germans to establish their own parish and dedicated their first church in 1844 toward the end of his episcopate. During the early efforts to establish a German parish in Boston, there was constant wrangling between the High Germans and Low Germans, reflective of two distinct dialects of the German language within the congregation. A succession of pastors tried to bring some sense of unity of purpose to the divided German community, which must have sorely tried the patience of the bishop on numerous occasions.

The Germans, unlike the Irish, immmigrated to the United States with a tradition of lay involvement in parish administration and the appointment of pastors that was already familiar to them. "Independence, self-government, and a community closely bound together by consenus were trademarks of the German hometown."[30] Some of the most intense trustee controversies in the United States were hard-fought battles between German parishes and Irish bishops. The German population in Boston was never very large. The Holy Trinity parish represents the only longstanding German national parish within the Archdiocese of Boston. The relentless challenge of German Catholics to the control of their parishes by Irish bishops never reached the same dimension in Boston as in New York, Philadelphia, and the Midwest.

Convinced of the importance of the parish in the smooth transition of immigrants to a new homeland, Bishop Fenwick envisioned the foundation of an idyllic Catholic community for Irish immigrants in the remote environs of Aroostook County, Maine. He established "Benedicta" as a wholesome alternative to the teeming tenement districts of the North End and the Boston waterfront for the destitute Irish immigrants who arrived in Boston in ever-increasing numbers. Fenwick recognized the unhealthy sanitary conditions and the spiritual dangers of the tenement districts and saw the prospect of a self-contained community of Irish immigrants ensconced in a rural setting as a preferable alternative. Fenwick's initiative was reflective of other utopian community experiments of his day, like the Brook Farm community in West Roxbury. Fenwick set before the Irish immigrants the prospect of gainful employment, healthful housing, educational opportunity, and spiritual support. Fenwick took the initial steps in the construction of "Benedicta" with the completion of a sawmill, school, and church. He soon realized, however, that the Irish who had been driven from their homeland by the agrarian woes in Ireland were not eager to return to the vagaries and loneliness of a rural setting. The day-labor opportunities and the close-knit society of the city were preferable to an isolated existence in rural Maine. Bishop Fenwick reluctantly abandoned his project and moved on to other projects, which included the foundation of the College of the Holy Cross in 1843.

While there were only eight Catholic churches within the diocese at the time of Bishop Fenwick's arrival in 1825, there were established during Bishop Fenwick's tenure more than fifty parishes within the assigned territory of the Diocese of Boston, a territory significantly reduced by the establishment of a new diocese for Connecticut and Rhode Island in 1843.[31] The Fenwick era was punctuated by some of the most virulent anti-Catholic demonstrations in the history of American Catholicism, most notably the burning of the Ursuline Convent in Charlestown by a nativist mob on August 11, 1834. An exhausted Bishop Benedict Fenwick passed away on August 11, 1846, the twelfth anniversary of this nadir point of his twenty-year tenure as bishop of Boston.

Parishes as Sanctuaries

When John Bernard Fitzpatrick succeeded Bishop Fenwick as the third bishop of Boston in 1846, his greatest challenge was the construction of even more churches to accommodate the burgeoning Catholic population of Boston. At the onset of the potato famine in Ireland, during the single year of 1847, the city of Boston, which had been absorbing immigrants at the rate of four or five thousand a year, was overwhelmed by over thirty-seven thousand new arrivals. Most of these new arrivals were unofficially categorized as "laborers," which was understood to be descriptive of the destitute and physically debilitated new Irish immigrants in distinction from the healthy, skilled refugees who had arrived in more restricted numbers during the earlier decades of the nineteenth century.[32] Bishop Fitzpatrick turned to the parishes and their priests as his primary means to respond to the needs of the new immigrants, who were predominantly Catholic. His overriding concern was the provision of parish churches and pastors to assist them in their assimilation into an alien culture. Their unease with the unfamiliar democratic government and the Protestant culture of Yankee Boston would be offset by their recognition of the parish as a familiar institution that could ease their transition to life in the United States. The Catholic Church was responsive to the needs of the new immigrants, building churches in the neighborhoods in which they settled and representing a familiar reality within a strange environment.[33]

Bishop Fitzpatrick successfully petitioned for two new dioceses to be created in Maine, New Hampshire, and Vermont in 1851. His diocese numbered ninety-five churches at that time, which represented an increase of forty-seven over the course of the previous seven years.[34] The Diocese of Boston was now delineated for the first time by the territory of the Commonwealth of Massachusetts, with sixty-three churches in the state and nine Catholic churches in the city of Boston.

The parish became the religious and social center of Irish immigrant life.[35] Clustering in the older and poorer sections of the cities, the Irish became objects of fear, scorn, and ridicule for the established American community. Fear of the effects that such large numbers of Irish immigrants would have on American society resulted in a marked increase in a nativist invectives during the years leading up to the Civil War. Catholic Boston held in fresh and painful memory the burning of the Ursuline Convent by a nativist mob in Charlestown on August 11, 1834, and the Broad Street Riot precipitated by a nativist attack on a Catholic funeral procession on June 11, 1837. The emergence of the even more vehement anti-Catholic rhetoric of the Know-Nothing Party in the 1850s placed the Irish Catholics of Boston in a situation in which they felt like a people under siege by the social, economic, religious, and political community that surrounded them. Bishop Fitzpatrick successfully cautioned his flock that they must not respond violently to the provocative attacks of nativists, who sought to confirm the prevalent opinion that the Irish were an inherently lawless, dangerous, and violent people. At the same time, Fitzpatrick encouraged his people to organize night watches during times of increased tension to prevent destructive attacks on Catholic churches and institutions. The Catholics of Boston definitely experienced themselves as a people under siege during the latter part of the nineteenth century, when walls of separation were constructed between Yankee Boston and Catholic Boston.

The number and size of Catholic parishes of Boston grew considerably during this period, but Catholic Boston itself maintained a quiet presence as a society parallel to the dominant Yankee Boston. Bishop Fitzpatrick and Archbishop Williams proved to be helpful bridges between the two cultures as their early education in the Boston Public Schools and cordial relations in later years with former schoolmates made them surprisingly accepted and highly esteemed within Brahmin society. For the most part, however, the Catholics in their parishes lived separate lives within the wider world of Yankee Protestant Boston. The parish was experienced as a refuge and safe sanctuary within a hostile environment. It was the supportive community of the neighborhood parish that enabled the Catholic immigrants to survive and eventually prosper in their new homeland. Some of the church architecture of this period, especially the new Cathedral of the Holy Cross and St. John's Seminary, evinced a stolid, fortress-like appearance that would bring some sense of security to a people living under siege.

The tenures of Bishop Fitzpatrick and Archbishop Williams seem to blend smoothly from the third bishop of Boston to the fourth bishop of Boston as

Father John Williams stepped in as early as 1857 to assist Bishop Fitzpatrick in his deteriorating state of health. He assumed increasing responsibility for the diocesan administration right up until the time of his succession to the See of Boston upon the death of Bishop Fitzpatrick in 1866. There were 109 parishes within the Diocese of Boston when John Williams began his forty-year tenure as bishop, a period when the parishes grew larger and the pastors grew more influential within their communities. Legendary pastors dominated the neighborhoods of their parishes and the lives of their parishioners.

The priestly career of Father James Fitton assumed legendary status as he established myriad mission centers that grew into parishes in Rhode Island and Connecticut, as well as throughout central and western Massachusetts, before he assumed a twenty-six-year pastorate of St. Nicholas parish (later Most Holy Redeemer) in East Boston in 1855. He brought the same unbridled energy to the East Boston community that had marked his earlier missionary career. His parishioners extolled his virtues on a granite monument erected at Holy Cross Cemetery in Malden after the death of this pioneer priest on September 15, 1881:

> Long a missionary throughout New England. He labored with zeal for the spread of Catholicity and erected many churches to the glory of God. Twenty-six years pastor of Most Holy Redeemer parish, East Boston and an early supporter of Catholic schools. He had a large and benevolent heart, especially devoted to the youth of his flock. Beloved by all and loving all.

Father Manassas Dougherty served as pastor of St. John's parish (later Sacred Heart) in East Cambridge while attending to Catholics in a wide arc of towns adjacent to Cambridge that included Arlington, Lexington, Medford, and Woburn. Father John O'Brien succeeded Father Dougherty and built an impressive complex of buildings at Sacred Heart parish, East Cambridge, while also founding a parish magazine, *The Sacred Heart Messenger,* which garnered a wide national readership until Cardinal O'Connell demanded its suppression as a rival publication to the archdiocesan-owned *Boston Pilot.* Another Father John O'Brien established an "O'Brien Line" of pastors, which provided perduring leadership for St. Patrick parish, Lowell, for more than half a century.

Father John McElroy, S.J., served as the first Jesuit pastor of St. Mary's parish in the North End before he took up his pivotal role in the construction of the Immaculate Conception Church in the South End of Boston and the founding of Boston College on the same property in 1863. Father John Roddan began his tenure as pastor of St. Mary's parish, Quincy, in 1848 with pastoral responsibility for a major portion of the present-day South Region of the archdiocese. He proved to be personally instrumental in the establishment of St. John's parish, Quincy, as well as parishes in Weymouth, Randolph, Abington, Stoughton, Cohasset, and Hingham. What is most remarkable about all of his pastoral achievement is that Father Roddan accomplished it while also serving as editor of the *Pilot*.[36]

Father Peter Ronan became pastor of the newly created parish of St. Peter in Dorchester when Father Bernard McNulty of St. Gregory parish ceded the northern section of Dorchester to this new parish, which would eventually spawn five daughter parishes of its own. Father Ronan was twenty-eight years old when in 1872 he was appointed founding pastor of St. Peter's parish by Bishop Williams. He constructed a cathedral-like edifice that bespoke the message that "the Catholics are here to stay" as it loomed above the colonial-era, white clapboard First Parish Church on the Dorchester town common. Father Ronan himself would dominate the North Dorchester neighborhood for a pastorate of half a century. Henry Towle, a parishioner, declared of Father Ronan on the occasion of his sixtieth Jubilee of priestly ordination: "Great emperors have preserved their memory by colossal tombs. A great priest has chosen better in leaving as his monument buildings which by perpetuating his memory as long as they stand, shall be used for the eternal salvation of all succeeding generations."[37]

The pastors of the territorial parishes were complemented by an extraordinary group of pastors who established the national parishes (later called personal parishes) that served the immigrant communities that arrived in Boston during the late nineteenth and early twentieth centuries.

Father Ernest Reiter, S.J., brought some measure of harmony to the Holy Trinity German parish, and a succession of Jesuit pastors would lead this parish in the completion of a magnificent stone church in the early German Gothic style, which cost this erstwhile bankrupt congregation well over $150,000. Father Francis Xavier Nopper, S.J., played a pivotal role as pastor from 1877 to 1892 in the provision of three Catholic grammar schools at different sites in South Boston, the South End, and Roxbury, along with a girls high school in Roxbury, as well as a poorhouse, an orphanage, and an old age home (the Altenheim) in Roxbury. Holy Trinity parish provided its parishioners with services from womb to tomb as the German section of Holyhood Cemetery in Brookline testifies. German language and traditions were carefully preserved with special attention to Christmas customs such as Christmas trees, Christmas cards, Christmas caroling, and the crèche.[38] Puritan Boston, which had eschewed the "pagan papist debauchery" and "drunken revelry" of Christmas celebrations from 1620 until the mid-nineteenth century, gradually came to embrace the celebration of Christmas through the influence of the Germans at Holy Trinity Church, which came to be popularly considered Boston's "Christmas Church." Many Jesuit vocations from the Archdiocese of Boston were sons of Holy Trinity parish. Their gravestones at the Jesuit cemetery in Weston display a panoply of German surnames that were familiar at Holy Trinity parish, but were never reflected in great numbers within the ranks of the diocesan clergy of Boston.

The second wave of non-Irish immigration began in concurrence with the beginning of the forty-year tenure of John Williams as bishop of Boston with a significant migration of French Canadians into the industrial cities of Lowell, Lawrence, Haverhill, Lynn, Salem, Marlboro, and Brockton. The

French Canadians came with a tenacious will to maintain their language and traditions in order to preserve their faith. "Qui perd sa langue, perd sa foi"[39] became the rallying cry of the French Canadian Catholics. Like the Germans, the French recognized the importance of maintaining the familiar language and customs of an immigrant people if they were to maintain their Catholic faith in their new homeland. The genesis of the French national parishes depended upon the ready response of the Oblates of Mary Immaculate and the Society of Mary (Marists) to the plea of Archbishop Williams for French-speaking priests to staff parishes in the Merrimack Valley. There would ultimately be twenty-one French national parishes established within the Archdiocese of Boston. The French parishes built churches that looked like cathedrals as if to say to the Irish parishes surrounding them, we can place our churches side-by-side with yours and feel proud.

The Portuguese migration to the Boston area was also concurrent with the succession of Archbishop Williams to the See of Boston in 1866. As with so many immigrants, the first place of concentration for the Portuguese community was the North End of Boston. The Portuguese shared with the Italian Catholics the former Free Will Baptist Church, which was procured by the archdiocese and dedicated as the Church of St. John the Baptist. Father Anthony Joachim Pimental would provide a strong anchor for the Portuguese Catholic community for half a century. He would follow the shift of the Portuguese population from the North End to Cambridge and East Boston. There would eventually be six Portuguese national parishes in Cambridge, East Boston, Lowell, Lawrence, Gloucester, and Peabody serving a vital community of Portuguese people of enduring faith. There were also a number of Portuguese chaplaincies attached to territorial parishes. A special joy of the Portuguese Catholic community was the dedication of the new St. Anthony Church, Cambridge, on June 18, 1980, by Humberto Sousa Cardinal Medeiros, a native son of the Azores.

The Italian immigration to Boston began during the final years of the nineteenth century. Between 1898 and 1910 more than 150,000 Italians settled in Massachusetts. The first Italian national parish was situated in the North End, an area recognized as the cradle of national parishes for the Archdiocese of Boston. The parish of St. Leonard of Port Maurice was staffed by the Franciscan Friars of the Immaculate Conception province with Father Joachim Guerrini as the founding pastor. Archbishop Williams would subsequently experience his only trustee controversy during his prolonged episcopate when a group of parishioners at St. Leonard parish formed the San Marco Society with the express intention of establishing an alternative Italian parish in North Square in Father Taylor's Seamans Bethel, a former Methodist chapel for seafaring men, that would be established under the *fabbriceria* (trustee) system they had known in Italy. Archbishop Williams was not happy with the desertion of parishioners from the Franciscan parish and would absolutely not consider establishing a new parish unless the property was deeded unconditionally to the archbishop of Boston like all other properties in the archdiocese by that time. The impasse was finally resolved through the intercession of the Pious Society of the Missionaries of St. Charles (Scalabrini), who convinced the San Marco Society to cede the title to the archbishop. They also agreed to staff the new parish, which celebrated the dedication of Sacred Heart Church on May 25, 1890.[40] Eventually fourteen Italian national churches would come to grace the Archdiocese of Boston. The Italian societies of the North End organize colorful festivals in honor of their patron saints each summer to the delight of Italians and non-Italians alike.

The Polish Apostolate began in 1893 in the North End with a meeting of Polish Catholics at a hall on Hanover Street. The pioneer of the Polish parishes, Rev. John Chmielinski, petitioned Archbishop Williams for permission to attend to the pastoral care of the Polish Catholics. He soon turned his attention to the large Polish community on the border of Dorchester and South Boston, where the first Polish parish was established and the Church of Our Lady of Czestochowa was dedicated on November 18, 1894. Father Chmielinski addressed the needs of Polish Catholics widely scattered throughout the area and played an instrumental part in establishing five new Polish parishes between 1903 and 1906. There would eventually be fourteen Polish parishes within the Archdiocese of Boston. A special point of pride for the Polish Catholics of the archdiocese was their privilege of welcoming Cardinal Karol Wojtyla to Boston twice prior to his election as Pope John Paul II in 1978.

The early Lithuanian immigrants in the United States fraternized easily with the Poles and often joined them in founding and maintaining parishes. Historically, religiously, and culturally very closely connected with the Poles, but later separated from them by a determined effort to establish their own national identity, Lithuanians in the United States were encouraged to separate themselves from the Polish parishes and to establish parishes of their own language and culture. Father John Zilinskas was the founding pastor of St. Peter's parish, South Boston, the first Lithuanian parish in Boston. It would later be joined by sister parishes in Brockton, Cambridge, Lowell, Norwood, and Lawrence.

The final set of national churches established during the Archbishop Williams era were the Maronite and Melchite Churches, which celebrate the Byzantine Rite in union with the Holy See. The Maronites were originally established in the South End in 1899 as the Church of Our Lady of the Cedars of Lebanon, which later moved to a larger facility in Jamaica Plain. Additional Maronite parishes would be established in Lawrence in 1903 and in Brockton in 1932. The Melchite community was originally established in Lawrence in 1896. The Eparchy of Newton of the Melchite Rite would later be established at the Cathedral of the Annunciation in Roslindale.

"The initiative and expense of founding or enlarging parishes, both territorial and national, were frequently carried by the laity. Archbishop Hughes of New York pointed out that American Catholicism was uniquely established by the laity and not the clerical missionary coming to convert a pagan population."[41] The motivation of the laity in the mid-nineteenth century for the foundation of new parishes in their hometowns was the long distance that they usually needed to travel to attend Sunday Mass. In the 1850s, for example, the Catholics of Hingham had to walk many miles to the nearest church in Quincy or Weymouth.[42] The Catholics of Newton, Wellesley, and Needham traveled by horse-drawn wagon or by foot to St. Joseph Parish, Roxbury, until the establishment of the Parish of Mary Immaculate of Lourdes in Newton Upper Falls in 1870. The Catholics from Stoneham, Wakefield, and Reading made the long trek to St. Mary's Parish, Charlestown, for many years until the more accessible Immaculate Conception Parish, Malden, was established in 1854. It was a challenge and a sacrifice for the Catholics of this era to fulfill their Sunday Mass obligation. The round-trip excursion took up the better part of their Sunday.

The late nineteenth-century pastors were larger-than-life figures who built imposing churches, along with rectories, schools, and convents. The parish plants became the center points of their neighborhoods. While Bishops Fitzpatrick and Williams encouraged the construction of simple churches that would not attract inordinate attention from Yankee Boston, some parishes constructed architectural marvels that proudly proclaimed the presence of the Catholic Church in Boston.

> Magnificent churches could be seen for miles around. It mattered that St. Francis de Sales Church in Charlestown raised its spire "on a par with the Bunker Hill Monument" and that the dome and twin spires of Mission Church "could dominate the skyline of Roxbury." The fact that St. Peter's in Dorchester occupied a "commanding presence" with a 150-foot tower "visible out to sea" announced to the Yankees that the Irish were here to stay. For people crushed economically and despised for both their religion and ethnic origins, such visibility became a psychological necessity. The financial respectability that they could not achieve as individuals could be simulated collectively through their churches. Even the Catholic critics of monumentalism recognized the powerful compulsion to appear affluent. In a Yankee society that equated wealth with virtue, a few opulent churches seemed necessary. The squat "school churches" of other dioceses, utilitarian but ugly, would never do in Boston.[43]

The new Cathedral of the Holy Cross in the South End was consecrated by Archbishop Williams on December 8, 1875, just seven months after he received the pallium as the first archbishop of Boston with New England as his province. The construction plans for the cathedral reflected the conflicted views of the church leaders of the time concerning the statement that church architecture made to the wider community. "The plan for the building was drawn along impressive lines, and the grand scale was deliberate," according to historian James O'Toole.

> Anti-Catholic and anti-immigrant sentiments were still a very recent memory in Boston, and construction of the new cathedral could signal the end of one era and the dawning of a new one. Some bricks from the ruins of the Ursuline convent in Charlestown, destroyed by a nativist riot in 1834, were included in the arch over the front door, but the scale of the structure would speak more loudly of the permanence and success of the Roman Catholic Church in spite of opposition.

The rector of the cathedral, Father James Healy, liked to point out to his parishioners that

> the spires would become, with the exception of the gilded dome of State House, the most prominent object of view for miles around.[44]

Perhaps indicative of the reluctance of Archbishop Williams to upset Yankee Boston, the towering spires of the new cathedral were never completed.

While Bishops Cheverus and Fenwick were viewed directly and personally by earlier generations of Catholics as the pastors of the entire Boston Catholic community, the greatly increased number of Catholics in the nineteenth century and the subsequent proliferation of parishes meant that Catholics now related routinely to the pastors of their own parishes as the early Catholics of Boston had related to their first bishops. It was the pastor who was generally considered to be the best educated and most influential figure in the neighborhood, and the people of the parish came to depend more and more upon his judgment and guidance in the myriad concerns of their daily lives. The parishes became personal fiefdoms to many of these pastors, who ruled their parochial domains with a strong and confident hand. Bishop Fitzpatrick and Archbishop Williams did not tend to impose administrative decisions from the center, allowing pastors the freedom to make the decisions they deemed best for their parishes. Bishop Fitzpatrick and Archbishop Williams saw themselves as active pastors of the cathedral parish working in close communion with the pastors of the other parishes. The laissez-faire administrative style of the nineteenth-century bishops would later be strongly censured by Cardinal O'Connell.

The combined tenure of Bishop Fitzpatrick and Archbishop Williams represents an important bridge between the first bishops of Boston and the bishops of the twentieth century. Bernard Fitzpatrick and John Williams were the first Bostonians to serve as bishops of Boston. They were both born in Boston and were baptized at the old Cathedral of the Holy Cross on Franklin Street during the tenure of Bishop Cheverus. Their vocations to the priesthood were nurtured under the careful tutelage of Bishop Fenwick within the cathedral parish. Their reserved, genteel personalities enabled them to become useful bridges between Catholic Boston and Protestant Boston during the second half of the nineteenth century when a great expansion of the Catholic population took place. They maintained careful watch over the city during that volatile period of transition for immigrants and for longtime Boston residents. They neutralized a number of dangerous situations that might have engaged the Catholic and Protestant communities in hostile confrontations. Archbishop Williams also served as a bridge within the American church as the great conciliator among the various factions of American bishops during the Americanist controversy. Archbishop Williams passed away peacefully at the cathedral rectory on August 30, 1906, and was entombed in the crypt of the Cathedral of the Holy Cross alongside Bishop Fitzpatrick.

A Catholic Culture in Boston

The centennial celebration of the Archdiocese of Boston in 1908 found the Catholic Church in Boston flexing its new-found muscle as Catholics were entering into a new era of influence in the public sector and near dominance in the political sphere. The election of successive Irish Catholic mayors of Boston at the beginning of the twentieth century marked a transition from Yankee Protestant to Irish Catholic dominance of the city government. Archbishop O'Connell proclaimed with great satisfaction at the October 28, 1908, Cathedral celebration of the diocesan centenary, "The Puritan has passed. The Catholic remains." This was a new and exhilarating experience for the long-suppressed and cruelly maligned Catholics who now held their heads high as they entered into positions of power and influence that had been jealously guarded as the preserve of Brahmin aristocracy.

William Henry O'Connell was appointed coadjutor archbishop of Boston on January 22, 1904, and took formal possession of the archdiocese on January 29, 1908, after the death of Archbishop Williams on August 30, 1907. The number of parishes in the archdiocese had nearly doubled to 194 during the Williams era. While Archbishop Williams was described as "reserved, silent, distantly polite and adverse to all publicity,"[45] O'Connell arrived in Boston like the roaring lion, which would become a familiar statuary addition to his grandest building projects. O'Connell began his tenure as archbishop of Boston with the pronounced intention of raising the profile of the Catholic Church in Boston.

The appointment of William O'Connell has been characterized as a response from Rome to the Americanist controversy that had pitted conservative prelates such as Archbishop Michael Corrigan of New York and Bishop Bernard McQuaid of Rochester against the more liberal Americanist prelates in the persons of Bishop John Ireland of Minneapolis–St. Paul and Cardinal James Gibbons of Baltimore. The Americanists wanted the church in the United States to be "radically different from what it had been in the Old World. It had to be open to the uniqueness of its new milieu and reflect that milieu. For these clergymen this definitely meant more democracy in a church whose bishops had become increasingly authoritarian."[46] Working closely with his Vatican allies, Cardinal Merry Del Val and Cardinal Francesco Satolli, O'Connell strove to restore the influence of Rome in the affairs of the American church. He emerged from the fray victorious in his new appointment as archbishop of Boston and as the great defender of the prerogatives of the Holy See. O'Connell's well-honed skills of *Romanità*, derived from his years of study and service in Rome, helped to assure Vatican hegemony in the administration of the American church, while also serving O'Connell's personal ambitions for advancement in the hierarchy.[47]

The strengthening of Roman supervisory authority over the local autonomy of the American bishops found its corollary in O'Connell's determination to diminish the autonomy of his local pastors and transfer much of their authority to the curial offices of the archdiocese. Donna Merwick chronicles this progression in *Boston Priests, 1848–1910: A Study of Social and Intellectual Change*.[48] After extolling the intellectual brilliance and administrative acumen of the impressive pastors of the Williams era, Merwick characterizes the early years of the O'Connell era as a carefully planned campaign to wrest authority from the local pastors and bring it under curial control. There was significant resistance to this effort on the part of the pastors, but by the end of his first decade as archbishop, O'Connell managed to shift the base of power in the archdiocese from the parishes to the chancery. While the attitude of the parishioners would not change greatly, as they continued to view their pastor as the ultimate authority, the pastors would learn to be careful to defer to the supervisory authority of the archbishop in the administration of their parishes.

There were still some extraordinarily resolute and independent pastors during this era, such as Monsignor Richard Neagle of Immaculate Conception, Malden. Monsignor Neagle was a former chancellor of the Archdiocese of Boston and a local favorite to succeed Williams as archbishop. Monsignor John P. Carroll grew up in the Immaculate Conception parish, Malden, during his pastorate and recalled that "in the minds of the parishioners, the hierarchy consisted of Monsignor Neagle, the Pope and the Cardinal in that order."[49] Monsignor Neagle gave nominal assent to Cardinal O'Connell's new directives that restricted the authority of the pastors, especially in the areas of the expenditures of funds and construction of buildings, but he managed to continue to hold sway as master of his own domain. Cardinal O'Connell was unpleasantly surprised to read in a newspaper account one morning of Monsignor Neagle's construction of a new boys high school at Immaculate Conception parish (later Malden Catholic) that would be staffed by the Xaverian Brothers. This was the first that O'Connell had heard about the project. When confronted by O'Connell for his failure to seek permission for this undertaking, Monsignor Neagle responded in a deliberately casual way: "As they [that is, the Xaverians] are already in the diocese, I assumed your approval, but it is no harm to ask it formally."[50] O'Connell had little choice but to extend his blessing to the new high school, but he was sorely reminded that after twenty-five years as archbishop he still had not managed to get all his pastors under control. Pastors would never again, however, be as free from episcopal control as the pastors of the Archbishop Williams era. This meant that the laity was now one step further removed from the sphere of influence and decision-making within the church of Boston. As time went on, the younger clergy would be less inclined to challenge O'Connell in any manner because of a well-based fear of later recrimination in the arena of priestly preferment and pastoral appointments.

Cardinal O'Connell sought to diminish the authority of his most influential pastors by the reduction of the size of their parishes and the creation of smaller parishes where, O'Connell asserted, a pastor could hope to know all of his parishioners by name. Many new parishes were carved from the mammoth parishes of the nineteenth century during the O'Connell era. Typical of this development was the appointment of Father James H. O'Connell (no relation to the cardinal) to the pastorate of a new parish in Hyde Park in 1938. Father O'Connell, fresh from an extended tenure as senior curate at St. John the Evangelist parish in Swampscott, went hat-in-hand to the pastors of St. Angela parish in Mattapan, Most Precious Blood parish in Hyde Park, and Sacred Heart parish in Roslindale to ascertain the particular streets that they were willing to cede from their territories. These pastors gave careful consideration to retaining their most generous benefactors in determining which streets would be relinquished to the new parish. Father O'Connell then visited every Catholic family within his assigned territory and invited them to become members of the new parish. Mass was celebrated during the early days of the parish on the upper floor of an old mill with oil-soaked floors and walls freshly white-washed by parish volunteers. A simple chapel was soon constructed as a temporary St. Joseph Church in a sparsely inhabited area that would see the rapid development of single-family homes over the ensuing years. Finally, a permanent church was dedicated on April 19, 1956, by Archbishop Cushing. The stated intention of Cardinal O'Connell was fulfilled as St. Joseph parish, Hyde Park, remained small enough that Monsignor O'Connell knew every parishioner by name and was well acquainted with the particular situation of each parish family during a tenure as pastor that spanned thirty-four years from 1938 to 1972. Cardinal O'Connell increased the number of parishes in Boston to 325 over the course of his episcopate, an increase of 131 parishes.

The term "megachurch" might be of recent vintage, but it accurately describes the Catholic parishes in Boston during the period of the two World Wars, separated by the Great Depression. Unprecedented numbers of Catholics attended Mass, confessed their sins, and participated in popular devotions at an ever-growing number of parish venues. The laity found its opportunity for active participation in the church in lay societies such as the Holy Name Society, Our Lady's Sodality, the Society of St. Vincent de Paul, and the Legion of Mary. There was a spiritual, apostolic, and social dimension to each of these parish societies that afforded the laity the opportunity to assume positions of leadership within the parish community. This was also the period of the great flowering of the elements of devotional Catholicism that had been imported from Europe with the nineteenth-century immigrants and were now implanted as key components of lay participation in the life of the church: Forty Hours Devotion, First Friday Masses, the Stations of the Cross along with a wide range of novenas focused on the Sacred Heart of Jesus, various titles of the Blessed Mother, and especially popular saints such as St. Anthony, St. Francis Xavier, St. Rita, and St. Therese of Lisieux.[51] Thousands of people thronged Mission Church each Wednesday for the Novena to Our Lady of Perpetual Help. The scapular, the rosary, and the miraculous medal became staples of the devotional life. Catholic culture in Boston was as readily accessible as the air you breathed.

From the Cities to the Suburbs

The appointment of Archbishop Richard Cushing as the sixth bishop of Boston following the death of Cardinal O'Connell on April 22, 1944, co-incided with the end of World War II and the postwar migration of the newly emerging Catholic middle class from the cities to the suburbs. The educational opportunities afforded by the G.I. Bill enabled Catholics in significant numbers to secure college degrees and to gain access to professional careers that were unimaginable for their parents and grandparents. There were also home loans available for veterans, which enabled young families to leave the triple-decker homes of their youth as part of a massive migration to the suburbs. Rural towns that had been safe and secure Yankee havens for generations now witnessed the rapid construction of Catholic churches and schools, while the ultimate brick-and-mortar bishop, Cardinal Richard Cushing, constructed a gleaming Catholic infrastructure of new central high schools, colleges, hospitals, shrines, and social service institutions that extended the visible presence of the Catholic Church from its traditional urban enclaves to the suburban communities.

The Cushing era was punctuated by gigantic Catholic spectacles such as the Holy Name Holy Hours that filled Fenway Park and Braves Field during the years following World War II. The CYO Parade in 1948 was an enormous undertaking that involved hundreds of parishes in the preparation of colorful floats and the recruitment of parish contingents of marchers. The parade garnered more than sixty thousand young people, who marched through the Yankee bastion of the Back Bay in a procession that took eight hours to pass the reviewing stands. All of this took place before more than a million spectators at the same time that the Red Sox were taking on the Cleveland Indians at Fenway Park in the World Series.

The Catholic Youth Organization was emblematic of the tenor of the Cushing era. Monsignor John P. Carroll coordinated a multifaceted program for the young people in parishes and Catholic high schools to fill the leisure time of Catholic youth with wholesome and productive spiritual, social, cultural, and athletic activities. Father Peter Hart developed a CYO Program at St. William parish, Dorchester, that rivaled the activity level of many diocesan programs, including an impressive newsletter that was published by the teenagers. Hundreds of basketball, baseball, softball, and hockey teams competed in CYO Leagues across the archdiocese. Catholics followed with eager interest the high drama that unfolded on the CYO Page of the *Boston Pilot* each week as Father Edmund Sviokla's upstart band from St. Thomas Aquinas parish, Jamaica Plain, managed to pursue and eventually dethrone the perennial championship band from St. William parish, Dorchester, under the direction Dominic Bianculli. Father J. Joseph Kierce of St. Kevin parish, Dorchester, orchestrated a spectacular CYO Week each fall in South Suffolk I Deanery. It included a deanery convention, a Holy Hour, and a "King & Queen Ball" at the Bradford Hotel, which offered a cotillion for the more formally clad couples representing their parishes as well as a record hop for the hundreds of teenagers who came to join the festivities. The Search for Christian Maturity retreats introduced thousands of teenagers to the experience of a spiritual retreat.

The waning years of the Cushing era were also the years of Vatican Council II (1962–65), which ushered in a rapid and radical transformation of the manner in which Catholics practiced their faith at the parish level. The liturgical changes of the 1960s had actually been presaged by the earlier liturgical movement that began with Pope Pius X and continued through the first half of the twentieth century. Pope Pius X transformed Catholic Mass practice with his encouragement of frequent reception of Holy Communion, a marked departure from a long period when Catholics attended Mass regularly, but received Holy Communion infrequently and then only after confessing their sins the day before to present themselves worthy at the Communion rail.

Following the National Liturgical Week Conference that took place in Boston in 1948 the parishes of the archdiocese stood at the forefront of the implementation of liturgical reform during the 1950s, particularly the Dialogue Mass, which invited the congregation to give voice to the Latin responses that had been formerly reserved to the altar servers. Few parishioners were really prepared, however, for the dramatic liturgical changes of the late 1960s that translated the Latin text of the Mass into English, turned the altar around so that the priest faced the people, and invited lay participation in the liturgy as lectors and extraordinary ministers of Holy Communion. The parishioners were encouraged now to "full, conscious and active participation"[52] in the liturgy in contrast to their earlier stance as passive participants in a mysterious ritual that was followed silently with the assistance of the English translation in their well-worn Latin missals. The Eucharist took place within the sacred confines of the sanctuary as the privileged domain of the priests and servers. One might consider with wonder today the graceful transition of priests who had celebrated the Latin Mass of Trent for forty years and then kept step with the church in the implementation of the *Novus Ordo* of Pope Paul VI in 1970. It is evident today that the liturgical reforms of Vatican II were implemented much too quickly before priests and parishioners were properly prepared for the changes, but it is a testament to the faithful parishioners of that era that the implementation of such radical changes in centuries-old Catholic practice occurred as smoothly as it did.

As Cardinal Cushing strode slowly and painfully down the center aisle of the Cathedral of the Holy Cross on October 9, 1970, at the installation of his successor, he raised his crimson biretta above his head and tipped his hat to the Catholic Boston that had known some glorious days and was entering upon challenging times. Cardinal Cushing's death, less than a month later, on November 2, 1970, marked the end of a remarkable era.

New Challenges in the Cities

The appointment of Humberto Sousa Medeiros as the seventh bishop of Boston on September 8, 1970, took place within a major transition period in the social, political, and religious order of Boston and the nation. The Vietnam War and the Watergate scandal left the American people with a pervading sense of distrust of institutional authority. The court-ordered busing of schoolchildren within the Boston public schools would accelerate the rate of "white flight" from urban neighborhoods during the 1970s, and many once-flourishing parishes in the Boston neighborhoods found their congregations reduced to such a degree that they struggled to pay their bills. The financially strapped archdiocese assisted parishes as best it could to maintain a Catholic presence in the inner-city neighborhoods, but Cardinal Medeiros was also struggling mightily to pay off the $48 million debt that he inherited from his bricks-and-mortar predecessor.

The migration of religious institutions and their members from the cities to the suburbs has been closely chronicled by Gerald Gamm in *Urban Exodus: Why the Jews Left Boston and the Catholics Stayed*. He examines the neighborhoods of Mattapan and Dorchester and the movement of residents from these urban neighborhoods to the suburbs during the 1950s–1970s. Gamm contrasts the response of the Jewish synagogues and Catholic parishes in the wake of the urban flight of major portions of their congregations from Boston neighborhoods to the suburbs. He notes that the Jewish temples and synagogues uprooted themselves physically from their urban neighborhoods and followed their congregations to their new suburban communities. The Catholic parishes remained in place in their urban neighborhoods with a redefined mission.[53]

The Catholic parishes of Dorchester and Mattapan experienced rapid social change during the 1960s and 1970s, which witnessed the departure to the suburbs of a major segment of the Irish, German, Italian, Polish, Lithuanian, and French Canadian parishioners who had packed these churches to capacity during the 1940s and 1950s. The homes within these neighborhoods would progressively be inherited by a population of African Americans, Hispanics, Haitians, Vietnamese, Cape Verdeans, and other peoples who were part of a new wave of immigration during the latter part of the twentieth century. Catholic parishes and schools in the neighborhoods were retooled to receive and respond to the needs of the new immigrants. Incredibly generous priests, sisters, and lay ministers were ready to shift gears and step forward to learn the languages and appreciate the cultures of their new parish communities. An Association of Urban Priests and an Association of Urban Sisters spearheaded this effort.

The response of the Catholic Church in Boston over the past thirty years to the new waves of immigration from Europe, Latin American, Asia, and Africa has not been the establishment of new personal parishes, but the creation of chaplaincies within territorial parishes and existing personal parishes. These chaplaincies provide priests and pastoral ministers who can minister to the new peoples in their own language with an appreciation of their particular devotional traditions. As the Archdiocese of Boston observes its two hundredth year it coordinates twenty-seven ethnic apostolates committed to the pastoral care of immigrants and refugees. The Eucharist is celebrated in approximately twenty languages each Sunday within the Arch-diocese of Boston. Many of these recent immigrants will assimilate quickly into territorial parishes. Most of the new immigrant groups are not able to assume the financial responsibility for their own personal parishes. The ethnic apostolates have generated a number of creative ways in which the church of Boston can welcome communities of new peoples of diverse lan-guages and cultures to celebrate their Catholic faith as they traverse the transition to a new homeland. This has been a road well traveled by ear-lier generations of immigrants who have successively enriched the church of Boston with their faith and traditions.

Cardinal Medeiros addressed the challenging mission of the church in urban neighborhoods in his 1971 pastoral letter *Man's Cities and God's Poor,* which called for a renewed commitment of the Catholic Church to the inner-city neighborhoods. His message was rooted in the social justice teach-ing of the church and his own pastoral solicitude for the poor, a hallmark of his ministry as bishop. American cities witnessed scenes of horrific violence and civil unrest during the time of Cardinal Medeiros. Racial tensions within the city of Boston were exacerbated by the imposition of a court-ordered plan of forced busing of school children to redress a systemic pattern of de facto segregation in the Boston public schools. The support of the Catholic Church for the Racial Imbalance Act of 1965 and the court-ordered bus-ing that followed left many parishioners of Boston parishes feeling for the first time that they had been abandoned by their religious leaders during a time of crisis. Cardinal Medeiros urged compliance with the law and full acceptance of its social justice imperatives, including his controversial deci-sion that the parochial schools could not provide a haven for refugees from the court-ordered busing plan, even though the struggling parish schools in the city would have benefited greatly from the increased enrollment.[54] Some pastors defied the cardinal's directive and opened their schools to trans-fers from the Boston public schools. Other parish priests, such as Father Bob Boyle and Father Bill Joy at St. Mary's parish, Charlestown, were torn between their support of the cardinal and the social justice teachings of the church and the distress of parishioners who felt that they were being unfairly compelled to surrender their rights to make critical decisions concerning the education of their children. These city priests had longstanding relationships with their parishioners and knew them as devoted parents who desperately desired a secure educational environment for their children. They found themselves separated from these same parishioners by traffic barriers during "Rosary Marches" in South Boston and Charlestown.[55] When the passions subsided and forced busing was implemented as the norm for the Boston public schools, many parishioners found themselves distanced from their parishes as they felt that they had been abandoned by their church. Cardi-nal Medeiros bore the brunt of the resentment directed against the church, and he admitted to one newspaper reporter that he feared for his personal safety if he were to visit South Boston or Charlestown. He immediately regretted this comment and made pastoral visits to the parishes of those troubled neighborhoods.[56]

The Medeiros era was not only a period of societal unrest, but also a pivotal period for the implementation of the vision of Vatican II within the local church. Cardinal Medeiros encouraged the pioneering efforts of Bishop Daniel Hart in the Office of Pastoral Development to provide parishes with some of their earliest opportunities for long-range pastoral planning. The Cursillo retreat movement and the Catholic Charismatic Renewal echoed the call of Vatican II for personal and ecclesial renewal. Bishop John D'Arcy established the Office of Spiritual Development, which retooled the traditional parish mission as an instrument of spiritual renewal at the parish level. The restoration of the permanent diaconate following Vatican II afforded Cardinal Medeiros the opportunity to ordain the first class of permanent deacons for the Archdiocese of Boston on May 22, 1976, providing a significant new resource of ordained ministers for the parishes.

When Cardinal Medeiros died on September 18, 1983, he may have felt unaccepted and unappreciated by large segments of his flock. The long lines of people, however, who waited patiently for hours to pass by his bier at the cathedral testified to the love and respect of the Catholics of Boston for this gentle shepherd who served as archbishop during a tumultuous period.

The Parish as Pastoral Priority

Bernard Francis Law was installed as the eighth bishop of Boston on March 23, 1984, at the Cathedral of the Holy Cross. His first pastoral letter, *Sunday Liturgy: The Heart of the Parish*, was issued on the first anniversary of his installation and established the quality of Sunday liturgy in the parishes as his highest priority:

> The parish, a microcosm of the Church, needs to reflect the central importance of the Sunday liturgy. For the parish community, this celebration of the Sunday liturgy is the heart of its life. It is at the Sunday liturgy that the parish discovers its identity as a part of the Church. It is at the Sunday liturgy that the parish derives its strength for its mission.[57]

The parish was the place where Cardinal Law found his greatest satisfaction as a bishop. He customarily celebrated Sunday liturgy at a number of parish churches each weekend. He took the opportunity of these parish visits to encourage pastoral staffs and parishioners to strive continually toward a full implementation of the liturgical reforms of Vatican II with a personal emphasis upon effective preaching and the quality of liturgical music.

The pastoral staffs of parishes had taken on a very different look in the wake of Vatican II. Parishes that might have been routinely staffed by five or six priests during the 1950s were now staffed by varied constellations of priests, permanent deacons, religious women, and lay ministers. The growth in lay ministry that gathered steam during the 1970s was most readily evident in the Catholic schools and the religious education programs. The depleted ranks of religious women engaged in the educational mission of the parish opened the door for laymen and laywomen to assume responsibility for Catholic schools and the catechetical programs for public school students. Lay persons have also been welcomed into roles of pastoral ministry as pastoral associates and coordinators of various ministries within the parishes. Parish finance councils were mandated by Canon Law in 1983 so that the laity, once banned from involvement in the supervision of parish finances and temporalities, were now encouraged to share their fiscal expertise with pastors in the responsible utilization of parish resources for mission. As astounding as the premise might sound to Bishop Fenwick, fresh from the battles with parish trustees, it became commonplace for pastors to issue regular financial reports to their parishioners.

At a convocation of parishes at the World Trade Center in Boston on March 7, 1998, Cardinal Law looked ahead to the celebration of the bicentenary of the archdiocese:

> Look with me ten years ahead, to the year 2008, the bicentennial of the founding of the Diocese of Boston. How many parishes should we have by then? Today we have 738 diocesan priests. We can reasonably predict that in the year 2005 we will have 573 diocesan priests. Predicting the future of the Church must always allow for the surprising movement of the Holy Spirit. There is, however, a future that is foreseeable in terms of our seminarians preparing for ordination, and our experience with retirements and deaths. Beyond 2005 we cannot predict. We can say with reasonable certitude, however, that we will have less then 573 priests, and probably no more than 550 priests. Today we number 387 parishes, with 355 of these staffed by diocesan priests.

Cardinal Law insisted that even if there were no shortage of priests, he would continue to encourage the greater utilization of lay people in church ministry. He saw this in keeping with the spirit of Vatican II, which called for a greater participation of the People of God in the life and mission of the church. He welcomed the empowerment of lay ministry as something that the church needs to do always in order to be fully church.[58]

The Convocation of Parishes was an essential step in the ongoing implementation of the Pastoral Plan for Mission adopted by the Eighth Synod of the Archdiocese of Boston on November 27, 1988. The Pastoral Plan was developed after extensive consultation with all the parishes of the archdiocese in a planning effort geared toward the delineation of pastoral priorities for the future of the church in Boston. This Eighth Synod of the archdiocese was unique in that it was the first time that deacons, religious, and laity were invited to join the bishops and priests within the synod deliberations. Cardinal Law and his regional bishops carried the Pastoral Plan of the Eighth Synod into an extensive program of parish visitations, which invited each parish to study and implement the synod documents within their own local community as part of their ongoing parish development.

Vatican II opened up an era that welcomed and encouraged the active engagement of the laity in the mission of the parish. This was a new day when the church as the Body of Christ would carry on the mission of Christ in the world through the priesthood of the baptized. While the Catholic Action initiatives of the 1940s and 1950s had encouraged the laity to assume a more active role in Christian service, the opportunities for lay involvement in the mission of the parish proliferated during the period following the Vatican Council. Basic catechist training for religious education teachers during the 1960s afforded some of the earliest opportunities for laity to deepen their understanding of church doctrine and prepare themselves for a more active role in the mission of the church. Parish councils were established in the 1960s to provide pastors with the advice and counsel of parishioners in the pastoral planning efforts that would set the course for parish programs and initiatives. The statutes approved by Eighth Synod of the Archdiocese of Boston mandated the establishment of a parish pastoral council in every parish.

A Shadow of Darkness

What had been looming as a dark shadow over the American church since the middle of the 1980s finally plunged the Catholic Church of Boston into darkness in 2001. The revelation that over the course of the second half of the twentieth century the Archdiocese of Boston had reassigned pedophile priests to parish ministry, with subsequent acts of abuse ensuing, enraged and humiliated the Catholic community in Boston. The scandal reopened grievous wounds in hundreds of victims of sexual abuse by priests. A significant number of Catholics severed their ties with the church for months and years. Some have not returned. Mass attendance plummeted in parishes. Cardinal Law tendered his resignation as archbishop of Boston to Pope John Paul II on December 13, 2002, acknowledging that he could no longer provide effective leadership for the church in Boston. The ensuing crisis of confidence and trust in the leadership of the Catholic Church continues to cast a dark shadow over the celebration of the second centenary of the Archdiocese of Boston, and the long-term impact of this crisis is still unknown.

"Rebuild My Church"

Seán Patrick O'Malley, O.F.M.Cap. was installed as the ninth bishop of Boston on July 30, 2003, accepting the mandate entrusted to St. Francis of Assisi to "rebuild my Church that is falling into ruin." Archbishop O'Malley addressed the need to respond immediately to the plight of the victims of clergy sexual abuse and committed himself to a lengthy process of healing within a Catholic Church that had been deeply traumatized and divided. Programs, policies, and procedures were implemented at the parish level to assure parishioners that the parish is a safe and secure environment for its young people.

Cardinal O'Malley is also grappling with one of the major preoccupations of Boston's early bishops: the provision of a sufficient number of priests to serve the parishes. An alarming drop in the number of priestly ordinations since the 1960s, coupled with the death, retirement, or resignation of many of the priests from the large ordination classes of the 1950s and 1960s, generates dire projections of a diminished number of priests to serve the parishes of the Archdiocese of Boston during the twenty-first century. The church of 2008 looks back to the Catholic communities during the time of Cheverus and Fenwick and wonders if circuit rider priests of early times will once again be needed to provide priestly service to parishes that will not be staffed by residential pastors.

The prospect of parishes without priests motivated Bishop Richard Lennon, apostolic administrator of the archdiocese during the interim between Cardinal Law and Cardinal O'Malley, to initiate an archdiocesan planning effort concerning the reconfiguration of parishes. All the parishes of the archdiocese convened in local clusters of three to eight parishes to consider the future of the parishes in their area. Consideration was given to the number of parishioners in each congregation, the ability of each parish to fund its mission, and a sacramental index that totaled the number of baptisms, weddings, and funerals that were celebrated in a parish each year. Geographical proximity to other parishes was also considered. Particular attention was focused on the personal parishes that ministered to earlier generations of immigrants, while identifying the parishes that are filling that role today for new generations. The final recommendations of the archdiocesan planning committee were accepted by Cardinal O'Malley in 2004. The announcement that eighty parishes would be merged or suppressed was received with shock and anger in many parishes, while some of the smaller parishes had already resigned themselves to the probable outcome. A council of parishes was organized by parish leaders to "support parishes subject to closure" and "to provide a forum for parishes and laity to communicate with the archdiocese about issues of concern." This was a new phenomenon of a voluntary association of parishes that, along with the Voice of the Faithful (see below page 273), communicated the concerns of the laity to the archdiocese outside the established structure of regions and vicariates. While some of the decisions on parish closures were reconsidered, seventy-five parishes were closed or merged. Fourteen of these closed parishes are presently engaged in some form of canonical appeal, while parishioners at five suppressed parishes have been occupying closed churches and maintaining vigils for over three years. Thirteen new parishes were established: seven by merger and six by the creation of new parishes. Many parishioners of suppressed parishes made smooth transitions to other parishes, while some are still looking for new spiritual homes.

It is a hopeful sign that a significant number of parishes of the archdiocese have responded affirmatively to the invitation of Cardinal O'Malley to begin a three-year period of parish renewal at the beginning of the third centenary. The Catholic Church of Boston, which has faced a host of crises and challenges over the course of two hundred years, has begun to look toward the future with hope. The well-placed emphasis upon the renewal of parishes may be the key to a successful inauguration of the next century of Boston Catholic history.

Conclusion

"There is always something fascinating about the history of a Catholic parish," wrote the late Archbishop Joseph Rummell of New Orleans in 1948. "Usually modest and humble in its beginnings, it grows larger, more dignified, more efficient with the years. It is almost human in its development, and quite understandably so, for it is composed of vibrant human beings."[59] Parishes are composed of human beings and are subject to all the faults and foibles of those human beings. The history of two hundred years of parish life in Boston is certainly reflective of that premise. There have been times when the inconsistency and insecurity of human beings has impeded the growth of parishes as communities where the faith is received from earlier generations, lived on a daily basis, and then passed on to succeeding generations. The parishes of Boston have been peopled sometimes by saints, sometimes by sinners, and most times by ordinary men and women who tried their best to fulfill their daily commitments.

There are 295 parishes that constituted the Archdiocese of Boston in 2008. As the archdiocese marks its bicentennial, however, it celebrates the history of more than four hundred parishes where people have lived their Catholic faith over the past two hundred years. Each of these parishes takes pride in its unique history, social context, personality, and achievements. Each of these parishes has played an important role in the two-hundred-year history of the Archdiocese of Boston.

The parishes of the Archdiocese of Boston are facing extraordinary struggles, disappointments, and challenges at the beginning of Boston's third centenary. Sunday Mass attendance on the part of Boston Catholics has dropped precipitously from more than 70 percent of baptized Catholics during the halcyon days of the 1940s and 1950s to less than 25 percent today. This depleted participation at Sunday Mass is certainly reflective of continuing anger over the clergy sex abuse scandal. It is also reflective of some deep distress with the closure of parishes. It would be inaccurate, however, to attribute the depleted numbers at Sunday Mass to these issues alone. There has indeed been a steady erosion of Sunday Mass attendance since the 1970s that is reflective of sweeping changes within the church and society.

The liturgical reforms that followed Vatican II left some Catholics wondering what had happened to the familiar traditions and consoling rituals that generations of Catholics had experienced as the fixed-point in their turbulent lives during the immigration period, the Depression, and two World Wars. Virulent demonstrations against an unpopular war in Vietnam, coupled with the Watergate crisis, contributed to a societal distrust of institutional authority that carried over into Catholic life. Widespread disappointment with the Catholic Church's reaffirmation of its traditional ban on artificial means of contraception in 1968 with the publication of *Humanae Vitae* set up an unfamiliar situation in which a significant number of Catholics questioned the teaching authority of the church on a matter of faith and morals. Disagreement with the church in one area of its teachings opened up the possibility of disagreement on other issues.

The decline in Sunday Mass attendance is also reflective of the rapid evolution of the economic, social, and cultural context of Catholics following World War II. "No longer a shunned, ghettoized, immigrant minority, Catholics today are largely a suburban population, better educated and more affluent than their grandparents," writes Paul Stonz in his recent study of priests.

> They have succeeded in joining the cultural mainstream, sending their children to public schools, and abandoning Sunday Mass in favor of soccer, TV, or shopping. The steep decline in religiosity among Catholic youth is also evidence of an acute crisis. The sociologist Christian Smith's analysis of the recent *National Study of Youth and Religion* is sobering. The massive study ranked U.S. Catholic teenagers well behind their Protestant peers in adherence to their religious tradition's beliefs, norms, practices, and commitments. Smith attributes this trend to a decline in practice among parents, a paucity of full-time youth ministers, the demise of Catholic schools and their replacement with weak CCD programs, and the upward mobility and acculturation of a once largely working-class immigrant population. According to this account, the financial success, social mobility, and cultural mainstreaming of American Catholics have led to the end of the urban parish-school-neighborhood enclaves that formed and cemented the communities and faith of immigrant Catholics. In other words, large social, cultural, and economic forces — and not simply the internal forces such as the alleged dilution of Catholicism by Vatican II reforms — have contributed to Catholicism's decline. And that decline is not about to reverse itself. It seems unlikely that young people who have only the foggiest understanding of Catholic tradition will suddenly return to the church as adults.[60]

Deficient catechetical methods in the past, coupled with a marked decrease in Sunday Mass attendance as an integral part of family life, point to a diminished number of those who will be actively engaged in parish life during the coming years. It seems likely that the parishes of the immediate future will be smaller, but hopefully those involved will be more fully engaged. The parishes of the first half of the twenty-first century will likely look very different from the enormous parishes of the first half of twentieth century, but tremendous growth in faith may take place within these smaller communities.

Pope John Paul II recognized the disheartening reality of diminished Catholic practice when he wrote:

> The sociology of religion does not help much here. As a basis for assessment, the criteria for measurement which it provides do not help when considering people's interior attitude. No statistic aiming at a quantitative measurement of faith (for example the number of people who participate in religious ceremonies) will get to the heart of the matter. Here the numbers alone are not

enough. From the point of view of the Gospel the issue is completely different. Christ says: *"Do not be afraid any longer, little flock, for your Father is
pleased to give you the kingdom"* (Luke 12:32).[61]

The Holy Father's pointed reference to the church as a "little flock" reflected his acceptance of the sociological projection that our parishes may be
smaller in the foreseeable future. At the same time his "little flock" citation
points back to the earliest Christian community in Jerusalem as the seedbed
of a prodigious evangelization that brought forth a flowering of Christianity throughout the world. Pope John Paul saw the new ecclesial movements,
along with the spectacular World Youth Day gatherings, as hope-filled indicators of a new evangelization at the beginning of the third millennium of
Christianity. He pointed emphatically to the large numbers of young people
who have embraced the Gospel challenge as a sign of hope for the church:

> Generations come and go which have distanced themselves from Christ and
> the Church, which have accepted a secular model of thinking and living or
> upon which such a model has been imposed. Meanwhile the Church is always
> looking toward the future. She constantly goes out to meet new generations.
> And new generations clearly seem to be accepting with enthusiasm what their
> elders seem to have rejected. What does this mean? It means that Christ is
> forever young. It means that the Holy Spirit is incessantly at work. Christ's
> words are striking: *My Father is at work until now, so I am at work* (Jn. 5:17).
> The Father and Son are at work in the Holy Spirit, who is the Spirit of truth,
> and truth does not cease to fascinate man, especially the hearts of the young.
> Therefore we should not consider statistics alone. Despite all of the losses the
> Church has suffered, it does not cease to look toward the future with hope.[62]

The Catholic parishes of the Archdiocese of Boston have assumed many
different forms over the past two hundred years. It is difficult to imagine what the parishes will look like a hundred years from now. Hopefully,
the parishes of Boston will continue to respond to current challenges and
will flourish as seedbeds of renewal within this local church. Confronting
daunting challenges, parishes will need to maintain an attitude of hopeful
realism.[63]

> Hope, which is distinguished from optimism, is ultimately based on the fidelity
> of God and the promise of Jesus to remain with the Church. Hope is nour-
> ished by prayer and reflection. It can flourish even when problems threaten to
> overwhelm us and solutions elude us. Hope enables us to sustain our ministry
> even in the midst of misunderstandings and failures. Christian hope strength-
> ens us to face our problems in all their harsh reality without escaping into
> utopian fantasies or repressing our anger and frustration. A hopeful attitude
> helps us appreciate the positive developments in the Church today, especially
> the tremendous growth in lay ministry and the vitality of good parishes. The
> dialectical virtue of hopeful realism enables us to hold together in a fruitful
> synthesis both trust in God and a realistic approach to Church problems. The
> severity of our current crisis moves us to put our hope in God rather than our-
> selves. This ultimate hope opens our eyes to the hopeful signs in the Church
> today.[64]

Parishes will prosper as they invite new generations of Catholics to a full
participation in the life of the church that they experience as the fulfillment

of a spiritual need rather than an obligation. A mobile Catholic population in the twenty-first century may need to travel greater distances to a smaller number of parishes.

Cardinal Joseph Ratzinger, now Pope Benedict XVI, seemed to envision this prospect in 1997, when he wrote:

> The Church, too, as we have said will assume different forms. She will be less identified with the great societies, more of a minority Church: she will live in small vital circles of really convinced believers who live their faith. But precisely in this way she will, biblically speaking, become the salt of the earth again.[65]

9

Boston's Catholics and Their Bishops

A Comparative View

JAMES M. O'TOOLE

Leadership is critical in any organization. The organization's survival, its ability to accomplish its mission and to thrive through time, depends to no small degree on the individuals who assume the responsibility for overseeing it. They are not alone, of course. In large and complex organizations, many other people also contribute to the effort, and broad support and participation are no less essential than direction from the top. What might be called "followership" is just as important, and cooperation between leaders and those who are led will determine success or failure. But leaders have a special responsibility, and the decisions they make will therefore determine the character and the work of the larger whole. For this reason, the history of any organization can be understood by studying the succession of leaders and their relationship to those below.

Such a historical viewpoint may be particularly useful in studying the history of the Roman Catholic Archdiocese of Boston on the occasion of its bicentennial. As an institution, the Catholic Church is organized hierarchically, with clear lines of authority that have developed over centuries. The personalities and abilities of the popes have determined the direction of the worldwide church at every historical turning point. Closer to home, the bishops and archbishops who have led the church in the greater Boston area have had an enduring impact. Not only did they make critical decisions concerning the parishes, schools, and social service agencies of the church, but most of them also served in their office for extended terms. In contrast to many other dioceses, Boston's bishops have generally had very long tenures. The result has been an administrative and historical continuity for the local church more seamless than that of other places and institutions. In the two centuries since the first one was appointed in 1808, there have been just nine bishops and archbishops of Boston. During that same span of two hundred years, there have been forty-one presidents of the United States and fifteen popes; France has had an empire, a restored monarchy, two revolutions, and five republics. In America, other Catholic dioceses have seen a swifter turnover in their leadership. The Archdioceses of New York, Philadelphia, and Louisville (originally Bardstown, Kentucky), all created along with Boston in 1808, have seen twelve, twelve, and ten bishops, respectively. Thus,

237

in Boston the leadership styles and administrative emphases of each bishop, once in place, have generally remained so for an extended period, sometimes for decades. For this reason, studying the history of the men who have led the Boston church is a particularly useful way of framing two centuries of historical experience.

From one perspective, the bishops and archbishops of Boston are a homogeneous group. All were white males; all were celibate Catholic priests. Allowing for their particular circumstances, they had all had a similar religious education and training, and their early priestly careers gave them many of the same experiences in serving the spiritual and other needs of Catholic lay people. Even so, each prelate had his own personality, his own strengths and weaknesses, and had to meet challenges that were peculiar to his own era. Each had his own administrative and pastoral style and his own conception of what the job of a Catholic bishop ought to be. Looking at each one on his own terms opens the way to understanding each of them, but it also contributes to the formation of a collective view. The experiences of each may describe the past, but they also mark out a path to the future, as the church of Boston faces new challenges in its third century.

John Cheverus

Jean Louis Anne Madeleine Lefebvre de Cheverus arrived in Boston during the first week of October 1796, and he almost immediately anglicized his name to the simpler "John Cheverus." He had been born twenty-eight years before at the home of his family in the town of Mayenne, in northwestern France, and he decided early to pursue a career in the priesthood. His decision was firm, but his timing was poor. He was ordained a priest right before Christmas 1790, just as the French Revolution, a year old by then, was about to turn in a violently anticlerical direction. Two months later, all priests in France were required to swear their primary loyalty to the state rather than the church, and like many of his fellow pastors Cheverus refused. Jailed for standing on principle, he managed to escape to England, where he picked up the language while working as a teacher and serving as a priest for the French émigré community in and around London. One of his former seminary professors, Father François Antoine Matignon, had already left for America, and he invited his pupil to join him there, so Cheverus secured passage to the new world, where Boston would be his home for the next three decades.[1]

The Catholic population of Boston in these years immediately after the American Revolution was small, and it seemed destined to remain so. The Puritans who founded the Massachusetts Bay Colony almost two hundred years before had been relentlessly hostile to anything or anyone connected to the "popery" of the church of Rome. They had even passed laws declaring all Catholic priests to be, by definition, "incendiaries and disturbers of the public peace," and such attitudes persisted for a long time. "Many here, even of their principal people," a Catholic visitor from Maryland told a friend in 1791, "have acknowledged to me that they would have crossed to the opposite side of the street rather than meet a Rom. Catholic. The horror which was associated with the Idea of a Papist is incredible." In the warming air of religious toleration that followed the Revolution, however, a small Catholic congregation had come together in Boston, buying an abandoned Protestant church and renaming it the Church of the Holy Cross. Matignon (who had already anglicized his name to Francis Anthony) began serving as pastor there on his arrival in the city in the summer of 1792, and Cheverus joined him four years later. Altogether, there were only about 120 Catholics in the city, the Marylander had guessed, though it was "probable there are more concealed, who, in consequence of intermarriages, long disuse and worldly motives, decline making an acknowledgement or profession of their faith." It would take the exertions of priests "of amiable, conciliatory manners, as well as of real ability," the visitor concluded, to begin to change local attitudes toward Catholics.[2]

"Real ability" is precisely what the parishioners of Holy Cross church got in Matignon and Cheverus. Their congregation was made up mostly of Irish and French immigrants to Boston, though there was even a population from the Caribbean. Trade routes between Boston and various islands there had brought significant numbers of free blacks to the city, enough so that one gallery of Holy Cross Church was reserved "exclusively for persons of color." The regular routines of parish work kept the two priests busy. In the year 1800, for example, the registers of the church recorded 77 baptisms, 9 marriages, and 7 funerals, but these increased to 93 baptisms, 17 marriages, and 18 funerals in 1810; the church's population had expanded to an estimated 720. In the next decade, the growth was even more impressive: 207 baptisms, 47 marriages, and 53 funerals, with a population of more than 2,100 in 1820. These numbers were small in comparison to later figures, but for the time they showed the effect that "amiable" priests could have in building up the community. Moreover, the work of the two clergymen was not confined to those who lived in the city. They regularly ventured farther afield in search of Catholics scattered along the New England coast from Cape Cod up to Maine. One of Cheverus's first assignments had been to travel through Maine and New Hampshire. There he sought out Irish and French settlers, and he also visited tribes of Native Americans. These had been converted to Catholicism long before by missionaries from Canada, and they had maintained their faith even though they had not seen a priest for generations. Such journeys became a recurring part of Cheverus's work in the ensuing years.[3]

In addition to work among their own people, Cheverus and Matignon promoted a rapprochement between Catholics and the wider community of Boston and New England. They sought in particular to win over the Yankee descendants of those earlier Puritans who crossed to the other side of the street when encountering a Catholic. The American Revolution had begun the thaw. In fighting for their independence from British colonial rule,

Americans had sought and received the aid of the king of France, a traditional Catholic enemy of his Protestant British cousin. Before falling to his own revolutionaries, Louis XVI had sent French soldiers and sailors to assist the Americans, and it had been in this connection that Mass was said in Boston, probably for the first time, in 1778, as the chaplain assigned to a French ship presided at the funeral of a crewman on board. The cooperation among the colonies during the Revolution had also contributed to an emerging spirit of religious toleration. Catholics from Maryland, embodied visibly in the prominent Carroll family, had been no less enthusiastic in the patriot cause than the Congregationalists of New England, the Presbyterians of New York, the Quakers of Pennsylvania, or the Anglicans of Virginia. This demonstrated that Americans could work together in public affairs even as they held on to their differing religious practices. Charles Carroll of Carrollton, the wealthy Maryland planter who was the only Catholic to have signed the Declaration of Independence, recognized this immediately, saying that his action promoted "not only our independence of England but the toleration of all sects professing the Christian religion and communicating to them all equal rights."[4] Locally, the change in attitude toward Catholics was not immediate: the Massachusetts constitution, adopted in 1780, still authorized the use of tax money for the support of "public, Protestant teachers of piety, religion, and morality" in all the towns of the Commonwealth. Even so, the two French Catholic priests who came to Boston a decade later had a new basis on which to establish closer relations with the surrounding community.

That improvement was evident in the building of a new church for the expanding congregation, which quickly outgrew the original Holy Cross on School Street. The two pastors shrewdly chose Charles Bulfinch, the most prominent architect and builder of his day and the scion of a wealthy local family, to draw the plans for a church on nearby Franklin Street. Bulfinch had just finished erection of the new State House at the top of Beacon Hill, and he would continue to remake the face of the city for another two decades, before leaving for Washington to become the architect of the Capitol. By choosing him to design their church, Catholics signaled that they would not be distinct from the rest of Boston: they would participate in the best the city had to offer, even as they maintained their own religious identity. They would be both fully Catholic and "fully Boston." The new Holy Cross that Bulfinch built for them resembled the other churches in town, built along simple, classical lines and resembling a Puritan meeting house more than a gothic Catholic cathedral. (This church was torn down in 1860 and, in any case, would have burned down in the great fire of 1872. Modern-day observers can get a sense of it, however, by visiting its "twin," St. Stephen's Church on Hanover Street in the North End.) Moreover, the two priests and their parishioners sought and secured broad support for their efforts. The list of financial subscribers to the new building project was headed by "The President of the United States," John Adams, who contributed $100, the largest amount of any single donor. The names of other Yankee contributors soon joined that of Adams in the church's account book: there were

Coolidges, Lymans, Peabodys, and Quincys recorded among the church's benefactors. Their ancestors would no doubt have been horrified at this support for popery, but Matignon and Cheverus had made it possible. They had demonstrated that Catholics were members of the larger community, that they shared with those who went to different churches a desire to contribute to the progress of society. "No person," a friend of Adams would later say of Cheverus, "could have been better adapted to establish the Church of Rome in the city of the Puritans."[5]

These abilities were recognized when, on the establishment of the new Diocese of Boston in April 1808, Cheverus was appointed its first bishop. The more logical choice, perhaps, would have been Matignon, but the older man would have none of it. (He was already fifty-five and thought himself too old; he would die ten years later.) If nominated for the position, Matignon said, he would "flee to the other end of the world." Instead, he recommended his younger colleague, even though, as he told Baltimore's Archbishop John Carroll, "if he knew that I am telling you this he would not thank me, for he is far from having any ambition." Given the difficulties of travel between the United States and Europe, convulsed at that time by the Napoleonic wars, it took almost a year after the creation of the new diocese for the official Roman documents to arrive so that Cheverus could be consecrated its bishop, but that ceremony was finally held in Baltimore in 1810. He had jurisdiction over all Catholics who lived in what were then the five New England states — Maine was still a part of Massachusetts — and from his earlier travels he knew that there were small communities scattered throughout the region. In Portsmouth, New Hampshire, for example, there were about a dozen Catholic families, and an equal number in Providence, Rhode Island. Within a decade, a congregation was gathering regularly in Vergennes, Vermont, on the shores of Lake Champlain. "The Catholics here have rented a room, erected an altar there, benches, etc., and have made a decent little chapel," Cheverus wrote to a friend after one visit to Vermont. Armed with the spiritual authority of a bishop, he could administer the sacrament of confirmation to these parishioners, something many of them had been awaiting for some time. He was traveling (without the conveniences of modern transportation, of course) as often as he was at home in Boston, but he was hopeful. "In this city and other places," he reported to a churchman in Rome, "where a few years ago, the name Catholic Church was, so to speak, infamous, and that of a Priest abhorred, we are now looked upon with veneration and friendship."[6]

Despite his new title, Cheverus's actual work changed very little. He was still as much a pastor as he was a bishop, and he continued to cherish the friendships he had made with parishioners, near and far. Nothing demonstrates the strength of these ties better than his long friendship with the family of Roger Hanly of Maine. He had met them and their neighbors for the first time on his initial visit along the coastline around Damariscotta in the summer of 1797, and a lifetime bond was formed. They regularly exchanged affectionate letters, in which Cheverus expressed his desire to be remembered between visits by the core of the small Catholic community there: "your son Roger, his dear wife & children, your respectable Sister Mrs. Hanly & family, old Mr. & Mrs. McGuire, Capt. Aikins & family," and others. None of these people is otherwise remembered by history, but the close personal connection between the bishop and these lay people is evident from the warmth of his correspondence with them. Cheverus said Mass for them whenever he was able to visit Maine, but he also gave them spiritual advice on how to sustain their faith in the meantime. "Every day," he wrote from Boston in one letter, "Say your prayers on your knees, morning & evening, with attention & devotion. Every Lords-day & Holyday, meet together morning & afternoon" to recite "the prayers at Mass with the Epistle & Gospel of the Day." Such family devotions might not be as good as having a priest regularly available to say Mass, but they would have to do until the next time, usually months away, that he or another clergyman could be with them. One spring, he wrote to the young daughter of one of the families who was preparing for her first communion, and he encouraged her in her prayers even though he himself would not be able to come to administer the sacrament to her for another two or three months. He even purchased gravestones for family members at his own expense, shipping them from Boston to Maine when the occasion warranted.[7] Here was a bishop who worked steadily at maintaining direct, personal connections to his flock.

Cheverus had originally come to the Catholics of Boston and New England as an outsider, but he purposely made himself one of them. From the very first — evident, for instance, in the conscious decision to sign his name "John" rather than "Jean" — he had made clear that he intended to remain an American in Boston for the rest of his life. Larger forces intervened, however, to remove him from what had become his home. The restoration of the monarchy and the church in France prompted repeated calls for him to return to the land of his birth. Baltimore's Archbishop Carroll was distressed at the prospect. "Considering the number of excellent clergymen in France [and] the resources of that populous country," Carroll wrote Cheverus, "there is but little danger of the faithful remaining destitute of the bread of Christian doctrine, and the graces of the sacraments." America needed him more. "What resources will remain for those whom you have begun to train here in the principles and duties of true religion? . . . The claims of charity are assuredly stronger in their behalf, than in behalf of those who are not, and probably never will be, in the same extreme necessity." Even so, Cheverus could not resist demands, coming from the restored Bourbon king himself, that he go back to France. In the summer of 1823, he finally gave in, departing Boston to become the bishop of Montauban, near Toulouse; in 1826, he moved again, becoming the archbishop of Bordeaux. It was there that he was elevated to the rank of cardinal in 1835, just a year before his death.[8]

The Catholics of Boston had lost their first bishop, and they felt the loss sharply. "Your departure," a committee of the parishioners of Holy Cross church told him, "is to us a most afflicting dispensation, . . . a wound whose anguish time may assuage, but can never heal."⁹ Together they had worked to establish a foundation for Catholicism in New England. Success had come because the bishop and the Catholic people had forged a strong bond so as to advance the common goal of building up the church. Had Cheverus been absorbed in less important matters, his departure would not have been the occasion for "anguish." As it was, he had succeeded because he remembered that a bishop was first and foremost a pastor. In later decades, it would become increasingly difficult for Boston's bishops to do this, as the administrative duties of their office became more complex. But Cheverus had worked amid complexity, too. The long distances he had to travel between pastoral visits around New England did not distract him from the importance of continuing to act as a pastor. Future bishops would succeed to the extent that they maintained that sense of priorities, that same conception of the responsibilities of their office.

Benedict Fenwick

More than two years intervened between the departure of Bishop Cheverus and the arrival of his successor. In that interim, the Catholics of Boston were served by Father William Taylor, and the bond that formed between them was no less strong than that tying them to their former bishop. Taylor had been born in Ireland, trained for the priesthood there, and came to America, where he was assigned to the small Catholic parish in New York for a time before coming to Boston in 1821. He had a somewhat volatile temperament, but he proved popular with the Catholics of the Boston diocese, in part because of his relentless missionary efforts. In his first two years, he had said Mass and helped organize parishes in places as widely scattered as Claremont, New Hampshire, and Hartford, Connecticut.¹⁰ Cheverus had come to know him well and may have wanted the Irishman to be his successor, but the choice went instead to a descendant of one of the oldest of Maryland Catholic families, Benedict Fenwick.

It was a fortuitous choice, for Fenwick's abilities were many. No less than his predecessor, he came as an outsider to Boston, and to the end of his days there were things about New England he found hard to take. His diaries are filled, for example, with almost daily complaints about the cold and snowy winters: his southern blood apparently never got used to them. But also like Cheverus, Fenwick threw himself into the work of building up Catholicism across the region that was his diocese, and his earlier career had suited him to the task. He had been born on one of his family's estates in St. Mary's County, Maryland, on the western shore of Chesapeake Bay at the mouth of the Potomac River. He studied first at Georgetown College in the nation's new capital, and, after the previously suppressed Jesuit order was restored, he joined it and was ordained in 1808. He then embarked on a varied pastoral career that exposed him to virtually every issue facing the country's fledgling Catholic community. First came a posting to New York City, where he served with another Jesuit in St. Peter's parish, the original church in the city at the lower tip of Manhattan Island. He helped establish a school called the New York Literary Institute, which eventually grew to become Fordham University. That effort prepared him for appointment as president of Georgetown in Washington, D.C. He served two separate terms in that capacity, interrupted by several years of parish work in Charleston, South Carolina. When he arrived in Boston as bishop in November 1825, he had had a broader experience of work for the church than almost any other priest in America.[11]

The Diocese of Boston remained small in institutional structure but large in geographic extent. It still encompassed all of New England, in which there were just six churches, starting with Holy Cross and the newly opened St. Augustine's in South Boston. Elsewhere in Massachusetts, there was a church in Salem — a building that was "finished in a very superior style," an early account reported — and another at New Bedford. In Maine, there was a church that the Hanlys and their neighbors had built at Damariscotta and another further inland at Whitefield. Drawing an unusual comparison, this account noted that in the Boston diocese, "as in that of Kentucky, there is a tribe of Indians, professing the Catholic religion, whose orderly conduct and sincere piety astonish, as well as edify, all who travel through their settlement." Those travelers included Fenwick himself, who like Cheverus periodically went to Maine to visit tribal settlements at Old Town, near Orono, and Pleasant Point, up the coastline on Passamaquoddy Bay. These natives had been visited occasionally by Protestant missionaries, "in the hope," Fenwick said, "of seducing them from the faith and of inoculating them with their various errors," but those efforts had been unsuccessful. The tasks ahead of Fenwick were daunting, and, he recalled later, he was "in a situation far from being enviable." Still, he trusted in God to "furnish him, in due time, with all the means requisite" for fulfilling his duties.[12]

The bishop had few priests at his disposal — by the middle 1830s, there were still just sixteen of them in all of New England — but the work of the church was advanced now by the coming of the first communities of women religious. A group of Ursuline Sisters had arrived in Boston in 1820, and they opened an academy for young women, at first adjacent to Holy Cross Cathedral downtown and then on a high hill in Charlestown, overlooking Boston harbor. These nuns were joined in 1832 by several Daughters of Charity, a community founded by the prominent convert to Catholicism (and later saint) Elizabeth Seton. The Charity sisters were led by Sister Ann Alexis Shorb, the daughter of a wealthy Philadelphia family. She was "a lady of noticeable refinement and education," one priest said of her, but more important she was a woman of tireless ability. For four decades she directed the work of the St. Vincent Orphan Asylum, an institution that originally served both boys and girls before eventually concentrating on girls only. Thousands of young girls passed through the orphanage's doors before it closed more than a century later in 1949. Fenwick found much-needed community with these growing numbers of sisters. He regularly said Mass for them, and he seems to have spent whatever free time he allowed himself in their company, sharing the burden of church work with them. This was understandable, but it may also have led to the opening of an unfortunate distance between the bishop and the lay Catholics of the diocese. Pressed by growing demands, Fenwick was able to be less of a pastor to the people of his own cathedral church than Cheverus had been. Cheverus had regularly administered the sacraments personally — he performed almost one-third (41 of 131) of the baptisms at Holy Cross in 1815, for example, and more than two-thirds (17 of 26) of the marriages — but this was increasingly impossible for Fenwick. In 1830 he performed only 4 of the nearly 500 baptisms and none of the 92 marriages in his cathedral.[13] Though he retained the affection of the Catholics of Boston, he was more unfamiliar to them personally than his predecessor had been, thereby risking a loss of commonality that would be exacerbated in later eras.

Even so, Fenwick's tenure witnessed an important transition for the Catholics of the Boston diocese. To a degree that had not been possible for them before, they became what may for the first time be recognized as a churchgoing people. Whereas the laity, especially those scattered across the countryside, had once experienced long fallow periods between the visits of traveling priests, they were now able to count on regularly scheduled Masses and other services. At the cathedral in Boston in the 1830s, for example, Mass was said every Sunday at 6:00, 7:00, and 10:00 a.m. (7:00, 8:00, and 10:00 during the winter months, when the sun rose later), and there were also other places where parishioners had their choice of services. St. Mary's, the new parish in Burlington, Vermont, for example, had Sunday Mass at ten o'clock, but afternoon vespers at two o'clock for those who could attend only that service. Moreover, the experience of going to church was steadily enhanced for lay people. An immigrant violinist and choirmaster, Luigi Ostinelli, oversaw the music of the Catholic churches in Boston, and he led their combined choirs in public concerts as well. After one Christmas Day Mass, Fenwick noted in his diary that the choir had "give[n] excellent music," and, perhaps partly as a result, "the church is crowded to suffocation." Lay people were also able for the first time to internalize the routines of regular church attendance and to adhere more closely to the clergy's expectations about their religious and sacramental duties. Nothing shows this more clearly than the customs that developed surrounding the baptism of children. The theology of the day encouraged Catholics to have infants baptized as soon after birth as possible, but the earlier irregularity with which lay people saw a priest often meant that years might pass before the ceremony could be performed. By the time of Fenwick's tenure as bishop, however, this was changing. St. Mary's Church in the North End of Boston, for example, located in one of the densest immigrant neighborhoods of the city, was the site of 335 baptisms in 1837, the parish's first year. Of these, just over half were performed within three days of the child's birth, and almost one-third of them were performed on the very day of birth or the day after.[14] Even in the midst of all the household turmoil that came with a newborn, these Catholics were careful to fulfill the demands of church membership.

For all the growth of the church under Fenwick, however, there were difficult times as well. The interreligious amity that had characterized the Revolutionary era was giving way to more troubled public attitudes; with these came increased suspicion of and hostility toward the Catholic Church and its people. At first, the threat was thought to be small. Catholics had "made little progress in this state," a gazetteer of Massachusetts reassured its readers shortly after Fenwick's arrival in Boston. "Their sentiments are well known, and few in America are in any danger of embracing doctrines so at variance with their habits and modes of thinking." Such Catholics as there were in New England had, the writer thought, "abate[d] much of the extravagance of the former pretensions of that church." Other observers took a more sinister and conspiratorial view, and they focused their attention on convents of sisters. In an era when society prescribed very limited roles for women, there was something deeply subversive about convents and schools, run by and for women. What exactly went on behind those mysterious walls? Some were only too willing to provide the answer. A woman with the too-coincidental name of Maria Monk had published an expose of the supposed abominations at a convent in Montreal, and this inflamed the public imagination. (Monk was an imposter, and her book had been ghostwritten by a team of evangelical ministers.) On a steamy August night in 1834, a mob attacked the convent of the Ursuline Sisters in Charlestown, drove sisters and their pupils alike into the night, and burned the place to the ground. The elite of Boston society denounced the outrage, but anti-Catholicism had found a broader popular base. Trial of the self-declared ringleaders resulted in acquittal, and Fenwick spent most of his remaining years in Boston in an unsuccessful attempt to recover monetary damages for the destruction. The episode left a lasting impression on the bishop, and he found it impossible to forget or entirely forgive. He left the burned-out shell of the convent standing, a visible but silent reproach to the Bunker Hill monument, then just going up on an adjacent hill.[15]

There were also successes for Fenwick. In 1843, after an extended search for an appropriate site — including a personal ascent of Mount Ascutney in Vermont, an escapade Fenwick described in his diary in positively comical terms — he established the College of the Holy Cross, a school for boys, in the central Massachusetts city of Worcester. This would, he hoped, begin to train an adequate number of priests for the church in New England, but it would also help expand the educated Catholic laity in the region. He continued to encourage the formation of new parishes, both in the city of Boston and around the region. Holy Trinity Church, a parish for German-speaking immigrants, opened in 1836, for example, and parishes were established quickly in the newly created towns of Lowell and Lawrence, bursting with Irish and French Canadian workers in the textile mills there. There was also growth elsewhere in the region. In northern Maine, for instance, Fenwick bought land for an agricultural community, named Benedicta in his honor, where young farmers hungry for land could set themselves up. So steadily were the numbers of Catholics growing that in 1844 the boundaries of the Boston diocese shrank for the first time, a process that would be repeated again and again until the end of the century. A new diocese was created at Hartford, comprising all of Connecticut and Rhode Island and leaving Fenwick with jurisdiction over the four northern New England states.

Throughout, Fenwick remained an active promoter of the spread of the church, and his time as bishop must be judged a success. At the same time, he encountered the problems that came with success. He had to work on many fronts at the same time, and he was never reluctant to do so. The role of a bishop was expanding. He found less time to serve personally as pastor to his parishioners and had to devote more energy to administering a growing and complex institution. Necessity had forced the shift, but it also underlined the danger of losing contact with the men and women in the pews who were the church. Fenwick was able to balance those demands reasonably well. He was personally gregarious and eager always for human contact. But his tenure as bishop also foreshadowed the difficulties that future bishops might have in combining their pastoral and their administrative roles. The need to strike that balance became all the more pressing with the demographic crisis that hit the church of Boston almost immediately after Fenwick's death in 1846.

John Fitzpatrick

When Bishop Fenwick died, Catholics in the Boston diocese probably thought that their future would be a more or less orderly continuation of their past. Their population would continue to grow slowly, they might well have believed, and new churches would be formed in a deliberate way once a substantial number of parishioners could be found in any locality, a process that would more than likely take a while. There were still not enough priests to meet the demand, but their numbers, too, were growing at a slow and steady pace, and the increase of sisters was proceeding in the same way. And then suddenly, everything changed.

Boston had depended on its port from its earliest days, and in the nineteenth century the harbor continued to be the center of local economic life. Goods and people from all over the world came into the country through Boston, and its proximity to Europe made it a logical entry point for those who wanted to move to America. Until the 1840s, however, the numbers of such people remained small. In 1821, for example, only about 2,200 foreign passengers had debarked on Boston's wharves, a statistically insignificant number in a city whose population was more than 43,000. The largest single group (a little over 800 that year) of them had come from Ireland, but a substantial number (more than 500) had also come from "British North America," that is, Canada. It was easy for the city to absorb these newcomers, some of whom remained in town while others moved into the interior of the country in search of opportunity. By the middle 1840s, however, the repeated failure of the potato crop in Ireland, coupled with political turmoil on the continent of Europe, sent these numbers skyrocketing, practically overnight. In the single year of 1846, the number of immigrants coming through Boston had jumped to almost 113,000, a fiftyfold increase over the figure from a quarter-century before. Moreover, half of the newcomers came from Ireland, and these were among the poorest of the poor. Dispossessed of farms at home, they were ill prepared for the emerging urban and industrial economy of the United States, and they were thus subject to all the social ills that came with poverty. Their suddenly substantial presence in the city caused alarm among the more established citizenry. A century later, one observer was still labeling these immigrants "a massive lump in the community, undigested, undigestible."[16]

Because so many immigrants were Catholics — not just from Ireland, but from Germany, French Canada, and elsewhere — it fell to the church to meet their needs, and it was no doubt a good thing that Boston Catholicism was presided over now by the first of its bishops to have been born here, one who knew the city intimately. The son of earlier Irish immigrants, John Fitzpatrick was born in 1812 and received his primary education in the city's public schools. He graduated from the Boston Latin School, the oldest public school in the country, and in his years there he forged strong personal friendships with those who would later be the leaders of Yankee Brahmin politics and society. These ties would prove useful again and again during his work as a pastor and bishop. After studies for the priesthood in Montreal and then in Paris, Fitzpatrick was ordained in 1840 and returned to America. In a quick succession of parish assignments — first at the cathedral, then at St. Mary's in the North End, then as the founding pastor of St. John's Church in Cambridge — he acquired the pastoral experience that was the foundation of every priest's life. Offering the Mass and the sacraments for his parishioners was his daily routine, but he also began to attract notice as a preacher. A local Congregational minister, hearing of Fitzpatrick's reputation, attended one service and pronounced the young priest "eloquent and accomplished" in the pulpit. Bishop Fenwick came almost immediately to rely on this capable young assistant, and by 1843 he had decided that Fitzpatrick should be his own successor in Boston. A few months later, Fitzpatrick was consecrated a bishop — he was just thirty-two years old — and when Fenwick died in the summer of 1846, Fitzpatrick assumed his responsibilities.[17]

Continuity with the expanding program of the Fenwick years marked Fitzpatrick's work, but the pace at which he had to accomplish it was redoubled because of the ever insistent demands that the thousands of new Catholic immigrants presented. It became a commonplace for Bostonians to speak of the influx of newcomers by resorting to the language of natural disaster: the immigrants were a "flood" or a "tidal wave." This only underlined the urgency with which Fitzpatrick had to work to expand the church's presence throughout his diocese. Churches had to be opened almost everywhere as quickly as it was possible to do so, a process that the later archdiocesan historians would describe as a matter of "addition, multiplication, and division." In and around the metropolis itself, new parishes were established, and the priests assigned to them usually had responsibilities for outlying missionary districts as well. The priests at St. Joseph's in Roxbury (still a separate town, not yet incorporated into Boston proper), a church that was dedicated by Fitzpatrick just two weeks after he became bishop, regularly traveled a wide circuit that included Brookline, Dedham, Walpole, and Taunton. Eventually, these mission stations would grow into distinct parishes of their own. Priests from New Bedford visited the towns of Cape Cod and would cross over to the islands of Martha's Vineyard and Nantucket. A mission center in the Blackstone River Valley sent priests into central and western Massachusetts, while parishes in Lowell and Lawrence, already growing themselves, also had charge of the surrounding towns, as well as places in New Hampshire. No wonder, a friend of Fitzpatrick's teased him, "We wake up in the morning and hear of two or three churches" that had gone up overnight.[18]

Like his predecessor, Fitzpatrick also gave attention to meeting the needs of his parishioners in this world. In rapid succession, several institutions that saw to the material wants of immigrants and their families were opened, starting with the House of the Angel Guardian in 1851. This was an orphanage for boys, a parallel facility to the St. Vincent Asylum for girls, which Fenwick had started two decades earlier and for which Fitzpatrick built a new building. Within just two years, the Angel Guardian was housing more than two hundred boys, to whom it offered a comfortable home and training in such employable skills as printing. A decade later, the bishop opened yet a third orphanage, the Home for Destitute Catholic Children. Despite its forbidding name, this too was a place where children could be protected from the physical and moral dangers of the streets while learning a useful trade they could take with them into adulthood. At about the same time, a hospital was opened in South Boston and named in honor of its principal benefactor, Andrew Carney, an immigrant who had made a fortune, at first in the tailoring business and then through shrewd investments. To staff these and other institutions, Fitzpatrick welcomed new communities of sisters to the diocese, and the church's workforce became ever more decisively a female one; indeed, sisters in the Diocese of Boston had outnumbered priests working there at least since the 1820s, and the gap widened further during Fitzpatrick's time as bishop.[19]

To support this growing network, Fitzpatrick relied not only on thousands of small, regular donations from Catholics, but also on the generosity of his friends among the wealthier Boston Brahmins who would probably not otherwise have supported Catholic causes. Renewing the school ties of his younger days, the bishop was an active member of such stoutly Yankee organizations as the Thursday Evening Club, where he rubbed shoulders every week with such figures as the physician and poet Dr. Oliver Wendell

Holmes. In his effort to open a college in the city for Catholic boys — those who could not afford the high tuition ($75 per year) of Holy Cross down the road in Worcester — he won support from an impressive array of the local establishment: Robert C. Winthrop, a descendant of Boston's founder in the seventeenth century; Edward Everett, who had been both governor of Massachusetts and president of Harvard; several members of the Lawrence family, the industrialists who built the city that bears their name; and many others. These efforts paid off with the founding of Boston College in 1863. Two years earlier, these same proper Bostonians had arranged for Fitzpatrick to be awarded an honorary degree from Harvard, the first of only two Boston bishops ever to be so honored. But Fitzpatrick's associations among local Protestants did not separate him from his own parishioners. The British historian and amateur theologian Lord Acton called on Fitzpatrick in 1853 during a tour of America and was struck by his host's ability to find time for everyone. "I spent an hour with him," Acton noted in his diary, "and he was called out at least twenty times by poor people who wished to see him. This goes on all day; he cannot close his door." Nor did he give up the ties to his own family, including his sister Eleanor, who had married Thomas Boland of Cambridge and who often took in travelers or orphans whom the bishop had sent her way. Fitzpatrick was always eager for the comfort and familiarity of home: during one Christmas at the Boland house, for example, he participated so eagerly in the jostling of the gift grab-bag that a few heads knocked together.[20] He could preside at the formal liturgies and ceremonies of the church, but he could also remain, as many called him, "Bishop John."

He never lost sight, however, of the serious business that being the Catholic bishop of Boston had become, and the hostility immigrants faced had to remain on his agenda. The anti-Catholic fires of the Ursuline convent riot had been banked but not entirely extinguished, and for a time nativism reemerged as a political movement. In the 1854 elections, every statewide officer from the governor on down and all but two members of the legislature were members of the American Party, more popularly known as Know-Nothings from their vow to deny all knowledge of the party's activities. These lawmakers sought to choke off the number of new immigrants, most of them Catholics, who could come into the state, and they also sought to restrict the rights of those already here. One of their "reforms" called for an increase in the length of time an immigrant would have to wait before becoming a citizen. A child born in Massachusetts had to wait twenty-one years before being allowed to vote, their logic went; why shouldn't an immigrant adult have to wait that long, rather than the traditional seven years? The legislature also appointed a committee — the newspapers called it a "convent smelling committee" — to inspect and sniff out the nefarious activities that many still suspected were common within these religious communities of women. The committee was seriously embarrassed in 1855 when it was caught padding its expense account and the chairman was discovered in a hotel room with a woman who was not his wife. The attendant publicity led to his expulsion from the legislature and, more broadly, helped to dissipate much of the Know-Nothing energy. But disputes over the reading of the Bible in the public schools, still a daily practice, also exacerbated tensions. In 1859 a principled — or maybe just stubborn — Catholic lad at the Eliot School in the North End had refused to read from the King James Version of the Bible and was whipped for his trouble. The public clamor brought charges that Catholics were opposed to the Bible altogether, while Catholics made the boy a hero. Fitzpatrick defended his church and its people during these crises, and he was instrumental in convincing the Boston school committee to change the practice of demanding that Catholic students read from a Bible their pastors found unacceptable.[21]

More than anything else, it was the coming of the Civil War that killed off political nativism in Massachusetts. By the mid-1850s, it was apparent that slavery, not immigration, was the great public issue that had to be addressed. Those agitators who advocated outright and immediate abolition were still not entirely respectable politically, and Catholics had their own reasons to be suspicious of abolitionists. Too many of them had cut their political teeth as Know-Nothings. Why was it, a Boston priest wondered, that those "who pity the negro hate the church"? Bishop Fitzpatrick, like most American Catholics, was prepared to accept the continuation of slavery in states where it already existed, hoping for some future day when it would, in Abraham Lincoln's cautious phrase, be "put in the way of extinction." Catholic theology had long drawn a distinction between the slave trade, which was clearly wrong, and slavery itself, which was morally neutral. Once the secession of several southern states had forced the issue, however, both the Boston bishop and his parishioners joined in defense of the Union. "We have hoisted the American Stars and Stripes over the *Pilot* establishment," the editors of the local Irish newspaper, working closely with Fitzpatrick, editorialized, "and there they shall wave until the 'star of peace' returns." The bishop seemed to realize that the war would be a long one. "This thing has been long maturing," he was reported to have said; "we will be lucky to see it ended in five years," a prediction that proved remarkably accurate. Immigrants and their sons enlisted for service in such numbers that a distinct "Irish Regiment" (the Ninth Massachusetts Infantry) was formed, seeing action in Virginia and elsewhere. Catholic enthusiasm for the war diminished after Lincoln's Emancipation Proclamation of January 1863 — fighting to save the Union was one thing, dying to free the slaves another — but the war nonetheless gave Catholics the chance to demonstrate their loyalty to their adopted country.[22]

Fitzpatrick performed his own service for the nation during the conflict, and he was thus the first bishop of Boston to begin working on a larger, even international, stage. Despite his relative youth — still just thirty-nine at the outbreak of the war — and a robust appearance, he had been troubled by ill health and, in the 1850s, suffered from several episodes of what was called "cerebral congestion," most likely small strokes. Accordingly, in the spring of 1862 he sailed for Europe for a rest prescribed by his doctors. Traveling through Italy and France, he eventually made his way to Brussels, where he took up residence for the next two years. There, he would pursue informal diplomatic efforts on behalf of the Union. Leaders of the secessionist states had sent a number of representatives, including the Catholic bishop of Charleston, South Carolina, to various European capitals, seeking support for their new government. If foreign leaders, perhaps including the pope himself, were to recognize the Confederate States of America, it would be harder for the Northern government to insist that it was not a distinct nation. These Southern efforts were making some headway, but Fitzpatrick was in a position to counter them by arguing the Union's cause, and this he did effectively. "He has done us much good in strengthening our cause with that class which has been most prejudiced against us," the American ambassador to Belgium told Secretary of State William Seward. Fitzpatrick even took over day-to-day management of the American embassy in Brussels during the ambassador's absences for visits to other capitals on the continent. No recognition for the Confederacy came and, while many diplomatic hands had produced that result, Fitzpatrick's were among them. By the time he returned to Boston in the summer of 1864, the tide had turned in favor of the Union.[23]

The war had interrupted but not halted developments in Boston more directly related to Fitzpatrick's duties as bishop. One of his longstanding concerns had been the condition of his own church, the Cathedral of the Holy Cross, which had been both the liturgical and the emotional center of the diocese for decades. By the 1850s, however, the surrounding neighborhood was changing dramatically, the earlier homes and residences replaced by commercial buildings, leaving few parishioners behind. The structure itself was also showing the wear of use, and Fitzpatrick reluctantly concluded that the only solution was to abandon the old site and to construct a newer, grander cathedral. The final service in the Franklin Street church was an emotional one: the bishop was so overcome that his long farewell sermon was read by another priest of the rectory. Completion of the new cathedral would fall largely to Fitzpatrick's successor, but he was the one who chose the site on Washington Street in the fashionable South End and set the plans in motion. Bigger and better able to meet the demands placed on the "first church" of the diocese, the new, gothic-designed Holy Cross also served an important symbolic function for local Catholics. Its construction was a mark of their permanence in a community that had once been wary of them and a mark of their intention to continue to contribute to the city and the region. The building was, its rector said later, "grand enough to meet our wants and to satisfy our aspirations." The taller of its two towers, the same priest liked to point out, was, at three hundred feet, a full eighty feet taller than the Bunker Hill Monument in Charlestown.[24]

Though he drew its plans, Bishop Fitzpatrick would not live to occupy this new cathedral. His time in Europe had brought only temporary relief from his physical ailments, and soon after the end of the Civil War it became virtually impossible for him to celebrate Mass or attend to other public duties. He had arranged for his vicar general, Father John Williams, to be consecrated a bishop with the intention of serving as his successor, and that transition came quickly. By the middle of February 1866, Fitzpatrick's decline was irreversible, and he died quietly at age forty-four. His tenure had been marked by turmoil, but also by progress. The Boston diocese, now reduced geographically only to the state of Massachusetts, had expanded to 112 churches, with 11 more under construction, two colleges, three orphanages, and a host of other schools and agencies. Fitzpatrick had also begun to convert the position of bishop into more of a public one: in a way that his predecessors had not, he transformed his office into one that had a role beyond the bounds of the Catholic populace. Boston's bishop would always be a public figure thereafter, with a role to play in the wider local, national, and even international community. Balancing that role with the more immediate one of serving as leader of the Catholics of the diocese would be required of all bishops in the future.

John Williams

John Williams would serve as the leader of Boston's Catholics for more than forty-one years, longer than any other man before or since. Assuming office on Fitzpatrick's death in 1866, he held the post until his own death in 1907, after the turn of a new century. He oversaw the opening of new churches, schools, and charitable institutions, and he even prepared the way for future developments that he himself could not foresee. Well into the 1950s, his successors were building new parishes and agencies on land that he had purchased decades before, intuiting the need for expansion without being able to specify exactly what the later times would require. For all those accomplishments, however, he has too often been overlooked in accounts of local Catholic history. In person, he was unassuming and quiet: a priest who served with him in the cathedral rectory recalled that he disapproved of idle chat at the dinner table. He was always more disposed to deflect credit for accomplishments onto others than to claim it for himself. Despite the heritage of his Irish-born parents, his personality had much of the taciturn Yankee about it. A letter from his surviving correspondence typifies his modest, straightforward style. "Dear sir," it reads in its entirety, "please send me a hat."[25]

Williams's diffidence should not be misinterpreted, for he left his mark on local Catholic life from the beginning. He was born in April 1822, and he was thus only ten years younger than his predecessor. Also like Fitzpatrick, he first attended the city's public schools before departing for a Sulpician prepatory seminary in Montreal. That was followed by advanced clerical studies in Paris, where he was ordained in 1845. Returning to Boston, he took up his pastoral duties in the cathedral parish, and he also served as chaplain to the House of the Angel Guardian. Bishop Fitzpatrick came to rely on him in many things, and it was therefore not surprising that Williams was designated his successor. It was a popular choice. The new bishop was "well known to the Catholics of Boston," a newspaper said at the time. "He was born among them, has lived among them." His appointment was a "happy and judicious" one.[26] Perhaps as a signal that a new age of inter-religious and interethnic cooperation was dawning, Williams's installation as bishop was attended by several non-Catholic leaders of state and local government. Barely a decade before, the holders of those offices had done everything possible to limit the role of Catholics in the wider community; now, their successors welcomed it. Nor was their acclaim lessened when, in 1875, Boston was raised to the rank of an archdiocese, with Williams holding the title of archbishop, which his successors have retained since. At about the same time, with the creation of new dioceses in Springfield and Providence, the archbishop's jurisdiction assumed its current geographical size: all of eastern Massachusetts with the exception of Cape Cod and Bristol County.

Williams had to continue the program of expansion of the churches and agencies of the archdiocese because, after a brief hiatus during the Civil War, immigration to Boston once again assumed sizable proportions. As before, newcomers from Ireland were the most numerous, but the list of countries sending migrants to American shores was now a longer one. Southern and eastern Europe began to hemorrhage, with Italians, Portuguese, Poles, and Lithuanians coming in significant numbers. Those who came into New England from French Canada also increased steadily. There were even for the first time migrants from the Near East, including a measurable Lebanese population, often identified in official reports as "Syrians" because of the shifting political subdivisions in that part of the world. By the time of Williams's death, almost one of every three residents of Massachusetts had been born abroad. Not all of these immigrants were Catholics, of course: German Protestants joined German Catholics, and there were Jewish immigrants from Poland and other parts of the Russian empire, where they had been subject to near-constant persecution. There were fewer immigrants to Boston from central Europe (Hungarians, Czechs, Slovaks, Bohemians) than to other American cities, especially in the Midwest. Even so, the demands that these new people put on the church were insistent.[27]

For all those reasons and because of the natural growth in the Catholic population already here, Williams had to continue the efforts of earlier bishops in which expansion was the watchword for Catholicism in Boston. During the course of his tenure, Williams opened forty-four new parishes, most of which were territorial parishes serving a mixed (though usually predominantly Irish) ethnic population. Thirteen of these new churches, however, almost one-third of the total, were designated for members of what the later archdiocesan historians would call "the newer Catholic races." By the time of his death, the archdiocese had ten French-language churches, five churches each for Italian and Polish Catholics, four for Lithuanians, three for Portuguese, and two for Lebanese. At the time, of course, the Mass and the sacraments were conducted entirely in Latin, a language uniformly foreign to native-born and newcomer alike. But these so-called national parishes gave those who brought a foreign language with them in their immigrant baggage the chance to hear sermons in their mother tongue. Even more important, they could go to confession in a language in which they were more comfortable than English. In petitioning for establishment of a new parish, a community of Italians in the city of Everett would later express the desire that all groups felt for "a church of their own where they can . . . understand just what is going on."[28]

Archdiocesan personnel had to grow in order to staff these new parishes. Throughout the country, the church had long relied heavily on an influx of priests from abroad, and while most of these men were devoted to their work, some found it impossible to adjust to the American setting. As early as 1815, Archbishop John Carroll of Baltimore had complained about the "medley of clerical characters" from Europe that parishioners in this country often had to put up with. Foreign-born priests were still a presence in Boston, but Williams resolved to shift the balance more decisively toward his own native clergy. There were about 125 priests in the diocese when he took office, and the opening of a seminary to increase their ranks and to improve their education was a high priority for him. No more would seminarians have to follow the path to the priesthood he and Fitzpatrick had taken through Canada and France. In 1880 he purchased the Stanwood Estate, a farm and orchard in Brighton, with the intention of opening a seminary that would prepare priests for service both in Boston and in the other dioceses of New England. Though a district of the city today, Brighton was at the time a separate town with a decidedly rural flavor, and that recommended it as a site for the seminary. Priestly training was thought to benefit from isolation from the wider world, and young men could enter the grounds of the seminary, named St. John's after the archbishop's own patron saint, and leave behind the cares of the rest of the Catholic community. Twenty-eight students enrolled when classes began in the fall of 1884, but that number nearly tripled in the first five years. Throughout, Williams took a keen interest in the seminary, and he was especially eager that its library be fully supplied. A month after it opened, he boxed up most of his own books, together with some other books left behind in the cathedral rectory by several deceased priests, and sent them to Brighton for the students' use.[29] Until the middle of the twentieth century, the seminary would produce large numbers of priests to serve the Catholics of the Boston area.

Even more impressive was the growth in the number of religious sisters in the archdiocese during the Williams era. Communities of sisters had their own internal governance procedures, and they were responsible to their own leadership in motherhouses, either in this country or abroad. Thus, the archbishop had only indirect jurisdiction over them. Mostly, he was in the position of encouraging and facilitating their work rather than directing it himself. For Williams, that was a perfect arrangement, and the ranks of nuns in the Boston area grew steadily during his tenure, both from the arrival of new sisterhoods and the expanding population of those already here. Just a year after the seminary had opened, a census of church personnel showed how decisively the balance had tipped in favor of sisters. There were about 300 priests in the archdiocese by then, but there were already more than twice as many (about 650) sisters. That ratio persisted — by the time of Williams's death there were about 900 priests and 1,700 sisters — and the gap would grow wider still in the twentieth century. Some sisters lived in very large communities. The Sisters of Notre Dame, for example, had 64 nuns living at their convent on Berkeley Street in downtown Boston and 53 more at a convent in Roxbury; they also had 15 in Cambridge, 23 in Lawrence, and 36 in Lowell. Many of these women religious taught in the elementary and secondary schools of local parishes, but they also engaged in all sorts of charitable and social work. The Sisters of Charity, for instance, oversaw the Carney Hospital in South Boston, first opened in 1863, while Franciscan Sisters conducted the work of St. Elizabeth's Hospital, originally a "lying-in" facility for women but later a general hospital. In one year, the St. Elizabeth's "eye infirmary" treated more than 160 "out-door [i.e., out-patient] eye patients" for free. Through thousands of contacts such as those, together with the daily presence of sisters in parochial school classrooms, the face of the church for lay Catholics in the Williams era was most likely a woman's face.[30]

How ordinary lay people connected to these church institutions and personnel during the era of Archbishop Williams can be hard to describe. As we live through them, the routines of daily life seldom seem noteworthy enough for anyone to write them down. Nineteenth-century Boston Catholics, most of them situated in the working class, lacked both the leisure and the resources to engage in diary keeping. Nor were priests or sisters in the habit of keeping journals, though most convents of nuns did maintain a "house chronicle," an official record of the community's work that could be shared with sisters at the motherhouse or elsewhere. Fortunately, however, one of Archbishop Williams's priests was briefly a diarist, and the picture that emerges from its pages is one of intimate connection between parishioners and their local church. James Anthony Walsh had grown up in Cambridge, the son of a doctor, and he had briefly attended Harvard College before enrolling in St. John's Seminary, where he was ordained in 1892. He would later achieve national and even international prominence as one of the founders of the Maryknoll society, which sent missionary priests and sisters around the world. Before that, however, fresh out of the seminary, he served for eleven years in his first assignment as a curate at St. Patrick's parish in Roxbury, and from him we get an idea of what life was like for Catholics of this era.[31]

The life of a parish priest was not one of quiet contemplation and prayer. One day in March 1900, Walsh made dutiful notes on what was a more or less typical day in the parish. He said the early (6:00 a.m.) Mass that Thursday morning and later worked on his sermon for the coming Sunday. He was interrupted, however, by a steady stream of parishioners who rang the rectory doorbell, seeking his aid. With appropriate discretion, he recorded their concerns. First came "Mrs. S," who had a "meddlesome married step daughter." Then there was a young woman "who, with her sister, has been under the evil influence of a married man." She was followed by a young man, "previously engaged, now engaged to another, with prospect of trouble from no. 1," and then another young man, "excessively annoyed by scruples," who found it difficult to accept the forgiveness available in the confessional. The harsh realities of urban life and the role of the church in mediating them were also evident, as Walsh was visited for assistance by a social worker from a state agency who was working on a case involving a "wife with two black eyes, husband in jail, children in want." Nor did parishioners seek the comforts of their church only during normal working hours. Priests were regularly called out at any time of night to anoint the dying and comfort their families. One New Year's Eve, Father Walsh was roused from sleep at 1:30 a.m. — "in a blustering snowstorm, wind very cold," he noted — to anoint a parishioner thought to be near death. He suspected that the man in question was merely drunk, and, as it turned out, he was right. He went anyway, however, not returning to the rectory until about 2:30 and not getting back to sleep until an hour after that. Priests such as Walsh did this work with genuine devotion, and the attachment that developed between lay people and their clergy. After presiding at a funeral, Walsh spoke affectionately of the dead man, noting that many relatives who had been of little assistance to him in life nonetheless showed up at the funeral. The deceased had lost an arm in an industrial accident years before, and now, Walsh wrote, "Larry's corpus has followed his long-lost arm, and we hope for him the joys of the blessed. He was no saint, but he died well."[32] In the church of Boston in the era of Archbishop Williams, that typified the personal connection that parishioners had with their church.

The archbishop himself was largely removed from such direct contact with the people in his parishes. He met them mostly as he traveled the archdiocese administering confirmation, a task that was so time consuming that in 1891 he successfully petitioned Rome for the appointment of an auxiliary bishop (Father John Brady, pastor of St. Joseph's parish in Amesbury) to help him in this. Williams was the leader of a large and complex organization, and he saw his role as providing general direction for it, rather than hands-on management of every detail. He would attend to larger administrative matters, the kinds of things that had to be decided at the center — the opening of the seminary, for example, or the purchase of parish property — but he would leave to priests, sisters, and lay people themselves the day-to-day operation of those institutions once established. He had a fundamental confidence in those who were working with him to advance the church's programs. He was a co-owner of the *Pilot*, for example, a weekly newspaper that had been established by Bishop Fenwick in 1829. When the paper fell into financial trouble fifty years later, Williams provided the funds to keep it going. He was also persistent in raising funds to repay those who had invested in the paper during several years of financial uncertainty. He left all editorial decisions, however, entirely in the hands of its editor, the renowned poet and essayist John Boyle O'Reilly. A later archbishop would convert the newspaper into more of an "official organ" of the archdiocese, with editorials and other material written in the archbishop's office, but Williams was sure that, left to himself, O'Reilly could support the work of the church throughout the archdiocese no less effectively.[33] For Williams, being the archbishop did not require that he take visible credit for everything that happened in the local church.

Because he was the leader of an important Catholic center, however, Williams necessarily played a part in significant, even historic events in the life of the church. In 1869 and 1870 he was in Rome for the meetings of the First Vatican Council. This was the first time since the sixteenth century that bishops from around the world had gathered for such a council, and it had serious work on its agenda, most notably the question of whether to define as official church doctrine the infallibility of the pope. Characteristically, Williams was silent on most of the council's work. The little diary he kept during its proceedings is exasperating to the historian since it is filled with accounts of carriage rides and sightseeing but silent on the great events of the council, which coincided with the capture of Rome by Italian nationalist troops. Like many other American bishops, Williams may have had his doubts about infallibility or at least about the advisability of defining it as dogma. Father Sherwood Healy, a former seminary professor whom Williams brought along with him to serve as his theological adviser, was skeptical. "The preponderance of talent is decidedly on the side of the non-definitionists," Healy wrote to a friend back home, possibly echoing Williams's own sentiments, though "the preponderance of numbers is all on the side of definition." In the end, Williams voted in favor of the doctrine, though he left Rome the very next day to return to Boston. More than a decade later, he participated in the Third Plenary Council of Baltimore, a gathering of all bishops in the United States, which set consistent policies in many aspects of the religious life of the church in this country. Foremost of these was the establishment of parish schools. There ought to be, the bishops said, a desk in a Catholic school for every Catholic child, and severe penalties (including denial of the sacraments) were authorized for those parents who sent their children to public schools. Here again, though Williams went along with the decision, he had some doubts about its wisdom. Catholic teachers and principals were coming to dominate the public school system in Boston, and Williams thus devoted less attention to constructing a separate church school system than bishops elsewhere. He did not oppose the idea of parochial schools, but their growth in the Boston area was slower than in other dioceses around the country. At his death, only 35 percent of the two hundred parishes had schools, a marked contrast to places like Chicago, where the number approached 100 percent.[34] Here again, Williams was willing to trust the judgment of local pastors and people. If they wanted a school, they could have one, and he would support them; if they made another choice, that too won his approval.

Archbishop Williams celebrated the sixtieth anniversary of his ordination to the priesthood in 1905, and the ceremony provided the occasion for numerous expressions of affection from the people of the archdiocese. He was well into his eighties by then, but still resilient. Cataract surgery two years before had slowed him a little, but soon enough he was back at his many tasks. His approach to this work was that of a traditional bishop. He had his own duties to perform, but he was also responsible for encouraging the distinct work of priests, sisters, and lay people. Together, they would all contribute to the mission of the church. That humility, a humility that was personal to him but that also expressed a larger vision of how the church ought to work — officially, it would be called "subsidiarity," leaving decisions at the level closest to the question at hand — elicited the cooperation of the Catholics of the archdiocese. At his death in the summer of 1907, he was mourned by all.

William O'Connell

With Boston's next archbishop, we approach the realm of living memory, where the boundary line between the past and the present, between history and today, starts to blur. Our perspective on this era and those that follow is thus different, and the assessments we make are more tentative, more subject to revision as time goes on. Many people still alive remember the tenure of William O'Connell. His time in office marked a turning point in the history of the archdiocese, and he himself captured that transition in a handy aphorism. Reflecting on the history of Catholicism in Massachusetts on the centennial of the diocese in 1908, O'Connell had concluded, "The Puritan has passed; the Catholic remains." The place where Catholics had once been suspect was now dominated numerically by members of the Roman church. This was, he had no doubt, a cause for celebration, a triumph over the many adversities that immigrants and their children had faced. But the change also entailed responsibilities. Catholics now had the duty to uphold society's values, for themselves and for the community at large, and the role of the archbishop in that process was widely accepted. "Your influence," a Yankee investment banker told O'Connell in the 1930s, "has always been patriotic, honorable and clean in thought, expression, purpose and action. It has helped vastly in improving the situation within our Commonwealth." A newspaper concurred, editorializing that, under O'Connell, the church was "steady and steadying," even as so much else in modern life seemed to be in flux.[35] The cardinal's own formidable personality had contributed measurably to that influence.

What the historians he commissioned to write the official history of the archdiocese would call "the foundations of a great career" began for O'Connell in Lowell, to which his parents had emigrated from Ireland in 1851. Eight years later, on December 8, which is celebrated in the church calendar as the Feast of the Immaculate Conception, William O'Connell was born. Other members of the family found work in the many mills of Lowell or in other trades, but William, the youngest of eleven children, was destined for education and another career. After some time in the public schools and enrollment in a high school or "minor" seminary in Maryland, he matriculated at Boston College, from which he graduated with the class of 1881. From there it was on to a seminary in Rome, where he was ordained three years later. He returned to Boston for parish assignments, first in Medford and then in St. Joseph's parish in the West End of Boston. The latter was one of the busiest parishes in the archdiocese, with a population of about fifteen thousand, and the young curate was thrown into its busy routines. In his first two years in the parish, he performed almost one-third of all the baptisms, and soon he was officiating at nearly half the marriages. At the same time, the pastor gave him responsibility for overseeing the parish Sunday school, and O'Connell was also active in promoting the work of devotional and temperance societies. Much of this work, O'Connell would recall later in his autobiography, was "trying and even repulsive to mere human sensibilities, but the 'God bless you, Father' of the homeless and the friendless lightened our hearts and brightened our way."[36]

Unlike his predecessors, however, O'Connell's advancement would not derive from his parish work. Instead, he would be recognized and put forward by leaders of the church in Rome, and he would eagerly become the means for the implementation in the United States of papal programs that took decreasing account of the particularities of local churches. In 1895 he was chosen to become the rector of the American College in Rome, the seminary he himself had attended. Under its previous rector (whose name was Denis O'Connell, though the two were not related), the school had become tainted in the eyes of some in the Roman Curia with "Americanism," the idea that the church in the United States (or any other country, for that matter) had its own distinctive characteristics. This stood in contrast to the rising spirit within the church's hierarchy of what was called *Romanità* — "Roman-ness" — and O'Connell committed himself to advancing that program. In 1901 he returned to North America as the bishop of Portland, Maine, though he spent much of his brief tenure there on a special papal diplomatic mission to Japan. He saw himself increasingly as an embodiment of this new emphasis on absolute adherence to Roman policy in all things, great and small. "As I am an American in patriotism," O'Connell said on arriving in Portland, "so am I, and shall ever be, Roman in faith." Rome was a "second fatherland" to him, he went on, adding that he turned "Romeward as naturally...as the needle seeks the North."[37] This stance had consequences: turning Romeward necessarily meant turning away from Boston, at least to some degree. When he succeeded Archbishop Williams six years later, he further advanced that program, and Rome seemed to confirm it in 1911, when O'Connell was the first archbishop to be elevated to the rank of cardinal. This, too, set a pattern, for every one of his successors in Boston has been similarly honored by the pope.

His concentration on the center of the worldwide church was matched by O'Connell's emphasis on his own position at the center of the archdiocese. He had a completely different administrative style from that of his predecessor, whom he often damned with faint praise. Archbishop Williams had been "a man of the highest and most honest character," O'Connell wrote in his memoirs, but "a sort of *laissez-faire* attitude" toward administration had resulted in what he claimed was a nearly "complete disorganization" that was "almost incredible." The new archbishop established procedures that would bring his office much more closely into the day-to-day work of the parishes, schools, and charitable agencies of the church. Pastors were required to seek explicit permission to spend more than $100 on anything, and parish account books had to be submitted annually to the chancery office for inspection. Any decisions made in personal meetings with O'Connell were not considered official until they had been confirmed afterward in writing. In several important areas, some familiar features of local Catholic life were brought more directly under the scrutiny and control of the archbishop's office. In 1908 after less than a year in office, he bought the *Pilot,* converting it from the independent paper it had been into "a diocesan organ of news and proper publicity"; his office would determine what was "proper." In the spring of 1911, he announced that he was dismissing the entire faculty of the seminary, who were members of the Sulpician order of priests, and replacing them with Boston diocesan clergy. O'Connell had chosen the Latin phrase *Vigor in Arduis* ("Vigor in Difficulties") as the motto on his episcopal coat of arms, and his administration seemed characterized by nothing if not vigor.[38]

In fact, the parishes and agencies of the archdiocese had not been as badly managed as this vision made it appear. Archbisop Williams's administrative style had relied more on local intitiatives — Williams did not think he had to do everything — and even under O'Connell pastors and religious sisters mostly continued to do the work they had been doing for decades, no less successfully. But O'Connell deliberately constructed an image of himself as an active and important public figure, and this had broader uses for the local Catholic community. The children of immigrants were increasingly assuming professional positions in commerce, law, and the civil service, and O'Connell's self-assertion as a local leader reflected vicariously on them. This was particularly true in state and local politics, where Catholics were largely taking control of elective and appointive office. This was the era of such legendary figures as James Michael Curley and John ("Honey Fitz") Fitzgerald and, although O'Connell often had his disagreements with these shrewd politicos, he was, like them, a recognized public leader. What he had to say on any subject made news simply because he was the one who had said it, and Catholics were reassured that "one of their own" had such influence. He was not afraid to speak out on almost any matter, and he could often swing the outcome of elections or legislative deliberations. In 1924, for example, he forced Catholic candidates into an abrupt about-face on the question of restricting child labor — he thought the proposal gave the government powers that properly belonged to the family — and a decade later he short-circuited a proposal to institute a state lottery, which he denounced as "out-and-out gambling" and a form of regressive taxation. In 1942 voters also deferred to his position in beating back a referendum that would have liberalized the state's birth control laws. Local politicians were careful to stay on his good side. His nickname in the halls of the State House was "Number One," an accurate enough measure of the influence he had in virtue of his office.[39]

Cardinal O'Connell sought to exercise a similarly influential role in the church nationally and internationally, but without comparable success. His position demanded some deference from other churchmen — with the death of Cardinal James Gibbons of Baltimore in 1921, he was the senior American cardinal — but his reputation was seriously damaged in the 1910s and 1920s by a scandal in his own household. His nephew, Monsignor James O'Connell, served as chancellor of the archdiocese and right-hand man to his uncle, but he was also secretly married to a woman in New York; apparently, he was embezzling money from the archdiocese to support his elaborate double life. At the same time, Father David Toomey, a young priest whom O'Connell had made the editor of the *Pilot,* was also secretly married. The cardinal knew of these activities, but both priests remained in office for several years until forced by the Vatican to resign. Cardinal O'Connell was faced with the prospect of removal from office himself for having tolerated such behavior, but he managed to hold on to his position, and the scandal never became publicly known. Even so, his influence within the church was vastly diminished, and he never played the role within the church, at home or abroad, that he had sought for himself.[40]

In spite of these troubled personal affairs, O'Connell nevertheless articulated an important new style for the leader of Boston's Catholics, a new way of being the archbishop that his successors all assumed on taking office. He had turned the position of archbishop into that of a public personage who was recognized and acknowledged beyond the boundaries of his own church. He was a community leader, not just a denominational, religious leader. The cardinal archbishop of Boston was now a figure comparable to the mayor or the governor, and his support was sought for all kinds of civic projects, particularly those that went beyond the bounds of purely religious matters. O'Connell sat as a member of the board of trustees of the Boston Public Library, for example, and he took those duties quite seriously, viewing them as a service to the entire community, not merely his own people. Kings and dignitaries visited him, an acknowledgment of his status. Unfortunately, this public standing also served to separate him from ordinary Catholics. He was seldom seen in person; for most parishioners, he was a photograph in the newspapers, not a physical presence on the altar or in the pulpit. Even so, he had helped elevate the position of the Catholic people, offering immigrants and second-generation Americans an example of the achievement and self-respect that could be theirs. In this way, he helped lay to rest the nativist suspicions that had plagued the Catholics of Boston since the previous century. His tenure allowed them to glimpse a world in which they would be at the center of things, not at the margins. He was more respected than loved by his people, and his imposing personal style seems more than a little offputting today. The changes of the Second Vatican Council and the on-going movement of Catholics into the American mainstream have rendered his triumphalist approach to the church obsolete. For his own times, how-ever, he gave Boston's Catholics something to be proud of, and he embodied the possibilities that were newly theirs.

Richard Cushing

If Cardinal O'Connell could be imposing and even stiff, his successor is widely remembered still today for his breezy, approachable, and relentlessly democratic style. While he could officiate at solemn religious services in the impressive robes of his office, Richard Cushing was just as likely to be seen leading the residents of an old folks home in some Irish songs or ex-changing his cardinal's hat with the bonnet of a first-grader in a parochial school yard. The contrasts between the two men were partly natural and partly cultivated. To be sure, Cushing had a different personality from that of his predecessor, one that seemed more in sympathy with changing times for the Catholics of Boston. But he also consciously exaggerated his more open personality, using it as a means of making a new statement about the role Catholics were playing in American society at large. Assuming of-fice in the final year of the World War II, he would lead the archdiocese through the many changes that came in the postwar period. Once again, it would be the archbishop's task to expand the parishes and institutions of the church as the Catholic population of Massachusetts not only grew, but also moved from city to suburb. He would preside over the largest ordination classes of new priests in the history of Catholic Boston, and the number of sisters would achieve their historic highs during his tenure. He oversaw the initial changes in liturgy mandated by the Second Vatican Council, and he would also face the challenges of shifting moral and social values that were affecting all Americans.

Cushing was born in South Boston in August 1895. Like so many other local Catholics of that time, he was a child of the working class: his father, originally a blacksmith, was a repairman for the city's elevated railway. The young Cushing enrolled at Boston College but, conforming to what was then the usual pattern for those destined for the diocesan priesthood, he left after two years and moved literally across the street to St. John's Sem-inary in Brighton. There, the rector found him "intelligent, forceful, [and] mature,...a positive type, with good practical qualities." He was already being noticed for his skills as a preacher, and those parishioners who, in later years, heard one of his sermons, delivered always in his distinctive tones, never forgot it. On ordination, he was assigned first to a parish in Somerville and then to the cathedral in Boston, but he found his real calling in 1928, when he was chosen to direct the diocesan office of the Society for the Propagation of the Faith, the agency that supported church missionary efforts abroad. This work gave him a lifelong devotion to the missions: he would later found the Society of St. James the Apostle, which sent priests from the United States to work in remote areas of Latin America. That interest says something not only about him, but more generally about the Catholics of Boston. After a century of labor at establishing themselves in the once-hostile environment of Massachusetts, they were now firmly planted enough to think about contributing personnel and resources to the development of the church elsewhere. A generation earlier, this would not have been possible, but by Cushing's day, Catholics had advanced far enough to be on the giving rather than the receiving end of church support. Cushing's ability to assemble such resources led to his designation as an auxiliary bishop and then as O'Connell's successor in 1944; in 1958, he was made a cardinal by Pope John XXIII.[41]

The Boston church experienced almost breathtaking growth during Cushing's tenure as archbishop. By the time of World War II, three of every five people in Massachusetts were Catholic, and the population was moving around inside the state. Thanks to the G.I. Bill, thousands of returning veterans had access to the higher education that their parents could only have dreamed about, and this produced a widespread movement up into the middle class. As often as not, the figurative move up the ladder of success was accompanied by a literal move from the older cities to the suburbs, and the institutions of the church followed the people under Cushing's supervision. There were just over three hundred parishes when he took office and more than four hundred at his death. This general trend could be seen everywhere across the archdiocese. Many older towns that had once had a single parish (Andover, Hingham, and Westwood, for example) soon had two; towns that started with two parishes (Milton and Woburn, for example) soon had four. Towns without parishes got them for the first time: there was no separate parish serving Marshfield, for example, when Cushing assumed office, but there were three of them there at his death. Expansion of the parochial school system proceeded along similar lines. Only one parish (St. Stephen's) in Framingham, for instance, had a school in 1944 at the beginning of Cushing's tenure. It was of good size, with 450 children enrolled, but by 1970 two other parishes in town (St. Bridget and St. Tarcisius) had also opened schools, and enrollment in the three approached 1,200. The number of sisters in the archdiocese increased in that period from 4,000 to 5,700, but these schools were also staffed increasingly by lay teachers: just 180 of them in the entire diocese in 1944, nearly 1,600 in 1970. The Catholic health care system similarly expanded, treating 27,000 patients in Cushing's first year and almost 385,000 of them in his last year.[42]

It was easy for Boston's Catholics to think that this kind of expansion would continue indefinitely. Everything, one might well believe, would continue to get bigger and better, even as the church remained fundamentally unchanged throughout this expansion. This proved not to be the case, as

Cardinal Cushing's tenure was cut across its middle by the dramatic events of the Second Vatican Council. Pope John XXIII had surprised nearly everyone when, just a year after his election, he announced that he would assemble bishops from around the world for an "ecumenical" council. This was the first such council in a century and only the second one since the Reformation, four hundred years before. Expressing his desire to "throw open the windows" of the church, Pope John asked the council to reconsider church practices and the theology that underlay them. A rush of reform came with the council's opening in 1962 and did not abate even after its formal sessions concluded in 1965. Cushing dutifully attended the sessions of the gathering, which were held in St. Peter's Basilica in Rome over several months in each successive autumn, though he did not take an active role in speaking. He famously complained that his command of Latin, in which the official deliberations were conducted, was not sufficiently good for him to follow the arguments. His principal intervention came in shaping the statement on Catholic relations with the Jewish people, a document that specifically rejected the older belief that the Jews had been in a particular way responsible for the death of Jesus. Cushing's extensive work in helping reconcile the Catholic and Jewish populations of Boston had prepared him for this effort, and his own Jewish brother-in-law gave the discussion a personal dimension for him.[43]

The council's most visible impact on ordinary Catholic lay people was a remaking of the Mass and the other sacraments of the church. The weekly liturgy was now to be conducted in English or the other vernacular of local parishes, and the priest stood behind a new altar, facing the congregation. The singing of hymns was expected, and priests were required always to deliver a homily, explaining the scriptural readings that the people had just heard read aloud. Other changes in religious practice were urged — more frequent reception of communion by parishioners, for instance — while certain devotional practices (such as novenas and Benediction of the Blessed Sacrament) were deemphasized for their potential to distract attention from the centrality of the Mass. These changes came suddenly for most Catholics, particularly in the Boston area. Other parts of the country had done more experimenting in the 1950s with practices such as the "dialogue Mass," in which the entire congregation said the prayers and responses usually recited only by the altar boys, but this had been uncommon in Boston, where the liturgical gears shifted with less warning. It was left to Cushing to implement these changes, and he made it clear that he would do so. "The introduction of the new rite is not a matter of choice," he wrote to the priests of the archdiocese. "It is ordered by the Holy See and must be carefully implemented in all the churches and chapels of the archdiocese." To help in this, he conducted a series of training sessions for priests, offering "further guidance in the theological background to the liturgical renewal." He used the pages of the *Pilot* to run stories, with photographs, explaining and illustrating how the new services were to be conducted, and these helped ease acceptance of the new and unfamiliar forms. "I thought the Participated

Mass last Sunday was just great," a parishioner from Lynn said in a letter to the paper's editor, and the speed with which he and other lay Catholics accepted the new ways of worship was remarkable. Cushing was somewhat more reluctant to approve the option of attending Sunday Mass on Saturday afternoon or evening — "a real change in the practice of worship among our people," he observed correctly — but he authorized it quickly in response to lay demand.[44]

Changes in the church that came with the Vatican Council were paralleled by changes in the position of Catholics in society during the Cushing era. By the postwar period, Catholics had long since come to control state and local government. A sweep of statewide office by Catholic Democrats in the elections of 1948, together with Democratic control of the state House of Representatives for the first time in history, confirmed Catholic voting strength. Cushing himself had helped marshal this power at the ballot box. That year, he organized a very successful get-out-the-vote drive in parishes to beat back an attempt to liberalize the state's birth control laws. He was also an enthusiastic "Cold Warrior," giving countless speeches on the dangers of international communism and supporting the anti-communist crusade of Wisconsin's Joseph McCarthy, at least until the senator's methods turned in an extreme direction. The cardinal's most visible political connection, however, was with the Kennedy family. He worked with Joseph and Rose Fitzgerald Kennedy in endowing local Catholic schools and charities, particularly those that provided help for special-needs children, an enduring interest for all of them. (At his death, Cushing would be buried on the grounds of St. Coletta's School, for those he called "exceptional" children, in Hanover.) He presided at the wedding of John F. Kennedy, the state's junior senator, in 1953, and at the president's funeral a decade later. In between, he was an informal adviser. "Whenever he was home" from Washington, Cushing later told Kennedy's younger brother (and successor) Edward, "he never failed to contact me by a telephone call or a personal visit. Our conversations covered many subjects." The cardinal helped plan strategy for defusing the "Catholic issue" in the 1960 presidential campaign, and behind the scenes he helped Robert Kennedy raise money to ransom the prisoners taken in the unsuccessful Bay of Pigs invasion. When Cushing gave the invocation at the 1961 inauguration of President Kennedy, it was the first time a Catholic prelate had ever done so. A century before, nativists would have been horrified at the sight, thinking that it confirmed their worst fears about Catholic political power; by then, it was not even worthy of comment in the press.[45]

Because of these many successes and also because of Cushing's ability to draw broad public attention to them, his tenure as archbishop is still viewed by many Boston Catholics as a kind of golden age. Never had the identification of local Catholics with their church seemed stronger or more personally meaningful. Beneath the surface, however, lay the origin of many troubles that would come in subsequent years. The massive church building campaign had been conducted without proper financial and administrative controls, and by the 1960s local banks were increasingly unwilling to advance resources to the archdiocese. The cardinal could raise money successfully, but he could also apparently spend it even faster, and by his final years the church's debt exceeded $80 million. At the same time, his eagerness to admit large numbers of seminarians and then to ordain them — he approached but never actually achieved his often-stated goal of ordaining a hundred new priests in a single year — meant that some of those who, it was later clear, should have been excluded from the priesthood joined its ranks. The principal offenders in the scandal over priest sexual abuse of children and young people, revealed in 2002, for example, had been ordained by Cushing in the late 1950s and early 1960s. Social changes, particularly rising racial tensions, were also simmering across the city, and these would result in violence shortly after the cardinal's death, centering particularly around the desegregation of the public school system. All of these would mark the tenure of Cushing's successor, not always happily. While he lived, however, the cardinal presided over a thriving local church. He would be the last "local boy" to serve as archbishop, and this too perhaps contributed to the aura that still surrounds his tenure. Like all of his predecessors, he seemed to provide Boston's Catholics with the kind of leadership they needed at the time, a reflection of how they had come to view themselves in their own particular historical circumstances.

Humberto Medeiros

Like the contrast between Cardinal O'Connell and his successor, that between Cushing and the next archbishop was marked and immediately noticeable. Where Cushing was outgoing and even flamboyant, Humberto Medeiros was naturally private and shy. He was born in the Azores in 1915 and came to the United States with his family as an adolescent. A native speaker of Portuguese, he picked up English readily, and this talent for languages eventually led him to a fluency in several other tongues as well. This suited him for work amid the increasing ethnic diversity of the church, particularly after changes in federal immigration law in the mid-1960s reopened the doors to newcomers, doors that had been largely shut by restrictive legislation half a century before. Medeiros was perhaps the best educated of all of Boston's bishops, earning undergraduate and graduate degrees (including a Ph.D.) from Catholic University in Washington. He was ordained a priest in 1946 and served in several parishes in and around his adopted city of Fall River, Massachusetts. In 1966 he was taken from his pastoral and administrative duties and appointed the bishop of Brownsville, Texas. The appointment seemed an ideal matching of individual and assignment. Parishioners there were overwhelmingly poor Mexican and Mexican American farm workers, and Medeiros publicly supported their demands for a living wage. Growing awareness throughout the 1960s of the need for righting longstanding social wrongs confirmed the idea that the church had an active role to play in that process, and Bishop Medeiros was an embodiment of this approach. A national Catholic magazine named him one of the twelve bishops in the country with "the most promise for the future of the Church." When it was announced in September 1970 that he would come to Boston as Cushing's successor — Medeiros was installed a month later, and Cushing died another month after that — the news confirmed the perception that different times were ahead.[46]

From the first, it was apparent that the many serious challenges for the archdiocese that had been gathering during Cushing's final years were about to reach crisis proportions. Facing them had to be at the top of the new archbishop's agenda. Medeiros's first task was to pay off the debt that he inherited. Exercising financial restraint is always less glamorous than free spending, but Medeiros recognized that this job had to be done. With the help of tighter administrative oversight and increasingly successful (and professional) fundraising, the debt was liquidated without major cutbacks in programs or the sale of church property. At the same time, some of the slow-motion impact of Vatican II was starting to be felt in ways that did not bode well for the church as an institution. Across the country, large numbers of priests were deciding to leave the priesthood, some of them to marry, others simply to take up positions in the secular workforce. The total number of priests in Boston peaked early in Medeiros's tenure at just under 2,500 and then began a steady decline that continued, and indeed picked up speed, down to the present day. In the same way, the number of sisters began a decline from 5,700 when Medeiros arrived to only 4,800 (a drop of 15 percent) a decade later. Those priests and nuns who remained soon experienced a process that the sociologists called "graying," with the average age steadily rising, portending even further declines in the future.[47] The number of parishes in the archdiocese remained level — in fact, it increased slightly, with the addition of new churches in such still-growing far suburbs as Carver — but it was nonetheless clear that the constant expansion of earlier decades was now decidedly a thing of the past. For the first time since the founding of the Boston church, contraction rather than expansion seemed the more likely prospect for the future.

The social and political upheavals of American life would also mark the Medeiros tenure as a time of conflict. The presumption that Catholics would be unified in response to these crises, a presumption on which O'Connell and Cushing could depend, was no longer warranted. Evidence for the shattering of this consensus was everywhere. The long war in Vietnam divided Catholics no less than their fellow citizens, and by the early 1970s opposition to American involvement there was particularly strong in the Boston area. Catholics were active in the antiwar movement and even helped elect a Jesuit priest — Robert Drinan, the dean of the Boston College law school — to Congress from Massachusetts in 1970 on a platform that promised an immediate withdrawal of troops from the Asian conflict. Boston Catholics had also participated in civil rights marches in the South during the 1960s, and they had made common cause with people of other faiths in the process. In 1965 a crowd of forty thousand, most of them Catholics, had gathered on the Boston Common to mourn and protest the death of James Reeb, a Unitarian minister from Boston, who had been murdered by the Ku Klux Klan in Alabama following his participation in the historic march in Selma. As the civil rights movement turned its attention increasingly to cities in the North, however, support waned, and Medeiros faced the prospect that parishioners might be impeding racial equality rather than promoting it. "The white voters of Boston, overwhelmingly Catholic, seem to have locked the door of the ghetto and thrown away the key," a local parish interracial group had charged. Another blow to Catholic unity was the Supreme Court decision of 1973 removing most legal restrictions on abortion. Though many Catholic politicians initially denounced the decision — "not in accordance with the value which our civilization places on human life," said Senator Edward Kennedy — most of them soon followed the general trend of the Democratic Party toward support for unrestricted access to abortion, thereby setting themselves expressly at odds with the position of the church. By 1980 it was clear both that a common political and social program, uniting the religious and political leadership in Boston, and the deference once automatically accorded the archbishop were gone.[48]

The insistence of Archbishop Medeiros, who was elevated to the rank of cardinal in 1973, on stating church positions on these and other issues inevitably made him less popular than those among his predecessors who had been more in tune with the drift of their times. His views on issues of economic and racial justice were unwaveringly clear, but parishioners did not always adopt them as their own. In 1978, for example, he faced significant opposition from well-to-do landowners in the town of Scituate when his urban ministry office proposed a housing development there that included units for low- and middle-income tenants. "I don't have two sets of rules," he said sharply, "one for the wealthy, one for the poor." These tensions were a replay in the suburbs of the racial and economic turmoil that had been roiling the city of Boston itself in the aftermath of an order in 1974 by the federal court to desegregate the city's public schools. Most observers agreed that the court's decision had been entirely correct as a matter of law: the Boston school committee had indeed engaged in practices that effectively separated white and black students. But opposition to the prescribed remedy, the daily transportation of students from different districts on school buses to achieve racial balance, aroused passionate and sometimes violent opposition, particularly in the heavily Catholic neighborhoods of South Boston and Charlestown. Medeiros repeatedly expressed his support for the desegregation order, and he saw to it that the parish schools of the city were not used as "segregation academies" for those fleeing integration of the public schools. But some parishioners denounced his stance and that of his priests, openly defying their entreaties for calm and cooperation. During one anti-busing protest march, a group of women passed their parish church, defiantly praying the rosary at the top of their lungs. When one of the priests, gathered on the church steps to watch, told them

that they should not be praying for what the church considered unjust, they
jeered back, "See, we don't need you anymore. We deal with God directly."
Medeiros's frustration at this opposition boiled over: in an unguarded moment, he claimed that if he went into the resisting neighborhoods he would
be stoned, a statement for which he later apologized. But it was clearer than
ever that, by the late twentieth century, Boston's Catholics would not always
follow their archbishop's lead.[49]

Medeiros's time in Boston saw happier occasions than this, particularly
as the years went on. As a cardinal, he had participated in the two papal elections of 1978, that of John Paul I in August and, after that pope's
unexpected death, the election of John Paul II in September. (Each of the cardinal's predecessors had participated in one papal election each: O'Connell
in 1939, Cushing in 1963). A year later, Medeiros welcomed John Paul II
to Boston as the first stop on his historic tour of America, the first ever
by a reigning pontiff. A motorcade through the city and a prayer service for
priests in Holy Cross Cathedral were followed by an open-air Mass for thousands on the Boston Common, conducted in a driving rain that drenched all
those in attendance but did not dampen their enthusiasm. The pope spent
the night in the cardinal's residence in Brighton, speaking to seminarians
the next morning before traveling on to New York for an address to the
United Nations and then to other cities around the country. Medeiros also
welcomed Mother Teresa of Calcutta to Boston in 1982. Widely recognized
as a saint even in her own lifetime for her selfless devotion to the sick and
poor of India, she and the cardinal seemed kindred spirits in their personal
attention to those in need. More broadly, Medeiros had also continued the
work of implementing the reforms of Vatican II. He authorized the use of
lay Eucharistic ministers in all the parishes of the archdiocese, and in 1976
he ordained the first group of permanent lay deacons for service in local
parishes.[50]

The years of turmoil took their toll, however, and Medeiros's health
became uncertain. Robust in appearance, he suffered from a number of ailments, and in September 1983 he submitted to open heart surgery. Though
the procedure seemed successful, he died the following morning at age sixty-
seven, having served in Boston for just thirteen years, the shortest tenure of
any archbishop. In spite of the many controversies of his time, he is increasingly seen today as a tragic figure. Though he was a man of genuine
spirituality, his overt piety represented a departure from the cooler religious
style that Bostonians were used to in their archbishop. Before his surgery,
he had put himself in God's hands: "whatever God wants," he supposedly
told an associate. That was, of course, an appropriate sentiment under the
circumstances, but local Catholics were used to a less resigned, more self-
confident attitude from their spiritual leader. Lingering ethnic animosities
were also problematic, particularly among some of his own priests: the overwhelmingly Irish clergy always saw Medeiros as something of an outsider.[51]
He may have seen himself that way, too, choosing to be buried next to his
parents in the family plot in a cemetery in Fall River. With the exception

of Bishop Cheverus, Medeiros's predecessors had all chosen to be buried either in Holy Cross Cathedral or in another institution of their diocese. Cardinal Medeiros had been called upon to lead the Boston church during difficult times, and the task was sometimes literally a thankless one. Even his more popular predecessors would have been challenged by it. Larger social, political, and religious forces over which he had no control had presented persistent problems, but his unwaveringly pastoral approach also offered a different model of leadership. Though the archdiocese had long since become a complex institution, it remained first and foremost a church, offering both the comforts and the challenges of religion. Medeiros's focus on those dimensions of faith was his ultimate legacy.

Bernard Law

With Boston's next archbishop, we leave decisively the realm of history and enter that of still-current events. The tenure of Bernard Law, who was appointed to succeed Cardinal Medeiros in March 1984 and was himself elevated to the cardinalate a year later, began with great promise. The son of an officer in the U.S. military, he was born in Mexico in 1931, and he was thus considerably younger than his predecessor, apparently indicating a generational shift in the leadership of Catholic Boston. After earning an undergraduate degree at Harvard, he attended a seminary in Ohio and was ordained in 1961 for service as a priest in Mississippi. He arrived there just in time to play an active part in challenging the Jim Crow laws and customs that had kept African Americans in an inferior position for generations, and in his role as a priest and as editor of the diocesan newspaper he helped place the church firmly on the side of racial integration. A job in the offices of the National Conference of Catholic Bishops in Washington was followed by appointment as bishop of the Diocese of Springfield–Cape Giradeau in rural southern Missouri, where he served for a decade before coming to Boston as archbishop six months after Medeiros's death. Such a peripatetic career had become a common one by then. Particularly during the papacy of John Paul II, bishops in the United States were appointed largely without connections to the dioceses they were asked to lead, a practice that would often leave them isolated from their parishioners. Even so, Bernard Law seemed destined for success. "After Boston," a visiting Roman prelate told him at the installation ceremony, "there's only heaven."[52]

His style and abilities stood in contrast to those of his predecessor. Medeiros had always been a little uncomfortable in front of television cameras or reporters, but Law, as a former newspaperman himself, was entirely at home there. From his first press conferences, he was smooth and persuasive: even if reporters disagreed with his positions (on abortion, for instance) he could state them in ways that commanded respect nonetheless. He made news everywhere he went, often without intending to. While driving home from a local church ceremony in his early months in the city, for example, he and another priest came across a woman whose car had broken down; he called for a tow truck on his mobile telephone, still an uncommon device at the time, and drove the woman to her destination. He seemed likely to restore the public persona of the archbishop to the position it had held in the days of O'Connell and Cushing, and the timing seemed right for such a restoration. A new mayor, Raymond Flynn, had taken office just two months before Law's arrival in Boston, replacing Kevin White, who had held that position since 1967. Together, the two personalities apparently represented a return to the confidence that Bostonians in general, and Catholic Bostonians in particular, had once felt.[53]

Law could not, however, reestablish the role of the archbishop as a decisive arbiter of public questions, and the changed circumstances in which he was operating were evident in political battles early in his administration. The commonality of purpose that had once united Catholic religious and political leaders in Massachusetts was gone forever. The definitive evidence for this came in 1986, when Law tried to secure voter approval of two issues that were of particular importance to him. Referendum questions on the ballot that year asked for restrictions on public funding for abortion and for removal of the provision in the state constitution that blocked the granting of public moneys to religiously affiliated schools and institutions. The cardinal had mounted an extensive, if low-key, effort to secure adoption of both measures at the polls. Pastors were encouraged to organize their parishioners, and a tape-recorded message from Law himself was played at Sunday Masses a few weeks before election day. His position was soundly rejected on both counts. The restrictions on abortion funding were defeated by 58 percent to 42 percent, and the prospect of state aid to church schools lost by an even larger margin: 69 percent to 31 percent.[54] The experience apparently had a chastening effect on the cardinal. Though his position on both issues did not change, he no longer attempted to secure endorsement of them through the political process.

In managing the internal affairs of the archdiocese, Law had more than enough to occupy his attention. The declining numbers of clergy and religious continued, and this required greater attention to the marshalling of archdiocesan personnel. By the turn of the century, the number of diocesan priests had dipped below 1,000, down from more than twice as many just thirty years before. Even more telling, nearly 300 priests were already retired, and the yearly ordination classes of new priests were counted in the single digits. The number of sisters continued its parallel decline and even picked up speed, leaving only about 2,600. Partly in response, Law began to close a number of local parishes around the archdiocese, a clear indication that the age of contraction was well under way. For the most part, these were churches in old ethnic neighborhoods that had once served non-English-speaking populations whose children and grandchildren lost their mother tongue and moved to the suburbs. Parish closings would become a more pressing issue, and a more contentious one, in the administration of Law's successor, but he himself had begun the process. The archdiocese had 408 parishes when Law took office, but only 362 when he left it. At the same time, he was sympathetic to the needs of newer immigrant populations, helping churches that had formerly served one ethnic group meet the needs of another. St. Patrick's parish in Lawrence, for example, founded in the 1870s for Irish immigrants, came to have as many weekly Masses in Spanish and Vietnamese as in English.[55]

Most seriously of all, however, the crisis surrounding clergy sexual abuse, a scandal that would eventually prove Cardinal Law's undoing, began to gather in the final decades of the twentieth century. The problem had not been entirely unknown in the past. Scattered reports from various places around the country — Louisiana, Texas, Rhode Island — had occasionally made news, but these were usually viewed as disconnected, tragic exceptions that only proved the more common rule of dedicated priestly service. In 1992, however, the case of an abusive ex-priest from the Diocese of Fall River galvanized the attention of Catholics and others in Massachusetts, suggesting that the problem might be more widespread than anyone had imagined. The metaphorical floodgates opened a decade later, with Boston as the epicenter of what grew into a national crisis for the church. Newspaper reports detailed the crimes — they were sins, too, of course — of several priests who had molested children in their parish assignments in and around Boston for years. After each incident came to the attention of church officials, the offenders were sent to treatment centers, where psychologists would eventually attest that they had been "cured"; after that, they were reassigned to a new parish, without notification that there had been any problems. Most of the time, the offenses would then simply begin again. Cardinal Law had overseen this entire process and, as it came to light, his actions seemed inadequate to the seriousness of the problem. The letters of reassignment usually contained boilerplate language about "dedicated priestly service," phrases that were meaningless in themselves but that came to seem callous and sinister in retrospect.[56]

For lay people, shock quickly gave way to anger and then to a commitment to action. A group of parishioners at St. John's Church in Wellesley began holding weekly meetings in the church basement to commiserate with one another over the scandal and to pray for the victims. "We started as a group of heartbroken people who needed to talk," one participant said. Later, a more pointed program would emerge. As examples of similar actions by bishops elsewhere multiplied, one woman said that the group had a clear goal: "we are trying to save the hierarchy from itself." The numbers attending the Monday night meetings in Wellesley swelled, and those attending also began to think about what more, besides talking, they could do. An informal organization took shape, calling itself Voice of the Faithful and rallying behind a slogan: "Keep the Faith, Change the Church." They made contact with similarly disaffected Catholics in other parts of the country — eventually, they claimed a nationwide membership of thirty thousand — and organized a national convention of those who were facing their own version of the scandal in dioceses everywhere. On a Saturday in July 2002, nearly four thousand Catholics from across the United States gathered for a day-long meeting in Boston. Victims told their wrenching personal stories, and panels explored how lay people might demand greater accountability from their church leaders. Anger continued to focus locally on Cardinal Law, who became a kind of symbol for the crisis nationally. Pressure steadily built on him to resign as archbishop, and this he finally did in December 2002.[57] Not since Bishop Cheverus had resigned his position to return to France had a leader of Boston's Catholics stepped down, and never had this happened in response to a public scandal. Law retired first to a convent in Maryland and then to a position in Rome at the Basilica of St. Mary Major.

It is still too soon for us to gain historical perspective on all these events. We can nevertheless note some of the seeds of the crisis, particularly the chasm they exposed between Cardinal Law in his capacity as archbishop and the Catholics of Boston. This dated partially from his early career away from Boston and from the manner of his appointment: when he was first designated the leader of the Boston church, he had not lived in the city since his student days, more than thirty years before. He and Boston's Catholics thus began their association largely as strangers to one another. While this might not have been problematic in more peaceful times, here it proved disastrous, compounding the anger of the scandal itself. A return to the pattern of the nineteenth century, in which bishops generally came from the ranks of a diocese's own clergy, might have laid a better foundation for cooperation between the officials of the church and its broad membership. At the same time, the way in which the duties of the archbishop had come to be defined also worked to a disadvantage. As it approached its bicentennial, the archdiocese was undeniably a large and complex organization. It is unrealistic to suppose that we can go back to the days of Cheverus, Fenwick, Fitzpatrick, or Williams, when the archbishop was essentially a pastor or the "first among equals" of the pastors. But the archbishop's office is still principally a pastoral one and needs to be approached in that way. The model of the archbishop as CEO of a large corporation, while it had its uses in the days of O'Connell and Cushing, is now inadequate for the expectations of lay people. A new model of leadership — or, perhaps more precisely, a return to an older model of leadership — is needed.

Seán O'Malley

It is plainly beyond the historian's competence to say anything about Seán O'Malley, who became the ninth leader of Boston's Catholics in 2003 and was elevated to the cardinalate in 2006. Born in 1940, he joined the Capuchin Franciscan order and was ordained in 1970. His career as a bishop began in St. Thomas in the Virgin Islands, and he was transferred to Fall River, Massachusetts, in 1992. There, he resolved one of the early cases of clergy sexual abuse and thereby acquired a reputation in such matters. That suited him in 2002 for a year's reassignment to the Diocese of Palm

Beach, Florida, where he also oversaw the resolution of abuse cases, before his transfer to Boston in the aftermath of Cardinal Law's resignation.

Even as he presides over the bicentennial of the church in Boston, with its useful backward glance, Cardinal O'Malley's is a task for the future. History seldom offers clear-cut "lessons," but the experiences of his predecessors suggest ways of approaching the challenges that lie ahead. As several earlier bishops knew, the personal style is better than the imperial style. The turmoil and disaffection of the recent past among local Catholics will not be overcome by a leader who distances himself from his parishioners. The people who fill the pews of local parishes experience the church primarily through that local connection, and Cardinal O'Malley and his successors will have to find a way to maintain a sense of intimacy between themselves and the people of Catholic Boston, restoring connections that perhaps came more naturally in the smaller church of the past. Sustaining those links will be all the more important as the age of contraction of the church continues. For the foreseeable future, the institution of the church will continue to shrink, and the number of priests and sisters will become steadily smaller. Even as new forms of lay ministry expand, the reconfiguration of the institutions and agencies of the church will have to be accomplished cooperatively. For their part, lay people are eager to participate in this process of seeking new ways of "being the church." As time puts distance between ourselves and the events of the scandal, it seems increasingly significant that large numbers of Catholics did not simply abandon the church. That they stayed with it, even amid the heartbreaking scandal, evinces a desire to remain faithful members of the church. That commonality of faith has sustained them for the last two hundred years and will be essential for the next century — centuries — of Catholics in Boston.

Contributors

Elizabeth MacDonald Bischof is assistant professor of history at the University of Southern Maine. A recent recipient of a Ph.D. from Boston College, she has received fellowships from the Massachusetts Historical Society, the Bostonian Society, and the Georgia O'Keeffe Museum Research Center supporting her work on a study of friendship and collaboration among young authors and artists in late nineteenth-century Boston.

François Gauthier took office as the new consul general of France in Boston in 2005. He graduated from Paris I-Sorbonne University (History), the Institut d'Études Politiques (IEP, Strasbourg, Political Science), and the École Nationale d'Administration (ENA, Strasbourg, Public Administration). In 1983 he joined the Ministry of Overseas Development, starting his diplomatic career in Paris and in Abidjan, Ivory Coast. From 1989 to 1993 he worked at the Ministry of Internal Affairs as representative of the state in the Lorraine and Burgundy regions. Thereafter he returned to the Ministry of Overseas Development, where he assumed the position of deputy director of education, culture, and research. In 2004 he participated in the Weatherhead Center for International Affairs Fellows Program at Harvard University.

Carol Hurd Green currently teaches in the Capstone program and the English department at Boston College, where she had earlier been associate dean of the College of Arts and Sciences and director of the Donovan Urban Teaching Scholars Program in the Lynch School of Education. She was a senior Fulbright Scholar in the Czech Republic in 1996–97. A graduate of a Catholic women's college, faculty member in two others, and on the Boston College faculty before coeducation, she was also a contributor to a volume on Catholic Women's Colleges in America. She is coeditor of *Notable American Women: The Modern Period; Journeys: Spiritual Autobiographies by Women; American Women Writers V;* and coauthor of *American Women in the 60s: Changing the Future.*

J. Bryan Hehir is secretary for social services, Archdiocese of Boston, and the Montgomery Professor of the Practice of Religion and Public Life at the Kennedy School of Government, Harvard University. He served on the staff of the U.S. Conference of Catholic Bishops (1973–92) and as president of Catholic Charities (1984–92) and Harvard Divinity School (1993–2001). He is a member of the American Academy of Arts and Sciences and the American Philosophical Society. His writing and research engage issues of ethics and international politics and the role of religion in the United States and world politics. Essays include "The Moral Measurement of

War"; "Strategy Logic and the Killing of Civilians"; and "Catholicism and Democracy."

William C. Leonard is associate professor of history and chair of the department at Emmanuel College, having received his M.A. from Northeastern University and his Ph.D. from Boston College in 1999. Dr. Leonard has written several articles related to the history of Boston's Catholics, including "Growing Together: Blacks and the Catholic Church in Boston," *Historian,* 2004, and wrote a chapter, "The Failure of Catholic Interracialism in Boston before Busing," for *Boston Histories: Essays in Honor of Thomas H. O'Connor* (Northeastern University Press, 2003). He is currently researching the life of Charles Lenox Remond, a nineteenth-century black abolitionist from Boston.

Thomas H. O'Connor is professor of history emeritus and university historian at Boston College. A graduate of the Boston Latin School, Dr. O'Connor received his A.B. and M.A. degrees from Boston College, and his Ph.D. degree from Boston University. He began teaching at Boston College in 1950, and served as chairman of the history department from 1962 to 1970. He has written many articles and books, including *Religion and American Society* (Addison Wesley, 1975), *Fitzpatrick's Boston, 1846–1866: John Bernard Fitzpatrick, Third Bishop of Boston* (Northeastern University Press, 1984), and *Boston Catholics: A History of the Church and Its People* (Northeastern University Press, 1998).

Joseph M. O'Keefe is professor of education and dean of the Lynch School of Education at Boston College. A 1976 graduate of Holy Cross, Father O'Keefe received a master's degree from Fordham University and was awarded a doctor of education degree from the Harvard University Graduate School of Education. He later received the master of divinity degree and licentiate in sacred theology from Weston Jesuit School of Theology. He is editor or co-editor of twelve books, and author or co-author of more than thirty-five articles and book chapters on Catholic education and education administration. He has been co-director of Selected Programs for Improving Catholic Education since 1995, and has directed the NCEA's Center for Research in Catholic Education from 2001 to 2006.

James M. O'Toole is the Clough Millennium Professor of History at Boston College. In 1978 he was appointed the first professional archivist for the Archdiocese of Boston, and he published the *Guide to the Archives of the Archdiocese of Boston* (Garland, 1982). For fifteen years he directed the M.A. program in history and archives at the University of Massachusetts at Boston. He has written extensively on American Catholic history, including *Militant and Triumphant: William Henry O'Connell and the Catholic Church in Boston* (University of Notre Dame Press, 1992), and *Passing for White: Race, Religion, and the Healy Family* (University of Massachusetts Press, 2002). His most recent book is *The Faithful: A History of Catholics in America* (Belknap/Harvard, 2008).

Aubrey J. Scheopner is a doctoral student at Boston College in the Curriculum and Instruction program at the Lynch School of Education, and is also the managing editor of *Catholic Education: A Journal of Inquiry and Practice*. She has co-authored several other publications with Rev. Joseph M. O'Keefe, S.J., including features in the *International Handbook on Catholic Education* and *International Studies in Catholic Education*.

William T. Schmidt, a priest of the Archdiocese of Boston, has served as pastor of St. Patrick parish, Stoneham, since 1995. He previously served as a parochial vicar at Immaculate Conception parish, Everett, and St. John the Evangelist parish, Swampscott, as well as secretary of pastoral services for the Archdiocese of Boston from 1988 to 1995. He attended Boston Public Schools and graduated from Cathedral High School. Father Schmidt studied at Boston College and St. John's Seminary in preparation for ordination to priesthood on May 15, 1976. He received a master's degree in Christian spirituality from Creighton University in 1984.

Notes

Abbreviations

AAB   Archives of the Archdiocese of Boston

HAB   Robert H. Lord, John E. Sexton, and Edward T. Harrington, *History of the Archdiocese of Boston in the Various Stages of Its Development, 1604–1943,* 3 vols. (Boston: Pilot Publishing Co., 1944)

JA   Josephite Archives

SBSP   Sisters of the Blessed Sacrament Papers

SRPF   St. Richard's Parish Files

Chapter 1: François Gauthier / From Jean de Cheverus to Jacques Maritain

1. Annabelle M. Melville, *Jean Lefebvre de Cheverus 1768–1836* (Milwaukee: Bruce, 1958).

2. J. Huen-Dubourg, *Vie du Cardinal de Cheverus, archevêque de Bordeaux,* 3rd ed. (Paris: De Périsse Frères, 1842).

3. Michael C. White, *The Garden of Martyrs* (New York: St. Martin's Press, 2004)

4. Huen-Dubourg, *Vie du Cardinal de Cheverus,* 66.

5. Michel Gauthier, "Monseigneur de Cheverus, prélat transatlantique," in *Les mutations transatlantiques des religions,* dir. Christian Lerat and Bernadette Rigal-Cellard (Bordeaux: Presses Universitaires de Bordeaux, 2000).

6. Huen-Dubourg, *Vie du Cardinal de Cheverus,* 124.

7. Ibid., 122.

8. Ibid., 126.

9. Robert H. Lord, John E. Sexton, and Edward T. Harrington, *History of the Archdiocese of Boston,* 3 vols. (Boston: Pilot Publishing Co., 1945), 1:800.

10. Yves Roby, *Les Franco-Américains de la Nouvelle-Angleterre* (Sillery-Québec: Editions du Septentrion, 2000).

11. Yves Garon, "Religieuses franco-américaines: Les Sœurs de Sainte-Jeanne d'Arc," in *Religion catholique et appartenance franco-américaine,* ed. Claire Quintal (Worcester, Mass.: Institut Français, Assumption College, 1993).

12. Rev. John W. Lynch, S.M., *Parish History of Our Lady of Victories* (Boston: Our Lady of Victories, 1975).

13. Jacques Julliard and Michel Winock, *Dictionnaire des intellectuels français* (Paris: Le Seuil, 1975).

14. Quoted by Florian Michel (in correspondence with the author).

Chapter 2: Thomas H. O'Connor / Papism and Politics in Massachusetts

1. See Robert H. Lord, John E. Sexton, Edward T. Harrington, *History of the Archdiocese of Boston,* 3 vols. (Boston: Pilot Publishing Co., 1945), vol. 1,

for a general history of intolerance toward Roman Catholics in Massachusetts throughout the colonial period. Also see John Fiske, *The Beginnings of New England: The Puritan Theocracy in Its Relations to Civil and Religious Liberty* (Boston: Houghton Mifflin, 1898), 40–41.

2. *HAB*, 1:284.

3. Ibid., 1:286–87.

4. Francis N. Thorpe, ed., *The Federal and State Constitutions*, 7 vols. (Buffalo, N.Y.: W. S. Hein, 1993 [c. 1907], III, 1889–1890).

5. Cheverus to Bishop John Carroll, Boston, March 10, 1801, cited in William L. Lucey, *Edward Kavanagh* (Francetown, N.H.: Marshall Jones Company, 1946), 75–80.

6. Cheverus to Simon Gabriel Brute, December 17, 1820, cited in Annabelle M. Melville, *Jean Lefebvre de Cheverus, 1763–1836* (Milwaukee: Bruce, 1958), 222.

7. Joseph Charles, *The Origins of the American Party System* (Williamsburg, Va.: Institute of Early American History and Culture, 1959); John C. Miller, *The Federalist Era, 1789–1801* (New York: Harper, 1960).

8. Melville, *Jean Lefebvre de Cheverus*, 127–32.

9. Thomas H. O'Connor, *The Boston Irish: A Political History* (Boston: Northeastern University Press, 1995), 25–27.

10. Kerby Miller, *Emigrants and Exiles: Ireland and the Irish Exodus to North America* (New York: Oxford University Press, 1985), 170–71.

11. O'Connor, *The Boston Irish*, 383–40. See Marvin Meyers, *The Jacksonian Persuasion: Politics and Beliefs* (Stanford, Calif.: Stanford University Press, 1957); Edward Pessen, *Jacksonian Democracy* (Urbana: University of Illinois Press, 1969); Arthur M. Schlesinger Jr., *The Age of Jackson* (Boston: Little, Brown, 1945).

12. *Boston Courier*, November 3, 1828. See James B. Cullen, *The Story of the Irish in Boston* (Boston: James B. Cullen and Co., 1889), 41–43, for a description of Jackson's visit to Boston in 1833.

13. James Hennesey, *American Catholics: A History of the Roman Catholic Community in the United States* (New York: Oxford University Press, 1981), 93–100.

14. John T. McGreevy, *Catholicism and American Freedom* (New York: W. W. Norton, 2003), 21–22.

15. Peter Guilday, *The Life and Times of John England, 1786–1842* (New York: America Press, 1927), 1:362, cited by Francis A. Sullivan, S.J., "The Participation of the Laity in Decision-Making in the Church," *Inculturation and the Church in North America*, ed. T. Frank Kennedy, S.J. (New York: Crossroad, 2006), 227.

16. McGreevy, *Catholicism and American Freedom*, 22; *HAB*, 2:229–306, describes troubles over lay trusteeism in Boston. Also see Richard Shaw, *Dagger John: The Unquiet Life and Times of Archbishop John Hughes of New York* (New York: Paulist Press, 1977).

17. Samuel F. B. Morse, *Imminent Dangers to the Free Institutions of the United States through Foreign Immigration* (New York: E. B. Clayton, 1836), and Lyman Beecher, *A Plea for the West* (New York: Arno Press, 1977), were two of the most popular books that warned of the dangers of the Catholic revival in America.

18. *Boston Pilot*, May 20, May 27, July 15, November 11, 1843. See Nancy L. Schultz, *Fire and Roses: The Burning of the Charlestown Convent, 1834* (New York: Free Press, 2000), for a recent treatment of the attack.

19. *Boston Courier*, November 22, 1844. Also see O'Connor, *The Boston Irish*, 56–57.

20. Thomas H. O'Connor, "Irish Votes and Yankee Cotton: The Constitution of 1853," *Proceedings of the Massachusetts Historical Society* 95 (1983).

21. *Boston Pilot*, November 5, 1853.

22. Thomas H. O'Connor, *Fitzpatrick's Boston, 1846–1866: John Bernard Fitzpatrick, Third Bishop of Boston* (Boston: Northeastern University Press, 1984), 59.

23. Ibid., 100–102, 117–18, 151–52.

24. Ibid., 102–4.

25. Ibid., 106–8.

26. Ibid., 114–15.

27. George S. Boutwell, *Reminiscences of Sixty Years in Public Affairs*, 2 vols. (New York: Greenwood Press, 1968), 1:220; *Daily Commonwealth*, November 22, 1853.

28. John R. Mulkern, *The Know-Nothing Party in Massachusetts: The Rise and Fall of a People's Party* (Boston: Northeastern University Press, 1990); Ray Allen Billington, *The Protestant Crusade, 1800–1860* (New York: Macmillan, 1938), 8–79.

29. O'Connor, *The Boston Irish*, 78–80.

30. Thomas H. O'Connor, *Civil War Boston: Home Front and Battlefield* (Boston: Northeastern University Press, 1997), 78–79.

31. *Boston Pilot*, March 1, 1862.

32. O'Connor, *Civil War Boston*, 237–38; Sam Bass Warner Jr., *Streetcar Suburbs: The Process of Growth in Boston, 1870–1900* (Cambridge, Mass.: Harvard University Press, 1974).

33. O'Connor, *Civil War Boston*, 239; Dale Baum, *The Civil War Party System: The Case of Massachusetts, 1848–1876* (Chapel Hill: University of North Carolina Press, 1984), 108; Thomas N. Brown, *Irish-American Nationalism, 1870–1890* (Westport, Conn.: Greenwood Press, 1980), 40–41.

34. O'Connor, *The Boston Irish*, 101–3.

35. See Cullen, *The Story of the Irish in Boston*, for biographical sketches of the charter members of the Young Men's Democratic Club.

36. Michael P. Curran, *The Life of Patrick Collins* (Norwood, Mass.: Norwood Press, 1906); M. Jeanne d'Arc O'Hare, "The Public Career of Patrick Collins," diss., Boston College, 1959.

37. *HAB*, 3:388–89; *Boston Pilot*, May 3, 1873.

38. *HAB*, 3:388–89; O'Connor, *Boston Catholics*, 141.

39. Curran, *The Life of Patrick Collins*, 21–22.

40. Ibid., Appendix, 188–90.

41. Robert H. Wiebe, *The Search for Order, 1877–1920* (New York: Macmillan, 1966); Samuel P. Hays, *The Response to Industrialism, 1885–1914* (Chicago: University of Chicago Press, 1957); Walter Licht, *Industrializing America: The Nineteenth Century* (Baltimore: Johns Hopkins University Press, 1995).

42. Susan Walton, "To Preserve the Faith: Catholic Charities in Boston, 1810–1930," *Catholic Boston: Studies in Religion and Community*, ed. Robert E. Sullivan and James M. O'Toole (Boston: Archdiocese of Boston, 1985), 67–68. Also see Peter S. Holloran, *Boston's Wayward Children: Social Services for Homeless Children, 1830–1930* (Rutherford, N.J.: Farleigh Dickinson University Press, 1989); Eric C. Schneider, *In the Web of Class: Delinquents and Reformers in Boston, 1810s–1930s* (New York: New York University Press, 1992).

43. O'Connor, *The Boston Irish*, 141–48.

44. Lesley Ainley, *Boston Mahatma: Martin Lomasney* (Boston: Bruce Humphries, 1949), 86–90; John Henry Cutler, *"Honey Fitz": Three Steps to the White House* (Indianapolis: Bobbs-Merrill, 1962), 69–71.

45. Lawrence Goodwyn, *The Democratic Promise: The Populist Movement in America* (New York: Oxford University Press, 1976); John D. Hicks, *The Populist*

Revolt (Lincoln: University of Nebraska Press, 1931); Richard Hofstadter, *The Age of Reform* (New York: Vintage Books, 1955).

46. O'Connor, *The Boston Irish*, 126–27, 164–65. See also Geoffrey Blodgett, *The Gentle Reformers: Massachusetts Democrats in the Cleveland Era* (Cambridge, Mass.: Harvard University Press, 1966).

47. Curran, *The Life of Patrick Collins*, 116–17; Michael Kazin, *Godly Hero; The Life of William Jennings Bryan* (New York: Knopf, 2006).

48. Curran, *The Life of Patrick Collins*, 153–54; O'Connor, *The Boston Irish*, 163.

49. O'Connor, *The Boston Irish*, 163–65.

50. Paula Kane, *Separatism and Subculture: Boston Catholicism, 1900–1920* (Chapel Hill: University of North Carolina Press, 1991), 76.

51. Donna Merwick, *Boston Priests, 1848–1910: A Study of Social and Intellectual Change* (Cambridge, Mass.: Harvard University Press, 1973).

52. William F. Kenny, *Centenary of the See of Boston* (Boston: J. K. Waters, 1909), 50; James M. O'Toole, *Militant and Triumphant: William Henry O'Connell and the Catholic Church in Boston, 1859–1944* (Notre Dame, Ind.: Notre Dame University Press, 1992), 121.

53. Kane, *Separatism and Subculture*; Richard M. Abrams, *Conservatism in a Progressive Era: Massachusetts Politics, 1900–1912* (Cambridge, Mass.: Harvard University Press, 1964).

54. James M. O'Toole, "Prelates and Politicos: Catholics and Politics in Massachusetts, 1900–1970," *Catholic Boston*, 39–41, provides a discussion of O'Connell's opposition to "Caesarism" and "despotism." Also see O'Toole, *Militant and Triumphant*, 139–40, 141–42.

55. O'Toole, *Militant and Triumphant*, 130; James J. Kenneally, "Catholicism and Woman Suffrage in Massachusetts," *Catholic Historical Review* 53 (1967): 43–57.

56. O'Toole, *Militant and Triumphant*, 132–35; O'Toole, "Prelates and Politicos," 27–31.

57. William V. Shannon, *The American Irish* (New York: Macmillan, 1995), 295–96. Also see William M. Halsey, *The Survival of American Innocence: Catholicism in an Era of Disillusionment, 1920–1940* (Notre Dame, Ind.: Notre Dame University Press, 1955).

58. Robert D. Cross, *The Emergence of Liberal Catholicism in America* (Cambridge, Mass.: Harvard University Press, 1958); Aaron Abell, *American Catholicism and Social Action: A Search for Social Justice, 1865–1950* (Garden City, N.Y.: Hanover House, 1960); David O'Brien, *American Catholics and Social Reform* (New York: Oxford University Press, 1968); Francis L. Broderick, *Right Reverend New Dealer: John A. Ryan* (New York: Macmillan, 1963).

59. Shannon, *The American Irish*, 300–305, 310–13. Also see Timothy Meagher, ed., *From Paddy to Studs: Irish American Communities in the Turn of the Century Era, 1880–1920* (New York: Greenwood, 1986).

60. O'Toole, *Militant and Triumphant*, 138.

61. Robert A. O'Leary, "William Henry Cardinal O'Connell: A Social and Intellectual Biography" diss., Tufts University, 1980, says the cardinal looked down on James Michael Curley as a scheming politico who exploited ethnic and religious antagonisms for personal gain. Cited in O'Toole, "Prelates and Politicos," 20–21. Also see O'Toole, *Militant and Triumphant*, 124–25, 128–29.

62. O'Toole, *Militant and Triumphant*, 140–41; O'Toole, "Prelates and Politicos," 40–41.

63. O'Toole, *Militant and Triumphant*, 138–39; O'Toole, "Prelates and Politicos," 37–38.

64. O'Toole, *Militant and Triumphant,* 135–36; O'Toole, "Prelates and Politicos," 31–35.

65. O'Toole, *Militant and Triumphant,* 135–36; O'Toole, "Prelates and Politicos," 32–33.

66. Thomas H. O'Connor, *Boston Catholics: A History of the Church and its People* (Boston: Northeastern University Press, 1998), 254–58. Also see Joseph Dever, *Cushing of Boston: A Candid Portrait* (Boston: Bruce Humphries, 1965); John H. Fenton, *Salt of the Earth: An Informal Portrait of Richard Cardinal Cushing* (Garden City, N.Y.: Doubleday, 1965); John Henry Cutler, *Cardinal Cushing of Boston* (New York: Hawthorn Books, 1970).

67. Thomas H. O'Connor, *Building a New Boston: The Politics of Urban Renewal, 1950 to 1970* (Boston: Northeastern University Press, 1991).

68. O'Connor, *Boston Catholics,* 246–47.

69. O'Toole, "Prelates and Politicos," 53–54.

70. Ibid., 55–57.

71. O'Connor, *Boston Catholics,* 252–54.

72. *Time,* July 2, 2007, 56–57.

73. O'Connor, *Boston Catholics,* 266–68.

74. Ibid., 268–79.

75. J. Anthony Lukas, *Common Ground: A Turbulent Decade in the Lives of Three American Families* (New York: Knopf, 1985), 57–60, provides a convenient summary of the various African American groups in Boston. Nicholas Lemann, *The Promised Land: The Great Black Migration and How It Changed America* (New York: Vintage Books, 1991), traces the increase of black migration from the 1940s to the 1960s.

76. William C. Leonard, "A Parish for the Black Catholics of Boston," *Catholic Historical Review* (January 1997). Also see Leonard, "The History of Black Catholics in Boston, 1790–1840," M.A. thesis, Northeastern University, 1993.

77. O'Connor, *Boston Catholics,* 276–79.

78. Ibid., 282–88.

79. Ibid., 291–93.

80. Ibid., 294–96.

81. O'Connor, *Building a New Boston,* 261–63.

82. O'Connor, *Boston Catholics,* 299–300.

83. Ibid., 300–301. J. Anthony Lukas, in *Common Ground,* 372–404, has a chapter titled "The Cardinal," in which he offers a perceptive and generally sympathetic view of the failure of Cardinal Medeiros to find common ground in the racial disputes of the 1970s.

84. O'Connor, *Boston Catholics,* 303.

85. Ibid., 304–5.

86. Ibid., 306–9.

87. Ibid., 309–12.

88. Investigative Staff of the Boston Globe, *Betrayal: The Crisis in the Catholic Church* (Boston: Little, Brown, 2003), 149.

89. O'Connor, *Boston Catholics,* 321–22.

90. Maurice T. Cunningham, "The Church's Response to the Massachusetts Gay Marriage Decision," *Journal of Church and State* 47 (Winter 2005): 25. It is ironic that Margaret Marshall would later be the presiding justice in the controversial case of *Goodridge v. Department of Public Health.*

91. Special commemorative issue of the *Boston Pilot,* "Bernard Cardinal Law: Episcopal Ordination, Silver Jubilee, 1973–1998," December 4, 1998.

92. Globe, *Betrayal,* 122; O'Connor, *Boston Catholics,* 315–16.

93. Globe, *Betrayal,* 7–8, 48, 126.

94. Ibid., 48–49.

95. Ibid., 7–8, 132–33.
96. Ibid., 7.
97. Cunningham, "Gay Marriage Decision," 136–37.
98. Globe, *Betrayal,* 134.
99. Ibid., 105.
100. Ibid., 99, 163.
101. Cunningham, "Gay Marriage Decision," 26; Globe, *Betrayal,* 99, 154–57.
102. Globe, *Betrayal,*
103. Cunningham, "Gay Marriage Decision," 26–27.
104. Ibid., 26.
105. Ibid., 31.
106. Ibid., 26.
107. Ibid., 19–20.
108. Ibid., 20–21. See pages 21–23 for a comparison of Church philosophy regarding marriage and constitutional views of the subject.
109. Ibid., 25.
110. Ibid., 29–30.
111. Ibid., 30.
112. Ibid., 29–30.
113. Ibid., 33–34.
114. Maurice T. Cunningham, "A Christian Coalition for Catholics? The Massachusetts Model," unpublished manuscript, cited with permission of the author, Department of Political Science, University of Massachusetts at Boston.
115. Cunningham, "Gay Marriage Decision," 35–36, 37. According to statistical tables created by Professor Cunningham, the shift in Catholic attitudes between November 2003 and February 2004 in favor of a popular vote on the gay marriage issue dramatizes the success of the political tactic.
116. *Boston Pilot,* March 23, March 30, 2007.
117. *Quincy Patriot Ledger,* June 15, 2007.
118. *Boston Globe,* June 17, 2007.
119. Ibid.
120. See David Hollenbach, S.J., "Catholicism and American Political Culture," *Inculturation and the Church,* 7–22, for ideas concerning cultural transformation.

Chapter 3: J. Bryan Hehir / Charity, Justice, and the Church in Boston

1. Address of Professor Thomas O'Connor at Catholic Charities Dinner (June 1, 2006); also, Robert H. Lord, John E. Sexton, Edward T. Harrington, *History of the Archdiocese of Boston,* vol. 3 (Boston: Pilot Publishing Co., 1945), 418.
2. There are multiple sources for the documents and history of Catholic social teaching and its role in the life of the church. The most authoritative single summary is Pontifical Commission of Justice and Peace, *Compendium of the Social Doctrine of the Church* (Washington, D.C.: U.S. Conference of Catholic Bishops, 2005). See also Judith A. Dwyer, ed., *The New Dictionary of Catholic Social Thought* (Collegeville, Minn.: Liturgical Press, 1994); Joseph N. Moody, ed., *Church and Society: Catholic Political and Social Thought and Movements 1789–1950;* Adrian Hastings, ed., *Modern Catholicism: Vatican II and After* (New York: Oxford University Press, 1991); Kenneth R. Himes, O.F.M., ed., *Modern Catholic Social Teaching: Commentaries and Interpretations* (Washington, D.C.: Georgetown University Press, 2005).

3. Vatican II, *Gaudium et Spes,* in Austin Flannery, O.P., ed., *Vatican Council II: The Conciliar and Post and Conciliar Documents,* rev. ed., vol. 1 (Northport, N.Y.: Costello Publishing Co., 1982), 905.

4. Paul VI, *Populorum Progressio,* in David O'Brien and Thomas A. Shannon, eds., *Catholic Social Thought: The Documentary Heritage* (Maryknoll, N.Y.: Orbis Books, 1992), 240. This compendium of encyclicals and other official documents will be used throughout these endnotes: I will cite author and document and then give the page number from O'Brien and Shannon, *Catholic Social Thought.*

5. John Paul II, *Sollicitudo Rei Socialis, Catholic Social Thought,* 399.

6. Daniel Patrick Moynihan, *Miles to Go: A Personal History of Social Policy* (Cambridge, Mass.: Harvard University Press, 1996), 212, 215.

7. Benedict XVI, Encyclical Letter *Deus Caritas Est* (December 22, 2005), para. 22.

8. Synod of Bishops (1974), *Justice in the World, Catholic Social Thought,* 289.

9. John XXIII, *Pacem in Terris, Catholic Social Thought,* 136ff.

10. Pius XI, *Quadragesimo Anno, Catholic Social Thought,* 62.

11. Jean-Yves Calvez and Jacques Perrin, *The Church and Social Justice: The Social Teaching of the Popes from Leo XIII to Pius XII* (Chicago: Henry Regnery, 1961), 162–73; and D. B. Robertson, ed., *Love and Justice: Selections from the Shorter Writings of Reinhold Niebuhr* (Cleveland: Meridian Books, World Publishing Co., 1967), 25–29.

12. Benedict XVI, *Deus Caritas Est,* para. 28.

13. John Courtney Murray, "The Issue of Church and State at Vatican II," *Theological Studies* 27 (1966): 600.

14. Benedict XVI, *Deus Caritas Est,* para. 19.

15. John Courtney Murray, *We Hold These Truths: Catholic Reflections on the American Proposition* (New York: Sheed and Ward, 1960); and Donald Pelotte, *John Courtney Murray, Theologian in Conflict* (New York: Paulist Press, 1975), 27–74; 74–114.

16. For a survey of "the Catholic system" see Charles A. Fahey and Mary Ann Lewis, eds., *The Future of Catholic Institutional Ministries* (New York: Fordham University Press, 1992).

17. For Catholic Charities see Dorothy M. Brown and Elizabeth McKeown, *The Poor Belong to Us* (Cambridge, Mass.: Harvard University Press, 1997), 13–50.

18. See O'Connor, address at Catholic Charities Dinner, June 1, 2006.

19. Michael O'Neill, *Nonprofit Nation: A New Look at the Third America* (San Francisco: Jossey Bass, 2002), 17.

20. Lester A. Salamon, "The Resilient Sector: The State of Nonprofit America," in *The State of Nonprofit America,* ed. Lester A. Salamon (Washington, D.C.: Brookings Institution Press, 2003), 6.

21. Ibid., 3–4.

22. Ibid., 4.

23. Samuel H. Beer, "In Search of a New Public Philosophy," in Anthony King, ed., *The New American Political System* (Washington, D.C.: American Enterprise Institute, 1978), 7.

24. Brown and McKeown, *The Poor Belong to Us,* 4; Thomas Harvey, "The Catholic Charities Movement: The Roots and Flowering of Catholic Social Teaching," in Fahey and Lewis, *The Future of Catholic Institutional Ministries,* 116. Harvey's description of the origins and relationships of Catholic Charities with the social teaching parallels the account offered here.

25. Benedict XVI, *Deus Caritas Est,* para. 31.

26. Peter Steinfels, *A People Adrift: The Crisis of the Roman Catholic Church in America* (New York: Simon & Schuster, 2005); see the chapter "Catholic Institutions and Catholic Identity," 103–64.

Chapter 4: Joseph M. O'Keefe and Aubrey J. Scheopner / Catholic Schools

1. Jessica A. Greene and Joseph M. O'Keefe, "Enrollment in Catholic Schools in the United States," in *Handbook of Research on Catholic Education,* ed. Thomas C. Hunt, Ellis A. Joseph, and Ron J. Nuzzi (Westport, Conn.: Greenwood Press, 2001), 163.

2. Ibid., 164.

3. Sonia Nieto, *Affirming Diversity* (New York: Longman, 2000), 138.

4. Jim Cummins and Sandra R. Schecter, "Introduction, School-Based Language Policy in Culturally Diverse Contexts," in *Multilingual Education in Practice: Using Diversity as a Resource,* ed. Sandra R. Schetcer and Jim Cummins (Portsmouth, N.H.: Heinemann, 2003), 11.

5. Nieto, *Affirming Diversity,* 146.

6. Ibid., 152.

7. The Boston Foundation, "Racial and Ethnic Diversity, Boston," The Boston Indicators Project, 2007, *www.bostonindicators.org/IndicatorsProject/CivicVitality/Indicator.aspx?id=814&sc=578&sct=Race/Ethnicity* (October 23, 2007).

8. Anthony M. Stevens-Arroyo and Segundo Pantoja, "History and Inculturation: The Latino Experience of Catholic Education," in *One Hundred Years of Catholic Education: Historical Essays in Honor of the Centennial of the National Catholic Educational Association,* ed. John Augenstein, Christopher J. Kauffman, and Robert J. Wister (Washington, D.C.: National Catholic Educational Association, 2003), 257–83.

9. National Center for Education Statistics, *Characteristics of Private Schools in the United States: Results from the 2003–2004 Private School Universe Survey* (Washington, D.C.: U.S. Department of Education, 2006).

10. J. A. Burns, Bernard J. Kohlbrenner, and John B. Peterson, *A History of Catholic Education in the United States* (New York: Benziger Brothers, 1937), 49.

11. Ibid., 39.

12. Timothy Walch, *Parish School: American Catholic Parochial Education from Colonial Times to the Present* (New York: Crossroad, 1996), 29.

13. Burns, Kohlbrenner, and Peterson, *A History of Catholic Education in the United States.*

14. Robert H. Lord, John E. Sexton, and Edward T. Harrington, *History of the Archdiocese of Boston: In Various Stages of Its Development, 1604 to 1943* (New York: Sheed & Ward, 1944).

15. Richard M. Linkh, *American Catholicism and European Immigrants* (Staten Island, N.Y.: Center for Migration Studies, 1975), 50.

16. Samuel F. B. Morse, *Foreign Conspiracy against the Liberties of the United States* (New York: Leavitt, Lord and Company, 1835), 51.

17. Harold A. Buetow, *Of Singular Benefit: The Story of Catholic Education in the United States* (New York: Macmillan, 1970), 203.

18. Jay P. Dolan, *In Search of an American Catholicism: A History of Religion and Culture in Tension* (New York: Oxford University Press, 2002).

19. Linkh, *American Catholicism and European Immigrants,* 29.

20. John T. McGreevy, *Parish Boundaries: The Catholic Encounter with Race in the Twentieth-Century Urban North* (Chicago: University of Chicago Press, 1996), 11.

21. Linkh, *American Catholicism and European Immigrants,* 4.

22. James M. O'Toole, *Militant and Triumphant: William Henry O'Connell and the Catholic Church in Boston, 1859–1944* (Notre Dame, Ind.: University of Notre Dame Press, 1992), 148.

23. Buetow, *Of Singular Benefit,* 203.

24. Dolores Liptak, *Immigrants and Their Church: Bicentennial History of the Catholic Church in America* (New York: Macmillan, 1989), 94.

25. *HAB.*

26. Linkh, *American Catholicism and European Immigrants*, 40.

27. *HAB.*

28. Timothy J. Meagher, " 'Never Take Shame in Your Mother Tongue…and Your Fatherland in America': Catholic Schools and Immigrants," in *One Hundred Years of Catholic Education: Historical Essays in Honor of the Centennial of the National Catholic Educational Association*, ed. John Augenstein, Christopher J. Kauffman, and Robert J. Wister (Washington, D.C.: National Catholic Educational Association, 2003).

29. McGreevy, *Parish Boundaries.*

30. Linkh, *American Catholicism and European Immigrants.*

31. Armand B. Chartier, "The Spiritual and Intellectual Foundations of Schooling of Franco-Americans," in *Steeples and Smokestacks; A Collection of Essays on the Franco-American Experience in New England*, ed. Claire Quintal (Worcester, Mass.: Institut Français, Assumption College, 1996), 233–66.

32. Gerald J. Brault, *The French-Canadian Heritage in New England* (Hanover, N.H.: University Press of New England, 1986).

33. Liptak, *Immigrants and Their Church*, 84.

34. Ibid. Walch, *Parish School.*

35. Stevens-Arroyo and Pantoja, "History and Inculturation," 258.

36. Ibid., 259.

37. Buetow, *Of Singular Benefit.*

38. Walch, *Parish School*, 63.

39. Linkh, *American Catholicism and European Immigrants*, 125.

40. William O. Bourne, *History of the Public School Society of the City of New York* (New York: W. Wood & Co., 1870), 206.

41. Walch, *Parish School.*

42. Ibid.

43. Charles N. Lischka, *Private Schools and State Laws* (Washington, D.C.: National Catholic Welfare Conference Bureau of Education, 1926), 57.

44. Ibid.

45. Ibid., 159.

46. Ibid., 164.

47. Liptak, *Immigrants and Their Church*, 94.

48. Linkh, *American Catholicism and European Immigrants*, 4.

49. Chartier, "The Spiritual and Intellectual Foundations of Schooling of Franco-Americans," 233–66.

50. Gerald J. Brault, "The Achievement of the Teaching Orders in New England: The Franco-American Parochial Schools," in *Steeples and Smokestacks; A Collection of Essays on the Franco-American Experience in New England*, ed. Claire Quintal (Worcester, Mass.: Institut Français, Assumption College, 1996), 273.

51. Linkh, *American Catholicism and European Immigrants*, 128.

52. Liptak, *Immigrants and Their Church*, 85.

53. Walch, *Parish School*, 81.

54. Ibid.

55. Linkh, *American Catholicism and European Immigrants*, 139.

56. Ibid.

57. Eileen Mary Brewer, *Nuns and the Education of American Catholic Women, 1860–1920* (Chicago: Loyola University Press, 1987), 13.

58. Ibid., 14.

59. Linkh, *American Catholicism and European Immigrants*, 111.

60. Walch, *Parish School.*

61. Brewer, *Nuns and the Education of American Catholic Women*, 21.

62. A Member of the Congregation, *The American Foundations of the Sisters of Notre Dame de Namur, Compiled from the Annals of Their Convents* (Philadelphia: Dolphin Press, 1928), 46.

63. Ibid., 383.

64. Brewer, *Nuns and the Education of American Catholic Women*, 42.

65. Fayette Breaux Veverka, *For God and Country: Catholic Schooling in the 1920s* (New York: Garland, 1988), 152.

66. William P. Leahy, *Adapting to America: Catholics, Jesuits, and Higher Education in the Twentieth Century* (Washington, D.C.: Georgetown University Press, 1991), 70.

67. Ibid.

68. Commission on Coeducation, *Report of the Commission on Coeducation* (available from the Special Collections Department, Foley Center Library, Gonzaga University, Spokane, WA 99258-0001; McGoldrick Papers 2:15, 1940), D.

69. Ibid.

70. Leahy, *Adapting to America*.

71. Ibid., 74.

72. Ibid.

73. Veverka, *For God and Country*, 170.

74. Mary Bowler, *A History of Catholic Colleges for Women in the United States of America* (Washington, D.C.: Catholic University of America, 1933).

75. Veverka, *For God and Country*, 181.

76. Ellen Marie Kuznicki, "A Study of the Origin, Development, and Merits of the Educational System of the Felician Sisters in the Polish American Catholic Schools of Western New York" (diss., Kansas State University, 1972), 21.

77. Ibid., 54.

78. Ibid., 56.

79. Ibid., 53.

80. Ibid., 69.

81. Dolan, *In Search of American Catholicism*, 128.

82. Greene and O'Keefe, "Enrollment in Catholic Schools in the United States," 162.

83. Mary A. Grant and Thomas C. Hunt, *Catholic School Education in the United States: Development and Current Concerns* (New York: Garland Publishing, 1992).

84. Greene and O'Keefe, "Enrollment in Catholic Schools in the United States."

85. Grant and Hunt, *Catholic School Education in the United States*.

86. "Catholic School Closings and Openings" *National Catholic Reporter*, September 4, 1968, 3.

87. Greene and O'Keefe, "Enrollment in Catholic Schools in the United States."

88. Harold A. Buetow, *The Catholic School: Its Roots, Identity, and Future* (New York: Crossroad, 1988), 283.

89. Dale McDonald, *United States Catholic Elementary and Secondary Schools 2006–2007: The Annual Statistical Report on Schools, Enrollment and Staffing* (Washington, D.C.: National Catholic Educational Association, 2007).

90. National Center for Education Statistics, *Characteristics of Private Schools in the United States: Results from the 2003–2004 Private School Universe Survey* (Washington, D.C.: U.S. Department of Education, 2006).

91. Meagher, "Never Take Shame in Your Mother Tongue."

92. Buetow, *Of Singular Benefit*, 132.

93. James W. Sanders, "Catholics and the School Question in Boston: The Cardinal O'Connell Years," in *Catholic Boston: Studies in Religion and Community,*

1870–1970, ed. Robert E. Sullivan and James M. O'Toole (Boston: Roman Catholic Archbishop of Boston, 1985), 121–70.

94. Mary Xaveria Sullivan, *The History of Catholic Secondary Education in the Archdiocese of Boston* (Washington, D.C.: Catholic University of America Press, 1946).

95. Frances H. Early, "The Settling-In Process: The Beginnings of the Little Canada in Lowell, Massachusetts, in the Late Nineteenth Century," in *Steeples and Smokestacks; A Collection of Essays on the Franco-American Experience in New England,* ed. Claire Quintal (Worcester, Mass.: Institut Français, Assumption College, 1996), 89–108.

96. James W. Sanders, "Boston Catholics and the School Question, 1825–1907," in *From Common School to Magnet School: Selected Essays in the History of Boston's Schools,* ed. James W. Fraser, Henry L. Allen, and Sam Barnes (Boston: Trustees of the Public Library of the City of Boston, 1979), 46.

97. Sanders, "Boston Catholics and the School Question."

98. Sanders, "Catholics and the School Question in Boston," 164.

99. Sanders, "Boston Catholics and the School Question," 60.

100. Sanders, "Catholics and the School Question in Boston."

101. Ibid., 151.

102. Robert J. Sauer, *Holy Trinity German Catholic Church of Boston: A Way of Life 1844–1994* (Dallas: Taylor Publishing Company, 1994), 40.

103. Ibid.

104. Ibid.

105. *HAB.*

106. Ibid., 199.

107. Brault, *The French-Canadian Heritage in New England,* 92.

108. Kristen A. Petersen and Thomas J. Murphy, *Waltham Rediscovered: An Ethnic History of Waltham, Massachusetts* (Portsmouth, N.H.: Peter R. Randall Publisher, 1988), 283.

109. Brault, *The French-Canadian Heritage in New England.*

110. Brault, "The Achievement of the Teaching Orders in New England."

111. *HAB,* 3:190.

112. Ibid., 3:221.

113. Thomas H. O'Connor, *Boston Catholics: A History of the Church and Its People* (Boston: Northeastern University Press, 1998), 166.

114. Ibid.

115. *HAB.*

116. Ibid., 3:235.

117. Ibid.

118. Joseph Fenwick, "Memoranda of the Diocese of Boston from the Arrival of Bishop Fenwick or Rather from the Day of His Consecration," vol. 1 (Boston: Boston Archdiocese, 1825), 3.

119. *HAB,* vol. 2.

120. Sanders, "Boston Catholics and the School Question."

121. Thomas H. O'Connor, *Fitzpatrick's Boston 1846–1866: John Bernard Fitzpatrick, Third Bishop of Boston* (Boston: Northeastern University Press, 1984), 100.

122. Ernest Stabler, *Founders: Innovators in Education, 1830–1980* (Edmonton: University of Alberta Press, 1986), 73.

123. O'Connor, *Fitzpatrick's Boston;* Sanders, "Boston Catholics and the School Question."

124. O'Connor, *Fitzpatrick's Boston,* 101.

125. Sanders, "Boston Catholics and the School Question," 56–57.

126. Peter Guilday, *A History of the Councils of Baltimore (1791–1884)* (New York: Macmillan, 1932).

127. Sanders, "Boston Catholics and the School Question," 64.

128. O'Toole, *Militant and Triumphant.*

129. O'Connor, *Boston Catholics.*

130. Sanders, "Catholics and the School Question in Boston," 125.

131. Sanders, "Catholics and the School Question in Boston."

132. Sullivan, *The History of Catholic Secondary Education.*

133. Sanders, "Catholics and the School Question in Boston."

134. O'Toole, *Militant and Triumphant.*

135. Petersen and Murphy, *Waltham Rediscovered,* 140.

136. O'Connor, *Boston Catholics.*

137. Sanders, "Boston Catholics and the School Question," 50.

138. Ibid., 55–56.

139. Ibid.

140. Burns, Kohlbrenner, and Peterson, *A History of Catholic Education in the United States,* 82.

141. O'Connor, *Fitzpatrick's Boston,* 112.

142. Sullivan, *The History of Catholic Secondary Education.*

143. O'Connor, *Fitzpatrick's Boston,* 113.

144. O'Toole, *Militant and Triumphant,* 147.

145. Ibid., 169.

146. Ibid., 171.

147. A Member of the Congregation, *Sisters of Notre Dame de Namur.*

148. Ibid., 303.

149. Katherine E. Conway and Mabel Ward Cameron, *Charles Francis Donnelly: With an Account of the Hearings on a Bill for the Inspection of Private Schools in Massachusetts in 1888–1889* (New York: James T. White & Co., 1909), 31.

150. Ibid., 34–35.

151. Commonwealth of Massachusetts Department of Education, *General Laws Relating to Education: Enacted by the Legislature on December 7, 1920, to Take Effect January 1, 1921,* Whole number 129, Number 9 (Boston: Wright & Potter Printing Co, 1921), 74.

152. *HAB,* 2:218.

153. O'Toole, *Militant and Triumphant.*

154. Ibid.

155. Sauer, *Holy Trinity German Catholic Church of Boston.*

156. William Wolkovich-Valkavièius, *Lithuanian Religious Life in America: A Compendium of 150 Roman Catholic Parishes and Institutions,* vol. 1: *Eastern United States* (Norwood, Mass.: Lithuanian Religious Life in America, 1991).

157. O'Connor, *Boston Catholics,* 136.

158. Ibid.

159. Ibid., 137.

160. Ibid.

161. Ibid.

162. Mary J. Oates, " 'The Good Sisters': The Work and Position of Catholic Churchwomen in Boston, 1970–1940," in *Catholic Boston: Studies in Religion and Community, 1870–1970,* ed. Robert E. Sullivan and James M. O'Toole (Boston: Roman Catholic Archbishop of Boston, 1985), 197.

163. A Member of the Congregation, *Sisters of Notre Dame de Namur,* 196.

164. Ibid., 447.

165. Oates, " 'The Good Sisters,' " 178.

166. Ibid.

167. A Member of the Congregation, *Sisters of Notre Dame de Namur.*

168. Ibid., 196.

169. Oates, " 'The Good Sisters,' " 172.

170. Charles Hale, " 'Our Houses Are Castles:' A Review of the Proceedings of the Nunnery Committee, of the Massachusetts Legislature; and Especially Their Conduct and That of Their Associates on Occasion of the Visit to the Catholic School in Roxbury," *Boston Daily Advertiser*, March 26, 1855, 9.

171. Ibid., 15.

172. A Member of the Congregation, *Sisters of Notre Dame de Namur,* 252.

173. Oates, " 'The Good Sisters,' " 179.

174. Ibid.

175. David R. Dunigan, *A History of Boston College* (Milwaukee: Bruce, 1947), 247.

176. Ibid., 248.

177. Ibid.

178. Marie-Thérèse Fischer, *Anne-Victoire De Méjanès and the Sisters of St. Chretienne* (Strasbourg, France: Éditions du Singe, 2007), 6.

179. *Historique de la Paroisse Saint-Joseph Waltham, Mass 1894–1919* (Eglise Saint-Joseph, 1920).

180. Julie Tremblay, "Generosity in Abandonment 100 Years Later," *St. Chretienne Annals* 10, no. 1 (2003): 2.

181. Ibid.

182. "The Salem Saga," *Sisters of St. Chretienne Celebrating 100 Years of Ministry in the United States 1903–2003, St. Anne's Church, Salem, Massachusetts,* October 25, 2003, 1.

183. Ibid., 3.

184. "Amesbury, MA 1904–1982," *St. Chretienne Annals* 10, no. 2 (2003): 4.

185. "Shirley, MA 1908–1921," *St. Chretienne Annals* 10, no. 2 (2003): 5.

186. "Largest School System in New England," *Boston Archdiocese Department of Education Newsletter* 4, no. 2 (September 1957): 1.

187. Meitler Consultants, Inc., *Situation Analysis Report: The 2010 Initiative Catholic Schools Archdiocese of Boston* (Hales Corners, Wisc.: Meitler Consultants), 1.

188. Ibid.

189. These are categories as they appeared on parish websites. The distinctions between Brazilian and Portuguese and French-Creole, Creole, and Haitian are unclear.

190. U.S. Department of Education, National Center for Education Statistics (2001), *Private School Universe Survey* (Washington, D.C.: U.S. Government Printing Office).

191. *HAB*, 3:196.

192. Translated by Joseph M. O'Keefe from *Historique de la Paroisse Saint-Joseph, Waltham, Mass. 1894–1919* (Eglise Saint-Joseph, 1920), 70: Sise sur les bords de la rivière Charles, c'est la terre sur laquelle nous avons planté notre tente, et où nos familles se sont établies. C'est notre chez-nous, c'est notre patrie. Sous le drapeau étoilé, nous jouissons du libre exercice de notre religion. Avec notre clergé, nos écoles et nos sociétés nationales, nous espérons que nos enfants et petits enfants conserveront l'idôme de la mère patrie, ses traditions et le culte des ancêtres.

193. Cummins and Schecter, "Introduction, School-Based Language Policy," 1–5.

194. Jim Cummins, "Bilingual Education: Basic Principles," in *Bilingualism: Beyond Basic Principles*, ed. Jean-Marc Dewaele, Alex Housen, and Li Wei (Ontario, Canada: Multilingual Matters, 2003), 64.

195. Cummins and Schecter, "Introduction, School-Based Language Policy," 1–5.

196. Paula Menyuk and Maria Estela Brisk, *Language Development and Education: Children with Varying Language Experience* (New York: Palgrave Macmillan, 2005), 200.

197. Cummins, "Bilingual Education: Basic Principles," 64.

198. National Catholic Conference of Bishops, *The Hispanic Presence: Challenge and Commitment* (Washington, D.C.: National Catholic Conference of Bishops, 1983), 4.

Chapter 5: Libby MacDonald Bischof / *"I Am a Catholic Just as I Am a Dweller on the Planet"*

1. Details of the event were recorded in the *Boston Daily Globe* and *New York Times:* "Tribute to a Patriot," *Boston Daily Globe,* June 21, 1896, 9; "John Boyle O'Reilly's Memorial; Unveiled in Boston in Presence of Distinguished Gathering," *New York Times,* June 21, 1896, 24.

2. "Opening Exercises, Remarks By Mr. A. Shuman," in *An Account of the Exercises at the Dedication and Presentation to the City of Boston of the O'Reilly Monument* (Boston: Printed by Order of the City Council, 1897), 19–21.

3. Names of attendees taken from the list of "Prominent People Present" included at the end of *An Account of the Exercises at the Dedication and Presentation to the City of Boston of the O'Reilly Monument,* 67–69.

4. Rev. Dr. Elmer H. Capen, "The Eulogy," in *An Account of the Exercises at the Dedication and Presentation to the City of Boston of the O'Reilly Monument,* 54.

5. Much mourning occurred in Boston on the occasion of O'Reilly's death. Under the auspices of the mayor, a memorial meeting was held in Tremont Temple on September 2, 1890, where such notables as General Benjamin Butler, Col. Thomas Wentworth Higginson, and Patrick Collins made public remarks. The Boston City Council published a transcription of these proceedings: *A Memorial of John Boyle O'Reilly from the City of Boston* (Boston: Printed by Order of the City Council, 1890). It was at this meeting that a resolution was first passed to commission a public memorial to O'Reilly in Boston.

6. "Tribute to a Patriot," *Boston Daily Globe,* June 21, 1896, 9.

7. The description of O'Reilly was taken from "Address of Gen. Francis A. Walker," *An Account of the Exercises at the Dedication and Presentation to the City of Boston of the O'Reilly Monument,* 21. Van Wyck Brooks said of O'Reilly "He did more than anyone else, as editor of the *Pilot,* to reconcile the Catholics and Protestants in Boston" (Van Wyck Brooks, *New England: Indian Summer 1865–1915* (New York: E. P. Dutton and Co., 1940), 311).

8. Robert H. Lord, John E. Sexton, Edward T. Harrington, *History of the Archdiocese of Boston In the Various Stages of Its Development 1604 to 1943,* vol. 3: 1866–1943 (New York: Sheed and Ward, 1944), 404–5.

9. Paula Kane, *Separatism and Subculture: Boston Catholicism, 1900–1920* (Chapel Hill: University of North Carolina Press, 1994), 253; Donna Merwick, *Boston Priests, 1848–1910: A Study of Social and Intellectual Change* (Cambridge, Mass.: Harvard University Press, 1973), 162.

10. Paul Messbarger, in *Fiction with a Parochial Purpose: Social Uses of American Catholic Literature, 1884–1900* (Boston: Boston University Press, 1971), refers to the few turn-of-the-century Catholic authors who did not conform to the standard vision of the Catholic author who "wrote for an American Catholic audience, employing specifically Catholic materials, from a Catholic point of view" as "literary anomalies" (114–15). He cites two Boston authors as examples of a more independent vision — John Boyle O'Reilly and Mary Agnes Tickner. In this chapter I argue that in Boston these individuals were not anomalies, but rather examples of an alternative and exceptionalist vision of Catholic literature, albeit one that failed when William Henry O'Connell assumed control of the Archdiocese of Boston in 1907.

11. The term "exceptionalist" as it is used here refers to the fact that O'Reilly and the other Catholic authors did not conform to any literary "formula" prescribed by the Catholic hierarchy.

12. Merwick, *Boston Priests*, 167.

13. Messbarger, *Fiction with a Parochial Purpose*, 131.

14. Merwick, *Boston Priests*, 167; Kane, *Separatism and Subculture*, 255.

15. As cited in Merwick, *Boston Priests*, 189. For more on O'Connell's leadership style see James O'Toole, *Militant and Triumphant: William Henry O'Connell and the Catholic Church in Boston, 1859–1944* (South Bend, Ind.: University of Notre Dame Press, 1993).

16. Messbarger, *Fiction with a Parochial Purpose*, 135–45. Messbarger does a good job of placing the direction of Catholic literature in this era within the larger context of American Catholics struggling for an identity both as Americans and as Catholics while, at the same time, the church hierarchy was debating an American influence on Catholicism as a whole. Messbarger does excellent close readings of many Catholic novels of the era, and readers interested in a detailed discussion of the subject matter of nineteenth-century Catholic fiction will find the book very interesting. In this chapter I am more interested in how the Catholic authors saw themselves and their purposes, and so do not include as many close readings of fiction as Messbarger.

17. For a very well researched and interesting study of Catholic intellectuals and converts on both sides of the Atlantic, see Patrick Allitt, *Catholic Converts: British and American Intellectuals Turn to Rome* (Ithaca, N.Y.: Cornell University Press, 1997). Insofar as the book relates to Catholic literature in Boston, see particularly his discussion of Orestes Brownson and Isaac Hecker, two former Transcendentalists who converted to Catholicism in the 1840s, in chapter 4 "Tractarians and Transcendentalists in America" (61–85). For a detailed discussion of conversion and antebellum fascination with Catholic symbolism in America, especially among authors of fiction and literature, see Jenny Franchot, *Roads to Rome: The Antebellum Protestant Encounter with Catholicism* (Berkeley: University of California Press, 1994).

18. The fascinating lives of Brownson and Hecker and their contributions to American Catholicism are beyond the scope of this chapter. Interested readers should see David J. O'Brien, *Isaac Hecker: An American Catholic* (New York: Paulist Press, 1992); Arthur Schlesinger, *A Pilgrim's Progress: Orestes A. Brownson* (Boston: Little, Brown, 1966), or, more recently, Patrick W. Carey, *Orestes A. Brownson: American Religious Weathervane* (Grand Rapids, Mich: Wm. B. Eerdmans, 2004).

19. A thorough discussion of the role of the convert in Catholic Literature in Boston is beyond the scope of this chapter, but interesting nonetheless. Many Catholic intellectuals of this era were converts to the faith and as such worked to further the range, scope, and audience for Catholic literature. As Lord noted, "From the converts the Catholic literary movement of the time received a considerable impetus" (*HAB*, 3:410). Lord also explained in his section on converts that there was an unusually high number of "Puritan" converts to Catholicism during the tenure of Archbishop Williams and detailed the numerous contributions of these men and women as well as their often prominent New England lineage (407–15). Lathrop was a well-respected author and editor who married Nathaniel Hawthorne's daughter Rose in 1871 in London. When the couple returned to the United States, they took up residence in Boston, and in 1875 Lathrop became the associate editor of the *Atlantic Monthly* under William Dean Howells. In 1877 he left the *Atlantic Monthly* to edit the *Boston Sunday Courier*, a position he held until 1879. When Francis, the only child of George and Rose, died in 1881 at the age of five, the couple retreated to Europe, where Lathrop wrote travel essays for *Harper's*

Monthly. The couple converted to Catholicism together in 1891. Lathrop helped found the Catholic Summer School of America in New London, Connecticut, in 1892, and in 1894, the couple wrote and published *A Story of Courage,* an account of the order of the Sisters of the Visitation. When Lathrop died in 1898, Rose became a Dominican nun and founded the Congregation of St. Rose of Lima, later known as the Servants of Relief for Incurable Cancer. For Lathrop's interest in and promotion of Catholic literature, readers should see George Parsons Lathrop, "Catholic Tendency in American Literature," *American Catholic Quarterly Review* 18, no. 70 (April 1893): 372–91.

20. For more information on the young Boston Bohemians Guiney associated with, see my dissertation: Elizabeth MacDonald Bischof, " 'Against an Epoch': Boston Moderns 1880–1905," diss., Boston College, 2005. When Guiney was helping her close friend F. Holland Day with editing for Copeland and Day, she even suggested that Day produce a special catalogue of Catholic authors on their list that would feature "all the books eminently fit for Catholic schools and colleges." Copeland and Day did issue such a catalogue in 1897 and included Catholic authors such as Francis Thompson, John Bannister Tabb, Lionel Johnson, Katherine Tynan Hinckson, and Guiney herself. See Joe W. Kraus, *Messrs. Copeland and Day, 69 Cornhill, Boston 1893–1899* (Philadelphia: George S. MacManus Co., 1979), 37.

21. For a discussion of increasing ethnic diversity in the Archdiocese of Boston, see James O'Toole, " 'The Newer Catholic Races': Ethnic Catholicism in Boston, 1900–1950," *New England Quarterly* 65, no. 1 (March 1992): 117–34.

22. Cardinal James Gibbons, "Introduction," in James Jeffrey Roche and Mary Murphy O'Reilly, *Life of John Boyle O'Reilly, Together with His Complete Poems and Speeches* (New York: Cassell Publishing Co., 1891), vi.

23. Katherine E. Conway, "John Boyle O'Reilly," in *The Catholic Encyclopedia,* vol. 11, 1911.

24. We are still without a definitive biography of O'Reilly, but those interested will find the following works useful: James Jeffrey Roche, *Life of John Boyle O'Reilly;* Francis G. McManamin, *The American Years of John Boyle O'Reilly, 1870–1890* (Washington, D.C.: Catholic University of America Press, 1959); and most recently A. G. Evans, *Fanatic Heart: A Life of John Boyle O'Reilly* (Nedlands, W.A.: University of Western Australia Press, 1997).

25. *HAB,* 3:395.

26. As cited in Thomas H. O'Connor, *Boston Catholics: A History of the Church and Its People* (Boston: Northeastern University Press, 1998), 58. My summary of the *Pilot*'s early history was gleaned from O'Connor, *Boston Catholics,* 58–61, 142–47 and "A Brief History of the Boston *Pilot,*" *Information Wanted: A Database of Advertisements for Irish Immigrants Published in the Boston Pilot,* Chestnut Hill, Boston College. Webpage at *http://infowanted.bc.edu/history/briefhistory/* (accessed October 2, 2007). The "Information Wanted" searchable database is an amazing Internet resource for Irish immigration in America, providing readers access to thousands of "Missing Friends" columns printed in the *Boston Pilot* from 1821 to 1931.

27. *HAB,* 3:391. Lord claims the circulation of around 100,000 by 1866, but I have not been able to uncover exact statistics anywhere else.

28. It was not just the Great Fire of 1872 that bankrupted Donahoe and the *Pilot,* as Roche explained: "The large granite building, owned and occupied by the *Pilot* on Franklin Street, was entirely consumed. As soon as possible, new quarters were taken on Cornhill, which, by a strange fatality, was also burned to the ground eleven days later. Nothing daunted the *Pilot* resumed business again at No. 360 Washington Street. A little impatience was excusable in it when called upon to

announce, early in the following June, that the paper had been burnt out for a third time on May 30" (Roche, *Life of John Boyle O'Reilly*, 135).

29. The complete letter is cited in Roche, *Life of John Boyle O'Reilly*, 133–34.

30. *HAB*, 3:394.

31. Editorial of August 17, 1878, as cited in Roche, *Life of John Boyle O'Reilly*, 185.

32. *HAB*, 3:394.

33. "A Great Catholic Review," *Boston Pilot*, May 18, 1889, 4.

34. It is interesting to note that this practice, so prevalent under O'Reilly's leadership, did not continue in the same manner once Roche and Conway took over the editorship.

35. See "New Books," the *Boston Pilot*, January 24, 1880, November 27, 1880.

36. As cited in Katherine E. Conway, "John Boyle O'Reilly," *Catholic World* 53, no. 314 (May 1891): 208.

37. Conway, "John Boyle O'Reilly," *Catholic World*, 208.

38. John Boyle O'Reilly to the Boston Press Club, November 8, 1879, as cited in Roche, *Life of John Boyle O'Reilly*, 195.

39. See, for example, "The Papyrus," the *Boston Pilot*, March 5, 1881, 1–3. I would like to give special thanks to my research assistant, Matthew DaPrato, who helped me comb the pages of the *Boston Pilot*.

40. Thomas R. Sullivan, *Notes of My Own Life, 1891–1903*, 4 vols. Massachusetts Historical Society, Boston, Massachusetts. He wrote about attending the reading of Catholic authors in vol. 1, 6–7. Sullivan was devastated by O'Reilly's death and participated in authors' readings for memorial fundraising as well as in the planning of the Papyrus Club memorial to O'Reilly, a bust of the author placed in the Boston Public Library. Sullivan also gave an interesting account of the night O'Reilly took him to meet Walt Whitman when he was in Boston. See vol. 1, April 4, 1891, 27–29.

41. "Remarks of Col. Thomas Wentworth Higginson," *A Memorial of John Boyle O'Reilly from the City of Boston*, 40.

42. As cited in Conway, "John Boyle O'Reilly," *Catholic World*, 206.

43. As cited in Roche, *Life of John Boyle O'Reilly*, 377.

44. "The Eulogy," *An Account of the Exercises at the Dedication and Presentation of the O'Reilly Monument*, 60.

45. John Boyle O'Reilly, *Moondyne: A Story of Convict Life in Australia* (London: George Routledge and Sons, n.d.), 10. This book was published in many editions and is also sometimes titled, *Moondyne Joe* or *Moondyne Joe: A Story from the Underworld*.

46. "Current Fiction," *The Literary World; A Monthly Review of Current Literature* 10, no. 21 (October 1879): 326.

47. Not all Catholic reviews of the book were negative. The *Catholic World* reported: "*Moondyne* is a far better story than two thirds of those that come to our table from far more pretentious authors." See "New Publications," *Catholic World* 29, no. 173 (August 1879): 718.

48. O'Reilly, "Is 'Moondyne' a Bad Book?" editorial from the *Boston Pilot* as cited in Roche, *Life of John Boyle O'Reilly*, 186–87.

49. Messbarger, *Fiction with a Parochial Purpose*, 117.

50. As cited in Roche, *Life of John Boyle O'Reilly*, 377.

51. "The Warrior and the Poet," *Boston Daily Globe*, July 26, 1885, 6. Later, in 1885, he penned a poem "Grant–1885" on the occasion of the general's death.

52. "O'Reilly's Crispus Attucks," *Boston Daily Globe*, December 19, 1888, 5.

53. O'Reilly's poem "Crispus Attucks" can be read in full in Roche, *Life of John Boyle O'Reilly*, 408–14.

54. Mark Robert Schneider, *Boston Confronts Jim Crow, 1890–1920* (Boston: Northeastern University Press, 1997), 363.

55. John R. Betts, "The Negro and the New England Conscience in the Days of John Boyle O'Reilly," *Journal of Negro History* 51, no. 4 (October 1966): 246.

56. "A Superb Poem," *Boston Daily Globe,* August 4, 1889, 12.

57. John Boyle O'Reilly, "The Pilgrim Fathers," as quoted in "Plymouth's Greatest Day," *New York Times,* August 2, 1889, 1. The full poem was printed on the front page of the *Boston Pilot* on August 10, 1889.

58. *HAB,* 3:395.

59. "A Loss to the Catholic Church," *Boston Pilot,* August 16, 1890, 1.

60. "Tributes to His Memory," *Boston Pilot,* August 23, 1890, 4; "Messages of Sympathy," *Boston Pilot,* August 16, 1890, 4.

61. "Tributes to John Boyle O'Reilly," *Boston Pilot,* August 23, 1890, 4.

62. "His Unique Service to Ireland and the Catholic Church," *Boston Pilot,* August 23, 1890, 4.

63. Merwick, *Boston Priests,* 168.

64. Kane notes that although Conway was Roche's assistant, it was she who "did the majority of the editing and production work," and quotes from Conway's diary about Roche: "For seven years previous to his departure, he had been a good deal of an invalid, and I had often carried the paper along for considerable intervals" (Kane, *Separatism and Subculture,* 223). Kane also gives a detailed summary of Conway's career, see ibid., 221–31.

65. *HAB,* 3:395.

66. Roche, *Life of John Boyle O'Reilly,* ix.

67. Conway, "John Boyle O'Reilly," *Catholic World,* 215.

68. *HAB,* 3:397.

69. Louise Imogen Guiney, "James Jeffrey Roche," *Magazine of Poetry and Literary Review* 1, no. 2 (1889): 185. It was very typical for both popular and Catholic magazines to engage Catholic authors to write appreciations of one another.

70. Patrick Sarsfield Cunniff, "Catholic Poets of New England: James Jeffrey Roche," *Boston College Stylus* 9, no. 7 (April 1896): 2.

71. Roger Lane, "James Jeffrey Roche and the Boston Pilot," *New England Quarterly* 33, no. 3 (September 1960): 343. As Lane argues, one of the ways Roche changed the tone of the paper was to appeal to more popular culture and assume "a folksy Republican tone."

72. Lane, "James Jeffrey Roche," 362. For an excellent account of Irish politics in Boston during this era see Thomas O'Connor, *The Boston Irish: A Political History* (Boston: Northeastern University Press, 1995).

73. "Literary Fame Won in Boston," *Boston Daily Globe,* April 4, 1908, 3.

74. James K. Kenneally, *The History of American Catholic Women* (New York: Crossroad Publishing Company, 1990), 132. For more on Catholic women see also Karen Kennelly, *American Catholic Women: A Historical Explanation* (New York: Macmillan, 1989), a collection of essays.

75. These questions were the topics of *Boston Daily Globe* articles on November 8, 1903, September 18, 1904, August 27, 1905, and January 19, 1908, respectively.

76. Kane, *Separatism and Subculture,* 227.

77. "Decoration for Miss Katherine E. Conway," *Boston Daily Globe,* June 16, 1912, 55.

78. "The Columbian Reading Union," *Catholic World* 55, no. 328 (July 1892): 618. The *Catholic World* frequently excerpted Reading Circle reports from the *Pilot,* noting in the same issue: "We quote from the Boston *Pilot* some notices showing the excellent work accomplished by the reading circles. Our friends in the

rural districts will read with interest the account of what Catholics at Boston can do for literary advancement," 616.

79. "Miss Conway at Medford," *Boston Daily Globe,* January 10, 1895, 5.

80. "Notes in Season," *Publisher's Weekly* 43, no. 10 (March 1893): 415.

81. Mary Sarsfield Gilmore, "Katherine E. Conway," *Dominicana: A Magazine of Catholic Literature* 9 (September 1901): 464.

82. Gilmore, "Katherine E. Conway," 465.

83. "Presentation on Friday," *Boston Daily Globe,* May 13, 1907, 13.

84. Denis A. McCarthy, "Miss Katherine E. Conway Receives the Laetare Medal," *Rosary Magazine* 30, no. 4 (April 1907): 435.

85. Ibid., 436.

86. *HAB,* 3:405; Messbarger, *Fiction with a Parochial Purpose,* 100.

87. For Messbarger, Guiney's choice to leave America permanently made her "liable to a special criticism." He argues that while the other Catholic writers who remained in the United States were "trying mightily to discover and proclaim a meaningful relationship with American Catholicism . . . Miss Guiney simply broke off the conversation. The ultimate effect of her work on American Catholicism was negligible" (Messbarger, *Fiction with a Parochial Purpose,* 101). Although Guiney did move to England, she did not completely disengage with American Catholicism. She actively corresponded with her American friends and continued to publish frequently in American Catholic periodicals like the *Catholic World.* It is well documented that she did prefer England to America, but she always considered herself an American and encouraged American Catholics to look to England as a model. If her influence was negligible, then why do so many (Messbarger included) still consider her to have been the most promising of all the late nineteenth-century Catholic authors?

88. Brooks, *New England: Indian Summer,* 412.

89. Louise Imogen Guiney donated her father's papers to his alma mater, the College of the Holy Cross, in Worcester, Massachusetts, where the bulk of her own personal papers also reside. For more on General Guiney's career, see Christian G. Samito, ed., *Commanding Boston's Irish Ninth: The Civil War Letters of Patrick R. Guiney, Ninth Massachusetts Volunteer Infantry* (New York: Fordham University Press, 1998). For more on Guiney's life, career, and literary productions see Eva Mabel Tenison, *Louise Imogen Guiney: Her Life and Works* (London: Macmillan, 1923), and Henry G. Fairbanks, *Louise Imogen Guiney* (New York: Twayne, 1973). Many authors note the particular interest of Guiney's letters, many of which are reprinted in Grace Guiney, ed., *Letters of Louise Imogen Guiney,* 2 vols. (New York: Harper Bros., 1926).

90. Stephen Maxfield Parrish, *Currents of the Nineties in Boston and London: Fred Holland Day, Louise Imogen Guiney and Their Circle* (New York: Garland Publications, 1987), 15.

91. Ibid., 17.

92. The Boston Public Library has fifteen letters from Guiney to Fields and Jewett — the earliest dating from 1887. Guiney referred to Fields as "The Lady ever Dear," and contents of the letters include appreciations, invitations, and mutual health concerns. Guiney convinced Jewett to write a small piece on her travels in Venice for the Women's Rest Tour Association publication "The Pilgrim Scrip" that Guiney and Alice Brown edited. Guiney spent time recuperating from an illness in 1910 at Fields's Charles St. home, and Fields also remembered Guiney in her will. As far as Guiney's and Moulton's relationship, one quote in particular is exemplary of the relationship between the two women. Moulton wrote, "My own darling — There! That's what you are to me, even though you are a resuscitated Greek faun, without a heart — I am always so glad to hear from you — & this time I am

doubly glad, because you have given up that editorial notion, which did *not* suit well for you at all. A poet and essayist like you had no business to waste her best years reading and deciding on other people's manuscripts — and I'm heartily glad you've abandoned the idea." Moulton was referring to Guiney's editing stint with Copeland and Day. Moulton to Guiney, undated. Louise Imogen Guiney Collection, College of the Holy Cross Special Collections.

93. Ralph Adams Cram, *My Life in Architecture* (Boston: Little, Brown, 1936), 14.

94. Robert Fulton to Louise Imogen Guiney, February 20, 1888. Robert Fulton's President's Office Records, 1867–95, John J. Burns Library, Boston College. Fulton was president of Boston College from 1870 to 1880 and again from 1888 to 1891.

95. Although much of Paula Kane's *Separatism and Subculture* is exceedingly well done, she drastically misreads the relationship between Guiney and Day, detailed on pages 234–36. Kane described Day as Guiney's "soulmate with whom she shared a romantic relationship for about eight years," and of the reasons for their connection postulates, "Perhaps he needed her to mother him by introducing him to polite society and potential portrait clients," or, "Perhaps she needed a presentable escort in London, and not a demanding lover who might challenge the perfect memory of her father." Day and Guiney were distant cousins, best friends (never lovers), and exceedingly supportive of one another and were never, as Kane claims, engaged to be married. Day needed no introduction into polite society, and although Kane dismisses his importance, he was a prominent publisher and internationally acclaimed photographer at the turn of the century. Their abiding friendship, which continued until Guiney's death in 1920, is detailed in the nine hundred plus letters to Day from Guiney that Day donated to the Library of Congress upon his death in 1933. The richness and intimacy of their friendship inspired both Day and Guiney to push their creative limits. Theirs was not, as Kane implies, a friendship or romance based upon social mobility. Guiney and Day's friendship is more accurately presented in Patricia Fanning, "The Frame We Have Invented: Culture, Biography and the Friendship of Fred Holland Day and Louise Imogen Guiney," in *New Perspectives on F. Holland Day*, ed. Patricia Fanning (Norwood, Mass.: Massachusetts Foundation for the Humanities, 1998), 7–12.

96. Louise Imogen Guiney to F. Holland Day, May 5, 1892, Louise Imogen Guiney Collection, Library of Congress, Washington D.C.

97. For a full accounting of this incident see Patricia Fanning, " 'Boycott!' Louise Imogen Guiney and the American Protective Association," *Historical Journal of Massachusetts* 28, no. 2 (Summer 1999): 166–80.

98. "Miss Guiney Gets a Raise," *Boston Daily Globe*, June 22, 1895, 8.

99. Louise Imogen Guiney to Dora Sigerson, April 5, 1895, as cited in Grace Guiney, ed., *Letters of Louise Imogen Guiney*, 2:66–67.

100. Louise Imogen Guiney to Rev. W. H. Van Allen, July 5, 1897, as cited in Grace Guiney ed., *Letters of Louise Imogen Guiney*, 1:188.

101. Louise Imogen Guiney to Dora Sigerson, Autumn 1899, as cited in Grace Guiney ed., *Letters of Louise Imogen Guiney*, 2:7.

102. Louise Imogen Guiney to Charlotte E. Maxwell, August 13, 1903, as cited in Grace Guiney ed., *Letters of Louise Imogen Guiney*, 2:90.

103. Louise Imogen Guiney to Wilfred Meynell, March 5, 1906, as cited in Grace Guiney ed., *Letters of Louise Imogen Guiney*, 2:120–21. Meynell, and his wife, Alice, a poet (both friends of Guiney), were publishers of *Merry England*, a Catholic literary monthly in England, and Guiney wanted Meynell to speak at one of the Catholic gatherings.

104. Louise Imogen Guiney, "An Outdoor Litany," *The Martyrs' Idyl and Shorter Poems* (Boston: Houghton Mifflin, 1899), 50–51.

105. Bliss Carman, "Contemporaries: IV, Louise Imogen Guiney," *Chap-Book* 2 (November 1894): 34.

106. Ironically, Van Allen was actually the rector of the Anglican Church of the Advent in Beacon Hill—the same church Guiney could not attend with Day.

107. Louise Imogen Guiney to Rev. W. H. Van Allen, September 10, 1896, as cited in Grace Guiney ed., *Letters of Louise Imogen Guiney*, 1:134.

108. Alice Brown, *Louise Imogen Guiney* (New York: Macmillan, 1921), 54–55.

109. Brown, *Louise Imogen Guiney*, 62–63.

110. For a good and nearly comprehensive listing of Guiney's published works, including articles in Catholic and popular periodicals, see the "Selected Bibliography" in Fairbanks, *Louise Imogen Guiney*, 153–60. For more on Guiney's contributions to the *American Ecclesiastical Review*, a publication aimed at the clergy, see William L. Lucey, S.J., "Louise Imogen Guiney and the American Ecclesiastical Review," *American Ecclesiastical Review* (June 1957): 364–70.

111. Guiney included large excerpts from Smith's original article in her own rejoinder, assuming many readers would not have seen the original piece.

112. Guiney, "Catholic Writers and Their Handicaps," 205.

113. Ibid., 209, 211.

114. Ibid., 212.

115. Ibid., 213.

116. Louise Imogen Guiney to Coletta Ryan, November 12, 1899, as cited in Grace Guiney ed., *Letters of Louise Imogen Guiney*, 2: 9.

117. Guiney, "Catholic Writers and Their Handicaps," 214.

118. Above quotations taken from "The Future of Catholic Literature," *Boston Pilot*, January 16, 1909, 1. The promotion of Catholic authors by Catholic newspapers and journals was certainly not a new phenomenon, nor was the admonishment of a Catholic audience to do more to support Catholic authors. In 1892 the *Catholic World* reprinted "Our Obligations to Catholic Authors," a lecture given by the Rev. Thomas McMillan to the Catholic Summer School. Father McMillan wrote of Catholic authors, "Inasmuch as they belong to the household of the faith they have a claim on our attention which should be cheerfully recognized. They are the exponents of the highest culture of mind and heart. Consequently we should study their writings and manifest our appreciation of their efforts." Catholic readers could work to ensure that public libraries were stocked with examples of Catholic literature and do what they could to protect the integrity of the literature. Unlike the *Pilot*, however, McMillan never argued that Catholic writers had holy a Catholic audience. See "The Columbian Reading Union," *Catholic World* 56, no. 332 (November 1892): 289.

119. Merwick, *Boston Priests*, 169, 189–90. O'Connell also encouraged the selling of the newspaper in church vestibules and replaced Conway as editor with David J. Toomey, a priest. O'Toole, *Militant and Triumphant*, 82–83.

120. Merwick, *Boston Priests*, 162–63.

121. In his otherwise very nuanced and well-done study, Ross Labrie, *The Catholic Imagination in American Literature* (Columbia: University of Missouri Press, 1997), did limit himself to "authors who represent high intellectual and artistic achievement . . . authors who were practicing Roman Catholics . . . and literary works that center on Catholic belief and spirituality," ix. Despite the narrow definition, Labrie's historically grounded discussions of Catholic and Puritan stereotypes and ideals as well as his discussion of literary modernism and Catholicism will interest many readers.

122. Anita Gandolfo, *Testing the Faith: The New Catholic Fiction in America* (New York: Greenwood Press, 1992), xii.

123. Jeanna DelRosso, *Writing Catholic Women: Contemporary International Catholic Girlhood Narratives* (London: Palgrave Macmillan, 2005), 15–16.

124. DelRosso, *Writing Catholic Women*, 17.

125. Guiney, "Catholic Writers and Their Handicaps," 213.

Chapter 6: William C. Leonard / People of Faith, People of Color

1. For the purposes of the chapter I will follow the archdiocese's designation regarding the use of the term "Hispanic" and use it instead of "Latino." Hispanic will refer generally to Spanish-speaking immigrants from the Caribbean, Central, or South America, and their descendants living in the archdiocese. "Latino" is often used interchangeably with "Hispanic," and the two groups do overlap. "Latino" generally refers to people from Central and South America, which could include Brazilians. The term "Hispanic" would not include Brazilians although some researchers do include Brazilians under the term "Latino." The archdiocese places Brazilians under its Office of Ethnic Apostolates, which does not include Hispanics.

2. Michael Paulson, "Keeping the Faith, In Spanish: Catholic Church Hopes Newspaper Fills Hispanic Void," *Boston Globe*, April 29, 2000.

3. Bryan T. Froehle and Mary L. Gautier, *Catholicism USA: A Portrait of the Catholic Church in the United States*, Center for Applied Research in the Apostolate Georgetown University (Maryknoll, N.Y.: Orbis Books, 2000), 11–13.

4. Ibid. 16–18, 55–56.

5. Thomas H. O'Connor, *Boston Catholics: A History of the Church and Its People* (Boston: Northeastern University Press, 1998), 160–61.

6. Ibid., 162–68. See also James M. O'Toole, "Here and There: Looking at Catholicism in New England," *U.S. Catholic Historian* (Summer 2000): 13–27.

7. See William C. Leonard, "A Parish for the Black Catholics of Boston," *Catholic Historical Review* (January 1997): 44–68; "The Failure of Catholic Interracialism in Boston before Busing," *Boston Histories: Essays in Honor of Thomas H. O'Connor*, ed. James O'Toole and David Quigley (Boston: Northeastern University Press, 2003); "Growing Together: Blacks and the Catholic Church in Boston," *Historian* (June 2004): 254–77.

8. William Byrne, "The Roman Catholic Church in Boston," in *The Memorial History of Boston, Including Suffolk County, Massachusetts, 1630–1880*, ed. Justin Winsor (Boston: J. R. Osgood and Company, 1881), 515.

9. Robert H. Lord, John E. Sexton, and Edward T. Harrington, *History of the Archdiocese of Boston in the Various Stages of Its Development, 1604 to 1943* (Boston: Pilot Publishing Co., 1945), 1:545.

10. Ibid., 1:347–49.

11. Byrne, "The Roman Catholic Church in Boston," 516–17.

12. Boston Registry Department, *A Report of the Record Commissioners of the City of Boston Containing Selectmen's Minutes*, vol. 25 (Boston: Rockwell and Churchill, 1890), 78. The French influence in Boston and the church is well documented in *HAB*, vol. 1.

13. Ibid., 525; Annabelle M. Melville, *Jean Lefebvre de Cheverus, 1786–1836* (Milwaukee: Bruce, 1958), 208.

14. "Boston Cathedral of the Holy Cross: Baptisms, Marriages & Burials, 1789–1844," Archives of the Archdiocese of Boston (hereafter AAB). For the period after 1822, the sacramental register for deaths does not exist.

15. Albert J. Raboteau, "Black Catholics and Afro-American Religious History: Autobiographical Reflections," *U.S. Catholic Historian* 5 (1986): 120; Cyprian Davis, O.S.B., "Black Catholics in Nineteenth Century America," *U.S. Catholic Historian* 5 (1986): 7–8.

16. Davis, "Black Catholics in Nineteenth Century America," 2.

17. This data is only an estimate of the actual number of black Catholics. Not everyone who was baptized, married, buried, or confirmed made it into the sacramental or city registers.

18. Baptismal information compiled at the Archdiocese of Boston archives. Baptismal entries are listed chronologically and can be found in the first three volumes of the Cathedral of the Holy Cross sacramental register.

19. U.S. Department of Commerce Bureau of the Census, *Historical Statistics of the United States: Colonial Times to 1970*, 2 vols., 1:49. The information is listed for whites only, but we can assume that blacks and whites had similar birth rates.

20. John Daniels, *In Freedom's Birthplace; A Study of the Boston Negroes* (Boston: Houghton Mifflin, 1914), 457; *HAB*, 1:604. Based on Daniels's population estimate for 1800 of 1,174 blacks in Boston and estimates by Father Matignon of around 1,000 Catholics in Boston by 1803.

21. Byrne, "The Roman Catholic Church in Boston," 517; *HAB*, 1:585–86.

22. "Book of Receipts & Expenses & Other Matters for the Use of the Roman Catholic Church in the Town of Boston Beginning from January 1793," 162, AAB, Commonly known as and hereafter referred to as "Matignon's Account Book."

23. Leonard, "Growing Together," 261–75.

24. See James M. O'Toole, *Passing for White: Race, Religion, and the Healy Family, 1820–1920* (Amherst: University of Massachusetts Press, 2003); for Robert Ruffin's role in the Congresses see Congress of Colored Catholics of the United States, *Three Catholic Afro-American Congresses* (Cincinnati, 1893.)

25. For a complete history of the Vatican's interest in African American Catholics see Cyprian Davis, O.S.B., "The Holy See and American Black Catholics: A Forgotten Chapter in the History of the American Church," *U.S. Catholic Historian* 7 (1988): 157–81.

26. "Colorphobia," *American Catholic Tribune*, July 6, 1889.

27. "In Boston," *American Catholic Tribune*, March 23, April 27, May 11, and May 18, 1888.

28. "Negro Catholics," *Boston Pilot*, August 18, 1906.

29. O'Connor, *Boston Catholics*, 193–238; and see Paula M. Kane, *Separatism and Subculture: Boston Catholicism, 1900–1920* (Chapel Hill: University of North Carolina Press, 1994).

30. Cyprian Davis, O.S.B., *The History of Black Catholics in the United States* (New York: Crossroad, 1990), 135.

31. Robert Lord, John E. Sexton, and Edward T. Harrington, *History of the Archdiocese of Boston in the Various Stages of Its Development, 1604 to 1943* (Boston: Pilot Publishing Co., 1945), 3:574–75; John T. Gillard, S.S.J., *The Catholic Church and the American Negro* (Baltimore: St. Joseph's Society Press, 1929), 44–45, 122, 208.

32. Leonard, "A Parish for the Black Catholics of Boston," 46–49.

33. Gillard, *Catholic Church and the American Negro,* 121.

34. Drexel to O'Connell, February 12, 1913, Sisters of the Blessed Sacrament Papers (hereafter SBSP), AAB.

35. Sister Mary Leo to Drexel, September 15, 1914, SBSP, AAB.

36. Wooten to O'Connell, April 39, 1917, St. Richard's Parish Files (hereafter SRPF), AAB.

37. Wooten to O'Connell, August 2, 1920, SRPF, AAB.

38. Bonzano to O'Connell, May 28, 1921, SRPF, AAB; O'Connell to Bonzano, June 2, 1921, SBSP, AAB; Robert C. Hayden, *African-Americans in Boston: More Than Three Hundred Fifty Years* (Boston: Boston Public Library, 1992), 22.

39. Mary Charles to O'Connell, May 8, 1935, SBSP, AAB.

40. Mary Charles to Phelan, June 30, 1937, SBSP, AAB.

41. Marilyn Halter, *Between Race and Ethnicity: Cape Verdean American Immigrants, 1860–1965* (Chicago: University of Chicago Press, 1993), 4–8.

42. Leonard, "A Parish for the Black Catholics of Boston," 52.

43. Mercedes to Drexel, October 18, 1938, SRPF, Josephite Archives (hereafter JA), Baltimore.

44. "Sisters of the Blessed Sacrament," *Chronicle,* September 23, 1939.

45. "Jubilation," *Chronicle,* October 7, 1944.

46. Casserly to Early, November 20, 1944, SRPF, JA; Stephen J. Ochs, *Desegregating the Altar: The Josephites and the Struggle for Black Priests, 1871–1960* (Baton Rouge: Louisiana State University Press, 1990), 4.

47. "Letters," *Chronicle,* March 10, 1945.

48. "Negro Parish," *Chronicle,* April 21, 1945.

49. Thomas to Cushing, April 2, 1945, SRPF, AAB.

50. "Church Purchased," *Chronicle,* May 19, 1945.

51. Cushing, n.t., SRPF, AAB.

52. "Letters," *Chronicle,* May 19, 1945.

53. "Church Opening," *Chronicle,* April 6, 1946.

54. "Cardinal," *Boston Pilot,* April 6, 1946.

55. Coyne to McNamara, September 29, 1959, SRPF, JA.

56. See *Chronicle:* February 9, 1946; March 23, 1946; May 25, 1946; November 23, 1946; June 19, 1954; April 6, 1957; April 26, 1958; December 6, 1958; December 20, 1958.

57. Leonard, "A Parish for the Black Catholics of Boston," 58–59.

58. Ibid.; Mathews to Cushing, November 2, 1956, SRPF, AAB.

59. "Church Notes," *Chronicle,* September 29, 1956; December 1, 1956.

60. "Church Notes," *Chronicle,* March 12, 1960.

61. Mathews to Cushing, November 2, 1956, SRPF, AAB.

62. Cushing to Mathews, November 3, 1956, SRPF, AAB.

63. Risk to Schlichte, November 9, 1961, SRPF, AAB.

64. Leonard, "A Parish for the Black Catholics of Boston," 60–62.

65. Gerald Gamm, *Urban Exodus: Why the Jews Left Boston and the Catholics Stayed* (Cambridge, Mass.: Harvard University Press, 1999), 46–86; William C. Leonard, *Vigor in Arduis: A History of Boston's African-American Catholic Community, 1788–1988* (UMI, 1999), 291–92.

66. O'Connor, *Boston Catholics,* 279–87; J. Anthony Lukas, *Common Ground: A Turbulent Decade in the Lives of Three American Families* (New York: Vintage Books, 1986), 373–75.

67. Leonard, "The Failure of Catholic Interracialism in Boston before Busing," 238–39.

68. Lukas, *Common Ground,* 398; "Urban Apostolates," *Boston Pilot,* October 16, 1971.

69. Leonard, "The Failure of Catholic Interracialism in Boston before Busing," 240–42.

70. "R & D Committee Report on Recruitment from Minority Groups," January 1973, St. John's Seminary College–Brighton, in possession of the author.

71. Leonard, *Vigor in Arduis,* 296–97; see the profile of Father Best in the *Pilot,* December 23, 1988.

72. See various issues from the *Pilot,* February 28, 1975; June 27, 1975; March 26, 1976; March 11, 1977; March 18, 1977; December 10, 1982.

73. O'Connor, *Boston Catholics,* 304–6; "Cardinal Law," *Boston Pilot,* January 22, 1988.

74. See various articles from the *Pilot,* March 6, 1981; February 19, 1982; March 4, 1983; April 20, 1984; and February 8, 1985.

75. "Boston Delegates Report," *Boston Pilot,* September 3, 1982; Leo Donoghue, "Roxbury Cluster Shows Unity Amid Diversities," *Boston Pilot,* October 29, 1982; and "Roxbury Parish," May 31, 1985.

76. Robert Gittens, "Black Catholics Respond," *Boston Pilot,* October 10, 1986; "Local Black Catholics Prepare," *Boston Pilot,* January 16, 1987.

77. "Local Black Catholics Prepare," *Boston Pilot,* January 16, 1987; Julie Asher, "Black Catholics Say National Congress Overdue," *Boston Pilot,* May 22, 1987.

78. Leonard, *Vigor in Arduis,* 296–97.

79. Leila H. Little, "Gordon," *Boston Pilot,* March 4, 1988.

80. Diego Ribadeneira, "The Changing Face of Worship: Immigrants Bring Diversity, Breathe New Life into Declining Urban Churches," *Boston Globe,* March 22, 1998, B1; James L. Franklin, "Newcomers Find a Place at Mass in Holy Cross Cathedral," *Boston Globe,* January 6, 1992, 18; Mass Honors Ethnic Diversity, September 12, 1994, 1.

81. Michael Paulson, "Church Closings Alarm Immigrants — Parishes Help Save Culture," *Boston Globe,* May 9, 2004, A1.

82. Hoffsman Ospino, "Latino Catholics in New England," in *Latinos in New England,* ed. Andrés Torres (Philadelphia: Temple University Press), 204.

83. Hoffsman Ospino, interview with the author, September 6, 2007.

84. Ospino, "Latino Catholics in New England," 213.

85. Gloria Negri, "Trip to Dominican Republic Gives Young Mass. Hispanics New Outlook," *Boston Globe,* August 20, 1989, 37.

86. Ospino, "Latino Catholics in New England," 204–5.

87. James L. Franklin, "Bienvenido: Boston Gives Hearty Welcome to Bishop with Hispanic Beat," *Boston Globe,* October 4, 1988, 19.

88. James L. Franklin, *Boston Globe,* "Boston Bishop Is Appointed Coadjutor for Corpus Christi," May 17, 1995, 74.

89. Jennifer McKim, "Hub's Hispanic Bishop Transferred to Texas," *Boston Globe,* June 25, 1995, 10.

90. Don Aucoin, "This Enduring Eire Hub/Lessons for Future in City's Irish Past," *Boston Globe,* March 17, 1996, 1.

91. "Catholics Seen Switching Faith," *Boston Globe,* April 6, 1991, 7.

92. Diego Ribadeneira, "Two New Bishops Appointed by Pope, Hispanic Ministry a Key, Cardinal Says," *Boston Globe,* July 25, 1996, B1.

93. Tatiana M. Smith, "Cathedral's Commitment: Only the Faces Changed," *Boston Globe,* October 1, 1995, 1.

94. Ospino, "Latino Catholics in New England," 215–16.

95. Michael Paulson, "Keeping the Faith, in Spanish: Catholic Church Hopes Newspaper Fills Hispanic Void," *Boston Globe,* April 29, 2000, B1; Ospino, "Latino Catholics in New England," 213, 221n.

96. Franco Ordonez, "Many Latinos Switching to Evangelical Churches," *Boston Globe,* June 2, 2005, 14.

97. Michael Levenson and Yuxing Zheng, "Immigrant Numbers up 15 percent in State since 2000: Biggest Hike Comes from Latin America," *Boston Globe,* August 16, 2006, B1.

98. Irene Sege, "East Boston Negotiates Its Own Ethnic Truce," *Boston Globe,* April 17, 1991, 1.

99. Yvonne Abraham, "Faith in Numbers – East: Boston Church Swells with Influx of Latino Immigrants," *Boston Globe,* March 18, 2001, B1.

100. *HAB*; Halter, *Between Race and Ethnicity,* 4–5.

101. Bella English, "Cardinal Law Praises Diversity of Parish; St. Patrick's Celebrates 150th Anniversary," *Boston Globe,* October 6, 1986, 18.

102. Halter, *Between Race and Ethnicity*, 7–8, 146.

103. "Cape Verdeans' Faith," *Boston Globe*, June 11, 2003, A22.

104. Lames Franklin, "Homeland Troubles Bring Brazilian Influx to Boston," *Boston Globe*, February 3, 1992, 1.

105. Levenson and Zheng, "Immigrant Numbers up 15 percent in State since 2000," B1.

106. Doreen Ludica Vigue, "A Brazilian Community Thrives in Marlborough," *Boston Globe*, April 11, 1993, 1.

107. Dorie Clark, "St. Peter's New Flock," C1.

108. Phillip Bennett, "Keeping Faith with Change at St. Peter's in Dorchester, Immigrants Still Pray, but in Different Tongues," *Boston Globe*, October 26, 1992, 1.

109. Dorie Clark, "St. Peter's New Flock," *Boston Globe*, December 30, 2001, C1.

110. Yvonee Abraham, "Beacon for Cambodians Faces Dim Future," *Boston Globe*, March 3, 2005, 1; Christine Williams, "Lowell's St. Patrick Parish Celebrates 175 Years," *Boston Pilot*, December 23, 2005.

111. Alexander Reid, "Asian Influx Forging a New Community in Historic Quincy," *Boston Globe*, March 8, 1998, C1.

112. Monica Rhor, "Parishes Replenish from Other Shores," *Boston Globe*, July 29, 2003, A1.

113. See Angelyn Dries, O.S.F., "Korean Catholics in the United States," *U.S. Catholic Historian* (Winter 2000): 99–110, for a good overview of the Korean Catholic community in the United States.

114. Christine Williams, "Archdiocese Announces Merge of Newton Parishes," *Boston Pilot*, June 1, 2007, 1; Thomas J. Curry, "A Korean Catholic Experience: St. Philip Neri Parish in the Archdiocese of Boston," *U.S. Catholic Historian* (Winter 2000): 113–19.

115. Irene Sege, "Father Jack: A Priest of the Streets after 16 Years, He Leaves a Transformed Egleston Square," *Boston Globe*, November 5, 1992, 77.

116. Kevin Joy, "Haitians Look Forward and Back: With Bicentennial Celebration, Community Reflects on Future," *Boston Globe*, January 1, 2004, B1.

117. *www.ccab.org/locations/metro-boston/haitian-multi-service/*, accessed April 3, 2007.

118. Neil W. McCabe, "Haitian Catholic Youth Celebrate 'God's Love and Mercy,' " *Boston Pilot*, June 16, 2006; Joy, "Haitians Look Forward and Back," B1.

119. Carey Dade, "Reaching Out to Haitians: O'Malley Becomes First Catholic Leader in Boston to Offer Mass in Creole," *Boston Globe*, January 2, 2004, B1.

120. Adrienne P. Samuels, "O'Malley Gives Hope in Haitians Own Words: Archbishop Marks Independence Day with Creole Mass," *Boston Globe*, January 2, 2006, B2.

121. Paulson, "Church Closings Alarm Immigrants," *Boston Globe*, May 9, 2004, B1.

122. Ribadeneira, "The Changing Face of Worship," B1.

123. Rhor, "Parishes Replenish from Other Shores," A1.

124. Elizabeth New Weld, "St. Joseph's Church has Changed with the Point," *Boston Globe*, November 13, 1994, 16.

125. Kathy McCabe, "United by Hope, Heritage: Two St. Joseph's Parishes Threatened," *Boston Globe*, May 16, 2004, 1; Kathy McCabe, "At Catholic Schools, It's 'We are the World': A New Diversity Being Embraced," *Boston Globe*, February 13, 2005, 1.

126. Emily Sweeney, "Members of Closed Parishes Start Anew at Renamed Church," *Boston Globe*, November 21, 2004, 3.

127. *www.ctkp.org*, accessed April 4, 2007.

128. Michael Paulson, "O'Malley Plans Aggressive Cuts, Vows to Decide Church Closings as Early as June," *Boston Globe,* December 17, 2003, A1; "Church Closings Alarm Immigrants," A1.

Chapter 7: Carol Hurd Green / The Role of Women in the Archdiocese of Boston

1. On Sister Ann Alexis and Katherine Conway, see Thomas O'Connor, *Boston's Catholics* (Boston: Northeastern University Press, 1998). Paula Kane, *Separatism and Subculture: Boston Catholicism, 1900–1920* (Chapel Hill: University of North Carolina Press, 1994), discusses both Conway and Avery. On Avery see also James Shenton in Edward T. James and Janet Wilson James, eds., *Notable American Women* (Cambridge, Mass.: Harvard University Press, 1971), I, X.

2. See especially Mary J. Oates, "Sisterhoods and Catholic Higher Education, 1890–1960," in *Catholic Women's Colleges in America,* ed. Tracy Schier and Cynthia Russett (Baltimore: Johns Hopkins University Press, 2002), 161–94; *The Catholic Philanthropic Tradition in America* (Bloomington; Indiana University Press, 1995); "Catholic Female Academies on the Frontier," *U.S. Catholic Historian* 12 (1994): 121–38; "Catholic Laywomen in the Labor Force, 1850–1950," in *American Catholic Women: An Historical Exploration,* ed. Karen Kennelly, C.S.J. (New York: Macmillan, 1989), 81–124; " 'The Good Sisters': The Work and Position of Catholic Churchwomen in Boston, 1870–1940," in *Catholic Boston: Studies in Religion and Community, 1870–1970,* ed. Robert Sullivan and James M. O'Toole (Boston: Catholic Archdiocese of Boston, 1985); "Organized Voluntarism: The Catholic Sisters in Massachusetts, 1870–1940," in *Women in American Religion,* ed. Janet Wilson James (Philadelphia: University of Pennsylvania Press, 1980), 141–69; Mary J. Oates, ed., *Higher Education for Catholic Women: An Historical Anthology* (New York: Garland, 1987).

3. Kane, *Separatism and Subculture;* James Kenneally, *History of American Catholic Women* (New York: Crossroad, 1990); Paula Kane, Karen Kennelly, and James Kenneally, eds., *Gender Identities in American Catholicism* (Maryknoll, N.Y.: Orbis Books, 2001); Karen Kennelly, *American Catholic Women.* The three-volume *Women and Religion in America,* ed. Rosemary Radford Ruether and Rosemary Skinner Keller (San Francisco: Harper and Row, 1981–1986), is an invaluable history and collection of documents; Ruether's many important books of both history and theology define the emerging consciousness of American Catholic women.

4. A plaque in Glover's memory, placed at Our Lady of Victories on Isabella Street, is reproduced on *www.goodyglovers.com/history.html.* She was condemned by Cotton Mather, who called her a " 'scandalous old Irish-woman, very poor, a Roman Catholick and obstinate in idolatry.' " See also *www.geocities.com/scorgify/glover/html.*

5. Robert H. Lord, John E. Sexton, and Edward T. Harrington, *History of the Archdiocese of Boston in the Various Stages of Its Development, 1604 to 1943* (Boston: Pilot Publishing Co., 1945), 1:343–44.

6. Ibid., 1:355, 478, 676.

7. Kevin Kenny recounts the commonly accepted version of Irish inheritance and cultural patterns, but suggests that it is overdrawn and that the picture of the Irish roots of emigration is too pessimistic, that Irish emigrants had more freedom of choice than is often suggested. See Kevin Kenny, *The American Irish: A History* (New York: Longman, 2000), 134–37.

8. Bronwen Walter, *Outsiders Inside: Whiteness, Place and Irish Women* (New York: Routledge, 2001), 34–37 and passim.

9. Figures from Walter, *Outsiders Inside,* 54, and Hasia Diner, *Erin's Daughters in America: Irish Immigrant Women in the Nineteenth Century*

(Baltimore: Johns Hopkins University Press, 1983), xiv, 60–61. See also Thomas Dublin's *Women at Work: The Transformation of Work and Community in Lowell, Massachusetts 1820–1860* (New York: Columbia University Press, 1979); Colleen McDannell, "Catholic Domesticity, 1860–1960," in *American Catholic Women,* ed. Kennelly, 54.

10. Walter, *Outsiders Inside,* 55, 56; Diner, *Erin's Daughters,* 95.

11. See James W. Sanders, "Catholics and the School Question in Boston: The Cardinal O'Connell Years," in Sullivan and O'Toole, eds., *Catholic Boston,* 121–69.

12. A July 1986 article from the *Pilot,* found in the National Data Collection Agency (NDCA), notes that it was "not only the teenagers who came to the Sisters for help, but also the orphaned, the destitute, and alcoholic, the mentally disturbed and the aged. No one was turned away...."

13. "Maternal Affection," *Catholic Home Journal,* May 1, 1887, cited by McDannell, "Catholic Domesticity, 1860–1960," 48.

14. An article by Barbara Welter, "The Cult of True Womanhood," *American Quarterly* 18, no. 2 (1966), defined the term and became a touchstone for women's scholarship.

15. McDannell, "Catholic Domesticity, 1860–1960," 48ff.

16. It should be noted that the generalization about the increase in women's workforce participation is most relevant to white middle-class women. See Paula Giddings, *When and Where I Enter: The Impact of Black Women on Race and Sex in America* (New York: Morrow, 1984).

17. The *Boston Herald* captioned their 1946 photograph "Mrs. O'Neil and her six chicks" though husband and father Daniel O'Neil and oldest child, Lawrence, were there.

18. Statement of the Treasurer (Hugh Carey) in the *Pilot* (?), penciled date 1882, in Corporation Records, AAB. Unusual for most lists of Catholic laywomen, there were several single women at the tables for this event.

19. Rev. Mother Augustine of the Mother of God, S.C., "Life of Archbishop Williams" (Boston: Carmel of Boston, 1909?), 452–56, unpublished manuscript in AAB.

20. Ibid., 469–72.

21. Katherine E. Conway, *The Golden Year of the Good Shepherd in Boston: Compiled from the Annals of the Convent* (Boston: Flynn, 1918), 198–99.

22. Among them, in addition to Martha Moore Avery, was Emma Forbes Cary, founder of the Radcliffe Catholic Club and sister-in-law of the Harvard president, who was brought to Catholicism through the influence of her Irish hairdresser.

23. See membership lists for the League of Catholic Women (LCW), 1910–1915 in the LCW Papers, AAB. It is risky, of course, to make definitive statements from such lists, since there is only a small number of single women, as well as married women under their husband's name, until well into the 1970s.

24. A typescript article by Conway in the Boston College archives reviews her central role in the founding of Reading Circles and of the summer schools, which brought together laywomen and men for lectures and to study classic literary and theological texts.

25. Burke's report in the LCW papers is enlightening; unfortunately the League was able to afford her services for only a year. As Kane notes, several of the LCW women were involved in penal reform, suggesting a broader social role than is sometimes assumed. See Kane, *Separatism and Subculture,* 216.

26. LCW Papers, AAB; Kane, *Separatism and Subculture,* 217–18. On child labor law and Cardinal O'Connell, see Douglas J. Slawson, *Ambition and Arrogance: Cardinal William O'Connell of Boston and the American Catholic Church* (New York: Cobalt Productions, 2007), chapter 11.

27. Oates, "Catholic Women in the Labor Force."

28. For nursing and health care, see the discussion below of Catholic hospitals. Social work was not professionalized until the early 1920s with the founding by Edith Abbott of the School of Social Service Administration, the first graduate school of social work, at the University of Chicago. See Lela Costin, "Edith Abbott," *Notable American Women,* 1–3.

29. Mary Ann Hinsdale, I.H.M., *Women Shaping Theology: 2004 Madeleva Lecture in Spirituality* (New York: Paulist Press, 2006), 84–88.

30. Mary Daly, *The Church and the Second Sex* (New York: Harper and Row, 1968); reissued "with a new feminist postchristian introduction by the author" (New York: Harper and Row, 1975); *Beyond God the Father: Toward a Philosophy of Women's Liberation* (Boston: Beacon Press, 1973; reissued 1985). Other major works include: *Gyn/ecology: the Metaethics of Radical Feminism* (1979); *Pure Lust: Elemental Feminist Philosophy* (1984); *Webster's First New Intergalactic Wickedary of the English Language* (1987); *Outercourse: The Bedazzling Voyage Containing Reflections from My Logbook of a Radical Feminist* (San Francisco: HarperSanFrancisco, 1995). As Hinsdale notes, "Any religious feminist today, including Catholic feminists, must reckon with Daly's critique that patriarchal domination and symbols in Christianity are irreformable" (*Women Shaping Theology,* 59).

31. Lisa Sowle Cahill is a fellow of the American Academy of Arts and Sciences; she is a past president of the Catholic Theology Society of America and of the Society of Christian Ethics. *web.med.harvard.edu.healthcaucus/bg_cahill.html.* Her most recent book is *Family: A Christian Social Perspective* (New York: Fortress, 2000); she has published more than one hundred articles and is convenor of an international study group on Genetics, Theology, and Ethics.

32. M. Shawn Copeland, "Method in Emerging Black Catholic Theology," in *Taking Down Our Harps,* ed. Diana L. Hayes and Cyprian Davis, O.S.B. (Maryknoll, N.Y.: Orbis Books, 1998), 123.

33. Eleanor Flexner and Janet Wilson James, "Mary O'Kenney Sullivan," in *Notable American Women,* ed. Edward T. and Janet Wilson James (Cambridge, Mass.: Harvard University Press, 1971), 655–56. See also Allen F. Davis, *Spearheads for Reform: The Social Settlements and the Progressive Movement 1890–1914* (New York: Oxford University Press, 1967), 138–47. O'Sullivan's papers are in the Schlesinger Library at Harvard University.

34. Stephen Norwood, "Julia Sarsfield O'Connor Parker," *Notable American Women: The Modern Period,* ed. Barbara Sicherman and Carol Hurd Green (Cambridge, Mass.: Harvard University Press, 1980), 525–26. See also Norwood, *Labor's Flaming Youth: Telephone Operators and Worker Militancy 1878–1923* (Urbana: University of Illinois Press, 1990).

35. "Who Deserves a Memorial," *www.irishheritagetrail.com.* Foley's papers are in the Schlesinger Library, Harvard University.

36. In 2008 there are still more men than women on most college and university faculties. The numbers are changing, however, and graduate school enrollments show women in a very significant proportion. At Boston College there are 672 male faculty and 278 female, an improvement from the 20 percent of women that persisted for many years.

37. As a result of work by progressive reformers, in 1879 women in Massachusetts had been granted suffrage for school board elections only. Catholic publications and spokesmen opposed women's entrance into politics, as they would later oppose suffrage generally, but, as Polly Kaufman speculates, as a devout Catholic Duff would have seen it as her obligation to run to protect young Irish Catholic women against discrimination. Polly Welts Kaufman, *Boston Women and City School Politics 1872–1905* (New York: Garland, 1994), 232–33, 250–55. A plaque of

Duff is on the Boston Women's Heritage Trail, at Old City Hall, 45 School Street: *www.bwht.org.downtown4.html*.

38. Kaufman, *Boston Women,* 235. See also the somewhat more detailed account of Duff's career in Janet Nolan, *Servants of the Poor: Teachers and Mobility in Ireland and Irish America* (Notre Dame, Ind.: University of Notre Dame Press, 2004), 43–47.

39. Kaufman, *Boston Women,* 256 and 266, n. 33, 34, 35. Some of Dierkes's later career is told in these notes. Regarding Holy Trinity membership, see George E. Ryan, ed., *Figures in Our Catholic History* (Boston: Daughters of St. Paul, 1979), 66. See also Franz Xaver Nopper, S.J., *Concerning the History of the Catholic German Holy Trinity Parish in Boston Mass.,* trans. Martha C. Engler (Boston: Holy Trinity Church, 1992).

40. Mark Feeney, "Louise Day Hicks, Icon of Tumult, Dies," *Boston Globe,* October 22, 2003: *www.boston.com/news/local/massachusetts/articles/2003/10/22/louise_day_hicks_ic.* There is extensive writing on the school desegregation crisis: see particularly Anthony Lukas, *Common Ground: A Turbulent Decade in the Lives of Three American Families* (New York: Vintage, 1986), and Ronald P. Formisano, *Boston against Busing: Race, Class and Ethnicity in the 1960s and 1970s* (Chapel Hill: University of North Carolina Press, 2004).

41. The correspondence, audio tapes, newspaper clippings, and other items pertaining to the public career of Margaret Heckler are housed in the Archives of the Burns Research Library at Boston College.

42. Biography: Mary Ann Glendon, U.S. Department of State, February 14, 2008. *www.state.gov/r/pa/ei/biog/99576.htm.* "Most powerful," Don Lattin, "No easy choices ahead for next Pontiff," *San Francisco Chronicle,* April 17, 2005: *SFgate.com/cgi-bin/article.cgi?file.* Among her books on family law are *New Family and the New Property* (Toronto: Butterworth, 1981) and *Abortion and Divorce in Western Law* (Cambridge, Mass.: Harvard University Press, 1987); she has also published a study of Cardinal Bernard Law, *Boston's Cardinal: The Man and His Witness* (Lanham, Md.: Lexington Books, 2002). Mary Ann Glendon, "A Woman's Place," in *Why I Am Still a Catholic,* ed. Kevin and Marilyn Ryan (New York: Riverhead Books, 1998), 198–210.

43. See Nancy Lusignan Schultz, *Fire and Roses: The Burning of the Charlestown Convent, 1834* (New York: Free Press. 2000).

44. Ibid., 66–67.

45. When Elizabeth Seton first formed her American community of women, they were known as the Sisters of Charity of St. Joseph; they were the first American-founded religious community. Several orders of the Sisters of Charity followed on the Seton founding in Emmitsburg, Maryland. The decision in 1850 by the Emmitsburg community to affiliate with the French order of the Daughters of Charity of St. Vincent de Paul led both to the adoption of the distinctive blue dress and cornette (based on French peasant women's garb) and to the adoption of the name Daughters of Charity.

46. Cheverus to Seton, March 4, 1805. In Annabelle Melville, *Elizabeth Bayley Seton 1774–1821* (New York: Charles Scribner's Sons, 1951), 96. She made her formal declaration of faith on March 14: Melville, *Elizabeth Bayley Seton,* 97. On their first meeting, see Melville, *Elizabeth Bayley Seton,* 177–78, 332, n80.

47. "Sisters of Charity, the Golden Jubilee of Their Coming to Boston," *Boston Pilot,* May 1882. NCDA 11-11, 1-2, no. 8.

48. The story of the bishop coming to the sisters with the son and daughter of a "deranged woman," asking them to take the girl, has been frequently told. See, e.g., "The Work of Fifty Years" — mainly a tribute to Sister Ann Alexis on her upcoming golden jubilee (March 12) as a Sister of Charity. *The Sunday Herald,* February 28, 1875, in the NDCA 11-35-00, 1-1, 2a. She died on March 19, 1875.

49. Anon., "St. Vincent's Orphan Asylum," NDCA 11-91, 1-2, no. 6.

50. "Notes on Our Beloved Sister Ann Alexis Shorb, Who Died at St. Vincent's Asylum, Boston, Mass. (United States), on the 19th of March, 1875, Aged 70 Years, 50 of Vocation." Daughters of Charity, *Lives of Deceased Sisters*. NDCA, 11-35-00, 1-1, 1, 2, and passim.

51. For a discussion of Catholic women in nursing in the nineteenth century and the tensions between religious and scientific commitments during the years of intense development within the hospitals of the scientific model of health care, see Kathleen M. Joyce, "Science and the Saints: American Catholics and Health Care, 1880–1930," diss., Princeton University, 1995, 51ff. and 219–28.

52. For a brief overview of this history and of the persistence of hospital hierarchies, see Virginia Drachman, *Hospital with a Heart: Women Doctors and the Paradox of Separatism at the New England Hospital 1862–1969* (Ithaca, N.Y.: Cornell University Press, 1984), 76–84.

53. Quoted in Joyce, "Science and the Saints," 145–48.

54. Dr. Henry Christian quoted in Delphine Steele, comp., "The Carney Hospital," cover date "c. 1950," NDCA.

55. Ibid.

56. The physicians, all male for many years, had to be recruited, and the reputation of the hospital was involved with the degree of their prestige. Because Carney was not an establishment hospital, it had to work harder to recruit its doctors.

57. Sister Gonzaga McCormick to Cardinal William O'Connell, January 15, 1908. Records of Institution, Hospital Correspondence 6:1, AAB. Reprinted in Lorine Getz, "Women Struggle for an American Catholic Identity," in Rosemary Radford Ruether and Rosemary Skinner Keller, eds., *Women and Religion in America*, Vol. 3: *1900–1968* (New York: Harper and Row, 1986), 202–3. Also see Joyce, "Science and the Saints," 140–41.

58. Joyce, "Science and the Saints," 24–26.

59. The original nurses' training school for Carney had developed a variety of programs and gained the status of a college; it was named for Catherine Labouré (1807–76), a member of the Daughters of Charity, who had a vision of Mary that became the image for the very popular devotion of the Miraculous Medal.

60. Letter to Friends of Carney Hospital from Sister Louise Gallahue, DC, in NDCA.

61. The others to close were St. Mary's in Fall River, Cushing Hall in Scituate, and Madonna Hall in Marlborough, formerly a House of the Good Shepherd. Its current mission was with "teenage girls, most...victims of physical and sexual abuse." The new policy was to place children in foster families: pointing out the potential difficulties of that solution for very troubled children, the editorial sees the real reason as financial — foster care would be much cheaper for the state, which would not have to subsidize the institutions. See the *Boston Globe*, August 29, 1985, 22; *http://nl.newsbank.com/nl-search/we/Archives*.

62. Anon., *A History of St. Elizabeth's Hospital, Brighton, Massachusetts with an Account of the Great Ten-Day $200,000 Campaign Successfully Completed in Its Behalf* (Boston: n.p., n.d. [1914?]), 7, 9, 10. Other information from St. Elizabeth Hospital account books, AAB.

63. It is now called the Connell School of Nursing, in honor of late Boston College alumnus William Connell '59, who left a major bequest for the school in his will. The school now offers bachelor's, master's. and Ph.D. programs.

64. Mary Oates, "Sisterhoods and Catholic Higher Education," in *Catholic Women's Colleges in America*, ed. Tracy Schier and Cynthia Russett (Baltimore: Johns Hopkins University Press, 2002), 162, 164–95 passim. Some texts list Trinity

as the first, but scholars generally agree that Notre Dame of Maryland was the first Catholic institution for women to move fully into collegiate education.

65. Most of the early Catholic colleges envisioned a local clientele; part of their mission, as they understood it, was to make education available to daughters of the Catholic middle class. As in other institutions, the sisters' donated labors furthered this goal.

66. Historical information on Emmanuel College is drawn primarily from Mary Friel, "History of Emmanuel College, 1919–1974," diss., Boston College, 1980.

67. Emmanuel College Catalogue 1919–21, 9, quoted in Friel, "History of Emmanuel College," 39. Friel notes that O'Connell placed six novices from the Sisters of St. Joseph at Emmanuel; two went on to be among the first faculty members at Regis College. Friel, "History of Emmanuel College," 64n. On Emmanuel lay faculty, Friel, "History of Emmanuel College," 74–75. On lay faculty contributions see Karen Kennelly, "Faculties and What They Taught," in *Catholic Women's Colleges,* ed. Schier and Russett, 422, and Dorothy M. Brown and Carol Hurd Green, "Making It: Stories of Persistence and Success," in *Catholic Women's Colleges,* ed. Schier and Russett, 237–38, 248.

68. Friel, "History of Emmanuel College," 67–68, 95.

69. Kip Tiernan, "The Roots of Christianity," delivered at the Women and the Church conference, Emmanuel College, 1976. See Kip Tiernan and Fran Froelich, eds., *Urban Meditations* (Boston: Poor People's United Fund, 2006), 19.

70. See John Donnellan, "Underlying Issues Surrounding the Closing of a Private Women's College," typescript in the Newton College papers at BCA. Donnellan demonstrates that — despite early generous donors — the lack of an alumnae base and especially the opening of Boston College to undergraduate women made the continuation of Newton impossible.

71. See Brown and Hurd Green, *Catholic Women's Colleges,* 263–65. Graduate programs were coeducational, both because of federal regulations and in the hope of attracting a new group of students.

72. "The New Regis College," *Boston Pilot,* July 23, 1927. College History, Regis College Archives (RCA).

73. "Regis College: 50th Anniversary of the Charter" (February 12, 1977), typescript, History, RCA.

74. In addition to the colleges founded by women religious in the Boston area, two opened west of the city. The College of Our Lady of the Elms (now known as Elms College) in Chicopee followed a familiar pattern: from an academy for girls founded by the Sisters of St. Joseph in 1899 it evolved into a normal school in 1908, and became a four-year college in 1928. Anna Maria College in Paxton was founded in 1946 by the Sisters of St. Anne. They were following the directive of their founder "to make higher education available to women of modest means," a goal for the majority of the colleges founded by women religious. Both Elms and Anna Maria have become coeducational.

75. Manhattanville had opened on the Lower East Side in 1841 and moved in 1847 to a location near the village of Manhattanville; it was chartered as a college in 1917. The college moved to Purchase, New York, in 1952. It became coeducational in 1969 and came under lay control in 1971.

76. See Doris Kearns Goodwin, *The Fitzgeralds and the Kennedys* (New York: Simon and Schuster, 1987), and a chatty biography, by Charles Higham, *Rose* (New York: Pocket Books, 1995); comment on Sacred Heart education, chapter 2.

77. Eleanor Kenny, R.S.C.J., "Foundations," typescript in the Newton College Archives, Box 2, Folders 11 and 24; donations, Box 1, Folder 5, in BCA. Kenny, who held a Ph.D. in philosophy, was president of the college from 1946 to 1956.

78. Founded at Newton by longtime political activist Betty Taymor, it moved for a few years to Boston College after the merger. The Center for Women in Politics and Public Policy is now at the University of Massachusetts–Boston.

79. The School of Nursing moved to the Chestnut Hill campus in 1950; its building was named in honor of Cardinal Cushing.

80. Mary C. Mellyn, assistant superintendent of the Boston public schools and sister of the dean of the recently founded Boston College School of Education, was the first woman to receive a BC degree, an honorary doctorate in 1925.

81. On the history of professional accomplishment of graduates of women's Catholic colleges see Oates, "Sisterhoods and Catholic Higher Education."

82. Lukas, *Common Ground,* 363; Formisano, *Boston Against Busing,* 219–20.

83. On the Healys, see James O'Toole, *Passing for White: Race, Religion, and the Healy Family, 1820–1920* (2002)

84. M. M. Katharine (Drexel) to Cardinal William O'Connell, February 12, 1913, reprinted in "Boston Black Catholic Oral History Project" (Roxbury: St. Francis de Sales–St. Philip Parish, n.d. [1970s?]).

85. Interview in Black Catholic Oral History Project. Marie McLean, originally from Cape Verde, had similar memories: "What made the... Mission so special was that it was especially for black people. The Sisters of the Blessed Sacrament's mission was to Black and Indians. That is why the nuns came to Boston."

86. Quoted in John T. McGreevy, *Parish Boundaries: The Catholic Encounter with Race in the Urban North* (Chicago: University of Chicago Press, 1996), 162.

87. Ibid., 177.

88. See the article on Caroline (Mrs. Roger) Putnam, "And Call Her Blessed," in *Regis Alumnae Quarterly* (Spring 1964): 6, 14, in Regis College Archives (RCA). Information on Patricia Goler from RCA.

89. Patricia Goler, "Alien No Longer," RCA, n.d. She notes in the paper that African-Americans had been "discouraged or banned from joining most religious congregations and... directed to the Sisters of the Blessed Sacrament or Josephite priests."

90. The papers of the AUS are in the Archives of the Archdiocese of Boston (AAB). The material here is drawn from minutes of meetings between 1968 and 1973 and copies of printed documents, including the constitution and announcements of lectures.

91. The history of this period of Catholic activism is told by Charles Meconis, *With Clumsy Grace: The American Catholic Left, 1961–1975* (New York: Seabury Press, 1979). See also Murray Polner, *Disarmed and Dangerous: The Radical Lives and Times of Daniel and Philip Berrigan* (New York: Basic Books, 1987) and the many writings by both Daniel and Philip Berrigan, especially Daniel Berrigan, *The Trial of the Catonsville Nine* (Boston: Beacon Press, 1970; New York: Fordham University Press, 2004).

92. Tiernan and Froelich, *Urban Meditations,* 2–3.

93. While the doctrine and imagery of the Mystical Body is found in the New Testament, Pius XII's 1943 encyclical, *Mystici Corporis,* proclaimed it as official church teaching and led to greater awareness of it in the minds of many Catholics. It is clearly both belief and metaphor for the Catholic Worker and its emphasis on human communion.

94. Although the focus here is on Sister Marie Augusta and Kip Tiernan, whose public roles and extensive writings have had broad influence, there are many other Boston Catholic women who have taken risks for justice. Among them was Sister Jeanne Normandin (1929–2006), a Sister of St. Anne, who worked in prison ministry and was the founder of Ruah House in Cambridge, Massachusetts, for women with AIDS. See her obituary in the *Boston Globe,* June 2, 2006.

95. Mary Jo Weaver, *New Catholic Women: A Contemporary Challenge to Traditional Religious Authority* (New York: Harper & Row, 1985), 84–85.

96. See Marie Augusta Neal, SNDdeNamur, *Catholic Sisters in Transition* (Wilmington, Del.: Michael Glazier, 1984). The survey was repeated in 1982; this volume discusses the results of, and comparisons between the two.

97. Marie Augusta Neal, "Sociology and Community Change," *Themes of a Lifetime* (Boston: Emmanuel College, 1997), 20–21.

98. Ibid., "Prologue," 10. Among Sister Marie Augusta's many publications two in particular spell out this message: *A Socio-Theology of Letting Go: The Role of a First World Church Facing a Third World People* (New York: Paulist Press, 1977) and *The Just Demands of the Poor: Essays in Socio-Theology* (New York: Paulist Press, 1987).

Chapter 8: William T. Schmidt /
Changing Patterns of Parish Life

1. James A. Coriden, *The Parish in Catholic Tradition: History, Theology and Canon Law* (New York: Paulist Press, 1997), 3–4.

2. Ibid., 19.

3. John J. Hughes, *Pontiffs: Popes Who Shaped History* (Huntington, Ind.: Our Sunday Visitor, 1994), 64.

4. Joseph J. Casino, "From Sanctuary to Involvement: A History of the Catholic Parish in the Northeast," in *The American Catholic Parish*, vol. 1: *The Northeast, Southeast, and South Central States*, ed. Jay P. Dolan (New York: Paulist Press, 1987), 11.

5. Coriden, *The Parish in Catholic Tradition*, 31.

6. Casino, "From Sanctuary to Involvement," 11.

7. Constitution on the Church (*Lumen Gentium*), chapter 2, Documents of Vatican Council II.

8. The Code of Canon Law, Canon 515.

9. Gerald P. Fogarty, S.J., "The Parish and Community in American Parish History," in *Building the American Catholic City Parishes and Institutions*, ed. Brian C. Mitchell (New York: Garland Publishing, 1988), 255.

10. Ibid., 257.

11. Casino, "From Sanctuary to Involvement," 11.

12. Thomas H. O'Connor, *Boston Catholics: A History of the Church and Its People* (Boston: Northeastern University Press, 1998), 7–8.

13. James W. Sanders, "Boston Catholics and the School Question: 1825–1907," in *Building the American Catholic City*, ed. Brian C. Mitchell (New York: Garland Publishing, 1988), 46.

14. James M. O'Toole, "The Six Ages of Catholicism in America," in *Church Ethics and Its Organizational Context*, ed. Jean M. Bartunek, Mary Ann Hinsdale, and James F. Keenan (Lanham, Md.: Rowman and Littlefield, 2006), 52.

15. Robert H. Lord, John E. Sexton, Edward T. Harrington, *History of the Archdiocese of Boston: In the Various Stages of Its Development 1604–1943*, 3 vols. (New York: Sheed & Ward, 1944), 1:377.

16. Jay P. Dolan, *In Search of an American Catholicism* (Oxford and New York: Oxford University Press, 2002), 30.

17. *HAB*, 1:410.

18. Ibid., 1:478.

19. Ibid., 1:551.

20. Ronald D. Patkus, "Conflict in the Church and the City: The Problem of Catholic Parish Government in Boston, 1790–1865," *Historical Journal of Massachusetts* (Winter 2001).

21. Rev. Archie D. Gillis, *St. Patrick through the Years* (Newcastle, Maine: Lincoln County Publishing, 1991), 7–10.

22. "Sunday Obligation without a Priest," in *Prayer and Practice in American Catholic Community,* ed. Joseph P. Chinnici and Angelyn Dries (Maryknoll, N.Y.: Orbis Books, 2000), 12–13.

23. Annabelle M. Melville, *Jean Lefebvre de Cheverus* (Milwaukee: Bruce, 1958), 144.

24. James M. O'Toole, *From Generation to Generation* (Boston: St. Paul Editions, 1983), 33.

25. O'Toole, *From Generation to Generation,* 33.

26. Jay P. Dolan, *In Search of an American Catholicism* (Oxford and New York: Oxford University Press, 2002), 29–30.

27. Patkus, "Conflict in the Church and the City."

28. Brian C. Mitchell, *The Paddy Camps: The Irish of Lowell 1821–61* (Urbana and Chicago: University of Illinois Press: 1988), 39.

29. Ibid., 60.

30. Jay P. Dolan, *The American Catholic Experience* (Garden City, N.Y.: Image Books, 1985), 168.

31. *HAB,* 2:423.

32. Thomas H. O'Connor, *Fitzpatrick's Boston: 1846–1866* (Boston: Northeastern University Press: 1984), 82.

33. Robert R. Grimes, S.J., *How Shall We Sing in a Foreign Land? Music of Irish Catholic Immigrants in the Antebellum United States* (Notre Dame, Ind.: University of Notre Dame Press, 1996), 6.

34. *HAB,* 2:423.

35. Grimes, *How Shall We Sing in a Foreign Land?,* 7.

36. Ronald D. Patkus, *From Generation to Generation II: Stories in Catholic History from the Archives of the Archdiocese of Boston* (Hanover, Mass.: Christopher Publishing House, 1992).

37. Gerald Gamm, *Urban Exodus: Why the Jews Left Boston and the Catholics Stayed* (Cambridge, Mass.: Harvard University Press, 1999), 111.

38. Rev. Francis X. Weiser, S.J., *Holy Trinity Parish, Boston, Mass: 1844–1944* (Boston: Holy Trinity Rectory, 1944), 14–15.

39. "Who loses his language, loses his faith."

40. *HAB,* 3:225–26.

41. Casino, "From Sanctuary to Involvement," 17–18.

42. Ibid., 18.

43. James W. Sanders, "Boston Catholics and the School Question: 1825–1097," in *Building the American Catholic City,* ed. Brian C. Mitchell (New York: Garland Publishing, 1988), 56–57.

44. James M. O'Toole, "Race, Ethnicity and Class in Boston's Cathedral of the Holy Cross," in *Boston's Histories: Essays in Honor of Thomas H. O'Connor,* ed. James M. O'Toole and David Quigley (Boston: Northeastern University Press, 2004), 205.

45. Sanders, *The School Question,* 62.

46. Dolan, *American Catholicism,* 66.

47. O'Toole, *Militant and Triumphant,* 70.

48. Donna Merwick, *Boston Priests 1848–1910: A Study of Social and Intellectual Change* (Cambridge, Mass.: Harvard University Press, 1973), 190–93.

49. Rev. Msgr. John P. Carroll, *Golden Memories* (Boston, privately published, 1997), 173.

50. O'Toole, *Militant and Triumphant,* 213–14

51. Joseph P. Chinnici, O.F.M., "The Catholic Community at Prayer: 1926–1976," in *Habits of Devotion: Catholic Religious Practice in Twentieth-Century*

America, ed. James M. O'Toole (Ithaca, N.Y.: Cornell University Press, 2004), 52–53.

52. Constitution on the Sacred Liturgy (*Sacrosanctum Concilium*), article 14, Documents of Vatican Council II.

53. Gerald Gamm, *Urban Exodus,* 20–21.

54. James E. Glinski, "The Catholic Church and the Desegration of Boston's Public Schools," in *Boston Histories: Essays in Honor of Thomas H. O'Connor,* ed. James O'Toole and David Quigley (Boston: Northeastern University Press, 2003), 248.

55. J. Anthony Lukas, *Common Ground: A Turbulent Decade in the Lives of Three American Families* (New York: Alfred A. Knopf, 1985), 367–69.

56. Ibid., 369–71.

57. Cardinal Bernard F. Law, *Sunday Liturgy: The Heart of the Parish* (Boston: Daughters of St. Paul Press, 1985), 5.

58. O'Connor, *Boston Catholics,* 318.

59. Cited in Joseph Gremillion and Jim Castelli, *The Emerging Parish: The Notre Dame Study of Catholic Life Since Vatican II* (San Francisco: Harper and Row, 1987), 10.

60. Paul Stonsz, "The Other Health Crisis: Why Priests Are Coping Poorly," *Commonweal* 134, no. 20 (November 23, 2007).

61. Pope John Paul II, *Crossing the Threshold of Hope* (New York: Alfred A. Knopf, 1994), 102–3.

62. Ibid., 113.

63. James Bacik, "The Priest as Pastor: Rooted in Christ, the Holy Spirit, and the Church," in *Priests for the 21st Century,* ed. Donald Dietrich (New York: Crossroad, 2006), 63.

64. Ibid., 64.

65. Cardinal Joseph Ratzinger, *Salt of the Earth: The Church at the End of the Millennium* (San Francisco: Ignatius Press, 1997), 222.

Chapter 9: James M. O'Toole / Boston's Catholics and Their Bishops

1. The definitive biography remains Annabelle M. Melville, *Jean Lefebvre de Cheverus, 1768–1836* (Milwaukee: Bruce, 1958).

2. John Carroll to Charles Plowden, June 11, 1791, *The John Carroll Papers,* ed. Thomas O'Brien Hanley (Notre Dame, Ind.: University of Notre Dame Press, 1976), 1:505.

3. Sacramental activity in Boston between 1790 and 1829 is summarized in the *Boston Pilot,* January 16, 1830. On Cheverus's pastoral work, see Lord, Sexton, and Harrington, *History of the Archdiocese of Boston in the Various Stages of Its Development, 1604–1943* (Boston: Pilot Publishing Co., 1944), 1:520–87; hereafter cited as *HAB.* See also Thomas H. O'Connor, *Boston Catholics: A History of the Church and Its People* (Boston: Northeastern University Press, 1998), 21–28.

4. Quoted in Ronald Hoffman, *Princes of Ireland, Planters of Maryland: A Carroll Saga, 1500–1782* (Chapel Hill: University of North Carolina Press, 2000), 309.

5. On Bulfinch and the construction of the new Holy Cross church, see Thomas H. O'Connor, *Boston Catholics: A History of the Church and Its People* (Boston: Northeastern University Press, 1998), 23–24, and Lawrence W. Kennedy, *Planning the City upon a Hill: Boston Since 1630* (Amherst: University of Massachusetts Press, 1992), 24–25. See also Walter Muir Whitehill, *A Memorial to Bishop Cheverus* (Boston: Boston Athenaeum, 1951).

6. Matignon quoted in Melville, *Jean Lefebvre de Cheverus,* 113–14; Cheverus quoted in ibid., 127, 249. On the early years of Cheverus's work as a bishop, see *HAB,* 1:632–70.

7. Some of Cheverus's correspondence with various members of the Hanly and related families is preserved in the Cheverus Papers in the Archives of the Archdiocese of Boston (hereafter AAB). See especially the letters to Roger Hanly, January 18, 1815; Anastasia Cottrill, April 2, 1816; and John Hanly, December 7, 1818.

8. Carroll to Cheverus, April 9, 1803, *Carroll Papers,* 2:412. On Cheverus's later career in France, see Melville, *Jean Lefebvre de Cheverus,* chapters 17–28.

9. Quoted in Melville, *Jean Lefebvre de Cheverus,* 267–68.

10. Taylor is now something of a forgotten man in Boston Catholic history; see *HAB,* 1:731–32 and 792–96.

11. On Fenwick's origins and early career, see *HAB,* 2:7–27, and O'Connor, *Boston Catholics,* 41–43.

12. *The Laity's Directory to the Church Service for the Year of Our Lord M,DCCC,XXII* (New York: William H. Creagh, 1822), 102–3; Benedict J. Fenwick, *Memoirs to Serve for the Future Ecclesiastical History of the Diocess of Boston,* ed. Joseph M. McCarthy (Yonkers, N.Y.: U.S. Catholic Historical Society, 1978), 169, 182–83.

13. On the clergy assigned to New England, see *The United States Catholic Almanac; or, Laity's Directory, for the Year 1833* (Baltimore: James Myres, 1833), 40–55. On the Ursulines and Daughters of Charity, see O'Connor, *Boston Catholics,* 34–35 and 48–49. The sacramental activity of Cheverus and Fenwick is summarized in Ronald D. Patkus, "A Community in Transition: Boston Catholics, 1815–1845," diss., Boston College, 1997, 48 and 57.

14. *United States Catholic Almanac, 1833,* 46 and 54. On early church music in Boston, see Patkus, "Community in Transition," 306–18, and David McCowin, "A Medley of Meanings: Musical Culture and the Nuances of Bishop Fenwick's Catholic Boston, 1825–1840" (unpublished paper, in author's possession). The early sacramental registers of St. Mary's parish, North End, from which these baptismal figures are compiled, are in AAB.

15. The fullest treatment of the Ursuline convent episode is in *HAB,* 2:205–39; see also Nancy Lusignan Schultz, *Fire and Roses: The Burning of the Charlestown Convent, 1834* (New York: Free Press, 2000). On the assessment of Catholics in Boston, see Jeremiah Spofford, *A Gazetteer of Massachusetts* (Newburyport, Mass.: Charles Whipple, 1828), 109.

16. The most comprehensive study of this phenomenon remains Oscar Handlin, *Boston's Immigrants: A Study in Acculturation,* revised and enlarged edition (New York: Atheneum, 1977). See especially page 55 and Tables II and V.

17. Thomas H. O'Connor, *Fitzpatrick's Boston, 1846–1866: John Bernard Fitzpatrick, Third Bishop of Boston* (Boston: Northeastern University Press, 1984), is the fullest biography, placing Fitzpatrick clearly in the context of the city; quotation on page 37. See also *HAB,* 2:389–408, for his early life and career.

18. See *HAB,* 2:467–73, for an encyclopedic account of all these parishes and missions; quotation on page 473.

19. On these and other institutions, see Peter C. Holloran, *Boston's Wayward Children: Social Services for Homeless Children, 1830–1930* (Boston: Northeastern University Press, 1994), especially chapter 2. On Carney, see O'Connor, *Fitzpatrick's Boston,* 122–23.

20. O'Connor, *Fitzpatrick's Boston,* 60–63; James M. O'Toole, *Passing for White: Race, Religion, and the Healy Family, 1820–1920* (Amherst: University of Massachusetts Press, 2002), 38.

21. On the Eliot School case, see John T. McGreevy, *Catholicism and American Freedom: A History* (New York: Norton, 2003), chapter 1. On the bishop's role

in opposing nativism, see O'Connor, *Fitzpatrick's Boston,* chapter 6; see also Thomas H. O'Connor, "Irish Votes and Yankee Cotton: The Constitution of 1853," Massachusetts Historical Society, *Proceedings* 95 (1983): 88–99.

22. On the suspicion of abolitionists and nativists, see the comments of Father Sherwood Healy, quoted in O'Toole, *Passing for White,* 85. The *Pilot*'s editorial is quoted in O'Connor, *Fitzpatrick's Boston,* 190; the bishop's prediction of a long war is ibid., 193.

23. O'Connor, *Fitzpatrick's Boston,* 203–7; Ambassador Henry Sanford to William Henry Seward, January 16, 1863, quoted in *HAB,* 2:711.

24. On the planning and construction of the new cathedral, see O'Toole, *Passing for White,* 118–25, and O'Connor, *Fitzpatrick's Boston,* 185–86.

25. Williams to James G. David, August 5, 1872, Williams Papers, AAB. There are also two similar letters from Williams to Davis (a Boston haberdasher), May 15, 1877, and October 4, 1877.

26. *Boston Pilot,* February 17, 1866.

27. For an overview of immigration in this period and after, see James M. O'Toole, " 'The Newer Catholic Races': Ethnic Catholicism in Boston, 1900–1940," *New England Quarterly* 65 (March 1992): 117–34.

28. See *HAB,* 3:189–238, for a thorough treatment. On the petition of the Italians of Everett, see Rocco to O'Connell, September 28, 1927, Parish Correspondence Files 40:1, AAB.

29. For Carroll's complaints, see his letter to Grassi, July 24, 1815, *Carroll Papers,* 3:349. The founding, early years, and enrollments of the seminary are described in John E. Sexton and Arthur J. Riley, *History of St. John's Seminary, Brighton* (Boston: Archdiocese of Boston, 1945), chapter 2 and Appendix H. Williams notes his donation of books in the Episcopal Register, October 18, 1884, AAB.

30. The best summary view is provided by Mary J. Oates, "Organized Voluntarism: The Catholic Sisters in Massachusetts, 1870–1940," *Women in American Religion,* ed. Janet Wilson James (Philadelphia: University of Pennsylvania Press, 1980), 141–69. See also the statistics and other data compiled in *Hoffman's Catholic Directory, Almanac, and Clergy List* (Milwaukee: Hoffman Brothers, 1886), 50–53.

31. On Walsh, see Robert E. Sullivan, "Beneficial Relations: Toward a Social History of the Diocesan Priests of Boston, 1875–1940," *Catholic Boston: Studies in Religion and Community, 1870–1970,* ed. Robert E. Sullivan and James M. O'Toole (Boston: Archdiocese of Boston, 1985), 235–37.

32. James A. Walsh Diary, AAB, entries of March 15, 1900, January 1, 1899, and February 24, 1899.

33. Unfortunately, there is only fragmentary correspondence between Williams and O'Reilly in the Williams Papers, AAB. For a summary, see A. G. Evans, *Fanatic Heart: A Life of John Boyle O'Reilly, 1844–1890* (Boston: Northeastern University Press, 1997), 202–3.

34. On Vatican I generally, see James Hennesey, *The First Council of the Vatican: The American Experience* (New York: Herder and Herder, 1963); Sherwood Healy's sentiments are expressed in his letter to James Edwards, April 30, 1870, Edwards Collection, Archives, University of Notre Dame, South Bend, Indiana. On the question of parochial schools, see Peter Guilday, *A History of the Councils of Baltimore (1791–1884)* (New York: Macmillan, 1932), and James W. Sanders, "Boston Catholics and the School Question, 1825–1907," *From Common School to Magnet School: Selected Essays in the History of Boston Schools,* ed. James W. Fraser et al. (Boston: Boston Public Library, 1979), 43–75.

35. O'Connell's sermon on the centennial of the archdiocese is contained in *Sermons and Addresses of His Eminence, William Cardinal O'Connell, Archbishop*

of Boston (Boston: Pilot Publishing Co., 1922), 3:121–39. The praise for his role is in Minot to O'Connell, April 27, 1938, O'Connell Papers, AAB, and *Boston Herald,* June 9, 1934.

36. The fullest biography is James M. O'Toole, *Militant and Triumphant: William Henry O'Connell and the Catholic Church in Boston, 1859–1944* (Notre Dame, Ind.: University of Notre Dame Press, 1992); parish life in the West End is described on 19–23. See also the older study by Dorothy G. Wayman, *Cardinal O'Connell of Boston: A Biography of William Henry O'Connell, 1859–1944* (New York: Farrar, Straus and Young, 1955). See also William O'Connell, *Recollections of Seventy Years* (Boston: Houghton Mifflin, 1934), 147.

37. *Boston Pilot,* July 13, 1901. On O'Connell's role in this "Romanization" of the American hierarchy, see Gerald P. Fogarty, *The Vatican and the American Hierarchy, 1870–1965* (Wilmington, Del.: Michael Glazier, 1985), 195–207.

38. O'Connell, *Recollections of Seventy Years,* 271. On O'Connell's administrative energies, see O'Toole, *Militant and Triumphant,* especially chapter 5.

39. See James M. O'Toole, "Prelates and Politicos: Catholics and Politics in Massachusetts, 1900–1970," *Catholic Boston,* ed. Sullivan and O'Toole, 15–65.

40. For a narrative of these events, see O'Toole, *Militant and Triumphant,* chapter 8. They have also been recounted in minute detail in Douglas J. Slawson, *Ambition and Arrogance: Cardinal William O'Connell of Boston and the American Catholic Church* (San Diego, Calif.: Cobalt Productions, 2007).

41. Cushing still lacks an adequate biography. For the best overview of his career, see O'Connor, *Boston Catholics,* chapter 7. The early assessment of Cushing is given in Peterson to O'Connell, May 26, 1921, St. John's Seminary Records, AAB.

42. Compare the entries and statistics for Boston reported in the *Official Catholic Directory* (New York: P. J. Kenedy Co., for 1944 and 1970).

43. The document, called *Nostra Aetate* from its Latin opening phrase, is in *The Documents of Vatican II,* ed. Walter Abbot (New York: Guild Press, 1966), 660–68; see especially section 4. On Cushing's relations with the local Jewish community in Boston, see O'Connor, *Boston Catholics,* 256–58.

44. Cushing to pastors, February 4 and 11, 1965, Chancery Circulars 9:9, AAB; Stephen Vuono to editor, *Boston Pilot,* February 22, 1964; "Cardinal Polls Clergy on 'Saturday' Masses," *Boston Pilot,* March 22, 1969.

45. For the issues and campaigns of this era, see O'Toole, "Prelates and Politicos," *Catholic Boston,* ed. Sullivan and O'Toole, especially pages 42–65. See also the oral history interview Cushing conducted with Senator Edward Kennedy in 1966 in the oral history collections of the John F. Kennedy Library, Boston.

46. On Medeiros's background and early career, see O'Connor, *Boston Catholics,* 281–87.

47. See the statistical summaries in the *Official Catholic Directory* for 1970 and 1980. These national trends are charted in Bryan T. Froehle and Mary L. Gautier, *Catholicism U.S.A.: A Portrait of the Catholic Church in the United States* (Maryknoll, N.Y.: Orbis Books, 2000), chapters 6 and 7.

48. On the protest on the death of Reeb, see "Boston's Uncommon Tribute," *Boston Pilot,* March 20, 1965. The charge of institutional racism among Boston Catholics is quoted in John T. McGreevy, *Parish Boundaries: The Catholic Encounter with Race in the Twentieth-Century Urban North* (Chicago: University of Chicago Press, 1996), 195. Catholics and abortion politics are treated carefully in McGreevy, *Catholicism and American Freedom,* chapters 8–9; for the quotation from Senator Kennedy, see page 280.

49. There is now an extensive literature on school desegregation in Boston and the church's role in it. See Ronald P. Formisano, *Boston against Busing: Race, Class, and Ethnicity in the 1960s and 1970s* (Chapel Hill: University of North Carolina Press, 1991); Medeiros's quote is on page 219. See also the account, not

always accurate, of the cardinal's role in J. Anthony Lukas, *Common Ground: A Turbulent Decade in the Lives of Three American Families* (New York: Knopf, 1985); the protesting women are quoted on page 363. A common belief persists that the parochial schools were used as a refuge for those fleeing busing, but the evidence suggests otherwise: see James E. Glinski, "The Catholic Church and the Desegregation of Boston's Public Schools," *Boston's Histories: Essays in Honor of Thomas H. O'Connor,* ed. James M. O'Toole and David Quigley (Boston: Northeastern University Press, 2004), 246–69.

50. On these developments, see O'Connor, *Boston Catholics,* chapter 8. See also Matthew Kraycinovich, "A Servant Sign Unseen: The Restoration Experience of the First Class of Permanent Deacons in the Roman Catholic Archdiocese of Boston" (unpublished paper; in author's possession).

51. Lukas, *Common Ground,* 397–402; see also *Whatever God Wants: Pastorals and Addresses by Humberto Cardinal Medeiros* (Boston: St. Paul Editions, 1984).

52. Understandably, there is as yet no scholarly biography of Law, but see the uncritical work of Romanus Cessario, *Boston's Cardinal: Bernard Law, the Man and His Witness* (Lanham, Md.: Lexington Books, 2002).

53. O'Connor, *Boston Catholics,* 304–28, discusses the early years of Law's tenure.

54. "Bid to Inform Catholics on Ballot Issues Called Low-Key," *Boston Globe,* September 29, 1986; "Church Influence Questioned after Vote," ibid., November 7, 1986.

55. Once again, compare the statistical summaries in the *Official Catholic Directory* for 1984 and 2000.

56. The literature on these cases is now quite extensive. See Jason Berry, *Lead Us Not into Temptation: Catholic Priests and the Sexual Abuse of Children* (New York: Doubleday, 1992); David France, *Our Fathers: The Secret Life of the Catholic Church in an Age of Scandal* (New York: Broadway Books, 2004); and the compilation of newspaper stories, originally appearing in the *Boston Globe* on the scandal, *Betrayal: The Crisis in the Catholic Church* (Boston: Little, Brown, 2002).

57. The events of the scandal and its aftermath are summarized in James M. O'Toole, *The Faithful: A History of Catholics in America* (Cambridge, Mass.: Belknap Press, 2008), 269–77.

Index

Also in the Series

Robert P. Imbelli, ed.
HANDING ON THE FAITH
The Church's Mission and Challenge

Catholic Press Award Winner!

- ◆ What is the substance of Catholic faith and hope?
- ◆ What are the best means for conveying the faith, particularly in North America?

The Crossroad Publishing Company presents the first volume of The Church in the 21st Century series sponsored by Boston College. In *Handing on the Faith* Robert P. Imbelli, a renowned theologian and teacher, introduces the work of leading Catholic theologians, writers, and scholars to discuss the challenges of handing on the faith and the opportunity it creates for Catholics to rethink the essential core of their identity.

This volume includes original contributions by figures such as Robert P. Imbelli, Mary Johnson, William D. Dinges, Paul J. Griffiths, Luke Timothy Johnson, Robert Barron, Robert Louis Wilken, Michael J. Himes, Christopher and Deborah Ruddy, Terrence W. Tilley, Thomas Groome, Bishop Blase Cupich, and John C. Cavadini.

0-8245-2409-8, paperback

crossroad

Also in the Series

Priests for the 21st Century
Edited by Donald J. Dietrich

Inculturation and the Church in North America
Edited by T. Frank Kennedy, S.J.

Take Heart:
Catholic Writers on Hope in Our Time
Edited by Ben Birnbaum

Prophetic Witness:
Catholic Women's Strategies for Reform
Edited by Colleen M. Griffith

Check your local bookstore for availability.
To order directly from the publisher,
please call 1-800-707-0670 for Customer Service
or visit our website at *www.cpcbooks.com.*

crossroad